Microsoft® Official Academic Course

Microsoft SharePoint 2010 Configuration (70-667)

WILEY

Credits

VP & PUBLISHER	Don Fowley
EXECUTIVE EDITOR	John Kane
DIRECTOR OF SALES	Mitchell Beaton
EXECUTIVE MARKETING MANAGER	Chris Ruel
MICROSOFT PRODUCT MANAGER	Colin Klein of Microsoft Learning
DEVELOPMENT AND PRODUCTION	Box Twelve Communications, Inc.
EDITORIAL PROGRAM ASSISTANT	Jennifer Lartz
ASSISTANT MARKETING MANAGER	Debbie Martin
SENIOR PRODUCTION MANAGER	Janis Soo
ASSOCIATE PRODUCTION MANAGER	Joel Balbin
CREATIVE DIRECTOR	Harry Nolan
COVER DESIGNER	Jim O'Shea
TECHNOLOGY AND MEDIA	Tom Kulesa/Wendy Ashenberg

Cover photo: Color Blind/Blend Images/Getty Images, Inc.

This book was set in Garamond by Aptara, Inc. and printed and bound by Bind-Rite Robbinsville. The covers were printed by Bind-Rite Robbinsville.

Founded in 1807, John Wiley & Sons, Inc. has been a valued source of knowledge and understanding for more than 200 years, helping people around the world meet their needs and fulfill their aspirations. Our company is built on a foundation of principles that include responsibility to the communities we serve and where we live and work. In 2008, we launched a Corporate Citizenship Initiative, a global effort to address the environmental, social, economic, and ethical challenges we face in our business. Among the issues we are addressing are carbon impact, paper specifications and procurement, ethical conduct within our business and among our vendors, and community and charitable support. For more information, please visit our website: www.wiley.com/go/citizenship.

Library of Congress Cataloging-in-Publication Data
Microsoft SharePoint 2010 Configuration (70-667) : Microsoft official academic course.
   pages cm
   Includes index.
     ISBN 978-0-470-53867-8 (pbk.)
   1. Microsoft Office.   2. Microsoft SharePoint (Electronic resource)   3. Business—Computer programs.
I. John Wiley & Sons, issuing body.
   HF5548.4.M525.M547 2012
   006.7'8—dc23

                                                              2012005563

Printed in the United States of America

10 9 8 7 6 5 4 3 2 1

Foreword from the Publisher

Wiley's publishing vision for the Microsoft Official Academic Course series is to provide students and instructors with the skills and knowledge they need to use Microsoft technology effectively in all aspects of their personal and professional lives. Quality instruction is required to help both educators and students get the most from Microsoft's software tools and to become more productive. Thus our mission is to make our instructional programs trusted educational companions for life.

To accomplish this mission, Wiley and Microsoft have partnered to develop the highest quality educational programs for information workers, IT professionals, and developers. Materials created by this partnership carry the brand name "Microsoft Official Academic Course," assuring instructors and students alike that the content of these textbooks is fully endorsed by Microsoft, and that they provide the highest quality information and instruction on Microsoft products. The Microsoft Official Academic Course textbooks are "Official" in still one more way—they are the officially sanctioned courseware for Microsoft IT Academy members.

The Microsoft Official Academic Course series focuses on *workforce development*. These programs are aimed at those students seeking to enter the workforce, change jobs, or embark on new careers as information workers, IT professionals, and developers. Microsoft Official Academic Course programs address their needs by emphasizing authentic workplace scenarios with an abundance of projects, exercises, cases, and assessments.

The Microsoft Official Academic Courses are mapped to Microsoft's extensive research and job-task analysis, the same research and analysis used to create the Microsoft Certified Technology Specialist (MCTS) exam. The textbooks focus on real skills for real jobs. As students work through the projects and exercises in the textbooks, they enhance their level of knowledge and their ability to apply the latest Microsoft technology to everyday tasks. These students also gain resume-building credentials that can assist them in finding a job, keeping their current job, or in furthering their education.

The concept of life-long learning is today an utmost necessity. Job roles, and even whole job categories, are changing so quickly that none of us can stay competitive and productive without continuously updating our skills and capabilities. The Microsoft Official Academic Course offerings, and their focus on Microsoft certification exam preparation, provide a means for people to acquire and effectively update their skills and knowledge. Wiley supports students in this endeavor through the development and distribution of these courses as Microsoft's official academic publisher.

Today educational publishing requires attention to providing quality print and robust electronic content. By integrating Microsoft Official Academic Course products, *WileyPLUS*, and Microsoft certifications, we are better able to deliver efficient learning solutions for students and teachers alike.

Joseph Heider

General Manager and Senior Vice President

Welcome to the Microsoft Official Academic Course (MOAC) program for Microsoft SharePoint 2010. MOAC represents the collaboration between Microsoft Learning and John Wiley & Sons, Inc. publishing company. Microsoft and Wiley teamed up to produce a series of textbooks that deliver compelling and innovative teaching solutions to instructors and superior learning experiences for students. Infused and informed by in-depth knowledge from the creators of SharePoint 2010, and crafted by a publisher known worldwide for the pedagogical quality of its products, these textbooks maximize skills transfer in minimum time. Students are challenged to reach their potential by using their new technical skills as highly productive members of the workforce.

Because this knowledgebase comes directly from Microsoft, architect of SharePoint 2010 and creator of the Microsoft Certified Technology Specialist and Microsoft Certified Professional exams (www.microsoft.com/learning/mcp/mcts), you are sure to receive the topical coverage that is most relevant to your personal and professional success. Microsoft's direct participation not only assures you that MOAC textbook content is accurate and current; it also means that you will receive the best instruction possible to enable your success on certification exams and in the workplace.

■ The Microsoft Official Academic Course Program

The *Microsoft Official Academic Course* series is a complete program for instructors and institutions to prepare and deliver great courses on Microsoft software technologies. With MOAC, we recognize that, because of the rapid pace of change in the technology and curriculum developed by Microsoft, there is an ongoing set of needs beyond classroom instruction tools for an instructor to be ready to teach the course. The MOAC program endeavors to provide solutions for all these needs in a systematic manner in order to ensure a successful and rewarding course experience for both instructor and student—technical and curriculum training for instructor readiness with new software releases; the software itself for student use at home for building hands-on skills, assessment, and validation of skill development; and a great set of tools for delivering instruction in the classroom and lab. All are important to the smooth delivery of an interesting course on Microsoft software, and all are provided with the MOAC program. We think about the model below as a gauge for ensuring that we completely support you in your goal of teaching a great course. As you evaluate your instructional materials options, you may wish to use this model for comparison purposes with available products:

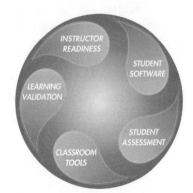

Illustrated Book Tour

▪ Pedagogical Features

The MOAC textbook for Microsoft SharePoint 2010 Configuration is designed to cover all the learning objectives for that MCTS exam, which is referred to as its "objective domain." The Microsoft Certified Technology Specialist (MCTS) exam objectives are highlighted throughout the textbook. Many pedagogical features have been developed specifically for *Microsoft Official Academic Course* programs.

Presenting the extensive procedural information and technical concepts woven throughout the textbook raises challenges for the student and instructor alike. The Illustrated Book Tour that follows provides a guide to the rich features contributing to *Microsoft Official Academic Course* program's pedagogical plan. Following is a list of key features in each lesson designed to prepare students for success on the certification exams and in the workplace:

- Each lesson begins with an **Objective Domain Matrix.** More than a standard list of learning objectives, the Domain Matrix correlates each software skill covered in the lesson to the specific MCTS "objective domain."

- Concise and frequent **step-by-step** exercises teach students new features and provide an opportunity for hands-on practice. Numbered steps give detailed, step-by-step instructions to help students learn software skills. The steps also show results and screen images to match what students should see on their computer screens.

- **Illustrations**—in particular, screen images—provide visual feedback as students work through the exercises. The images reinforce key concepts, provide visual clues about the steps, and allow students to check their progress.

- Lists of **Key Terms** at the beginning of each lesson introduce students to important technical vocabulary. When these terms are used later in the lesson, they appear in bold italic type where they are defined.

- Engaging point-of-use **Reader Aids**, located throughout the lessons, tell students why this topic is relevant (*The Bottom Line*), provide students with helpful hints (*Take Note*), or show alternate ways to accomplish tasks (*Another Way*). Reader Aids also provide additional relevant or background information that adds value to the lesson.

- **Certification Ready** features throughout the text signal students where a specific certification objective is covered. They provide students with a chance to check their understanding of that particular MCTS objective and, if necessary, review the section of the lesson where it is covered. MOAC provides complete coverage of the MCTS certification exam objectives.

- **Knowledge Assessments** provide three challenging lesson-ending activities.

- **Case Scenarios** provide workplace-based situations that test students' ability to apply what they've learned in the lesson.

www.wiley.com/college/microsoft *or*
call the MOAC Toll-Free Number: 1+(888) 764-7001 (U.S. & Canada only)

▪ Lesson Features

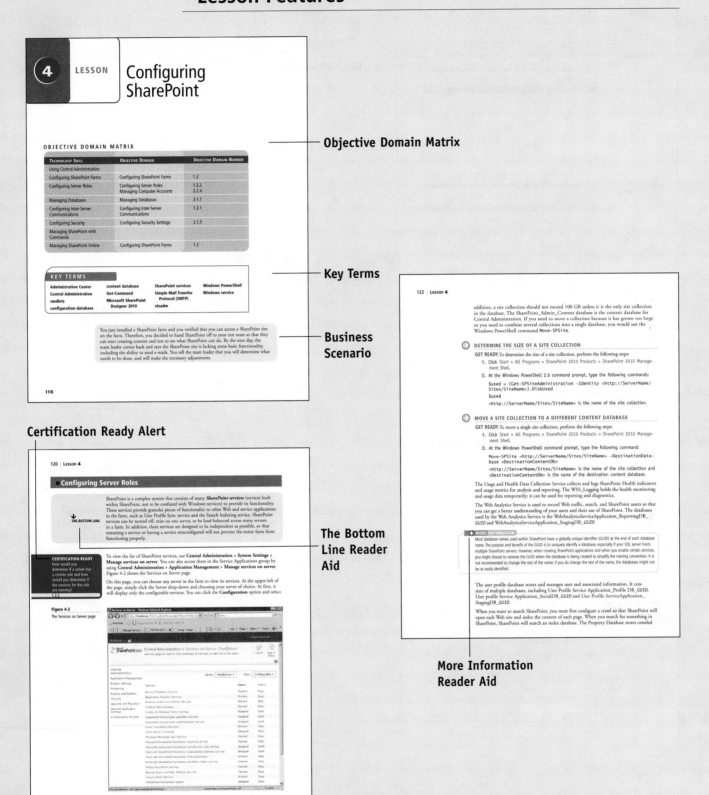

Objective Domain Matrix

Key Terms

Business Scenario

Certification Ready Alert

The Bottom Line Reader Aid

More Information Reader Aid

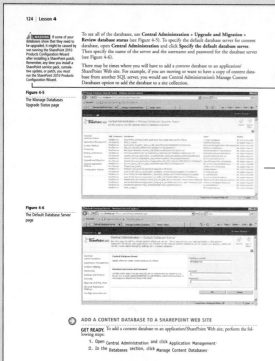

Warning Reader Aid

Screen Images

Certification Ready Alert

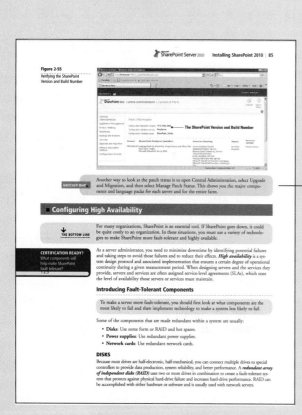

Another Way
Reader Aid

Step-by-Step
Exercises

Easy-to-Read Tables

240 | Lesson 7

Table 7-2
List Permissions

PERMISSION LEVEL	DESCRIPTION	DEPENDENT PERMISSIONS
Manage Lists	Creates or deletes lists, adds or removes columns in a list, and adds or removes public views of a list.	View Items, View Pages, Open, Manage Personal Views
Override Check Out	Discards or checks in a document that is checked out to another user without saving the current changes.	View Items, View Pages, Open
Add Items	Adds items to lists and adds documents to document libraries.	View Items, View Pages, Open
Edit Items	Edits items in lists, edits documents in document libraries, and customizes Web Part Pages in document libraries.	View Items, View Pages, Open
Delete Items	Deletes items from a list and deletes documents from a document library.	View Items, View Pages, Open
View Items	Views items in lists and views documents in document libraries.	View Pages, Open
Approve Items	Approves minor versions of list items or documents.	Edit Items, View Items, View Pages, Open
Open Items	Views the source of documents with server-side file handlers.	View Items, View Pages, Open
View Versions	Views past versions of list items or documents.	View Items, Open Items, View Pages, Open
Delete Versions	Deletes past versions of list items or documents.	View Items, View Versions, View Pages, Open
Create Alerts	Creates e-mail alerts.	View Items, View Pages, Open
View Application Pages	Views forms, views, and application pages. Enumerates lists.	Open

Table 7-3
List Permissions as they Relate
to Permission Level

PERMISSION	FULL CONTROL	DESIGN	CONTRIBUTE	READ	LIMITED ACCESS
Manage Lists	X	X			
Override Check-Out	X	X			
Add Items	X	X	X		
Edit Items	X	X	X		
Delete Items	X	X	X		
View Items	X	X	X	X	
Approve Items	X	X			
Open Items	X	X	X		
View Versions	X	X	X	X	
Delete Versions	X	X	X		
Create Alerts	X	X	X	X	
View Application Pages	X	X	X	X	X

158 | Lesson 5

Figure 5-4
Selecting the Authentication
Mode

4. In the **IIS Web Site** section, you can configure the settings for your new Web application by selecting either Use an existing web site or Create a new IIS Web site.
If you select **Create a new IIS web site**, it will ask for the name of the site, port number used by the site, the host header name and the path of where the Virtual Directory will be created. If you are creating a new Web site, this port field is populated with a random port number. If you are using an existing Web site, this field is populated with the current port number. Remember that you don't need to fill in the Host Header box unless you want to configure two or more IIS Web sites that share the same port number on the same server.
5. In the **Security Configuration** section, you would configure authentication and encryption for your Web application. For the Authentication Provider section, click Negotiate (Kerberos) or NTLM. The default value is NTLM authentication.
6. In the **Allow Anonymous** section, you can also choose to allow anonymous authentication or not by clicking Yes or No.

TAKE NOTE* If you want users to be able to access any site content anonymously, you must enable anonymous access for the entire Web application zone before you enable anonymous access at the SharePoint site level.

7. In the **Use Secure Sockets Layer (SSL)** section, if you require SSL, click Yes or No. If you choose to enable SSL for the Web site, you must configure SSL by requesting and installing an SSL certificate (see Figure 5-5).

**Take Note
Reader Aid**

156 | Lesson 5

SharePoint Web applications support both NTLM and Kerberos, which let clients seamlessly authenticate without being prompted for credentials (single sign-on). Typically, these credentials are the credentials that the user uses to log on to his or her computer.

NTLM (short for NT LAN Manager) is a suite of Microsoft security protocols that provides authentication, integrity and confidentiality to users. NTLM is an integrated single sign-on mechanism, which is probably best recognized as part of Integrated Windows Authentication for HTTP authentication. It provides maximum compatibility with different versions of Windows and compared to Kerberos, is the easiest to implement.

The *Kerberos* protocol is a secure protocol that supports ticketing authentication. While Kerberos is considered more secure than NTLM, it is more complicated than NTLM that requires additional configuration (such as requiring a service principal name (SPN) for the domain account that SharePoint is using).

Other authentication methods supported by SharePoint include the following:

- **Anonymous:** Allows a user to access SharePoint without providing any credentials for authentication. Instead, the computer-specific anonymous access account is used which is IIS_IUSRS. This is often used with public Web sites where access is giving to everyone.
- **Basic:** Authentication based on a user name and password that is transmitted clear-text (unencrypted). When security is necessary, Basic can be made secure by using SSL to encrypt authentication and Web traffic.
- **Digest:** A type of authentication that is similar to basic authentication except that the credentials are sent across the network encrypted. If you choose to use Digest, you will also need to enable Digest authentication for the IIS Web site.
- **Certificates:** Encryption is provided by SSL, which uses the exchange of public key certifications. Public key certificates are issued by a Certificate Authority (CA). If you choose to use Client Certificates, you will also need to configure the IIS Web site for certificate authentication.

X REF
Configuring Kerberos will be
discussed in Lesson 10.

Creating a Web Application

You can create a Web application by using the SharePoint Central Administration Web site or Windows PowerShell. After the Web site is created, you would then create one or several site collections on the Web application that you have created. You will not be able to access the SharePoint site until you create the collection.

X REF
Configuring and Managing
authentication providers
will be discussed in detail
in Lesson 10, including
configuring and managing
Claims-based authentication
and forms-based
authentication.

To create a Web application, you must be a member of the Farm Administrators SharePoint group and member of the local Administrator group on the computer running Central Administration.

X-Ref Reader Aid

**www.wiley.com/college/microsoft or
call the MOAC Toll-Free Number: 1+(888) 764-7001 (U.S. & Canada only)**

SharePoint Server 2010 Managing Authentication Providers | 451

G. To create the actually trusted identity token issuer (provider), execute the following command:

```
$ap = New-SPTrustedIdentityTokenIssuer -Name
"ADFSv2" -Description "ADFSv2 Federated Identity" -
Realm $realm -ImportTrustCertificate $cert -
ClaimsMappings $map1 -SignInUrl $signinurl -
IdentifierClaim $map1.InputClaimType
```

After SharePoint has been configured for AD FS, you can open Central Administration and click Manage Web Applications. When you click on a Web application and click the Authentication Providers button in the Ribbon, you can choose the zone you want to configure, select Trusted Identity Provider, and then select the AD FS identity provider.

SUMMARY SKILL MATRIX ———————————————— **Skill Summary**

IN THIS LESSON, YOU LEARNED:

- Authentication is the act of confirming identity of a user and is an essential part of authorization.
- Authentication providers are software components that support specific authentication methods. You can configure a Web application to support many different types of authentication depending on the access method.
- Classic-Mode Authentication is the same type of authentication used in SharePoint Server 2007.
- Claims-Based Authentication is a new authentication mode that is built on the Windows Identity Foundation (WIF) and that uses an identity system that allows users to present claims that include information about who the user is and what system and content the user can access.
- NTLM is slightly less secure than Kerberos. However, it is the easiest to set up since it works out of the box.
- The Kerberos protocol is a secure protocol that supports ticketing authentication. While Kerberos is considered more secure than NTLM, it is more complicated than NTLM in that it requires additional configuration (such as requiring a service principal name (SPN) for the domain account that SharePoint is using).
- Basic Authentication is a simple authentication protocol that sends a username and password over the network in clear text.
- Forms-based Authentication (FBA) is an identity management system that is based on ASP.NET membership and role provider authentication. When an unauthenticated user attempts to access a SharePoint Web application that is configured for FBA, the user doesn't see a popup login box; the user is redirected to a logon form/page to which the user submits credentials.
- The Secure Store Service is a service application that acts as a credential manager. It is needed by various service applications, including PerformancePoint, to connect to external data sources on behalf of users or groups using the unattended service account.
- Active Directory Federation Service (AD FS) provides secure sharing of digital identity and permissions across a security and enterprise boundaries. AD FS expands single sign-on (SSO) functionality within a single security or enterprise boundary or with Internet applications, customers and partners.

Knowledge Assessment

452 | Lesson 11

Knowledge Assessment

Fill in the Blank

Complete the following sentences by writing the correct word or words in the blanks provided.

1. _____ Authentication was also available in SharePoint Server 2007.

2. The Claims-Based Authentication is built on the _____ and uses an identity system that allows users to present claims which include information about who the user is.

3. _____ is an authentication type that is the easiest to implement and is the default authentication for SharePoint 2010.

4. When you configure Kerberos, the user connects to the service via _____.

5. The _____ mode sends a username and password over the network in clear text.

6. _____ is an identity management system that is based on ASP.NET membership and role provider authentication and it provides a Web form for users to supply usernames and passwords.

7. To enable Forms-based Authentication, you must configure the _____ file.

8. _____ provides secure sharing of digital identity and permissions across a security and enterprise boundary.

9. _____ are software components that support specific authentication methods.

10. To access a Web site or service through SharePoint using the same credentials but a different domain, you would use _____.

Multiple Choice

Circle the letter that corresponds to the best answer.

1. If you want a user to access SharePoint without logging in, you should use _____ authentication.
   a. anonymous
   b. digest
   c. NTLM
   d. Forms-Based

2. What account does the anonymous authentication use to access resources?
   a. domain\administrator
   b. computername\administrator
   c. IUSR_computername
   d. ASP_Net

3. What is used to enforce permissions across all sites in a Web application when using anonymous access?
   a. group policy
   b. anonymous access restrictions
   c. collection template
   d. access guideline

4. What command is used to add an SPN to an account?
   a. spn.exe
   b. setspnum.exe
   c. adsi.exe
   d. setspn.exe

Case Scenarios

454 | Lesson 11

Case Scenarios

Scenario 11-1: Switching to Kerberos

Your manager indicates a new directive came from the corporate office saying that whenever possible, you need to use Kerberos authentication. He would like to know which method is the default method, what advantage does Kerberos have, and what steps would you need to convert to Kerberos.

Scenario 11-2: Implementing SSL

Your manager tells you that he was at a customer site that uses SharePoint and they used a customized login page to access SharePoint. You tell your manager that they were most likely using Forms-Based Authentication. Your manager asks you to identify the basic steps in enabling Forms-Based Authentication (FBA). How do you respond?

www.wiley.com/college/microsoft or
call the MOAC Toll-Free Number: 1+(888) 764-7001 (U.S. & Canada only)

Conventions and Features Used in This Book

This book uses particular fonts, symbols, and heading conventions to highlight important information or to call your attention to special steps. For more information about the features in each lesson, refer to the Illustrated Book Tour section.

CONVENTION	MEANING
↓ THE BOTTOM LINE	This feature provides a brief summary of the material to be covered in the section that follows.
CLOSE	Words in all capital letters and in a different font color than the rest of the text indicate instructions for opening, saving, or closing files or programs. They also point out items you should check or actions you should take.
CERTIFICATION READY	This feature signals the point in the text where a specific certification objective is covered. It provides you with a chance to check your understanding of that particular MCTS objective and, if necessary, review the section of the lesson where it is covered.
TAKE NOTE*	Reader Aids appear in shaded boxes found in your text. *Take Note* provides helpful hints related to particular tasks or topics.
⬥ ANOTHER WAY	*Another Way* provides an alternative procedure for accomplishing a particular task.
X REF	These notes provide pointers to information discussed elsewhere in the textbook or describe interesting features of Windows Server 2008 that are not directly addressed in the current topic or exercise.
Alt + Tab	A plus sign (+) between two key names means that you must press both keys at the same time. Keys that you are instructed to press in an exercise will appear in the font shown here.
A *shared printer* can be used by many individuals on a network.	Key terms appear in bold, italic font when they are defined.
Key **My Name is.**	Any text you are asked to key appears in color.
Click **OK.**	Any button on the screen you are supposed to click on or select will also appear in color.

Instructor Support Program

The *Microsoft Official Academic Course* programs are accompanied by a rich array of resources that incorporate the extensive textbook visuals to form a pedagogically cohesive package. These resources provide all the materials instructors need to deploy and deliver their courses. Resources available online for download include:

- **DreamSpark Premium** designed to provide the easiest and most inexpensive developer tools, products, and technologies available to faculty and students in labs, classrooms, and on student PCs. A free 3-year membership is available to qualified MOAC adopters.

- The **Instructor's Guide** contains solutions to all the textbook exercises as well as chapter summaries and lecture notes. The Instructor's Guide and Syllabi for various term lengths are available from the Book Companion site (http://www.wiley.com/college/microsoft).

- The **Test Bank** contains hundreds of questions in multiple-choice, true-false, short answer, and essay formats and is available to download from the Instructor's Book Companion site (http://www.wiley.com/college/microsoft). A complete answer key is provided.

- **PowerPoint Presentations and Images.** A complete set of PowerPoint presentations is available on the Instructor's Book Companion site (http://www.wiley.com/college/microsoft) to enhance classroom presentations. Tailored to the text's topical coverage and Skills Matrix, these presentations are designed to convey key SharePoint concepts addressed in the text.

   All figures from the text are on the Instructor's Book Companion site (http://www.wiley.com/college/microsoft). You can incorporate them into your PowerPoint presentations, or create your own overhead transparencies and handouts.

   By using these visuals in class discussions, you can help focus students' attention on key elements of SharePoint and help them understand how to use it effectively in the workplace.

- When it comes to improving the classroom experience, there is no better source of ideas and inspiration than your fellow colleagues. The **Wiley Faculty Network** connects teachers with technology, facilitates the exchange of best practices, and helps to enhance instructional efficiency and effectiveness. Faculty Network activities include technology training and tutorials, virtual seminars, peer-to-peer exchanges of experiences and ideas, personal consulting, and sharing of resources. For details visit www.WhereFacultyConnect.com.

DREAMSPARK PREMIUM—FREE 3-YEAR MEMBERSHIP AVAILABLE TO QUALIFIED ADOPTERS!

DreamSpark Premium is designed to provide the easiest and most inexpensive way for universities to make the latest Microsoft developer tools, products, and technologies available in labs, classrooms, and on student PCs. DreamSpark Premium is an annual membership program for departments teaching Science, Technology, Engineering, and Mathematics (STEM) courses. The membership provides a complete solution to keep academic labs, faculty, and students on the leading edge of technology.

Software available through the DreamSpark Premium program is provided at no charge to adopting departments through the Wiley and Microsoft publishing partnership.

Contact your Wiley representative for details.

For more information about the DreamSpark Premium program, go to:

https://www.dreamspark.com/

Important Web Addresses and Phone Numbers

To locate the Wiley Higher Education Representative in your area, go to the following Web address and click on the "*Who's My Rep?*" link at the top of the page:

http://www.wiley.com/college

Or call the MOAC toll-free number: 1 + (888) 764-7001 (U.S. & Canada only).

To learn more about becoming a Microsoft Certified Professional and exam availability, visit www.microsoft.com/learning/mcp.

Book Companion Web Site (www.wiley.com/college/microsoft)

The students' book companion site for the MOAC series includes any resources, exercise files, and web links that will be used in conjunction with this course.

Wiley Desktop Editions

Wiley MOAC Desktop Editions are innovative, electronic versions of printed textbooks. Students buy the desktop version for 40% off the U.S. price of the printed text, and get the added value of permanence and portability. Wiley Desktop Editions provide students with numerous additional benefits that are not available with other e-text solutions.

Wiley Desktop Editions are NOT subscriptions; students download the Wiley Desktop Edition to their computer desktops. Students own the content they buy to keep for as long as they want. Once a Wiley Desktop Edition is downloaded to the computer desktop, students have instant access to all of the content without being online. Students can also print out the sections they prefer to read in hard copy. Students also have access to fully integrated resources within their Wiley Desktop Edition. From highlighting their e-text to taking and sharing notes, students can easily personalize their Wiley Desktop Edition as they are reading or following along in class.

Preparing to Take the Microsoft Certified Technology Specialist (MCTS) Exam

The new Microsoft Certified Technology Specialist (MCTS) credential highlights your skills using a specific Microsoft technology. You can demonstrate your abilities as an IT professional or developer with in-depth knowledge of the Microsoft technology that you use today or are planning to deploy.

The MCTS certifications enable professionals to target specific technologies and to distinguish themselves by demonstrating in-depth knowledge and expertise in their specialized technologies. Microsoft Certified Technology Specialists are consistently capable of implementing, building, troubleshooting, and debugging a particular Microsoft technology.

You can learn more about the MCTS program at www.microsoft.com/learning/mcp/mcts.

Preparing to Take an Exam

Unless you are a very experienced user, you will need to use a test preparation course to prepare to complete the test correctly and within the time allowed. The *Microsoft Official Academic Course* series is designed to prepare you with a strong knowledge of all exam topics, and with some additional review and practice on your own, you should feel confident in your ability to pass the appropriate exam.

After you decide which exam to take, review the list of objectives for the exam. You can easily identify tasks that are included in the objective list by locating the Objective Domain Matrix at the start of each lesson and the Certification Ready sidebars in the margin of the lessons in this book.

To take the MCTS test, visit www.microsoft.com/learning/mcp/mcts to locate your nearest testing center. Then call the testing center directly to schedule your test. The amount of advance notice you should provide will vary for different testing centers, and it typically depends on the number of computers available at the testing center, the number of other testers who have already been scheduled for the day on which you want to take the test, and the number of times per week that the testing center offers MCTS testing. In general, you should call to schedule your test at least two weeks prior to the date on which you want to take the test.

When you arrive at the testing center, you might be asked for proof of identity. A driver's license or passport is an acceptable form of identification. If you do not have either of these items of documentation, call your testing center and ask what alternative forms of identification will be accepted. If you are retaking a test, bring your MCTS identification number, which will have been given to you when you previously took the test. If you have not prepaid or if your organization has not already arranged to make payment for you, you will need to pay the test-taking fee when you arrive.

Acknowledgments

MOAC Instructor Advisory Board

We would like to thank our Instructor Advisory Board, an elite group of educators who has assisted us every step of the way in building these products. Advisory Board members have acted as our sounding board on key pedagogical and design decisions leading to the development of these compelling and innovative textbooks for future IT Professionals. Their dedication to technology education is truly appreciated.

Charles DeSassure, Tarrant County College

Charles DeSassure is Department Chair and Instructor of Computer Science & Information Technology at Tarrant County College Southeast Campus, Arlington, Texas. He has had experience as a MIS Manager, system analyst, field technology analyst, LAN Administrator, microcomputer specialist, and public school teacher in South Carolina. Charles has worked in higher education for more than ten years and received the Excellence Award in Teaching from the National Institute for Staff and Organizational Development (NISOD). He currently serves on the Educational Testing Service (ETS) iSkills National Advisory Committee and chaired the Tarrant County College District Student Assessment Committee. He has written proposals and makes presentations at major educational conferences nationwide. Charles has served as a textbook reviewer for John Wiley & Sons and Prentice Hall. He teaches courses in information security, networking, distance learning, and computer literacy. Charles holds a master's degree in Computer Resources & Information Management from Webster University.

Kim Ehlert, Waukesha County Technical College

Kim Ehlert is the Microsoft Program Coordinator and a Network Specialist instructor at Waukesha County Technical College, teaching the full range of MCSE and networking courses for the past nine years. Prior to joining WCTC, Kim was a professor at the Milwaukee School of Engineering for five years where she oversaw the Novell Academic Education and the Microsoft IT Academy programs. She has a wide variety of industry experience including network design and management for Johnson Controls, local city fire departments, police departments, large church congregations, health departments, and accounting firms. Kim holds many industry certifications including MCDST, MCSE, Security+, Network+, Server+, MCT, and CNE.

Kim has a bachelor's degree in Information Systems and a master's degree in Business Administration from the University of Wisconsin Milwaukee. When she is not busy teaching, she enjoys spending time with her husband Gregg and their two children—Alex, 14, and Courtney, 17.

Penny Gudgeon, Corinthian Colleges, Inc.

Penny Gudgeon is the Program Manager for IT curriculum at Corinthian Colleges, Inc. Previously, she was responsible for computer programming and web curriculum for twenty-seven campuses in Corinthian's Canadian division, CDI College of Business, Technology and Health Care. Penny joined CDI College in 1997 as a computer programming instructor at one of the campuses outside of Toronto. Prior to joining CDI College, Penny taught productivity software at another Canadian college, the Academy of Learning, for four years. Penny has experience in helping students achieve their goals through various learning models from instructor-led to self-directed to online.

Before embarking on a career in education, Penny worked in the fields of advertising, marketing/sales, mechanical and electronic engineering technology, and computer programming. When not working from her home office or indulging her passion for lifelong learning, Penny likes to read mysteries, garden, and relax at home in Hamilton, Ontario, with her Shih-Tzu, Gracie.

Margaret Leary, Northern Virginia Community College

Margaret Leary is Professor of IST at Northern Virginia Community College, teaching Networking and Network Security Courses for the past ten years. She is the Co-Principal Investigator on the CyberWATCH initiative, an NSF-funded regional consortium of higher education institutions and businesses working together to increase the number of network security personnel in the workforce. She also serves as a Senior Security Policy Manager and Research Analyst at Nortel Government Solutions and holds a CISSP certification.

Margaret holds a B.S.B.A. and MBA/Technology Management from the University of Phoenix, and is pursuing her Ph.D. in Organization and Management with an IT Specialization at Capella University. Her dissertation is titled "Quantifying the Discoverability of Identity Attributes in Internet-Based Public Records: Impact on Identity Theft and Knowledge-based Authentication." She has several other published articles in various government and industry magazines, notably on identity management and network security.

Wen Liu, ITT Educational Services, Inc.

Wen Liu is Director of Corporate Curriculum Development at ITT Educational Services, Inc. He joined the ITT corporate headquarters in 1998 as a Senior Network Analyst to plan and deploy the corporate WAN infrastructure. A year later he assumed the position of Corporate Curriculum Manager supervising the curriculum development of all IT programs. After he was promoted to the current position three years ago, he continued to manage the curriculum research and development for all the programs offered in the School of Information Technology in addition to supervising the curriculum development in other areas (such as Schools of Drafting and Design and Schools of Electronics Technology). Prior to his employment with ITT Educational Services, Wen was a Telecommunications Analyst at the state government of Indiana working on the state backbone project that provided Internet and telecommunications services to the public users such as K-12 and higher education institutions, government agencies, libraries, and healthcare facilities.

Wen has an M.A. in Student Personnel Administration in Higher Education and an M.S. in Information and Communications Sciences from Ball State University, Indiana. He used to be the Director of Special Projects on the board of directors of the Indiana Telecommunications User Association, and used to serve on Course Technology's IT Advisory Board. He is currently a member of the IEEE and its Computer Society.

Jared Spencer, Westwood College Online

Jared Spencer has been the Lead Faculty for Networking at Westwood College Online since 2006. He began teaching in 2001 and has taught both on-ground and online for a variety of institutions, including Robert Morris University and Point Park University. In addition to his academic background, he has more than fifteen years of industry experience working for companies including the Thomson Corporation and IBM.

Jared has a master's degree in Internet Information Systems and is currently ABD and pursuing his doctorate in Information Systems at Nova Southeastern University. He has authored several papers that have been presented at conferences and appeared in publications such as the Journal of Internet Commerce and the Journal of Information Privacy and Security (JIPC). He holds a number of industry certifications, including AIX (UNIX), A+, Network+, Security+, MCSA on Windows 2000, and MCSA on Windows 2003 Server.

Focus Group and Survey Participants

Finally, we thank the hundreds of instructors who participated in our focus groups and surveys to ensure that the Microsoft Official Academic Courses best met the needs of our customers.

Jean Aguilar, Mt. Hood Community College

Konrad Akens, Zane State College

Michael Albers, University of Memphis

Diana Anderson, Big Sandy Community & Technical College

Phyllis Anderson, Delaware County Community College

Judith Andrews, Feather River College

Damon Antos, American River College

Bridget Archer, Oakton Community College

Linda Arnold, Harrisburg Area Community College–Lebanon Campus

Neha Arya, Fullerton College

Mohammad Bajwa, Katharine Gibbs School–New York

Virginia Baker, University of Alaska Fairbanks

Carla Bannick, Pima Community College

Rita Barkley, Northeast Alabama Community College

Elsa Barr, Central Community College–Hastings

Ronald W. Barry, Ventura County Community College District

Elizabeth Bastedo, Central Carolina Technical College

Karen Baston, Waubonsee Community College

Karen Bean, Blinn College

Scott Beckstrand, Community College of Southern Nevada

Paulette Bell, Santa Rosa Junior College

Liz Bennett, Southeast Technical Institute

Nancy Bermea, Olympic College

Lucy Betz, Milwaukee Area Technical College

Meral Binbasioglu, Hofstra University

Catherine Binder, Strayer University & Katharine Gibbs School–Philadelphia

Terrel Blair, El Centro College

Ruth Blalock, Alamance Community College

Beverly Bohner, Reading Area Community College

Henry Bojack, Farmingdale State University

Matthew Bowie, Luna Community College

Julie Boyles, Portland Community College

Karen Brandt, College of the Albemarle

Stephen Brown, College of San Mateo

Jared Bruckner, Southern Adventist University

Pam Brune, Chattanooga State Technical Community College

Sue Buchholz, Georgia Perimeter College

Roberta Buczyna, Edison College

Angela Butler, Mississippi Gulf Coast Community College

Rebecca Byrd, Augusta Technical College

Kristen Callahan, Mercer County Community College

Judy Cameron, Spokane Community College

Dianne Campbell, Athens Technical College

Gena Casas, Florida Community College at Jacksonville

Jesus Castrejon, Latin Technologies

Gail Chambers, Southwest Tennessee Community College

Jacques Chansavang, Indiana University–Purdue University Fort Wayne

Nancy Chapko, Milwaukee Area Technical College

Rebecca Chavez, Yavapai College

Sanjiv Chopra, Thomas Nelson Community College

Greg Clements, Midland Lutheran College

Dayna Coker, Southwestern Oklahoma State University–Sayre Campus

Tamra Collins, Otero Junior College

Janet Conrey, Gavilan Community College

Carol Cornforth, West Virginia Northern Community College

Gary Cotton, American River College

Edie Cox, Chattahoochee Technical College

Rollie Cox, Madison Area Technical College

David Crawford, Northwestern Michigan College

J.K. Crowley, Victor Valley College

Rosalyn Culver, Washtenaw Community College

Sharon Custer, Huntington University

Sandra Daniels, New River Community College

Anila Das, Cedar Valley College

Brad Davis, Santa Rosa Junior College

www.wiley.com/college/microsoft *or*
call the MOAC Toll-Free Number: 1+(888) 764-7001 (U.S. & Canada only)

Susan Davis, Green River Community College

Mark Dawdy, Lincoln Land Community College

Jennifer Day, Sinclair Community College

Carol Deane, Eastern Idaho Technical College

Julie DeBuhr, Lewis-Clark State College

Janis DeHaven, Central Community College

Drew Dekreon, University of Alaska–Anchorage

Joy DePover, Central Lakes College

Salli DiBartolo, Brevard Community College

Melissa Diegnau, Riverland Community College

Al Dillard, Lansdale School of Business

Marjorie Duffy, Cosumnes River College

Sarah Dunn, Southwest Tennessee Community College

Shahla Durany, Tarrant County College–South Campus

Kay Durden, University of Tennessee at Martin

Dineen Ebert, St. Louis Community College–Meramec

Donna Ehrhart, State University of New York–Brockport

Larry Elias, Montgomery County Community College

Glenda Elser, New Mexico State University at Alamogordo

Angela Evangelinos, Monroe County Community College

Angie Evans, Ivy Tech Community College of Indiana

Linda Farrington, Indian Hills Community College

Dana Fladhammer, Phoenix College

Richard Flores, Citrus College

Connie Fox, Community and Technical College at Institute of Technology West Virginia University

Wanda Freeman, Okefenokee Technical College

Brenda Freeman, Augusta Technical College

Susan Fry, Boise State University

Roger Fulk, Wright State University–Lake Campus

Sue Furnas, Collin County Community College District

Sandy Gabel, Vernon College

Laura Galvan, Fayetteville Technical Community College

Candace Garrod, Red Rocks Community College

Sherrie Geitgey, Northwest State Community College

Chris Gerig, Chattahoochee Technical College

Barb Gillespie, Cuyamaca College

Jessica Gilmore, Highline Community College

Pamela Gilmore, Reedley College

Debbie Glinert, Queensborough Community College

Steven Goldman, Polk Community College

Bettie Goodman, C.S. Mott Community College

Mike Grabill, Katharine Gibbs School–Philadelphia

Francis Green, Penn State University

Walter Griffin, Blinn College

Fillmore Guinn, Odessa College

Helen Haasch, Milwaukee Area Technical College

John Habal, Ventura College

Joy Haerens, Chaffey College

Norman Hahn, Thomas Nelson Community College

Kathy Hall, Alamance Community College

Teri Harbacheck, Boise State University

Linda Harper, Richland Community College

Maureen Harper, Indian Hills Community College

Steve Harris, Katharine Gibbs School–New York

Robyn Hart, Fresno City College

Darien Hartman, Boise State University

Gina Hatcher, Tacoma Community College

Winona T. Hatcher, Aiken Technical College

BJ Hathaway, Northeast Wisconsin Tech College

Cynthia Hauki, West Hills College – Coalinga

Mary L. Haynes, Wayne County Community College

Marcie Hawkins, Zane State College

Steve Hebrock, Ohio State University Agricultural Technical Institute

Sue Heistand, Iowa Central Community College

Heith Hennel, Valencia Community College

Donna Hendricks, South Arkansas Community College

www.wiley.com/college/microsoft *or*
call the MOAC Toll-Free Number: 1+(888) 764-7001 (U.S. & Canada only)

Judy Hendrix, Dyersburg State Community College

Gloria Hensel, Matanuska-Susitna College University of Alaska Anchorage

Gwendolyn Hester, Richland College

Tammarra Holmes, Laramie County Community College

Dee Hobson, Richland College

Keith Hoell, Katharine Gibbs School–New York

Pashia Hogan, Northeast State Technical Community College

Susan Hoggard, Tulsa Community College

Kathleen Holliman, Wallace Community College Selma

Chastity Honchul, Brown Mackie College/ Wright State University

Christie Hovey, Lincoln Land Community College

Peggy Hughes, Allegany College of Maryland

Sandra Hume, Chippewa Valley Technical College

John Hutson, Aims Community College

Celia Ing, Sacramento City College

Joan Ivey, Lanier Technical College

Barbara Jaffari, College of the Redwoods

Penny Jakes, University of Montana College of Technology

Eduardo Jaramillo, Peninsula College

Barbara Jauken, Southeast Community College

Susan Jennings, Stephen F. Austin State University

Leslie Jernberg, Eastern Idaho Technical College

Linda Johns, Georgia Perimeter College

Brent Johnson, Okefenokee Technical College

Mary Johnson, Mt. San Antonio College

Shirley Johnson, Trinidad State Junior College–Valley Campus

Sandra M. Jolley, Tarrant County College

Teresa Jolly, South Georgia Technical College

Dr. Deborah Jones, South Georgia Technical College

Margie Jones, Central Virginia Community College

Randall Jones, Marshall Community and Technical College

Diane Karlsbraaten, Lake Region State College

Teresa Keller, Ivy Tech Community College of Indiana

Charles Kemnitz, Pennsylvania College of Technology

Sandra Kinghorn, Ventura College

Bill Klein, Katharine Gibbs School–Philadelphia

Bea Knaapen, Fresno City College

Kit Kofoed, Western Wyoming Community College

Maria Kolatis, County College of Morris

Barry Kolb, Ocean County College

Karen Kuralt, University of Arkansas at Little Rock

Belva-Carole Lamb, Rogue Community College

Betty Lambert, Des Moines Area Community College

Anita Lande, Cabrillo College

Junnae Landry, Pratt Community College

Karen Lankisch, UC Clermont

David Lanzilla, Central Florida Community College

Nora Laredo, Cerritos Community College

Jennifer Larrabee, Chippewa Valley Technical College

Debra Larson, Idaho State University

Barb Lave, Portland Community College

Audrey Lawrence, Tidewater Community College

Deborah Layton, Eastern Oklahoma State College

Larry LeBlanc, Owen Graduate School– Vanderbilt University

Philip Lee, Nashville State Community College

Michael Lehrfeld, Brevard Community College

Vasant Limaye, Southwest Collegiate Institute for the Deaf–Howard College

Anne C. Lewis, Edgecombe Community College

Stephen Linkin, Houston Community College

Peggy Linston, Athens Technical College

Hugh Lofton, Moultrie Technical College

Donna Lohn, Lakeland Community College

Jackie Lou, Lake Tahoe Community College

Donna Love, Gaston College

Curt Lynch, Ozarks Technical Community College

Sheilah Lynn, Florida Community College– Jacksonville

Pat R. Lyon, Tomball College

Bill Madden, Bergen Community College

Heather Madden, Delaware Technical & Community College

Donna Madsen, Kirkwood Community College
Jane Maringer-Cantu, Gavilan College
Suzanne Marks, Bellevue Community College
Carol Martin, Louisiana State University–Alexandria
Cheryl Martucci, Diablo Valley College
Roberta Marvel, Eastern Wyoming College
Tom Mason, Brookdale Community College
Mindy Mass, Santa Barbara City College
Dixie Massaro, Irvine Valley College
Rebekah May, Ashland Community & Technical College
Emma Mays-Reynolds, Dyersburg State Community College
Timothy Mayes, Metropolitan State College of Denver
Reggie McCarthy, Central Lakes College
Matt McCaskill, Brevard Community College
Kevin McFarlane, Front Range Community College
Donna McGill, Yuba Community College
Terri McKeever, Ozarks Technical Community College
Patricia McMahon, South Suburban College
Sally McMillin, Katharine Gibbs School–Philadelphia
Charles McNerney, Bergen Community College
Lisa Mears, Palm Beach Community College
Imran Mehmood, ITT Technical Institute–King of Prussia Campus
Virginia Melvin, Southwest Tennessee Community College
Jeanne Mercer, Texas State Technical College
Denise Merrell, Jefferson Community & Technical College
Catherine Merrikin, Pearl River Community College
Diane D. Mickey, Northern Virginia Community College
Darrelyn Miller, Grays Harbor College
Sue Mitchell, Calhoun Community College
Jacquie Moldenhauer, Front Range Community College
Linda Motonaga, Los Angeles City College
Sam Mryyan, Allen County Community College
Cindy Murphy, Southeastern Community College
Ryan Murphy, Sinclair Community College

Sharon E. Nastav, Johnson County Community College
Christine Naylor, Kent State University Ashtabula
Haji Nazarian, Seattle Central Community College
Nancy Noe, Linn-Benton Community College
Jennie Noriega, San Joaquin Delta College
Linda Nutter, Peninsula College
Thomas Omerza, Middle Bucks Institute of Technology
Edith Orozco, St. Philip's College
Dona Orr, Boise State University
Joanne Osgood, Chaffey College
Janice Owens, Kishwaukee College
Tatyana Pashnyak, Bainbridge College
John Partacz, College of DuPage
Tim Paul, Montana State University–Great Falls
Joseph Perez, South Texas College
Mike Peterson, Chemeketa Community College
Dr. Karen R. Petitto, West Virginia Wesleyan College
Terry Pierce, Onandaga Community College
Ashlee Pieris, Raritan Valley Community College
Jamie Pinchot, Thiel College
Michelle Poertner, Northwestern Michigan College
Betty Posta, University of Toledo
Deborah Powell, West Central Technical College
Mark Pranger, Rogers State University
Carolyn Rainey, Southeast Missouri State University
Linda Raskovich, Hibbing Community College
Leslie Ratliff, Griffin Technical College
Mar-Sue Ratzke, Rio Hondo Community College
Roxy Reissen, Southeastern Community College
Silvio Reyes, Technical Career Institutes
Patricia Rishavy, Anoka Technical College
Jean Robbins, Southeast Technical Institute
Carol Roberts, Eastern Maine Community College and University of Maine
Teresa Roberts, Wilson Technical Community College
Vicki Robertson, Southwest Tennessee Community College
Betty Rogge, Ohio State Agricultural Technical Institute

Lynne Rusley, Missouri Southern State University

Claude Russo, Brevard Community College

Ginger Sabine, Northwestern Technical College

Steven Sachs, Los Angeles Valley College

Joanne Salas, Olympic College

Lloyd Sandmann, Pima Community College–Desert Vista Campus

Beverly Santillo, Georgia Perimeter College

Theresa Savarese, San Diego City College

Sharolyn Sayers, Milwaukee Area Technical College

Judith Scheeren, Westmoreland County Community College

Adolph Scheiwe, Joliet Junior College

Marilyn Schmid, Asheville-Buncombe Technical Community College

Janet Sebesy, Cuyahoga Community College

Phyllis T. Shafer, Brookdale Community College

Ralph Shafer, Truckee Meadows Community College

Anne Marie Shanley, County College of Morris

Shelia Shelton, Surry Community College

Merilyn Shepherd, Danville Area Community College

Susan Sinele, Aims Community College

Beth Sindt, Hawkeye Community College

Andrew Smith, Marian College

Brenda Smith, Southwest Tennessee Community College

Lynne Smith, State University of New York–Delhi

Rob Smith, Katharine Gibbs School–Philadelphia

Tonya Smith, Arkansas State University–Mountain Home

Del Spencer, Trinity Valley Community College

Jeri Spinner, Idaho State University

Eric Stadnik, Santa Rosa Junior College

Karen Stanton, Los Medanos College

Meg Stoner, Santa Rosa Junior College

Beverly Stowers, Ivy Tech Community College of Indiana

Marcia Stranix, Yuba College

Kim Styles, Tri-County Technical College

Sylvia Summers, Tacoma Community College

Beverly Swann, Delaware Technical & Community College

Ann Taff, Tulsa Community College

Mike Theiss, University of Wisconsin–Marathon Campus

Romy Thiele, Cañada College

Sharron Thompson, Portland Community College

Ingrid Thompson-Sellers, Georgia Perimeter College

Barbara Tietsort, University of Cincinnati–Raymond Walters College

Janine Tiffany, Reading Area Community College

Denise Tillery, University of Nevada Las Vegas

Susan Trebelhorn, Normandale Community College

Noel Trout, Santiago Canyon College

Cheryl Turgeon, Asnuntuck Community College

Steve Turner, Ventura College

Sylvia Unwin, Bellevue Community College

Lilly Vigil, Colorado Mountain College

Sabrina Vincent, College of the Mainland

Mary Vitrano, Palm Beach Community College

Brad Vogt, Northeast Community College

Cozell Wagner, Southeastern Community College

Carolyn Walker, Tri-County Technical College

Sherry Walker, Tulsa Community College

Qi Wang, Tacoma Community College

Betty Wanielista, Valencia Community College

Marge Warber, Lanier Technical College–Forsyth Campus

Marjorie Webster, Bergen Community College

Linda Wenn, Central Community College

Mark Westlund, Olympic College

Carolyn Whited, Roane State Community College

Winona Whited, Richland College

Jerry Wilkerson, Scott Community College

Joel Willenbring, Fullerton College
Barbara Williams, WITC Superior
Charlotte Williams, Jones County Junior
    College
Bonnie Willy, Ivy Tech Community College
    of Indiana
Diane Wilson, J. Sargeant Reynolds
    Community College
James Wolfe, Metropolitan Community
    College
Marjory Wooten, Lanier Technical
    College
Mark Yanko, Hocking College
Alexis Yusov, Pace University

Naeem Zaman, San Joaquin Delta College
Kathleen Zimmerman, Des Moines Area
    Community College

We also thank Lutz Ziob, Don Field, David
Bramble, Rob Linsky, Keith Loeber, Mike
Mulcare, Colin Klein, Joe Wilson, Jim
Clark, and Scott Serna at Microsoft for their
encouragement and support in making the
Microsoft Official Academic Course program
the finest instructional materials for master-
ing the newest Microsoft technologies for
both students and instructors.

Brief Contents

Contents

Introducing SharePoint 2010

OBJECTIVE DOMAIN MATRIX

Technology Skill	Objective Domain
What is SharePoint?	Supplemental
Exploring SharePoint	Supplemental
Understanding SharePoint's Components	Supplemental
Understanding SharePoint's Identities and Profiles	Supplemental
Using SharePoint's Configuration Tools	Supplemental
SharePoint Online and Office 365	Supplemental

TAKE NOTE*

The information in this lesson is not part of the 70-667 exam objectives. The information provided in this lesson serves as a basis of fundamental knowledge for the student to more effectively understand and work with SharePoint in the subsequent lessons.

KEY TERMS

Active Directory

alerts

Blank Site

Blog Site

Client Access License (CAL)

cloud computing

collection

database server

Document Center

Document Workspace Site

farm

Group Work Site

Internet Information Services (IIS)

libraries

lists

Meeting Workspace Site

Microsoft .NET Framework

Microsoft Office SharePoint Server (MOSS) 2007

Microsoft SharePoint Foundation

Microsoft SQL Server

MySites

Office 365

Ribbon

SharePoint

SharePoint Central Administration

SharePoint Foundation 2010

SharePoint Online

SharePoint Server 2010

Site Actions menu

Site Settings

Team Site

Uniform Resource Locator (URL)

views

Web Parts

Windows Internal Database

Windows SharePoint Services (WSS)

workflows

Your manager wants to organize a lot of information, including several hundred documents, and he wants to make that information easy to retrieve. He would like to automate some forms that need to be reviewed and approved by several people before certain actions are implemented. You advise him that SharePoint 2010 can handle all of this—and even more.

What Is SharePoint?

THE BOTTOM LINE

Microsoft SharePoint is a popular Web platform developed by Microsoft that offers a powerful, flexible, and scalable centralized Web application. Although SharePoint looks like a typical Web site, it's actually a Web content management system, a document management system, and a collaboration tool.

SharePoint is a suite of services that provides a Web site/portal that allows users to organize and retrieve information; using SharePoint, users can easily collaborate on projects. SharePoint also allows the tracking and management of projects and business processes. To accomplish all of this, SharePoint provides the following:

- A central repository for information that can be easily organized and retrieved
- An easy-to-use and familiar environment
- A flexible, customizable platform
- Tools to create information easily
- Tools to share and exchange information
- Controls to protect data
- Tools to track tasks and processes
- Tools to manage workflows

SharePoint allows for quick learning, lower support costs, effective management, improved security, and easy growth. Of course, the trick to working with SharePoint is to configure SharePoint in a way that organizes the organization's data and communicates the right information in a timely manner. It should also be noted that users get just the right amount of information—not too little and not too much. Since SharePoint displays as a Web site/portal, users need only use a Web browser to access SharePoint. Figure 1-1 shows the default team site.

The Evolution of SharePoint

SharePoint Foundation and SharePoint 2010 are not the first versions of SharePoint. The first version was SharePoint 2001, which allowed administrators to quickly create fully functional Web sites/portals. Of course, by today's SharePoint standards, these Web sites were very basic.

As SharePoint 2001 started to become popular and users wanted to develop internal and external sites based on SharePoint, Microsoft eventually released *Windows SharePoint Services (WSS)* 2.0 and 3.0 as free add-ons for Windows Server 2003. With WSS 3.0, users could:

- Store documents
- Store announcements
- Store news and information articles
- Create and manage tasks and calendar appointments
- Collaborate on documents, tasks, and projects

Figure 1-1

The SharePoint 2010 default team site

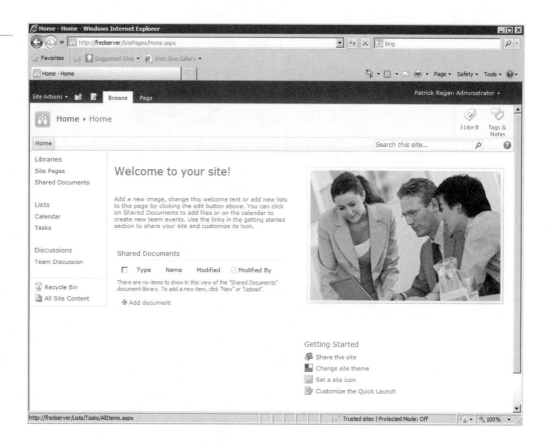

Eventually, SharePoint WSS 3.0 could be upgraded to ***Microsoft Office SharePoint Server (MOSS) 2007***, which provided an Enterprise version of SharePoint. MOSS 2007 is sometimes referred to as just SharePoint 2007. While WSS 3.0 provided the framework for SharePoint 2007, SharePoint 2007 added new features, including:

- The MySite personal site gave users the ability to create personal Web sites about themselves.
- Users could subscribe to RSS feeds to notify them when content was changed.
- Users had the ability to create User Profiles in the User Profile Store, which integrated with and automatically updated personal information (including telephone numbers, email addresses, and many other fields).
- Users could target content based on their group or audience.

WSS 3.0 was eventually superseded by SharePoint Foundation, and SharePoint Server 2007 was replaced by SharePoint Server 2010. Similar to WSS 3.0 and MOSS 2007, SharePoint Foundation is a free add-on for Windows servers. SharePoint Server 2010 must be licensed.

Introducing SharePoint 2010

SharePoint Foundation 2010 (sometimes just referred to as SharePoint Foundation) is the free version of SharePoint and is named differently from SharePoint Server 2010 to avoid confusion. The two licensed editions of ***SharePoint Server 2010*** are Standard and Enterprise. Of course, for the most functionality, you must purchase the Enterprise edition.

SharePoint Foundation 2010 is the small-business version of the SharePoint platform that includes tools and features such as basic lists (data arranged in a simple row and column format), document storage, and basic team collaboration services. When used with SQL Server Express,

SharePoint Foundation allows an organization to set up a single server with a minimum investment, which allows SharePoint to be competitive with open-source collaboration tools.

SharePoint Server 2010 expands the functionality of SharePoint Foundation by including numerous enterprise features. Depending on the organization needs, SharePoint 2010 can be purchased based on licensing (Client Access License or Internet licenses) and functionality (Standard or Enterprise editions):

- **SharePoint Server 2010 Enterprise Client Access License** and **SharePoint Server 2010 Standard Client Access License.** *Client Access License (CAL)* is based on the number of users that you have within your organization who use SharePoint. If you want to implement SharePoint Server 2010 Client Access License features, you must purchase a Microsoft Office SharePoint 2010 Server License just to run it on a server. To implement SharePoint 2010 Enterprise, you must purchase SharePoint 2010 Enterprise. Lastly, you must purchase the number of Client Access Licenses (CALs) for each user (or device) accessing the server. Keep in mind that you cannot mix Standard and Enterprise CALs when using multiple SharePoint servers to work together.

- **SharePoint Server 2010 for Internet Sites, Enterprise Edition** and **SharePoint Server 2010 for Internet Sites, Standard Edition.** The Internet edition has an open license, which means it doesn't limit how many users can access SharePoint. A license is required for each Internet facing server. You do not have to purchase CALs.

SharePoint 2010 Enterprise has more features than SharePoint 2010 Standard, and SharePoint 2010 Standard has more features than SharePoint Foundation. Enterprise versions feature additional functionality, including interoperability with external line-of-business applications, Web services, and Microsoft Office client applications. Enterprise versions also include better decision tools, more robust forms, and enhanced workflows compared. Table 1-1 shows the features available for the different editions of SharePoint.

Table 1-1

SharePoint Features

	FOUNDATION	STANDARD	ENTERPRISE
Access Services	No	No	Yes
Audience Targeting	No	Yes	Yes
Blogs	Yes	Yes	Yes
Business Connectivity Services	Yes	Yes	Yes
Business Data Integration with the Office Client	No	No	Yes
Business Data Web Parts	No	No	Yes
Business Intelligence Center	No	No	Yes
Calculated KPIs	No	No	Yes
Chart Web Parts	No	No	Yes
Connections to Microsoft Office Clients, Office Communications Server and Exchange	Yes	Yes	Yes

Content Organizer	No	Yes	Yes
Dashboards	No	No	Yes
Data Connection Library	No	No	Yes
Discussions	Yes	Yes	Yes
Duplicate Detection	No	Yes	Yes
Enterprise Wikis	No	Yes	Yes
Excel Services	No	No	Yes
Federated Search	No	Yes	Yes
InfoPath Forms Services	No	No	Yes
Managed Metadata Service	No	Yes	Yes
MySite, My Content, My Newsfeed, and My Profile	No	Yes	Yes
PerformancePoint Services	No	No	Yes
Photos and Presence	Yes	Yes	Yes
PowerPivot for SharePoint	No	No	Yes
Ratings	No	Yes	Yes
Rich Media Management	No	Yes	Yes
Rich Web Indexing	No	No	Yes
Sandboxed Solutions	Yes	Yes	Yes
Searching	Basic Site Search	Basic Site Searches and Search Scopes	Basic Site Searches, Search Scopes, and Contextual Searches
Secure Store Service	No	Yes	Yes
Sorting	No	Basic	Advanced
Tags	No	Yes	Yes
Thumbnails and Previews	No	No	Yes
Visio Services	No	No	Yes
Web Analytics	No	Yes	Yes
Web Parts	Yes	Yes	Yes
Wikis	Yes	Yes	Yes
Word Automation Services	No	Yes	Yes
Workflow	Yes	Yes	Yes
Workflow Templates	No	Yes	Yes

Because a SharePoint site can grow to include hundreds of lists, with each list containing hundreds of items and hundreds or maybe even thousands of documents, you need a simple way to search for and find information. You therefore have the following search options for SharePoint Server 2010:

- **Microsoft SharePoint Foundation 2010 Search.** Although included with SharePoint Foundation, Microsoft SharePoint Foundation 2010 Search can only index and search a single site collection and it cannot index external data. It also has a limit of 10,000 items that can be indexed.

- **Microsoft Search Server 2010 Express.** This is an enhanced, but free, search server that allows you to index external content. If you are using Microsoft SQL Server, you can search up to 10 million items. In addition, it provides a smarter search engine that can modify information presented based on previous searches and selections, and has the ability to provide query suggestions.

- **Microsoft Search Server 2010.** This is a search server that extends the search functionalities beyond site search, and provides the ability to deploy across multiple servers. It is limited to 500,000 items and a single index database. Microsoft Search Server 2010 must be licensed.

- **Microsoft SharePoint Server 2010.** This is the standard search engine that is part of SharePoint 2010 Server; it has the same capabilities of Microsoft Search Server 2010 but allows you to search up to 100 million items.

- **FAST Search Server.** This server provides full Enterprise search features for multiple SharePoint servers working together, including the ability to search content based on context, to view document thumbnails, and to scroll previews of documents without opening the documents. To use FAST Search Server, you must purchase a SharePoint Enterprise CALs license.

+ **MORE INFORMATION**

For more information about the various SharePoint 2010 editions and licenses, visit http://sharepoint.microsoft.com/en-us/buy/Pages/Editions-Comparison.aspx or http://sharepoint.microsoft.com/en-us/buy/Pages/default.aspx

When assessing the total cost of ownership, SharePoint 2010 can be relatively expensive. You will need to include the following cost items:

- Server hardware, which can range from a single server to multiple servers. A *farm* is the term used to describe multiple servers that work together to provide a SharePoint environment.
- Server operating systems for each server, including the SQL Server.
- SQL Server licensing.
- SharePoint Server licensing.
- SharePoint CALs (Standard and Enterprise).

Understanding the SharePoint Suite

SharePoint is not just a simple program, service, or protocol. It is a suite of programs and services that begins with the Windows server and expands to the SharePoint architecture (see Figure 1-2) consisting of various technologies that are combined to provide the SharePoint services. You can then use your browser or an Office application to access the SharePoint environment.

A server is a computer that provides services. SharePoint is a suite of services. Therefore, SharePoint 2010 needs to run on a 64-bit server (such as Windows Server 2008 (x64) with Service Pack 2, or Windows Server 2008 R2).

Figure 1-2

The SharePoint 2010
architecture

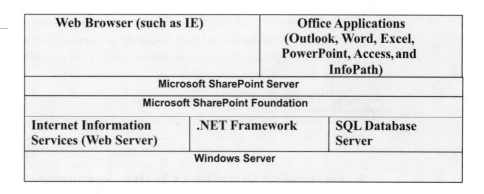

Web Browser (such as IE)		Office Applications (Outlook, Word, Excel, PowerPoint, Access, and InfoPath)
Microsoft SharePoint Server		
Microsoft SharePoint Foundation		
Internet Information Services (Web Server)	.NET Framework	SQL Database Server
Windows Server		

TAKE NOTE * Starting with SharePoint Foundation and SharePoint 2010, you can install SharePoint on a computer running the 64-bit version of Windows Vista or Windows 7. However, this is only supported as part of a development environment.

Since SharePoint is accessed as a Web site, it runs on Microsoft's Web server, which is called *Internet Information Services (IIS)* and is included with Windows servers. You also need to install the *Microsoft .NET Framework*, which is a software framework for Windows operating systems. Microsoft .NET Framework includes a large library—which SharePoint accesses—and it supports several programming languages. The .NET Framework allows the creation of SharePoint Web Parts, which contains document libraries and lists. .NET Framework 3.5 is also included with Windows Server 2008.

The component that makes SharePoint powerful, flexible, and customizable is the use of a Microsoft database server known as *Microsoft SQL Server*. A *database server* is a server that specializes in storing, organizing, and retrieving data (including large lists, files, tasks, and so on). By using a SQL server to provide content, each site and page loaded is dynamic—which means the content of each page varies according to which page you go to, which user you logon as, and which options you select.

The basic services are derived from the *Microsoft SharePoint Foundation*, which provides the interface with the operating system via IIS. If you install SharePoint Standard edition, SharePoint Standard works on top of SharePoint Foundation. If you install SharePoint Enterprise, SharePoint Enterprise works on top of SharePoint Standard (which works on top of SharePoint Foundation).

After SharePoint is installed, an organization can customize SharePoint by using the following options:

- Your organization can use themes and branding to customize the look and feel of SharePoint sites.
- Your organization can use out-of-the-box solutions, templates, and Web Parts to deliver rich functional solutions.
- Your organization can deploy a wide range of technologies that provide a variety of Web services and application program interfaces (ranging from simple "no-code" solutions to complex Visual Studio solutions) to help you create and deploy solutions.
- Your organization can create and implement both simple and complex Workflows.
- Your organization can use Microsoft Visio Services, Microsoft Excel Services, and Microsoft Access Services to share documents and allow documents to be automatically refreshed and updated from various data sources.
- Your organization can connect data sources to SharePoint by using Business Connectivity Services.
- Your organization can use SharePoint Designer to design and customize Microsoft SharePoint Web sites.

- Your organization can create and implement forms by using InfoPath Services.
- Your organization can use PerformancePoint Services to create interactive dashboards that display key performance indicators (KPIs) and data visualizations in the form of scorecards, reports, and filters.

+ MORE INFORMATION

For more information about the SharePoint 2010 architecture, visit http://msdn.microsoft.com/en-us/library/ gg552610.aspx

Understanding SharePoint's System Requirements

SharePoint is not intended to run on a desktop operating system such as Windows 7. Instead, it should be installed on a server. Therefore, you must understand the minimum and recommended system requirements for SharePoint.

The minimum hardware required for a single server installation are:

- Four cores or more, 64-bit processor
- 4 GB of RAM
- 80 GB free disk space

If SharePoint is going into a production environment where it will be used by 100 or more users every day, you should consider a minimum of 8 cores and 8 GB of memory. You may also need lots more disk space based on how much you need to store. If you have many more users, you might consider using multiple servers to create a farm to break up the workload. To play with or simply practice with SharePoint, the minimums listed here are fine.

To install SharePoint 2010, you must have the 64-bit version of Windows Server 2008 with Service Pack 2 (SP2) or Windows Server 2008 R2 (Standard, Enterprise, Data Center, or Web Server editions). As previously mentioned, you must install IIS and the Microsoft .NET Framework.

To load SharePoint, you must have one of the following SQL servers:

- The 64-bit version of Microsoft SQL Server 2005 with Service Pack 3 (SP3) and cumulative update package 3 for SQL Server 2005 Service Pack 3
- The 64-bit version of Microsoft SQL Server 2008 with Service Pack 1 (SP1) and Cumulative Update 2
- The 64-bit version of Microsoft SQL Server 2008 R2

Unfortunately, for larger deployments, you must install one of the licensed editions—and that could cost thousands of dollars.

Windows Server 2008 and Windows Server 2008 R2 include *Windows Internal Database*, which is an SQL-based data store for Windows roles and features. You can also download and install the newest free version of SQL Server 2008 R2 Express. However, by using the free versions, you have limited capabilities, including supporting only up to 10 GB in databases. While that might seem like a lot, a busy SharePoint site can easily grow well beyond the 10 GB limit. Of course, that is enough for you play with and practice with.

+ MORE INFORMATION

For more information about the SharePoint 2010 system requirements, visit http://technet.microsoft.com/en-us/ library/cc262485.aspx

Accessing a SharePoint Site

Since SharePoint is presented as a Web site for the users, users need only browsers in order to access the site. SharePoint 2010 supports more browsers than previous versions of SharePoint.

Since SharePoint provides a Web interface, SharePoint is accessed using a browser such as Internet Explorer (IE). Therefore, most systems should have the components to access SharePoint. SharePoint 2010 supports more browsers (such as FireFox and Safari) than previous versions supported. With some browsers, you might only have basic read, write, and administrative activities. At the time of this writing, it is recommended to use Internet Explorer 7.0 or higher, or Mozilla Firefox 3.5 or higher. It should also be noted that IE 6.0 is not supported.

While users need only browsers to access a SharePoint site, they can do more if they have Office 2010 Professional Plus or Enterprise. If they don't have Office 2010, they can't open or edit Office files (such as Word documents or PowerPoint documents) unless Office Web App was installed on SharePoint Server. In addition, without Microsoft Office, users can't access the datasheet view for a list nor can they open certain forms. The datasheet view allows you to access multiple records at once because the records are displayed like a spreadsheet. Lastly, if users use Microsoft Outlook, Outlook can connect to a calendar in SharePoint and users can configure their SharePoint tasks to appear in Outlook.

■ Exploring SharePoint

THE BOTTOM LINE

Before you learn how to configure SharePoint, you should familiarize yourself with how it works. To access a SharePoint site, you just need to open your Internet browser and visit the Web address—or *Uniform Resource Locator (URL)*, as it's known. If this becomes a page that you visit often, you can save this page in your Favorites list or even make the page your default page for your browser. Depending how the site was created, you may or may not be asked to enter your user name and password.

When you visit a SharePoint site, there is no way to tell which version or edition of SharePoint is installed. However, SharePoint 2010 has a newer looking interface compared to older versions of SharePoint.

The main part of the page is the page body, which contains the information for the page. At the top of the page, you will find the *Ribbon* (including the Ribbon tab bar and the Ribbon body), which is the primary method for controlling what you want to do in SharePoint. The Ribbon body changes according to what you are trying to do. For example, when you access a document library, you have one Ribbon bar. Figure 1-3 shows the Calendar Tools Ribbon, which displays only when you are accessing a Calendar list within SharePoint. Figure 1-4 shows the Library Tools Ribbon, which displays when you are accessing a Document Library.

Figure 1-3

The Calendar Tools Ribbon

Figure 1-4

The Library Tools Ribbon

The **Site Actions menu** (see Figure 1-5) provides shortcuts to commands commonly used by administrators, contributors, and designers. For example, the Site Actions menu allows you to create new subsites and pages, add lists or libraries to the current page, edit the page, and access site permissions and site settings.

Figure 1-5

The Site Actions menu

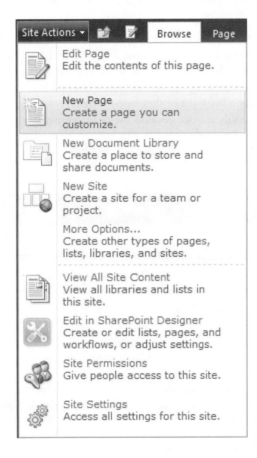

TAKE NOTE* The Site Actions menu is available only to users who are members of the Site Members group, which is a special group defined within SharePoint. SharePoint groups will be discussed in Lesson 7.

The Navigate Up button (see Figure 1-6) provides you with a means to navigate up in the site hierarchy, possibly to the parent site. As shown in the figure, the Navigate Up button opens a tree that is representative of the current location.

Microsoft **SharePoint** Server 2010 **Introducing SharePoint 2010 | 11**

Figure 1-6

The Navigate Up button

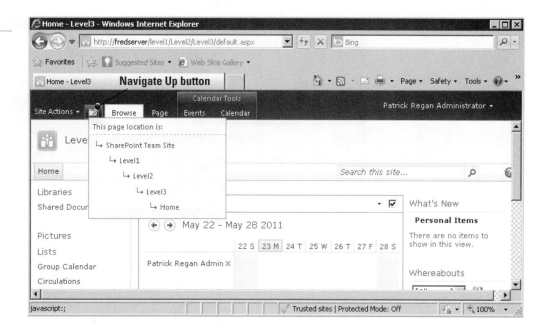

The Edit button (see Figure 1-7) allows you to open the Editing Tools, which puts the page into editing mode (see Figure 1-8). In editing mode, you can add, delete, and rearrange content.

Figure 1-7

The Edit button

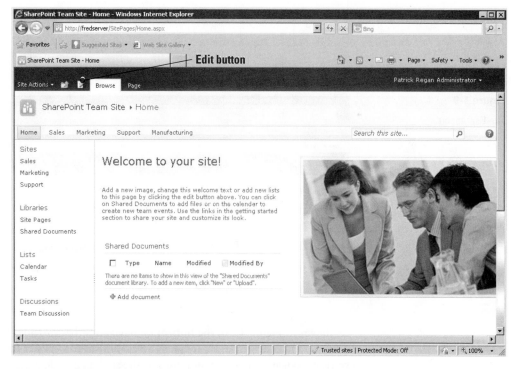

The Browse tab is the default view of a SharePoint page. At the top-right of the window (see Figure 1-9), users can click the User down-arrow to display a menu of personal options and settings (including signing in as a different user and signing out of the Web site).

The Page tab allows you to save and close Edit mode, check out the page (a SharePoint process that prevents multiple people from making changes to the same document), see a page history of what has been changed recently, as well as configure other options.

Figure 1-8

Editing mode

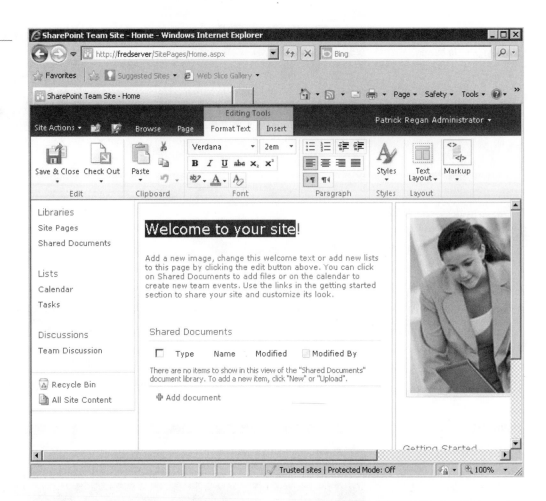

Figure 1-9

The User menu

As shown in Figure 1-10, the horizontal navigation bar provides links to the site's home page, subsites, and other pages that you, as an administrator, specify for users. The Quick Launch vertical navigation bar provides links to the site's pages, documents, lists, discussions, and Recycle Bins. Each navigational bar can be customized by an administrator.

Since a SharePoint server can host such a large volume of information, users will eventually need to use a quick search to find the information they're looking for. SharePoint includes a search box (see Figure 1-11) to simplify that task.

Figure 1-10

The Horizontal navigation bar
and the Quick Launch vertical
navigation bar

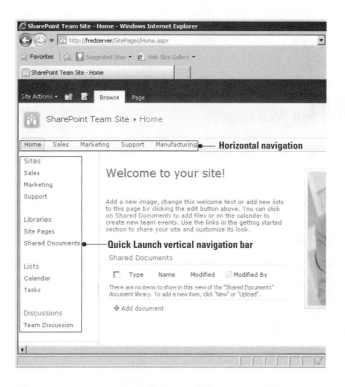

Figure 1-11

The search box

■ Understanding SharePoint's Components

THE BOTTOM LINE

Now that you have learned what makes up a SharePoint server, how to access it, and how to navigate it, this section explains the various components within SharePoint. Before learning how to install and configure SharePoint, you should have an understanding of what you are trying to configure.

When creating content using SharePoint, you will be using the following parts:

- Sites and Web pages
- Lists
- Libraries
- Views

- Web parts
- Workflows
- Alerts

Sites and Web Pages

Sites and Web pages are the first basic building block of SharePoint.

Sites are collections of Web pages. The Web pages are what the users create, manage, and view. The *Web pages* then contain lists, libraries, and other Web Parts arranged to provide the desired content. A site can contain just one Web page, or hundreds of Web pages.

Since companies have multiple departments or run multiple projects, a single site can also link to subsites for the various departments or projects. Depending on how the sites are created and linked, the subsites may or may not share the same attributes including what activities a user is allowed to do on a site or subsite, and may include common navigation tools to quickly and easily move within the site.

The easiest way to create sites and Web pages is to use one of the many templates that are provided as part of SharePoint. Some of the popular site templates include:

- A *Team Site* used to collaborate on projects and documents using lists and libraries.
- A *Document Workspace Site* that focuses on creating and collaborating on documents.
- A *Document Center* that allows a user to create, update, store, and manage documents.
- A *Group Work Site* to provide basic functions needed for a group to function effectively including contacts, calendars, general documents, and other lists.
- A *Meeting Workspace Site* to set up and document meetings.
- A *Blog Site* for users to post ideas, suggestions, and brainstorming.
- A *Blank Site* for users to create a custom site.

 CREATE A SITE

GET READY. To create a SharePoint site using the Site Actions menu, perform the following steps:

1. Navigate to the page where you want to place a subsite.
2. Click Site Actions to open the Site Actions menu and click the New Site option (see Figure 1-12). The Create dialog box appears.
3. Click the site template you want to use (see Figure 1-13).
4. In the Team Site Name box, type the title for the site.
5. Press the Tab key and, in the <URL name> box, type the name of the page.
6. Click Create. Your new site will open.

A *collection* is a grouping of sites in SharePoint. Every site collection has a single root site under which the other sites are built. In addition, the site collection has some attributes for all sites within a collection, including sharing the same Recycle Bin for deleted items.

Figure 1-12

Selecting the New Site option

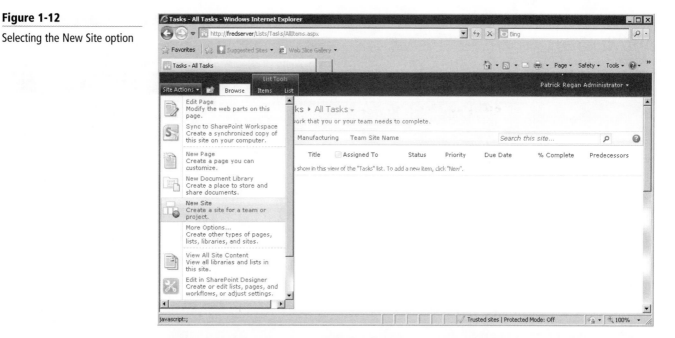

Figure 1-13

Using a site template

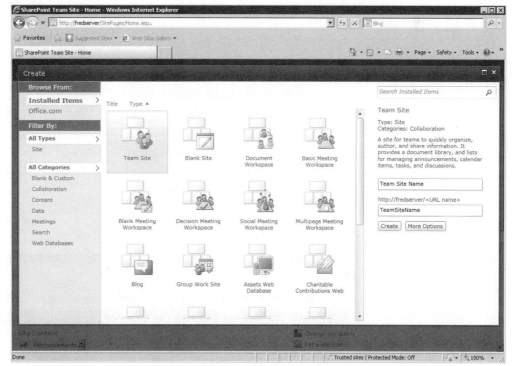

Lists

SharePoint allows you to save and retrieve large amounts of data. A list is a common method to organize data.

Lists are used to store, manage, organize, and share information and are a basic component used often in sites and Web pages. A list is information arranged in rows and columns, as shown in Figure 1-14. Similar to a spreadsheet, a list can also do mathematical calculations. Some commonly used lists are announcements, calendars, links, tasks, and discussions. Similar to sites or Web pages, you use templates to create lists, which can then be customized as needed by adding columns and mathematical functions.

Figure 1-14

A task list

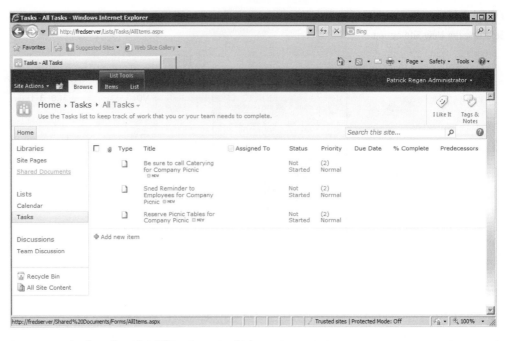

Some popular lists found in SharePoint include:

- Announcements for news messages on the Home page
- Calendars that show meetings and other events
- Contact information, including names, companies, email addresses, and phone numbers
- Discussions for threaded comments on a subject
- Issue Tracking for issues that need to be resolved
- Links for linking pages to the site
- Reports that display and index reports
- Status updates that track the accomplishment of goals
- Tasks for what needs to be done
- Custom lists to which you can add columns

Figure 1-15 shows the default lists used on a team site.

Figure 1-15

Default lists used in a SharePoint site

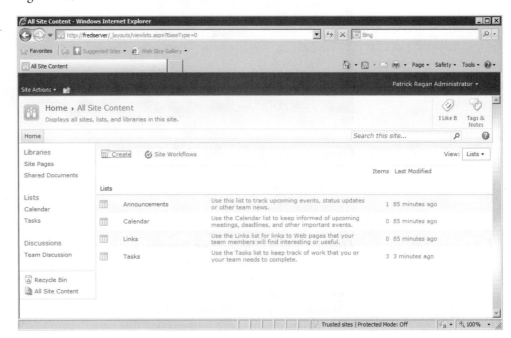

 CREATE A LIST

GET READY. There are several ways to create lists, including editing a page, adding a Web Part, or using the Site Actions menu. To create a list using the Site Actions menu, perform the following steps:

1. Navigate to the page where you want to place a list.
2. Open the Site Actions menu and click More Options (see Figure 1-16).

Figure 1-16

Selecting More Options

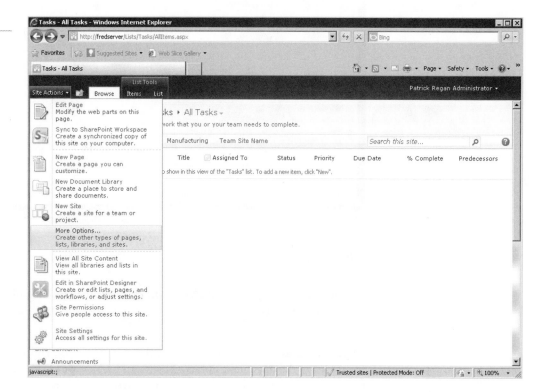

3. Click List to show only the List templates (see Figure 1-17). Then click the template you want to use.
4. In the ListName box in the right pane, type a name for the title of the list and click Create. The list is created.

Figure 1-17

Selecting the template

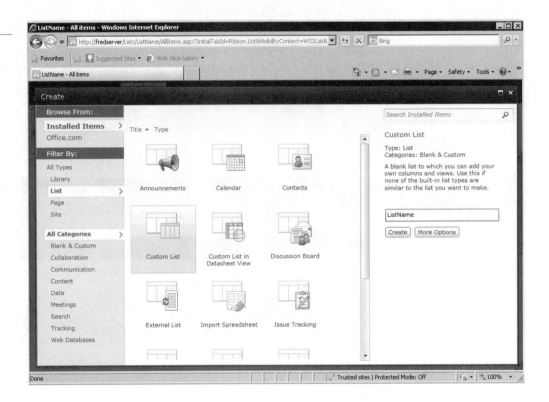

Libraries

Besides organizing raw data, SharePoint can also store and organize documents, forms, and wikis via libraries.

Libraries are used to store and organize documents, forms, and wikis. A commonly used library list is the document library, which can include word-processing documents, PDF files, notes, drawings, diagrams, forms, pictures, spreadsheets, videos, and presentations. Figure 1-18 shows a document library. Libraries also give you the ability to display the

Figure 1-18

A document library

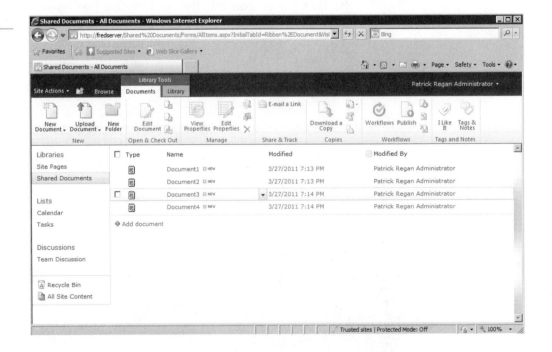

library in different ways, track versions of documents, and provide the ability for users to check in and check out documents so that you don't have multiple users changing the same document at the same time.

 CREATE A DOCUMENT LIBRARY

GET READY. Just like there are several ways to create a list, there are several ways to create a library. If you use the Site Actions menu, you can easily access templates to create items such as sites, lists, and libraries. To create a document library using the Site Actions menu, perform the following steps:

1. Navigate to the page where you want to place the library.
2. Open the Site Actions menu and click New Document Library (see Figure 1-19).

Figure 1-19

Creating a document library

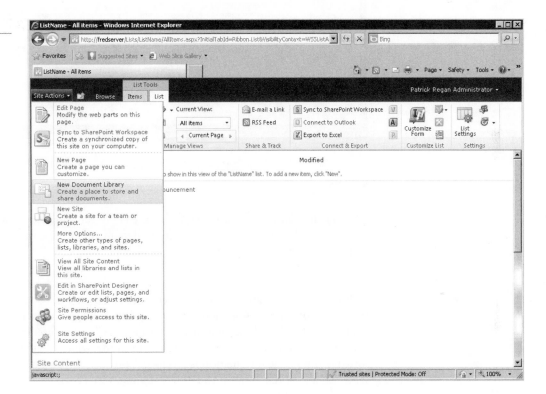

3. In the Name box, type a name for the library. In the Description box, type a description of the library (see Figure 1-20).
4. In the Navigation area, choose whether you want the library to display on Quick Launch.
5. In the Document Version History area, choose if you want to create a version each time you edit a file in this document library.
6. Click the Create button. The Document Library is created.

Figure 1-20

Configuring your Document Library

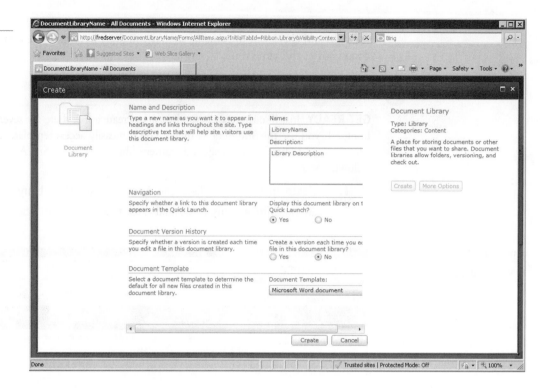

Views

SharePoint can retrieve, store, and organize large amounts of data, and you often need a way to quickly show a particular piece of data in an effective way so that you can make effective decisions.

As lists and libraries are created and used, some of these will contain hundreds, maybe even thousands, of entries. When looking at large lists and libraries in their raw form, it can be difficult to find and read the data that a user needs. *Views* are used to control what information is filtered based on the desired columns and records, while specifying how the information is sorted and how the information is grouped. Fortunately, you can create multiple views for the same list and switch between the different views very easily.

 CREATE A VIEW

GET READY. To create a view, perform the following steps:

1. Navigate to the list that you want to create a view for.
2. At the top of the window, click the DefaultView down arrow and then click Create View (see Figure 1-21).
3. In the Choose a view format area, click Standard View (see Figure 1-22).
4. In the View Name box, type the name of the view (see Figure 1-23). If you want to make this view the default view when viewing this list, select the Make this the default view option.
5. If you want you to be the only one to use the view, select Create a Personal View.

Figure 1-21

Selecting the Create View option

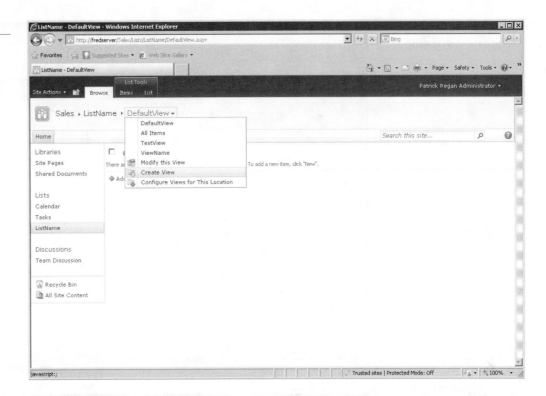

Figure 1-22

Choosing the view format

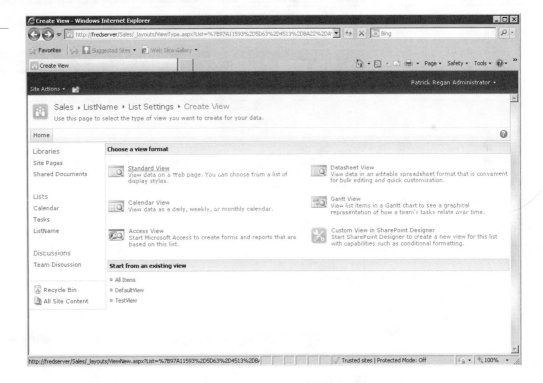

6. Select each of the columns you want to show in the view. You can also specify the order that the columns show by selecting the appropriate number using the Position from Left option. Optionally, you can create sort, filter and grouping options.

7. Click OK to create the view.

To select a view, click the current view and then choose the view you want to select (see Figure 1-24).

Figure 1-23

Selecting the view options

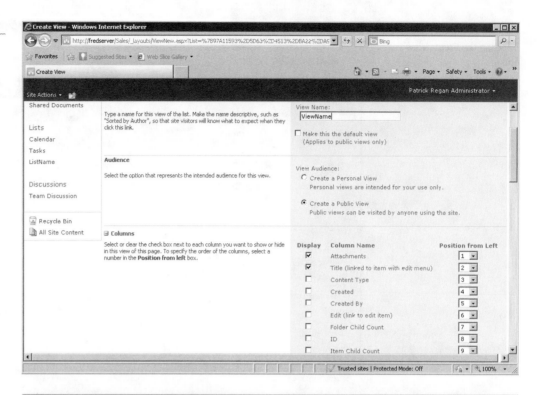

Figure 1-24

Selecting the view

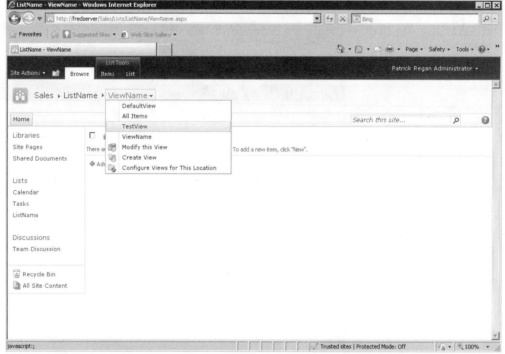

Web Parts

While SharePoint offers many templates and allows you to organize its content in many ways, each Web page can be further customized with Web Parts.

Web Parts are customizable SharePoint components that allow you to add custom elements to a page or allow existing information to be presented in an organized way that incorporates business logic and applications. While common Web Parts are lists and libraries,

SharePoint also provides several ready-made Web Parts; still yet, many others are available from third-parties. In addition, customized Web Parts can be created with a variety of programing languages.

 ADD A WEB PART TO A SITE

GET READY. To add a Web Part, perform the following steps:

1. Navigate to the page on which you want to add a Web Part.
2. Click the Edit Page icon on the Ribbon (see Figure 1-25). The Editing Tools tabs (the Format Text tab and the Insert tab) open.
3. Click the Insert tab and then click Web Part (see Figure 1-26). An Add Web Part area opens.

Figure 1-25

The Edit Page icon

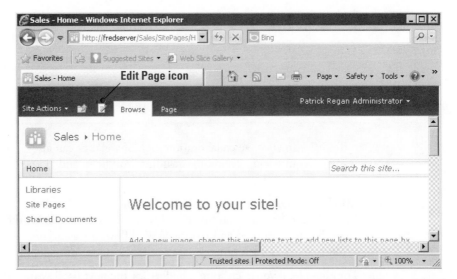

Figure 1-26

Adding a Web Part to a page

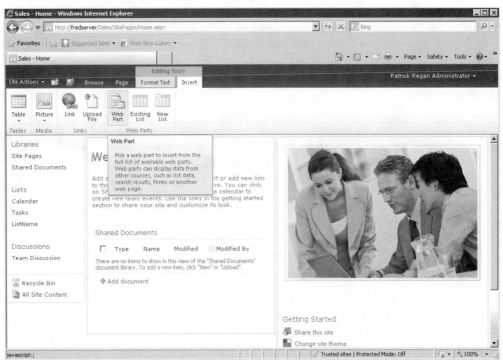

4. Click the Web Part that you want to add and then click Add (see Figure 1-27).

Figure 1-27

Selecting the Web Part

Workflows and Alerts

To make an effective collaboration tool, SharePoint can also notify you of events that might require your attention, including workflows and alerts.

Workflows allow you to manage information within SharePoint via a defined process, or can be used to add application functionality within SharePoint. Workflows divide a process into steps that are measured and reported. Workflows are associated with lists, libraries, list items, or documents to track progress, approval, or disposition/deletion of the items.

For example, if you're creating a budget for the next fiscal year, and the budget must be approved by several people, you can define workflows that will ensure that each person reviews and approves the budget before it is considered final. Another common use of workflows is to have a document reviewed before being published. Table 1-2 shows the SharePoint Workflows that are included with SharePoint Server 2010.

Table 1-2

SharePoint Workflows

WORKFLOW	DESCRIPTION	AVAILABILITY
Approval	Routes a document for approval by one or more people. Documents can be approved, rejected, reassigned, or have changes requested.	SharePoint Server 2010 and SharePoint Foundation
Collect Feedback	Routes a document to one or more people so they can review documents and leave comments for the originator.	SharePoint Server 2010 and SharePoint Foundation
Collect Signatures	Routes a document to gather signatures for the final completion of a document	SharePoint Server 2010 and SharePoint Foundation
Disposition Approval	Keeps track of how old a document is so that it can be deleted when it expires.	SharePoint Server 2010 and SharePoint Foundation
Three-State	Tracks the status (assigned, completed, or accepted) of an item as being in a list.	SharePoint Foundation

Alerts empower SharePoint to automatically notify a user when information has been added or changed. In addition, tasks and calendar items can be established to send out reminders when a task event or other event is due.

 ADD A WORKFLOW TO A LIBRARY OR LIST

GET READY. To add a workflow to a library or list, perform the following steps:

1. Navigate to the site with the library or list.
2. Under the Library Tools tabs, click the Library tab, and then click Workflow Settings. Figure 1-28 shows the Workflow Settings button.
3. By default, in the These workflows are configured to run on items of this type option (see Figure 1-29), all items are selected. If you want the workflow to affect only documents or folders, select either Documents or Folders.

Figure 1-28

The Workflow Settings button

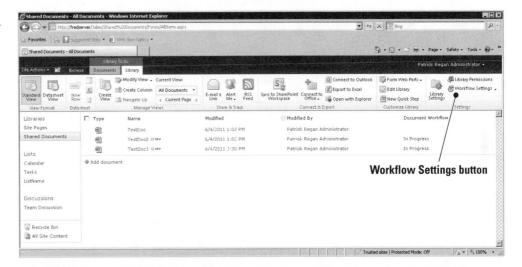

Figure 1-29

The Add a workflow option

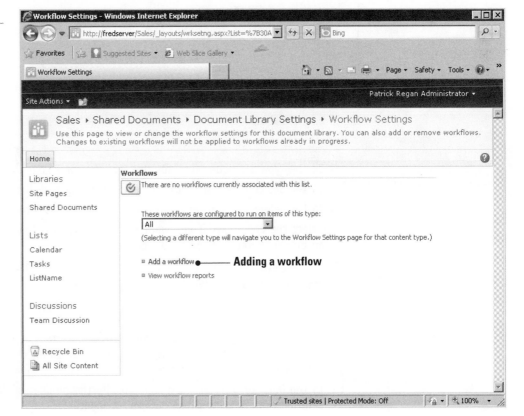

4. Click the Add a workflow option (see Figure 1-29).

5. If you wish for the document to be approved before being published, select Approval–SharePoint 2010 (see Figure 1-30).

Figure 1-30

Selecting the type of workflow

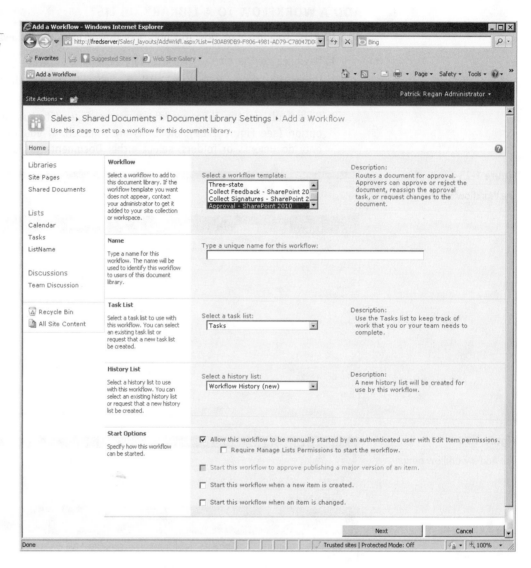

6. In the Type a unique name for this workflow box, type your unique name.

7. In the Select a task list box, select an existing task list.

8. In the Select a history list box, select a list to keep track of the history.

9. Select the check box if you want to Allow this workflow to be manually started by an authenticated user with Edit permissions.

10. To complete the settings, click Next (or, if you choose Disposition Approval, click OK).

11. When the Document Workflow page displays, type the name of the Approvers (see Figure 1-31). If you have more than one user, separate the users with a semicolon (;).

12. In the Order drop-down, select One at a time (serial) if you want all of the approvers to be notified in the order specified, or select All at once (parallel) if you want to all of the approvers to be notified together.

13. In the Duration Per Task text box, specify the number of days and then select the duration units (such as days, weeks, or months).

Figure 1-31

Selecting approvers and
notification settings

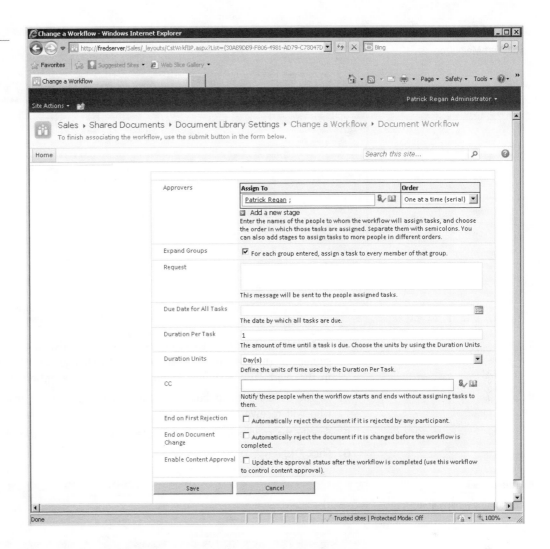

14. If you want yourself or others to be notified when a workflow begins, type the name of the users in the CC text box.

15. In the End on the First Rejection area, if you want the document to be rejected if any reviewer rejects it, select the Automatically reject the document if it is rejected by any participant option.

16. In the End on Document Change area, if you want to reject the document if it was changed while the workflow was running, select the Automatically reject the document it is changed before the workflow is completed option.

17. In the Enable Content Approval area, if you want it to be automatically approved when the workflow is successfully completed, select the Update the approval status after the workflow is completed option.

18. Click Save.

 ADD AN ALERT

GET READY. To set up an alert for a list or library, perform the following steps:

1. Navigate to the list or library.

2. In the Share & Track group, click the List or Library tab, click the Alert Me button (see Figure 1-32), and then click Set Alert On This List or Set Alert On This Library.

Figure 1-32

The Alert Me button

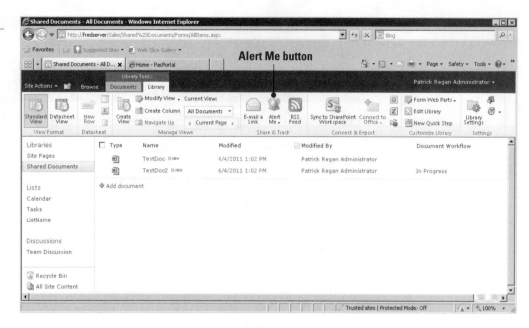

3. A default alert title consists of the name of the list or library, which is used as the subject of the alert e-mail. If you want to change the title, type the new alert title in the Alert Title text box. Figure 1-33 shows the options to configure a new alert.

4. In the Send Alerts To box, type the name of the users or e-mail addresses of those who will receive the alerts.

5. Specify the conditions for which an alert will be sent and how often the alerts will be sent.

6. Click OK.

Figure 1-33

Configuring a new alert

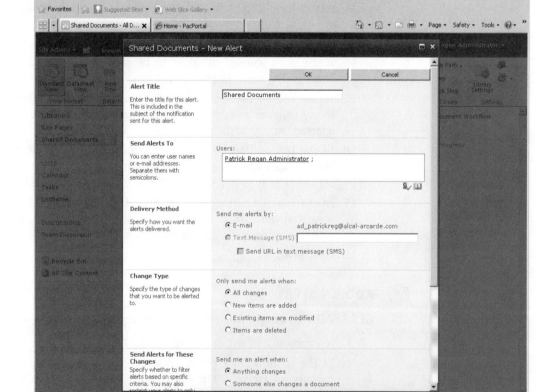

■ Understanding SharePoint's Identities and Profiles

THE BOTTOM LINE

Social networking allows users to find and connect with one another. SharePoint offers multiple social networking tools—not to have fun, necessarily, but to allow users within an organization to collaborate more effectively. These tools include User Profiles and MySites.

Active Directory is the directory service that contains accounts for users within your organization; these accounts are used for authentication, authorization, and auditing. User profiles in SharePoint contain contact and other personal information that can be searched through and used by SharePoint users. SharePoint can synchronize the user profiles with Active Directory user accounts and their attributes (such as email addresses, phone numbers, addresses, managers, job titles, and so on). You don't have to constantly update hundreds (sometimes thousands!) of user attributes; SharePoint frequently synchronizes information with Active Directory.

With SharePoint, users can upload pictures of themselves that will display with their user profiles. This way, users can visually see what other users look like. In addition, if your organization uses Office Communicator, SharePoint can connect to Office Communicator so that SharePoint can show if a user is online or not.

Lastly, SharePoint offers *MySites*, which allows users to customize their individual SharePoint pages. These sites can be used to establish relationships between users and to connect people in an organization.

■ Understanding SharePoint's Configuration Tools

THE BOTTOM LINE

After you install the SharePoint program (which will be covered in Lesson 2), you will have to configure SharePoint as a whole and you will have to configure sites, pages, lists, and so on from time to time. The two primary tools to configure SharePoint are SharePoint Central Administration and SharePoint Site Actions.

This lesson is a simple introduction to SharePoint. In Lesson 2, the SharePoint installation and initial configuration will be discussed. With Lesson 2 and beyond, SharePoint Central Administration and SharePoint Site Actions will be used to configure SharePoint.

To this point, the SharePoint components have been introduced, including an introduction to how to use SharePoint. While you will need to know how to use SharePoint to configure, administer, test, and troubleshoot, it is not the main focus of this book. Instead, you will be focusing on installing and configuring SharePoint. Therefore, you will be using SharePoint Central Administration and SharePoint Site Settings (which are located within the Site Actions menu).

SharePoint Central Administration

SharePoint Central Administration is a separate Web site running on the same IIS server as the SharePoint site.

During the installation and initial configuration of SharePoint Server 2010, the Windows SharePoint Services setup program assigns a random port number greater than 1024 to the administration site to keep it separate from the user site (which uses the standard HTTP port number of 80). Therefore, you usually must type the following:

http://NameOfServer:portnumber

For example:

http://winserver:27167

Figure 1-34 shows SharePoint Central Administration.

Figure 1-34

SharePoint Central
Administration

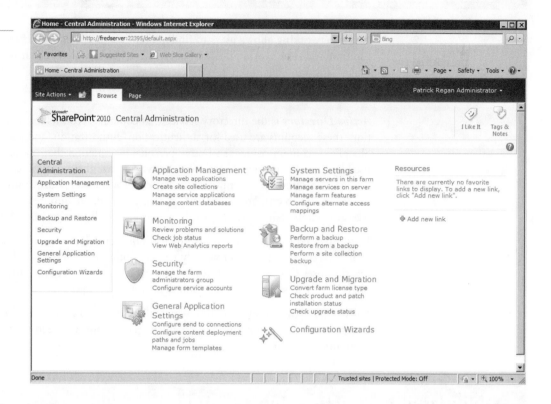

Fortunately, since the port number is sometimes difficult to remember, you can open
SharePoint Central Administration by logging on to the server where SharePoint is installed,
clicking the Start button, selecting Microsoft SharePoint 2010 Products, and then selecting
SharePoint Central Administration.

 OPEN SHAREPOINT CENTRAL ADMINISTRATION

GET READY. To open the SharePoint Central Administration on the server running SharePoint,
perform the following steps:

1. Login as a SharePoint administrator on the server that is running SharePoint.
2. Click Start > All Programs.
3. Click Microsoft SharePoint 2010 Products and then choose SharePoint 2010 Central
   Administration (see Figure 1-35). SharePoint Central Administration opens.

The quickest way to get a SharePoint site up and running is to run the Configuration
Wizards. However, if you select the Standalone option during installation, the SharePoint
service will automatically be installed using the default settings.

The rest of SharePoint Central Administration is divided into the following areas:

- **Application Management:** Allows you to manage Web applications, create site collec-
  tions, manage service applications, and manage content databases.
- **Monitoring:** Allows you to track, view, and report the health and status of your
  SharePoint farms.
- **Security:** Allows you to configure security setting for users and the entire SharePoint
  environment.
- **General Application Settings:** Allows you to configure external service connections,
  SharePoint Designer settings, and settings to integrate Reporting Services.

Figure 1-35

Opening SharePoint Central
Administration

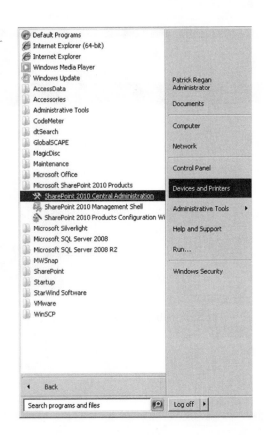

- **System Settings:** Allows you to manage the SharePoint servers, including the SQL server and SMTP server. It also allows you to manage features, solutions, and farm-wide settings.
- **Backup and Restore:** Allows you to perform backups and restores.
- **Upgrade and Migration:** Allows you to upgrade SharePoint, add licenses, and enable Enterprise Features.
- **Configuration Wizards:** Provides wizards that allow you to easily and quickly configure SharePoint.

Most of these options will be covered in the following lessons.

SHAREPOINT SITE SETTINGS

SharePoint Central Administration is usually used to configure SharePoint Web sites and services. To configure settings with a SharePoint site, you will use Site Settings. *Site Settings*, accessed through the Site Actions menu (see Figure 1-36), is the primary interface to configure site settings, including setting the site-specific permissions, determining the look and feel of the site, as well as configuring other miscellaneous settings.

Figure 1-37 shows the Site Settings page.

The right side of the screen displays the Site URL and Mobile Site URL for the site. The Mobile Site URL is used for handheld devices, such as smart phones.

The rest of the page includes the following categories:

- **Users and Permissions:** Provides options for managing people, groups, administrators, and permissions.
- **Galleries:** Allows you access libraries of reusable content (including Web Parts, list templates, themes, and solutions) that is available to a site or sites within a site collection.

Figure 1-36

Opening Site Settings

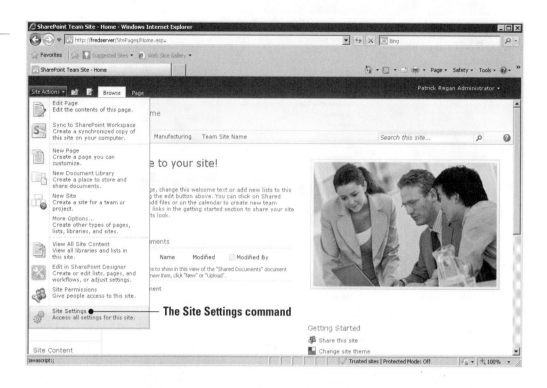

Figure 1-37

The Site Settings page

- **Site Administration:** Allows you to manage the site structure, including regional settings (language, time zone, days that make up a work week, and time format), site libraries, lists, user alerts, RSS feeds, sites, workflows, and work flow settings.

- **Site Collection Administration:** Allows you to configure options for the Recycle Bin, site hierarchy, site collection features, and help settings.

- **Look and Feel:** Allows you to configure the default page layouts and overall appearance of the SharePoint site.

- **Site Actions:** Allows you to save sites as a template, view site Web Analytics Reports, delete a site, and manage site features.

- **Reporting Services:** Allows you to connect to a Microsoft SQL Report Server to generate complex reports.

■ Understanding SharePoint Online and Office 365

THE BOTTOM LINE

Office 365, which includes *SharePoint Online* (see Figure 1-38), is a cloud-based service that helps an organization create sites share documents and insights with colleagues, partners, and customers. Rather than install and deploy SharePoint Server 2010 at the organization's physical site, organizations subscribe to SharePoint Online to provide employees with collaboration and information management capabilities that work with familiar Office applications.

Over the past couple of years, there has been a lot of buzz around cloud computing. *Cloud computing* is the delivery of computing as a service rather than a product. For the most part, with cloud computing, you access the service over the network (usually over the Internet). Most are not concerned with how it works in the background. Instead, they know that they log on using a browser or local application and then access whatever services needed. Since this is a service instead of a product, you typically sign up for the service. For many of these, you must pay a monthly fee. In return, you simply use the service; the hosting company handles installation, initial configuration of the product, maintenance, and upgrades. They might also handle backups and forensics services as needed. Cloud computing offers ease of use, scalability, and virtualized resources at a reasonable price.

Office 365 is Microsoft's hosted software and service delivered and accessed over the Internet. It includes the Microsoft Office suite of desktop applications and hosted versions of Microsoft server products, including Exchange Server, SharePoint Server, and Lync Server.

TAKE NOTE*

For more information about Microsoft Office 365 and SharePoint Online, visit the following Web sites:

http://www.microsoft.com/en-us/office365/hosted-solutions.aspx

http://sharepoint.microsoft.com/en-us/SharePoint-Online/Pages/default.aspx

http://technet.microsoft.com/en-us/sharepoint/gg144571

Figure 1-38

The Microsoft Office 365
SharePoint Team Site

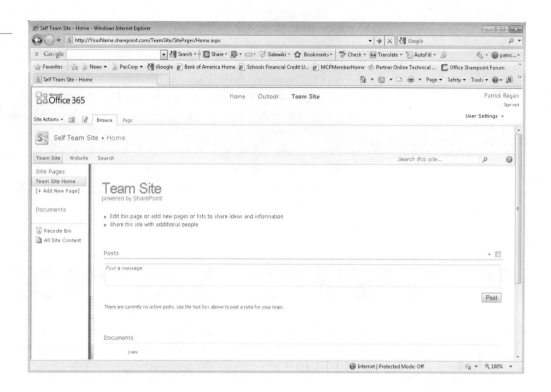

SKILL SUMMARY

IN THIS LESSON YOU LEARNED:

- SharePoint is a suite of services that provides a Web site/portal that allows users to organize and retrieve information and allows a team to easily collaborate and work together.

- SharePoint Foundation 2010 is the free version of SharePoint and is named differently from SharePoint Server 2010 to avoid confusion.

- Microsoft released two editions of SharePoint Server 2010: Standard and Enterprise. Of course, for the most functionality, you must purchase the Enterprise edition.

- SharePoint is not just a simple program, service, or protocol; it's a suite of programs and services that starts with the Windows server up to the SharePoint workspace.

- Since SharePoint is presented as a Web site for the users, the user needs only a browser to access it.

- Sites are collections of Web pages. The Web pages are what the users create, manage, and view. The Web pages then contain lists, libraries, and other Web Parts arranged to provide the desired content.

- Lists are used to store, manage, organize, and share information; they are a basic component used often in sites and Web pages.

- Libraries are used to store and organize documents, forms, and wikis.

- You can create multiple views for the same list and easily switch between the different views.

- Web Parts allow you to add custom elements to a page or allow existing information to be presented in an organized way that also incorporates business logic and applications.

- Workflows allow you to manage information within SharePoint via a defined process or can be used to add application functionality within SharePoint.

- After installing the SharePoint program, you will have to configure SharePoint as a whole and you will have to configure sites, pages, lists, and so on from time to time. The two primary tools to configure SharePoint are SharePoint Central Administration and SharePoint Site Actions.

- Office 365, which includes SharePoint Online, is a cloud-based service that helps an organization create sites to share documents and insights with colleagues, partners, and customers.

■ Knowledge Assessment

Fill in the Blank

Complete the following sentences by writing the correct word or words in the blanks provided.

1. _____ are a collection of Web pages used in SharePoint 2010.

2. _____ contain lists, libraries, and other Web Parts.

3. A _____ is a grouping of sites with a single root site.

4. _____ allow you to manage information by executing a defined process when information is added to a Web site or list.

5. The _____ is the control that has most of the buttons and menus used to control a SharePoint component.

6. _____ is a separate Web site used to configure SharePoint.

7. _____ are used to store, manage, and organize large amounts of information as a table.

8. _____ is a suite of services that allows you to organize and retrieve information and allows team members to collaborate.

9. SharePoint Foundation replaced _____.

10. SharePoint runs on top of _____ and the .NET Framework.

Multiple Choice

Circle the letter that corresponds to the best answer.

1. Which of the following is the free version of SharePoint 2010?
   a. SharePoint Foundation 2010
   b. SharePoint Server 2010 for Internet Sites
   c. SharePoint Services 2010
   d. SharePoint Site Enterprise 2010

2. Which of the following is not the minimum hardware required for a single server installation of SharePoint 2010?
   a. 2 or more core processors
   b. 4 GB of memory
   c. 80 GB free disk space
   d. 64-bit processors

3. Which of the following SQL versions can you *not* use with SharePoint Server 2010?
   a. 64-bit version of SQL Server 2005 with SP2
   b. 64-bit version of SQL Server 2008 with SP1 and cumulative update 2
   c. 64-bit version of SQL Server 2008 R2
   d. 64-bit version of SQL Server 2008 R2 Express

4. Which of the following is used to store and organize documents and forms?
   a. views
   b. wiki
   c. Web Part
   d. library

5. Which of the following allows you to add custom elements to a page?
   a. views
   b. lists
   c. Web Parts
   d. library

6. Which of the following allows you to create new subsites and pages, add lists or libraries, or edit a page?
   a. Ribbon
   b. SharePoint Central Administration
   c. Site Actions menu
   d. library manager

7. SharePoint requires _____ to provide a software framework that includes a large library that allows you to create SharePoint Web Parts.
   a. IIS
   b. SQL Server
   c. The .NET Framework
   d. DCOM

8. Which of the following are used to install SharePoint 2010?
   a. 64-bit version of Windows Server 2008 with SP2
   b. 64-bit version of Windows Server 2008 R2 with no SP
   c. 64-bit version of Windows Server 2008 R2 with SP1
   d. 32-bit version of Windows Server 2008

9. What is the disadvantage of using SQL Server 2008 R2 Express?
   a. The size of the databases is limited.
   b. Performance will be slow.
   c. SharePoint Server 2010 will not run on the SQL Server 2008 R2 Express.
   d. It requires an extremely large paging file.

10. Site Settings is accessed through the _____.
    a. Ribbon
    b. Site Actions menu
    c. Gallery Editor
    d. Web Site Editor

True / False

Circle T if the statement is true or F if the statement is false.

T | F **1.** You can only use Internet Explorer to access a SharePoint site.

T | F **2.** SharePoint Foundation includes a MySite personal site.

T | F **3.** By default, SharePoint Central Administration uses a random port.

T | F **4.** When you use SharePoint over the Internet for your corporate users, it is best to use the SharePoint 2010 for Internet Sites, Enterprise edition.

T | F **5.** SQL Server 2008 R2 Express is limited to 10 GB in databases.

■ Case Scenarios

Scenario 1-1: SharePoint as a Communication

The CEO informs you that he isn't pleased with the communication between the various departments and within the team. He says that another project failed because of poor communication. He wants to know what can be used to help with this problem, and how it would help. What do you tell him?

Scenario 1-2: Skills Needed for SharePoint

The IT manager for your company informs you that he has been reading about SharePoint's capabilities and features. He is interested in using SharePoint to its fullest capabilities and asks you about the specialized skills that would be required to maintain a full implementation of SharePoint to support 2,000 users. What do you tell him?

2 LESSON

Installing SharePoint 2010

OBJECTIVE DOMAIN MATRIX

TECHNOLOGY SKILL	OBJECTIVE DOMAIN	OBJECTIVE DOMAIN NUMBER
Deploying New Installations and Upgrades	Deploying New Installations and Upgrades	1.1
Scripting Installations	Scripting Installations	1.1.6
Installing Language Packs	Installing Language Packs	1.1.5
Troubleshooting SharePoint Installation Problems	Analyzing ULS Logs, Installation Error Logs, and Event Logs	1.1.7
	Repairing Installation Errors	1.1.8
Activating Enterprise Features		
Applying and Managing Patches	Applying and Managing Patches	1.2.8
Configuring High Availability	Configuring High Availability	1.2.3

KEY TERMS

active-passive cluster

cumulative updates (CU)

database mirroring

detect method

domain controller

failover cluster

Farm Configuration Wizard

high availability

language packs

network fault-tolerance

Network Interface Card (NIC) teaming

network load balancing (NLB)

redundant array of independent disks (RAID)

service accounts

service packs

SharePoint preparation tool

SharePoint Products Configuration Wizard

tier 2 farm

tier 3 farm

uninterruptible power supply (UPS)

During a meeting, you explained to management the benefits of using SharePoint. Now, your manager would like you to create a SharePoint environment so that a team can investigate the possible uses of SharePoint for the company. Therefore, you need to acquire the necessary resources and install SharePoint.

■ Deploying New Installations and Upgrades

THE BOTTOM LINE

When installing SharePoint, you have a choice of multiple environments. SharePoint can be installed on a single server with its own internal database, to a single server with separate installation of SQL Server, or it can be installed as a farm consisting of multiple servers. However, when you are first learning about SharePoint, the best way to start is to install a simple installation of SharePoint and eventually expand to creating a multi-server farm.

CERTIFICATION READY
What are the general steps to Install SharePoint 2010?
1.1

When you perform a SharePoint installation, you typically follow these steps:

1. Plan your installation.
2. Install Windows Server.
3. Install SQL Server if necessary.
4. Install any prerequisites.
5. Install SharePoint binaries.
6. Run the SharePoint 2010 Products Configuration Wizard to configure the SharePoint server and farm.
7. Perform the initial configuration, including configuring services and applications on the farm.

Before discussing the steps of installing SharePoint, there is one more point that should be made. As you install and configure, it is very important that you document each step that you perform. This will allow you to duplicate the SharePoint environment in the future and it can become quite valuable when you want to migrate or upgrade in the future.

Preparing for Installation

When preparing for an installation, you should plan your installation, acquire the necessary resources, install the operating system, install SQL server (if necessary), and then start installing SharePoint.

Planning is essential for every part of implementing SharePoint 2010, and a crucial part of preparing for the installation. Even the simplest installation still requires some planning. For SharePoint 2010, you will need to:

- Know the minimum requirements for SharePoint.
- Add additional resources to make sure that you have a minimum performance level.
- Determine the minimum storage you will need to store the SharePoint files and any data that you want to put in SharePoint.
- Determine where you are going to install SharePoint.
- Determine the licensing you will need.
- Determine what features you will need to install or enable.
- Determine the SQL Server server name and instance name.
- Determine the product key or trial key, which must be entered during setup.

TAKE NOTE*

For the sake of the 70-667 exam, you should only be concerned with the basics, such as knowing the minimum system requirements needed to install SharePoint and the components needed on the server for SharePoint to run. The 70-668 exam emphasizes capacity planning, performance tuning, and topology design.

UNDERSTANDING THE MINIMUM REQUIREMENTS

CERTIFICATION READY
What are the minimum requirements to install SharePoint 2010?
1.1

According to Microsoft, the minimum hardware requirements for Web servers, application servers, and single server installations are as follows:

- **Processor**: 64-bit, four cores
- **RAM**: 4 GB for developer or evaluation use, or 8 GB for production use in a single server or multiple server farm
- **Hard disk**: 80 GB for system drive

The minimum hardware requirements for the database server are as follows:

- **Processor**: 64-bit, four cores for small deployments and 64-bit, eight cores for medium deployments
- **RAM**: 8 GB for small deployments and 16 GB for medium deployments

The operating system that you need for a single server with a built-in database, front-end Web server, and application servers in a farm are as follows:

- The 64-bit edition of Windows Server 2008 Standard, Enterprise, Data Center, or Web Server with SP2. If you are running Windows Server 2008 without SP2, the Microsoft SharePoint Products Preparation Tool installs Service Pack 2 for Windows Server 2008 automatically.
- The 64-bit edition of Windows Server 2008 R2 Standard, Enterprise, Data Center, or Web Server; or the 64-bit edition of Windows Server 2008 R2 Service Pack 1 (SP1) Standard, Enterprise, Data Center, or Web Server.

For the database server in a farm, you will need one of the following:

- The 64-bit edition of Microsoft SQL Server 2008 R2.
- The 64-bit edition of Microsoft SQL Server 2008 with Service Pack 1 (SP1) and Cumulative Update 2. It is recommended that you use Cumulative Update 5 or higher.
- The 64-bit edition of Microsoft SQL Server 2005 with Service Pack 3 (SP3) and Cumulative update package 3 for SQL Server 2005 Service Pack 3.

TAKE NOTE * When you install Microsoft SQL Server 2008 SP1 on Windows Server 2008 R2, you might receive a compatibility warning. You should disregard this warning and continue with your installation.

A free evaluation copy of Windows Server 2008 R2 is located at http://www.microsoft.com/windowsserver2008/en/us/trial-software.aspx. You must create a Windows Live ID account, which takes only a couple of minutes. You then save the ISO file to your hard drive and burn the ISO image to a DVD, which will be used for installation. Of course, you need a DVD burner. Fortunately, the downloading and burning of the DVD does not have to be done on the computer that you are going to perform the installation on.

In addition, you will need to download and install the following .NET Framework 3.5 SP1 hotfix for Windows Server 2008 and Windows Server 2008 R2 before you run Setup:

KB979917 - QFE for SharePoint issues - Perf Counter fix & User Impersonation (http://go.microsoft.com/fwlink/?LinkId=192577)

 INSTALL WINDOWS SERVER 2008 R2

GET READY. To install Windows Server 2008 R2, perform the following steps:

1. Insert the Windows Server 2008 R2 installation media and power on the physical server. You might be prompted to press any key to install from the DVD. If so, press the space bar.

The initial installation screen displays (see Figure 2-1).

2. Configure the following three items:

- **Language to install:** For example, English or German.
- **Time and currency format:** For example, English (United States) or French (Switzerland).
- **Keyboard or input method:** For example, US or United Kingdom.

Figure 2-1

The initial Windows install screen

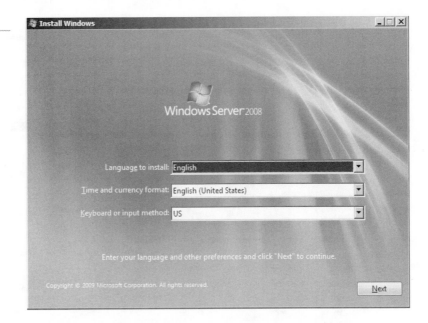

3. Click Next and then click Install now (see Figure 2-2).

Depending on the type of media you are using to install the software, you might be prompted to enter the Windows product key.

Figure 2-2

The Windows Server Install Now option

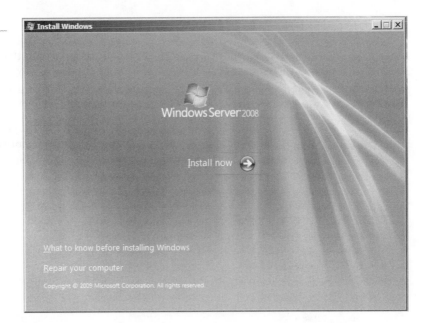

4. If prompted, type a Windows product key and then click **Next**. (If you're using an evaluation copy, you will not be prompted.)

   You're prompted to install either the full version of Windows Server 2008 or Server Core and then choose the edition of Windows. You will need to choose a full installation and either Standard or Enterprise edition depending on the hardware requirements that you need to use.

5. Select a Standard (Full Installation), as shown in Figure 2-3.

Figure 2-3

Selecting the operating system to install

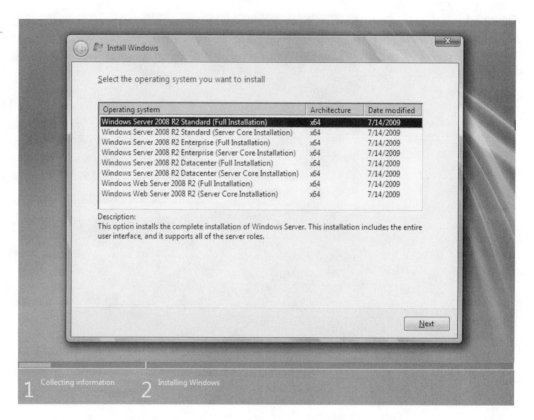

6. Click Next.

   On the subsequent screen, you are prompted to accept the Windows Server 2008 R2 license terms.

7. Read the licensing terms and then place a checkmark next to I accept the license terms. Click Next to continue the installation.

   You are prompted to select an upgrade installation or a clean install. If you are installing Windows onto brand new hardware, you will notice that the Upgrade option is grayed out; only the Custom option is available.

8. Select the Custom (advanced) installation option (see Figure 2-4).

Figure 2-4

The Custom (advanced) install option

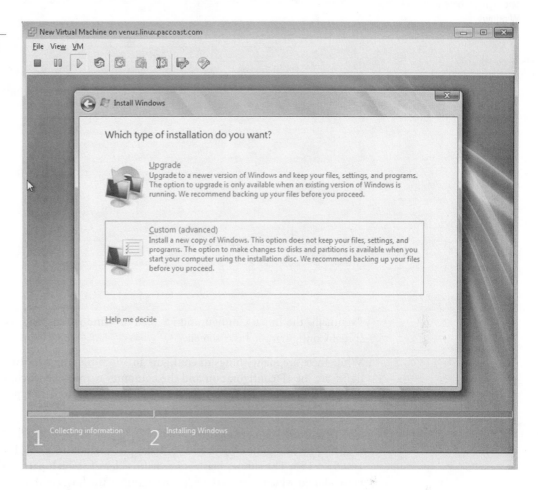

On the subsequent screen, you are prompted to select the hard drive partition on which to install Windows.

9. Select the appropriate partition (see Figure 2-5) and click Next.

TAKE NOTE*

If it is a new system, you will only have unallocated space, which will have to be used to create necessary partitions.

At this point, the installation process begins. The remainder of the installation is largely automated.

After a final reboot, you will be prompted to establish a complex password.

10. Click OK.

11. Type a password (such as Password01) twice in the appropriate boxes and press Enter.

TAKE NOTE*

Normally, you would choose a stronger password, but this password will suffice for a practice environment.

---

12. Once the password is changed, click OK.

Figure 2-5

Specifying where to install
Windows

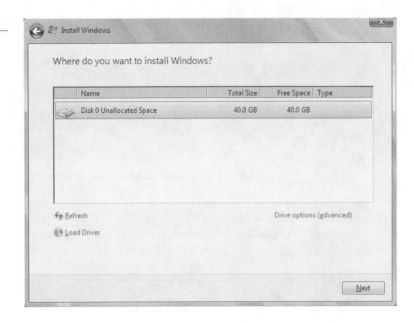

Eventually, the Initial Configuration Screen in Windows displays. Be sure not to close the Initial Configuration Tasks screen.

While there are many things to configure in Windows, the two things you should first configure are the IP configuration and the computer name. The IP configuration enables the computer to communicate on the network. The computer name helps you easily get to it remotely.

The IP address uniquely identifies a computer on a network. Each address consists of four numbers ranging from 0 to 255. Examples include 192.168.1.120, 10.24.42.23, and 140.55.4.154. The subnet mask is needed to identify which part of the address identifies the network and which part of the address identifies the host on the network.

The default gateway is the address of the nearest router. It needs to know the default gateway because when it has to send packets to another network, it automatically forwards packets to the router so that they can be forwarded to the appropriate network.

Lastly, the DNS server address is used to provide naming resolution for host and domain names to IP addresses. For example, when you type www.microsoft.com, it translates that address to an IP address of a Microsoft server.

 CONFIGURE WINDOWS NETWORKING

GET READY. With the Initial Configuration Tasks screen open from the previous steps still open, you can configure Windows networking by following these steps:

1. Click the Configure networking option (see Figure 2-6).

   The Network Connections screen opens (see Figure 2-7), displaying the available network connections.

Figure 2-6

The Initial Configuration Tasks window

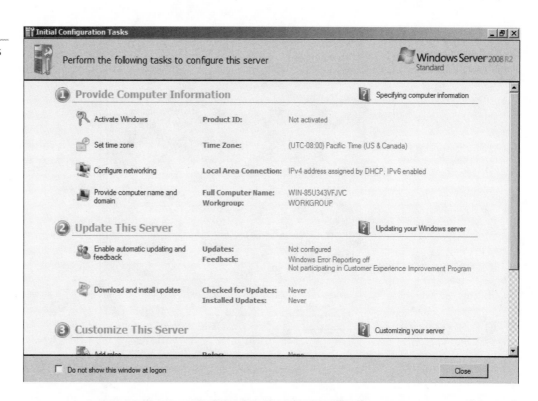

Figure 2-7

The Network Connections screen

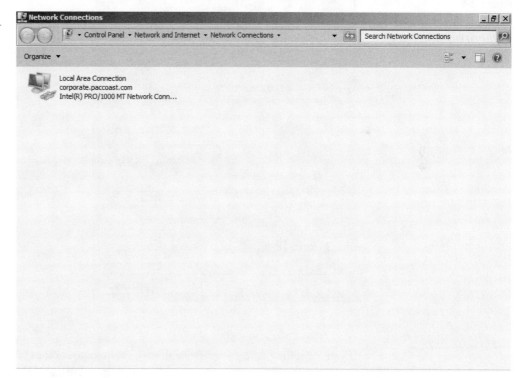

2. Double-click Local Area Connection. The Local Area Connection Status dialog displays (see Figure 2-8).

3. Click Properties. The Internet Protocol Version 4 (TCP/IPv4) Properties dialog displays (see Figure 2-9).

4. Select the Use the following IP address option.

5. Type the appropriate IP address, Subnet mask, Default gateway, and Preferred DNS server.

Figure 2-8

The Local Area Connection
Status dialog

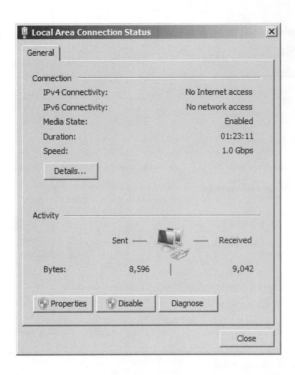

Figure 2-9

The Internet Protocol Version 4
(TCP/IPv4) Properties dialog

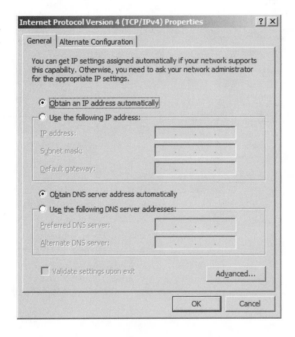

TAKE NOTE*

If you are setting up a computer within your company, talk to your network administrator to acquire the IP address, subnet mask, default gateway, and DNS Server address. If you are setting up a computer at home, you will most likely connect to a router that allows you to connect multiple computers to the Internet. Most likely, you can type in the following:

IP address: 192.168.1.120
Subnet mask: 255.255.255.0
Default gateway: 192.168.1.1
Preferred DNS server: 192.168.1.1

Figure 2-10 shows an example of configured IPv4 settings.

Figure 2-10

The IPv4 configuration with addresses

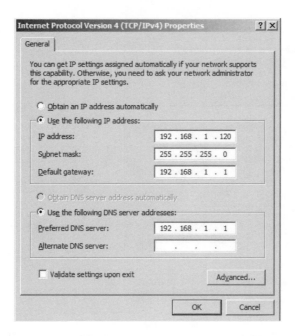

6. Click OK to accept your settings and to close the Internet Protocol Version 4 (TCP/IPv4) Properties dialog box.

 DEFINE COMPUTER NAMES

GET READY. During this section, you will change the computer to a domain. In addition, if you have a **domain controller** (a popular centralized server that provides authentication and authorization services), you can add the computer to a domain.

1. Go back to the Initial Configuration Tasks screen and click the Provide computer name and domain option. The System Properties dialog box (see Figure 2-11) displays.

Figure 2-11

The System Properties dialog

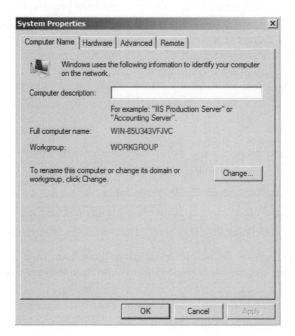

2. Click Change. The Computer Name/Domain Changes dialog box opens (see Figure 2-12).

Figure 2-12

The Computer Name/Domain
Changes dialog

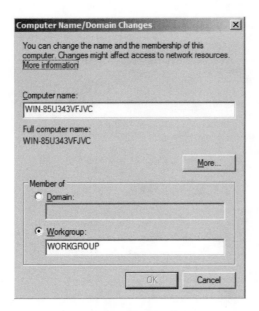

3. In the Computer name box, type your computer name. If you are using a home computer, you might use WinServer.

4. To add the computer to a domain, select the Domain option and type the name of your domain.

You are then prompted for the username of a domain account and a password.

5. When you are finished, click OK.

You are prompted to reboot your computer.

Running the Installation Program for a Stand-alone Single-Server Deployment with Built-In SQL Server

> Installing and configuring SharePoint is a multistep process. Of course, the simplest and quickest method to deploy SharePoint is to install SharePoint as a *single-server deployment* that does not require separate database server setup. This type of deployment is suitable for evaluating SharePoint, learning SharePoint, and testing SharePoint solutions. However, for many organizations, this installation cannot be used for production because of its performance limitations, including the fact that it's limited to one processor, 1 GB for a buffer pool, and the maximum size of the SharePoint databases is 4 GB.

To install SharePoint Server 2010 on a single server with a built-in database, the installation process is broken into the following stages:

1. Install SharePoint Server 2010 Prerequisites.

2. Install SharePoint Server 2010 (with the built-in database).

3. Run the SharePoint Products and Technologies Configuration Wizard.

When performing the stand-alone installation, SharePoint installs Microsoft SQL Server 2008 Express. In addition, the SharePoint Products and Technologies Configuration Wizard creates the configuration database and content database for SharePoint sites and then installs the SharePoint Central Administration Web site. Because it is a single server installation with a built-in database, it also creates your first SharePoint site collection.

TAKE NOTE★
A Standalone installation cannot be converted to a Server Farm installation. Therefore, if you think you might need to expand to multiple servers to create a server farm, you should choose the Server Farm installation. If you do choose Standalone installation now and you want to convert to a Server Farm, you will need to uninstall SharePoint and then reinstall with the Server Farm installation type.

To install SharePoint, you must download the SharePoint installation program. A free evaluation copy can be acquired from http://www.microsoft.com/downloads/en/details.aspx?FamilyID=43162af5-5b7b-40e0-b879-a77dac8f58bc&displaylang=en

TAKE NOTE★
When you perform the download, jot down the license key. You will need the license key during installation.

TAKE NOTE★
For more information about deploying SharePoint 2010, visit http://technet.microsoft.com/en-us/library/cc262957.aspx

For more information about installing SharePoint 2010, including an Installing SharePoint 2010 video, visit http://technet.microsoft.com/en-us/library/ff607866.aspx

UNDERSTANDING ACTIVE DIRECTORY AND SERVICE ACCOUNTS

As mentioned in Lesson 1, Active Directory provides identity and authentication services that usually use user names and passwords. In addition, these services also control access to SharePoint and SQL Services.

SharePoint 2010 requires dedicated Active Directory user accounts, called ***service accounts***, to run services and applications. Before creating your Active Directory accounts, you must plan for and create the service accounts that will be used with SharePoint and then assign the proper rights and permissions to communicate with Active Directory, SQL Server, and SharePoint. In addition, you should provide the minimal rights and permissions necessary to do their jobs while not providing more permissions than needed.

Before installing SharePoint, create the appropriate logon accounts and assign the proper rights and permissions. Create and configure the following service accounts:

- **SQL Server Services account**: The SQL Server service account is used to run SQL Server and SQL Server Agent services. While you can use either the Local System account or a domain user account, it is a best practice to use a domain user account. If the SQL Server is on a different computer than SharePoint, you are required to use a domain account.

- **SharePoint Setup User Account**: The SharePoint setup user account is the account that you should use to install and configure SharePoint. Since SharePoint needs to access an SQL server and create and modify SQL databases on the SQL server, the SharePoint setup user account must have the securityadmin and dbcreator roles on the SQL server and must be a member of the local Administrators group for any server that will run SharePoint.

- **Server Farm Account**: During installation and configuration, you will need to assign a service account for the SharePoint farm including configuring and managing the server farm. It is the identity used by the Central Administration site's application pool and the identity used by the SharePoint Timer service. The Service Farm Account must be added to the local Administrators group on each server on which SharePoint will be installed. The Server Farm Account is automatically added as an SQL Server login on the computer that runs SQL Server; it is assigned the SQL dbcreator fixed-server role and securityadmin fixed-server role, and is the db_owner fixed database role for all SharePoint databases in the server farm.

While these service accounts need to be created to properly install SharePoint, they are not the only service accounts that will be needed for SharePoint.

RUNNING THE PREPARATION TOOL

To simplify the installation process, the SharePoint installation disk includes the *SharePoint preparation tool*, which you can use to install all necessary prerequisites required for SharePoint 2010.

The preparation tool installs the following prerequisites:

- Web Server (IIS) role
- SQL Server 2008 Native Client
- Application Server role
- Microsoft .NET Framework version 3.5 SP1
- Microsoft Sync Framework Runtime v1.0 (x64)
- Microsoft Filter Pack 2.0
- Microsoft Chart Controls for the Microsoft .NET Framework 3.5
- Windows PowerShell 2.0
- Microsoft SQL Server 2008 Analysis Services ADOMD .NET
- ADO .NET Data Services Update for .NET Framework 3.5 SP1
- A hotfix for the .NET Framework 3.5 SP1 that provides a method to support token authentication without transport security or message encryption in WCF
- Windows Identity Foundation (WIF)

 INSTALL SHAREPOINT PREREQUISITES

GET READY. To install the SharePoint Server 2010 prerequisites, perform the following steps:

1. Log on to the server as an administrator.
2. Double-click the SharePoint executable that you downloaded.
3. If the Open File – Security Warning dialog box displays, prompting you to confirm that you want to run the file, click Run.
4. When the Microsoft SharePoint 2010 splash screen displays (see Figure 2-13), click the Install software prerequisites option.

Figure 2-13

The SharePoint 2010 splash screen

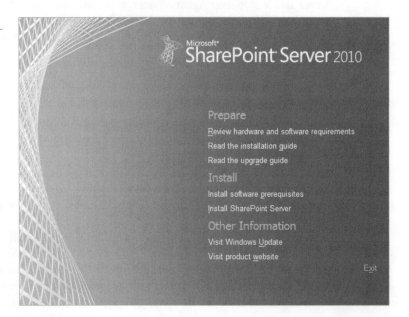

TAKE NOTE* Since the prerequisite installer downloads components from the Microsoft Download Center, you must have Internet access on the computer.

5. When the Microsoft SharePoint 2010 Products Preparation Tool wizard begins, click Next (see Figure 2-14).

Figure 2-14

The SharePoint 2010 Products Preparation Tool wizard

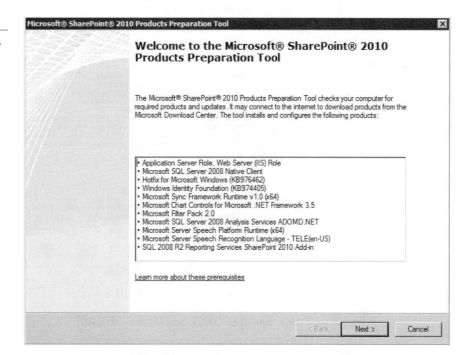

6. When the License Agreement displays (see Figure 2-15), select the I accept the terms of the License Agreement(s) checkbox and click Next.

Figure 2-15

SharePoint 2010 Products Preparation Tool license agreement

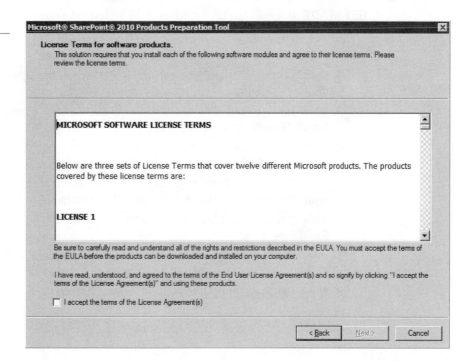

7. When the prerequisites are installed, click Finish (see Figure 2-16) and then reboot Windows.

Figure 2-16

The Installation Complete page

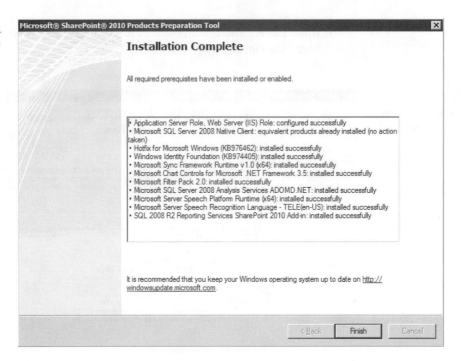

RUNNING THE SHAREPOINT SETUP PROGRAM

When you install SharePoint as a stand-alone server, the installation program simplifies the installation process by installing the SharePoint program (sometimes referred to as *SharePoint binaries*) and enabling common SharePoint services.

 INSTALL SHAREPOINT

GET READY. To install SharePoint Server 2010 for a stand-alone single-server deployment (with built-in SQL Server), perform the following steps:

1. Log on to the server as an administrator.
2. Double-click the SharePoint executable file. When the Open File Security warning displays, click Run.
3. When the Microsoft Windows SharePoint 2010 splash screen displays, click the Install SharePoint Server option.
4. When you are prompted for the Product Key (see Figure 2-17), type the key and then press Continue.
5. When the License Agreement displays, select the I accept the terms of this agreement checkbox (see Figure 2-18) and click Continue.
6. When you are prompted to choose your type of installation (see Figure 2-19), click Standalone.
7. When the Run Configuration Wizard box displays, make sure the Run the SharePoint Products Configuration Wizard now option is selected and then click Close.
8. When the SharePoint Configuration Wizard displays (see Figure 2-20), click Next.

Figure 2-17

Entering your product key

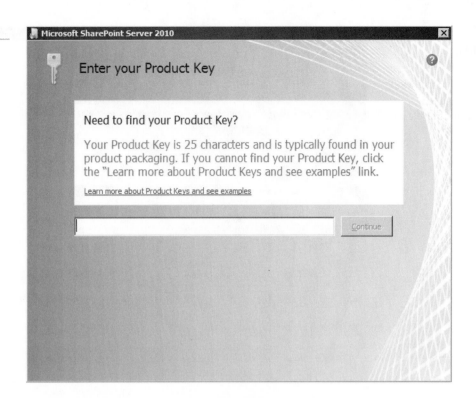

Figure 2-18

The SharePoint 2010 license agreement

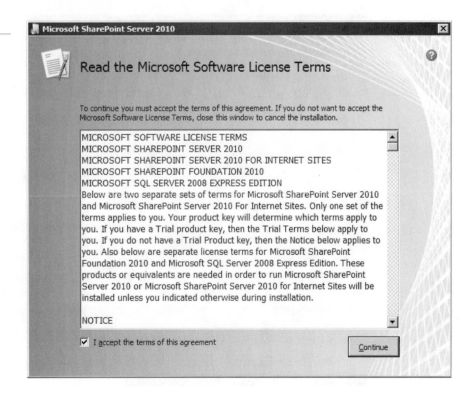

9. When a dialog warns you that it has to restart some services (see Figure 2-21), click Yes.

10. Click Next.

11. When the configuration is complete (see Figure 2-22), click Finish.

Figure 2-19

Choosing the type of
SharePoint installation

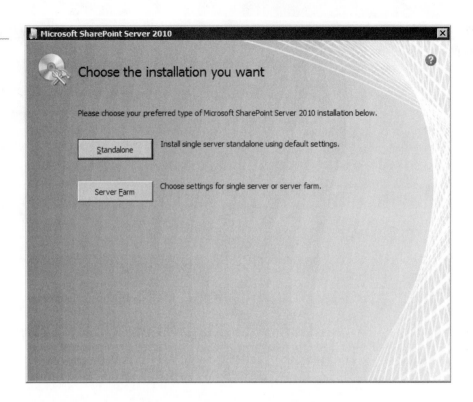

Figure 2-20

The SharePoint Configuration
Wizard

Figure 2-21

A warning stating that some
services need to be restarted

Figure 2-22

Confirmation that SharePoint configuration has finished successfully

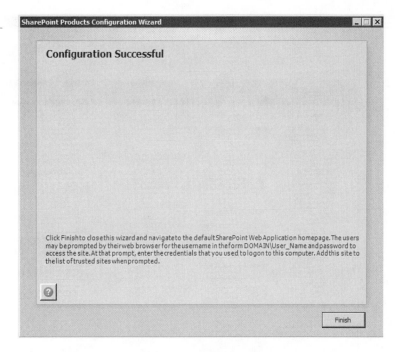

12. When browser opens to the new SharePoint site, you're prompted to provide a specific template for the initial site.
13. Click your template (see Figure 2-23) and then click OK.

Figure 2-23

SharePoint requesting the initial template

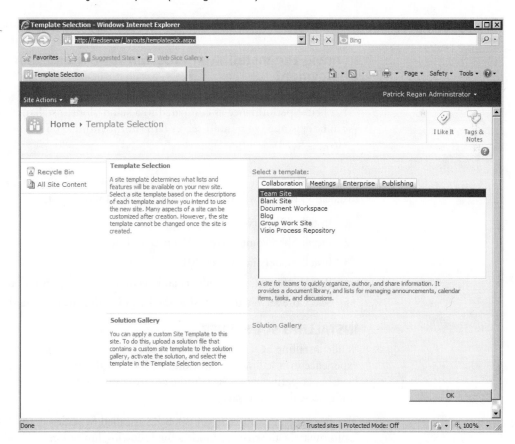

SharePoint prompts you to set up groups for the site (see Figure 2-24).

14. Keep the defaults and then click OK.

The SharePoint site home page opens.

Figure 2-24

Setting up groups for a SharePoint site

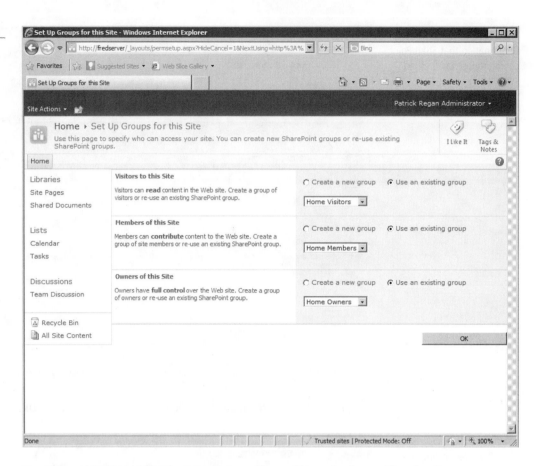

Running the Installation Program for a Stand-alone Single-Server Deployment

For better performance as compared to a stand-alone installation and for scalability that can be expanded to a multi-server farm in the future, you would choose the single-server farm.

To install SharePoint Server 2010 on a single-server with SQL Server already installed, the installation process will be broken down to the following stages:

1. Install SQL Server.
2. Install SharePoint Server 2010 prerequisites.
3. Install SharePoint Server 2010.
4. Run the SharePoint Products and Technologies Configuration Wizard.
5. Select the servers to run using the Farm Configuation Wizard or manually install them.

INSTALLING SQL SERVER

While installing SQL server is not a focus on the 70-667 exam, it is important to get some experience in installing and working with the SQL server. By having an SQL server, you will have better performance, have more control over your SharePoint environment, and have the ability to scale if necessary.

The free version of SQL Server 2008 R2 is called SQL Server 2008 R2 Express Edition. Unfortunately, the free version has the following limitations:

- 1 processor
- 1 GB of memory
- 10 GB Maximum Database Size (all databases)

If you choose to use SQL Server 2008 R2 Express Edition, download the version with the Management Tools at:

http://www.microsoft.com/download/en/details.aspx?id=23650&hash=uQ851KpkHnuQw8 QoN023X4tkqRt31vqSx2MGyKvLWOEd%2fZjLhGs4G5pxPRSWY9FMJElzfE5jj5rR4vzeZ BJ6pQ%3d%3d

SharePoint performance depends heavily on the performance of the SQL Server. Therefore, for higher performance, you might consider one of the non-free versions such as:

- Standard Edition allows up to 4 processors, 64 GB of memory, and 524 Petabytes for databases.

- Enterprise allows up to 8 processors, 2 TB of memory, and 524 Petabytes for databases and supports multiple high availability options such as database mirroring.

⊙ INSTALL SQL SERVER 2008 R2 EXPRESS WITH MANAGEMENT TOOLS

GET READY. To install SharePoint 2008 R2 Express, perform the following steps:

1. Log on to the server as an administrator.
2. Double-click the SQL Server executable that you downloaded. The SQL Server Installation Center opens (see Figure 2-25).

Figure 2-25

The SQL Server Installation Center

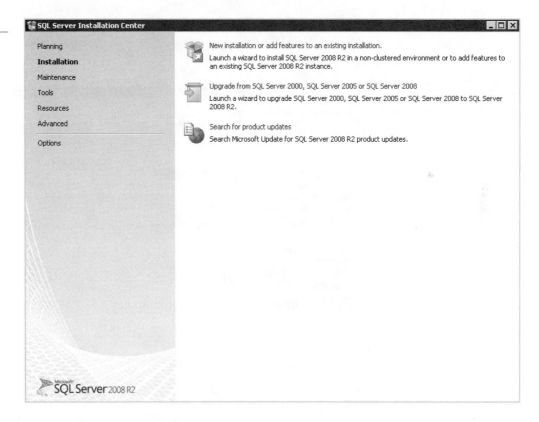

3. Click the New installation or add features to an existing installation option.
4. On the License Terms page (see Figure 2-26), select the I accept the license terms option and then click Next.
5. After the setup support files are installed, the Feature Selection page displays (see Figure 2-27). Click Next.

   SQL instances are multiple SQL Server services, each with their own ports, logins, and databases. They are used to isolate SQL environments. The default instance is MSSQLSERVER.

Figure 2-26

The SQL Server license agreement

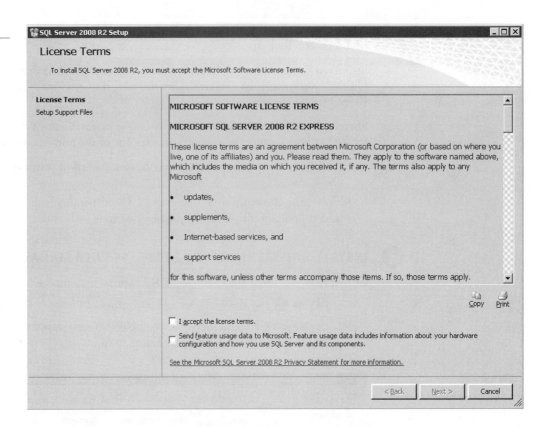

Figure 2-27

The SQL Feature Selection page

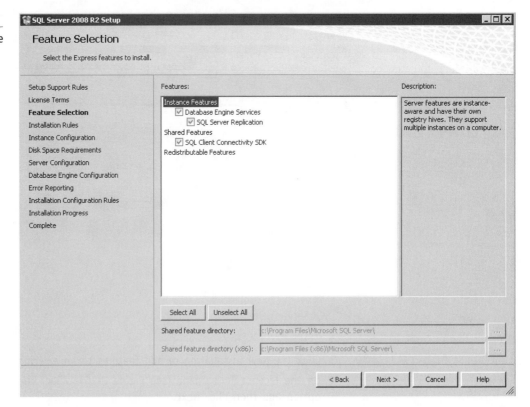

6. Select the Default Instance option.

   For a production environment, you might change the location of the SQL Instance root directory. (See Figure 2-28.)

7. For now, click Next.

Figure 2-28

Configuring the SQL Server instance

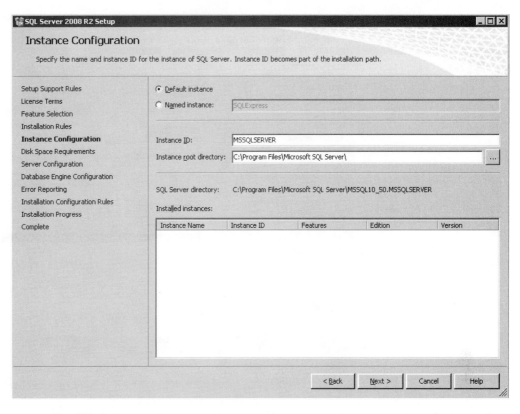

The SQL Server service accounts are used to use separate accounts and passwords for each of the SQL services (see Figure 2-29).

Figure 2-29

Configuring SQL Server service accounts

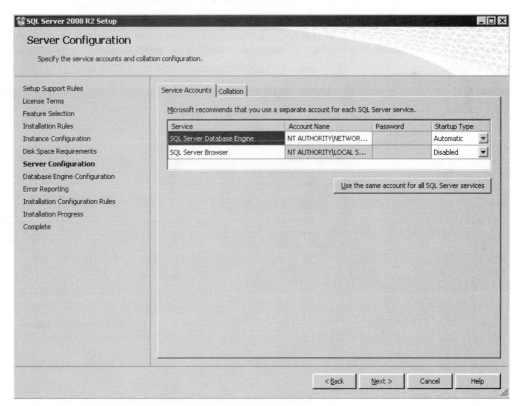

8. For the test environment, keep the default option and then click Next.

When the Database Engine Configuration page displays (see Figure 2-30), you can configure the authentication mode and location of the data directories.

Figure 2-30

Configuring SQL Server
account provisioning

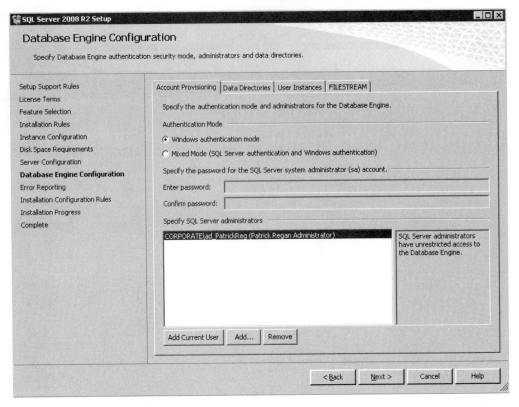

9. Since you are planning only to use SharePoint, keep Windows authentication mode.

10. Select the Data Directories tab.

Figure 2-31 shows the default folders used by the SQL Server.

11. For a production environment, you would often change the location of the data root directory, the log files, and the temp DB. However, for a learning environment, you can keep the default and then click Next.

Figure 2-31

SQL Server data directories

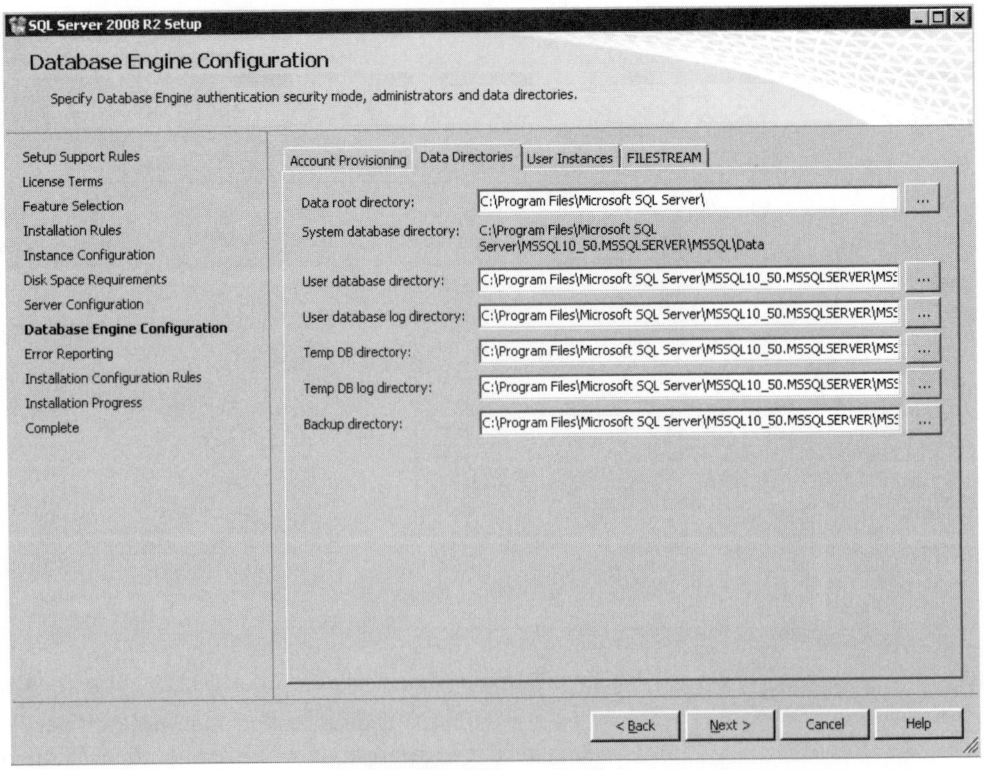

12. When the Error Reporting page displays, click Next.

13. When the installation is complete, click Close.

SQL Server and its databases are managed using the SQL Server Management Studio. Fortunately, you do not need to be a database administrator (DBA) to install and configure SharePoint. However, there are some options that a SharePoint administrator can perform using the SQL Server Management Studio, such as backing up the database and adding a database from another SharePoint environment.

INSTALLING SHAREPOINT PREREQUISITES AND SETUP PROGRAM

Installing the prerequisite for a single-deployment server is not different than installing the prerequisites for a stand-alone server with a built-in SQL server. However, by clicking the Server Farm button, you have an option to install a single farm.

 INSTALL SHAREPOINT

GET READY. To install SharePoint Server 2010 for a stand-alone single-server deployment (without SQL Server), perform the following steps:

1. Log on to the server as an administrator.

2. Double-click the SharePoint executable file.

3. When the Microsoft Windows SharePoint 2010 splash screen displays, click the Install SharePoint Server option.

4. When prompted for the Product Key, type the key.

5. When the License Agreement displays, select the I accept the terms of this License Agreement checkbox and then click Continue.

6. When prompted for the type of installation, click the Server Farm button.

7. Select the Complete – Install all components option (see Figure 2-32).

Figure 2-32

SharePoint Server 2010 server type

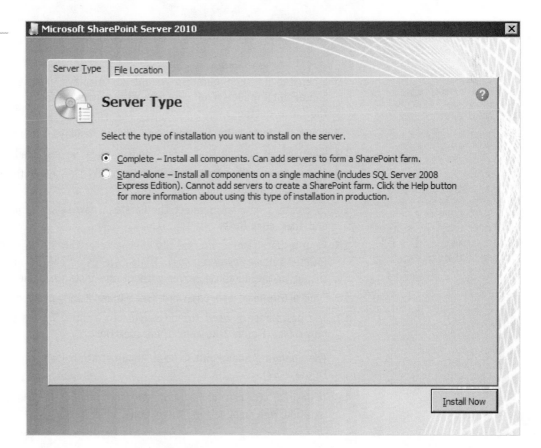

8. Click the File location tab. If you're administering a production environment, you might change the file location (see Figure 2-33).

9. Click Install Now.

Figure 2-33

Specifying the SharePoint file location

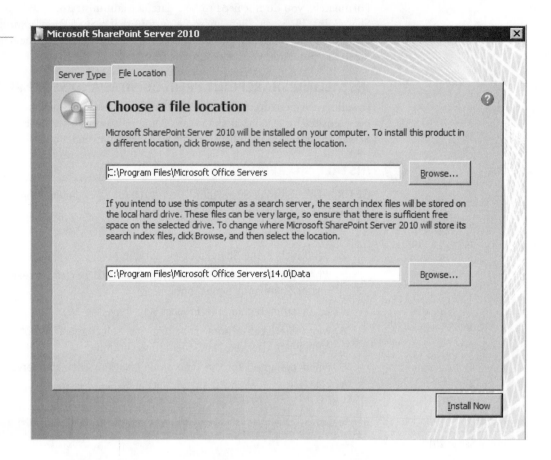

10. When the Run Configuration Wizard box displays, make sure the Run the SharePoint Products Configuration Wizard now option is selected and then click the Close button.

11. When the SharePoint Configuration Wizard displays, click Next.

12. When you're warned that some services must be restarted, click Yes.

13. If you have a SharePoint farm, you can add the server to the farm by selecting Connect to an existing server farm.

14. To create a new farm, select the Create a new server farm option (see Figure 2-34) and then click Next.

15. For the Database server, specify the name of the SQL server and its instance name (*SQLservername\instancename*). If you are using the default instance, you just have to put in the database server without the instance name.

16. Type a username and password (see Figure 2-35) and then click Next.

17. The passphrase is used to add servers to a farm. Type a passphrase in both text boxes (see Figure 2-36) and then click Next.

   The Configure SharePoint Central Administration Web Application page displays (see Figure 2-37).

18. If desired, you can manually Specify port number for the SharePoint Central Administration Web Application. When done, click Next.

Figure 2-34

Creating a SharePoint
Farm using the SharePoint
Configuration Wizard

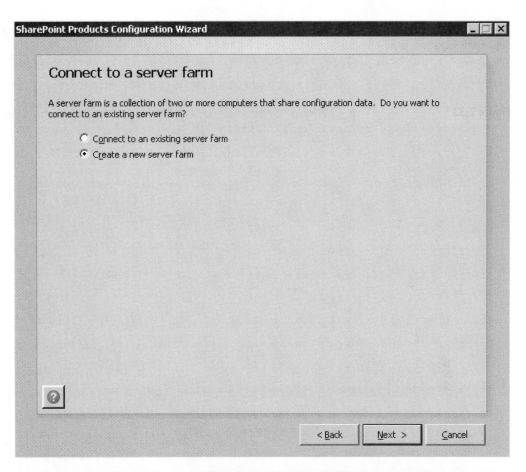

Figure 2-35

Specifying the configuration
database

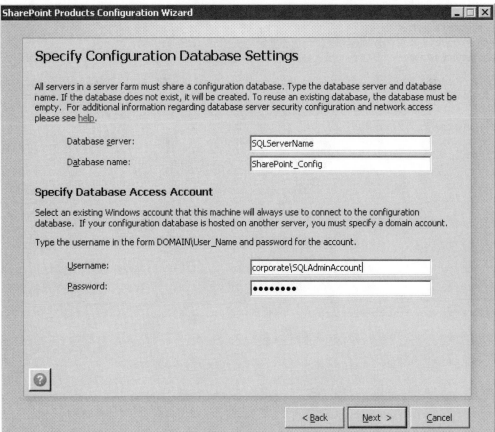

Figure 2-36

Setting the SharePoint farm passphrase

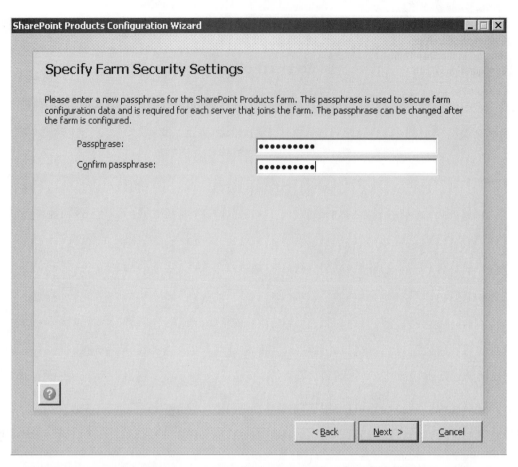

Figure 2-37

Configuring SharePoint Central Administration Web Application and security settings

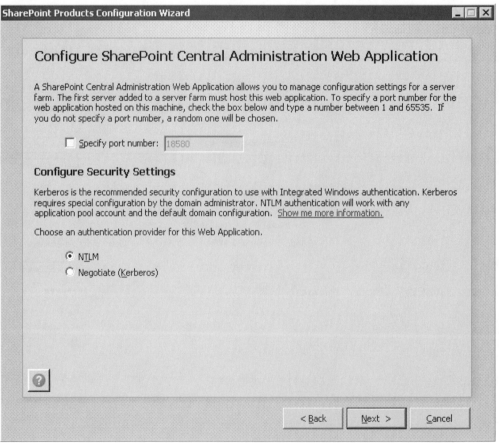

19. When the Completing the SharePoint Products Configuration Wizard displays, click Next.

20. When the configuration is complete, click Finish. The SharePoint Central Administration tool opens.

RUNNING THE FARM CONFIGURATION WIZARD

When you do a stand-alone installation, the appropriate SharePoint services are automatically installed and configured, and the default home site collection is created. When you perform the Complete Installation, you need to build and configure the SharePoint farm. One way to install the services or create the home site is to run the *Farm Configuration Wizard* at the end of the installation, or later from within Central Administration. If you decide not to do the wizard, you can install the additional services and create the home site manually with Central Administration.

 TAKE NOTE *

While the Central Administration Wizard simplifies the installation, Microsoft recommends not using Farm Configuration Wizard. Instead, Microsoft recommends installing and configuring the individual services and creating the top level site so that you have more control and flexibility with the SharePoint configuration.

You can run the Farm Configuration Wizard from within Central Administration at a later time. It is located under the Configuration Wizards group.

When SharePoint opens Central Administration for the first time, it will ask if you want to help make SharePoint better, and if you want to sign up for Customer Experience Improvement Program and automatically upload error reports to Microsoft. While it is recommended by Microsoft, it does not affect the way SharePoint runs; as such, participation is voluntary. So click Yes or No, and then click OK.

TAKE NOTE *

Of the services available, the User Profile Service Application is one of the more complicated and sensitive services to install and configure. If the wizard fails, it will most likely do so if you select the User Profile Service Application. Therefore, if you do choose to use the wizard, it is highly recommended that you deselect the User Profile Service Application option and continue with the wizard.

USE THE INITIAL FARM CONFIGURATION WIZARD

GET READY. To run the Initial Farm Configuration Wizard, perform the following steps:

1. If you just completed a Complete Installation and are asked how to configure your SharePoint farm, click Start the Wizard (see Figure 2-38).

2. When prompted for a service account, use an existing managed account or create a new one. Since you have just installed SharePoint, the only managed account is the account that you used to install SharePoint.

3. Select the services that you want to install, deselect the services you do not want to install, and then click Next (see Figure 2-39).

 X REF

Managed accounts will be discussed in Lesson 6.

Figure 2-38

Configuring a SharePoint Farm
with the built-in wizard

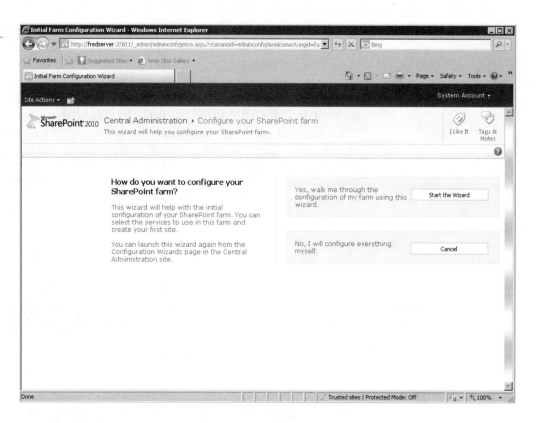

Figure 2-39

Specifying service account and
SharePoint services

After several minutes, you will be asked to create the top-level Web site. See Figure 2-40.

Figure 2-40

Creating the top-level Web site

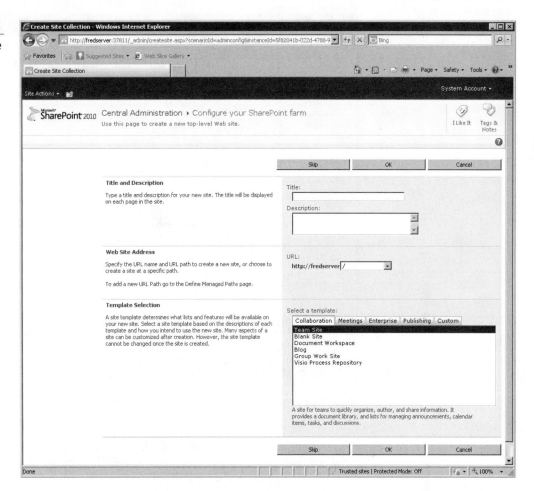

4. If you decide to create it at a later time, you can click Skip. If you decide to create it now, type a title, an optional description, select a template, and then click OK.

5. After the wizard completes, a summary screen displays (see Figure 2-41). Click Finish.

Creating a Multi-Server Farm

For larger deployments, you must install multiple servers to provide SharePoint services.

A **tier 2 farm** is a farm that includes one or more servers providing Web and application services and one or more servers offering database services. A **tier 3 farm** goes one step further by having one or more servers providing Web applications, one or more servers providing application services, and one or more servers offering database services.

Figure 2-41

Confirmation that the Farm
Configuration Wizard has
successfully completed

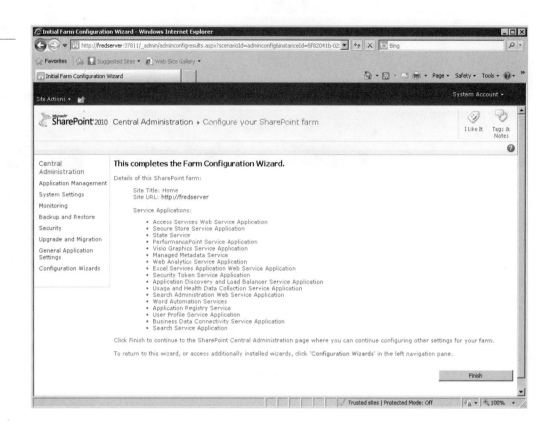

 CREATE A MULTI-SERVER FARM

GET READY. To install SharePoint as a multi-server farm, perform the following steps:

1. Install the SQL server with the appropriate service packs and cumulative updates.

   If you are using SQL Server 2005, you must have local and remote connections enabled and configured to use the TCP/IP protocol. If you are using SQL Server 2008, you must have the TCP/IP protocol enabled for the network configuration.

   Figure 2-42 shows how to enable the TCP/IP protocol for SQL Server 2008 R2 using the SQL Server Configuration Manager. Figure 2-43 shows that the default port used for the SQL Server is TCP Port 1433.

Figure 2-42

Enabling the TCP/IP for the SQL
Server Configuration Manager

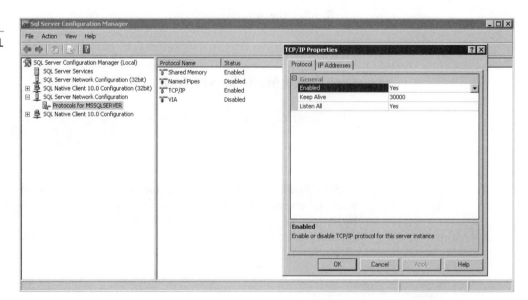

Figure 2-43

By default, SQL Server uses
TCP Port 1433

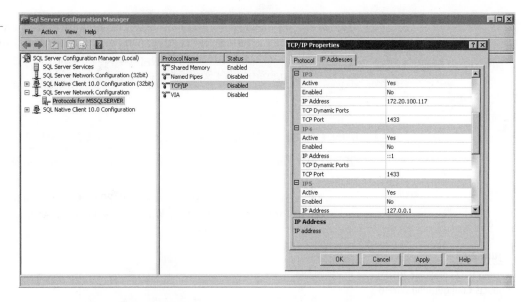

2. For the SharePoint servers, install Windows. You should then make sure that these machines are fully patched and updated.

3. Install the software prerequisites on all of the machines before installing SharePoint 2010.

4. After SharePoint 2010 is installed on all of the machines, run the SharePoint Products and Technologies Configuration Wizard to create the server farm. Whichever machine will host the SharePoint Central Administration should be the first server in which you run the SharePoint Products and Technologies Configuration Wizard, in which you will select the Complete Install option.

5. Lastly, run the SharePoint Products and Technologies Configuration Wizard on the remaining machines.

Running the SharePoint 2010 Products Configuration Wizard

The *SharePoint Products Configuration Wizard* performs basic tasks to initially configure SharePoint and to enable Central Administration. Of course, the Central Administration is used to configure your site. The SharePoint 2010 Products Configuration Wizard is also used to add additional servers to a farm and to complete SharePoint upgrades.

Besides performing the initial configuration, the configuration wizard will:

- Reconfigure access to Central Administration
- Identify missing components
- Validate your configuration
- Identify, repair, or reset security and low-level configuration settings

If you perform an upgrade to SharePoint or install a language pack, you must run the SharePoint Productions Configuration Wizard.

TAKE NOTE *

The SharePoint Products Configuration Wizard might have to start, stop, or reset the SharePoint Administration Service, the SharePoint Timer Service, Internet Information Services (IIS), and services from other applications that depend on Microsoft SharePoint and that are appropriately registered.

RUN THE SHAREPOINT 2010 PRODUCTS CONFIGURATION WIZARD

GET READY. To run the SharePoint 2010 Products Configuration Wizard, perform the following steps:

1. Click Start, click Microsoft SharePoint 2010 Products, and then choose SharePoint 2010 Products Configuration Wizard (see Figure 2-44).

Figure 2-44

Starting the SharePoint 2010 Products Configuration Wizard

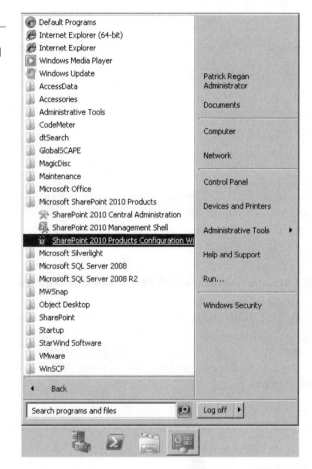

2. When the Welcome screen displays, click Next.
3. When you are prompted to restart services, click Yes.

4. When the Modify server farm Settings page displays (see Figure 2-45), click Next.

Figure 2-45

The Modify Server Farm
Settings page

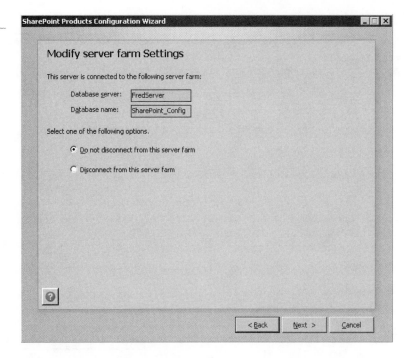

5. When the Modify SharePoint Central Administration Web Application Settings page
displays (see Figure 2-46), select No, this machine will continue to host the Web
site and then click Next.

Figure 2-46

The Modify SharePoint Central
Administration Web Application
Settings page

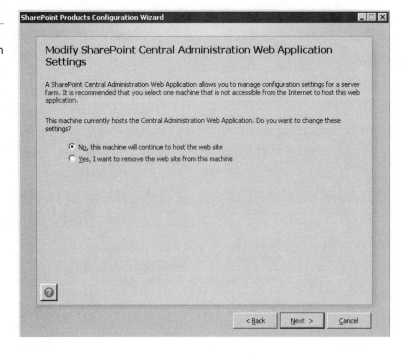

6. When the Completing the SharePoint Products Configuration Wizard page displays (see Figure 2-47), click Next.

Figure 2-47

Completing the SharePoint Products Configuration Wizard

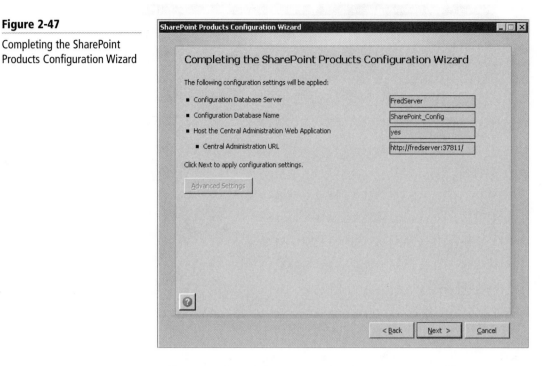

7. When the configuration is successful, click Finish (see Figure 2-48). The Central Administration Web site opens.

Figure 2-48

Confirmation that the SharePoint Product Configuration Wizard was successfully completed

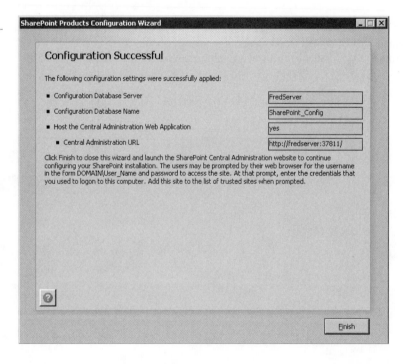

The Products Configuration Wizard (psconfig.exe) can be executed at the Windows command prompt to provide an alternative interface to perform several operations that control how SharePoint 2010 Products are configured. To use the psconfig.exe, you must be a member of the Administrators group on the local computer.

To run the Products Configuration Wizard at a command prompt, navigate to the C:\ Program Files\Microsoft Shared\Web server extensions\14\bin folder and then type the psconfig command with the appropriate parameters:

`psconfig.exe -cmd <command> [optional parameters]`

To view Help, at the command prompt, type:

`psconfig.exe -?`

To view Help about a specific command, type:

`psconfig.exe -help <command name>`

The commands in `psconfig` must be run in a specific order to run successfully.

1. `configdb` creates, connects, or disconnects this server from the server farm.
2. `helpcollections` manages help collections.
3. `secureresources` performs SharePoint 2010 Products resource security enforcement on the server.
4. `services` manages SharePoint 2010 Products services.
5. `installfeatures` registers any SharePoint Products and Technologies features located on the file system of this server with the server farm.
6. `adminvs` manages the SharePoint Central Administration Web application on the local computer.
7. `evalprovision` provisions this server as a stand-alone (evaluation mode) server.
8. `applicationcontent` manages shared application content.
9. `upgrade` performs an upgrade of SharePoint 2010 Products.

If you use the SharePoint Products Configuration Wizard to configure an installation, it calls the commands in the correct order for you. In addition, if psconfig detects that the server farm has to be upgraded, it automatically starts an upgrade when you run it (even if you did not select the upgrade command).

✚ MORE INFORMATION

For more information on using the `psconfig` command, visit http://technet.microsoft.com/en-us/library/cc263093.aspx

■ Scripting Installations

↓ THE BOTTOM LINE

Installation and configuration using the standard user interface can be time-consuming. Also, if you install multiple SharePoint services, they can be prone to inconsistent implementation. Similar to scripting an installation of Windows, you can also script the installation of SharePoint to simplify the installation and reduce the time to install a SharePoint server.

CERTIFICATION READY
What are the steps and commands used in scripting the installation of SharePoint 2010?

1.1.6

When you perform a scripted installation, you want to insert a disk into a server, turn on the server, and then SharePoint will automatically be installed. If you are responsible for a large data center with many SharePoint servers, or if you are configuring an environment for someone to install SharePoint with little to no user input, you could set up a scripted installation. With many servers to install, a little work to setup a scripted installation can go a long way toward saving you time and effort later on, and also reduces user error during the installation process.

A scripted installation is divided into two phases:

1. Perform a scripted installation of SharePoint prerequisites
2. Perform a scripted installation of SharePoint Server 2010 binaries

As mentioned previously in this lesson, when you perform a normal installation, you download the prerequisites from the Internet and install them using the Preparation Tool. To make a scripted installation a complete stand-alone package—and since some organizations do not allow servers to have direct access to the Internet—download the prerequisites and copy them to a network share (or an installation disk).

> **TAKE NOTE** ★ To get a list of all of the prerequisites and links to those files, visit http://technet.microsoft.com/en-us/library/cc262485.aspx

To install the prerequisites using scripted commands, use the PrerequisiteInstaller.exe, which supports parameters that specify the location of each prerequisite. The syntax of each parameter is:

```
/PrerequisiteName:PathToInstallationFile
```

For example, to execute sqlncli.msi, you would script the following command:

```
PrerequisiteInstaller.exe /SQLNCli:
"\\SPInstall\SPprereqs\sqlncli.msi"
```

\\SPInstall\SPprereqs is the name of the shared folder.

You can also use the PrerequisiteInstaller.exe to install multiple perquisites. For example, you could use:

```
PrerequisiteInstaller.exe
/SQLNCli:"\\SPInstall\SPprereqs\sqlncli.msi"
/ChartControl:"\\SPInstall\SPprereqs
\MSChart.exe" /W2K8SP2:"\\SPInstall\SPprereqs
\Windows6.0-KB948465-X64.exe"
/NETFX35SP1:"\\SPInstall\SPprereqs
\dotnetfx35setup.exe"
```

You can also add the /unattended parameter to run the Preparation Tool in silent, unattended mode whereby no prompts or messages are displayed during the installation.

To script the PrerequisiteInstaller.exe, create a batch file with the above command. You can also create a PrerequisiteInstaller.Arguments.txt file and place it in the same location as the PrerequisiteInstaller.exe with all of the parameters used above, but not actually include the beginning part, PrerequisiteInstaller.exe:

```
/SQLNCli:"\\SPInstall\SPprereqs\sqlncli.msi"
/ChartControl:"\\SPInstall\SPprereqs
\MSChart.exe" /W2K8SP2:"\\SPInstall\SPprereqs
\Windows6.0-KB948465-X64.exe"
/NETFX35SP1:"\\SPInstall\SPprereqs
\dotnetfx35setup.exe"
```

To script the installation of the SharePoint binaries, you use an Extensible Markup Language (XML) file named Config.xml by default. Microsoft provides the following sample Config.xml files in the SharePoint installation disk in the files folder:

- \Setup\Config.xml is for a stand-alone server installation using Microsoft SQL Server 2008 Express Edition.

- \SetupFarm\Config.xml is for a server farm installation.
- \SetupFarmSilent\Config.xml is for a server farm installation in silent mode.
- \SetupFarmUpgrade\Config.xml is for an in-place upgrade of an existing farm.
- \SetupSilent\Config.xml is for a stand-alone server installation using SQL Server 2008 Express Edition in silent mode.
- SetupSingleUpgrade\Config.xml is for an in-place upgrade of an existing single-server installation.

A sample config.xml file would be:

```
<Configuration>
<Package Id="sts">
<Setting Id="LAUNCHEDFROMSETUPSTS" Value="Yes"/>
</Package>
<Package Id="spswfe">
<Setting Id="SETUPCALLED" Value="1"/>
</Package>
<Logging Type="verbose" Path="%temp%" Template="SharePoint Server
Setup(*).log"/>
<PIDKEY Value="36BY2-DVVJY-6426X-PXWVQ-BM342" />
<Display Level="none" CompletionNotice="no" />
<Setting Id="SERVERROLE" Value="APPLICATION"/>
<Setting Id="USINGUIINSTALLMODE" Value="0"/>
<Setting Id="SETUP_REBOOT" Value="Never" />
<Setting Id="SETUPTYPE" Value="CLEAN_INSTALL"/>
</Configuration>
```

You then modify the XML file to match your environment, including removing the comment tags (<!–– and ––>) and typing a valid product ID.

To execute the stand-alone installation of \Files\Setup\Config.xml file, you would then execute the following command:

```
setup.exe /config:\Files\Setup\Config.xml
```

The **stsadm** command and PowerShell is covered in Lesson 3.

After the installation is complete, run the SharePoint Products Configuration Wizard to finalize the installation. After you have installed SharePoint, you can use the **stsadm** command and PowerShell to execute the SharePoint Products Configuration Wizard for the SharePoint server farm.

■ Installing Language Packs

↓ THE BOTTOM LINE
Many organizations deal with people from different countries, who speak and write in different languages. In these situations, SharePoint must be customized to support multiple languages so that it can reach a multinational audience.

Language packs are site templates that contain languages in addition to the default language. When you install a language pack, language-specific site definitions are added to the language templates folder of the server. The language templates folder is *%COMMONPROGRAMFILES%*\Microsoft Shared\Web server extensions\14\template\ LocaleID.

When you create a Web site, you select the language for the site you are creating. The default language is the language that was used when you installed SharePoint, including the site toolbars, navigation bars, list names, and column headings. In addition, a language might change the left-to-right orientation for those languages that use it.

To create a site or site collection in a language other than the default, you must install that language pack before creating those sites. You cannot change the language of a site after the site has been created.

CERTIFICATION READY?
What are the steps to support other languages in SharePoint 2010?
1.1.5

While the language changes for the SharePoint interface, it does not change for the content of the pages and it does not translate any of the files stored on the site. In addition, there are some UI elements (such as error messages, notifications, and dialog boxes) that do not change—specifically those that are generated by supporting technologies (for example, the .NET Framework, Windows Workflow Foundation, or SQL Server).

To install a language pack, do the following:

1. Install the Windows operating system language files.
2. Install SharePoint.
3. Run the SharePoint Products Configuration Wizard.
4. Download the language pack for SharePoint 2010.
5. Install the language back on all front-end SharePoint servers.
6. Run the SharePoint 2010 Products Configuration Wizard for each server.

Multilingual User Interface (MUI) Language Packs (Windows Server Language Packs) enable a multilingual user interface in a Windows Server 2008 environment. Before installing SharePoint, you must install the language files for the Windows operating system. While Windows includes language files for many languages, if you need to support East Asian languages (such Chinese, Japanese, or Korean) or complex script languages (such as Arabic, Hebrew, or Vietnamese), you must download and install the Windows language files by using the Regional and Language Settings application in Control Panel. The Multilingual User Interface (MUI) Language Packs can be found using the Microsoft Download Center Web site (http://www.microsoft.com/download).

 INSTALL THE WINDOWS SERVER LANGUAGE PACK

GET READY. To install the Windows Server Language Pack, perform the following steps:

1. Sitting at the server keyboard, click Start and then select Control Panel. In the Category view, click Clock, Language, and Region. Then click Region and Language (see Figure 2-49).

Figure 2-49

Accessing the Region and Language settings

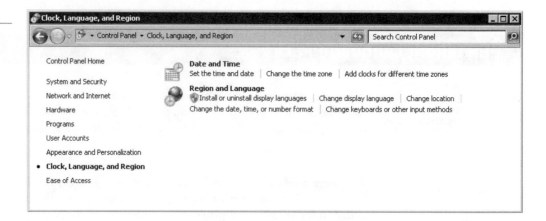

2. Select the Keyboards and Languages tab (see Figure 2-50) and then click Install/ Uninstall languages.

Figure 2-50

Configuring the Region and Language settings

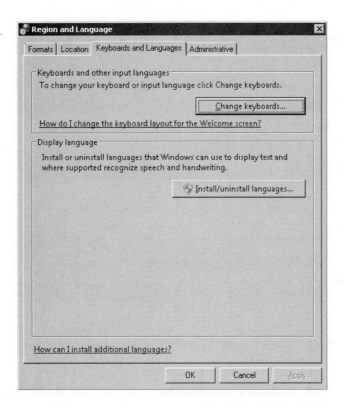

3. In the Install or Uninstall Display Languages dialog box (see Figure 2-51), click Install display languages.

Figure 2-51

Installing or uninstalling display languages

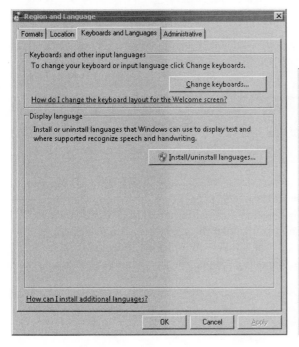

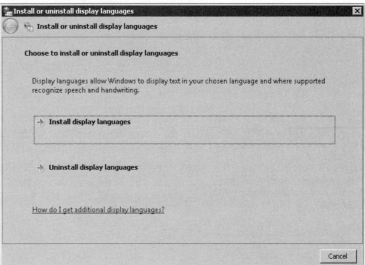

4. Select the desired languages from the list. If the language does not appear, click Browse to navigate to the location of the required .cab files and select the .cab file (see Figure 2-52). Click Next.

Figure 2-52

Choosing the language to install

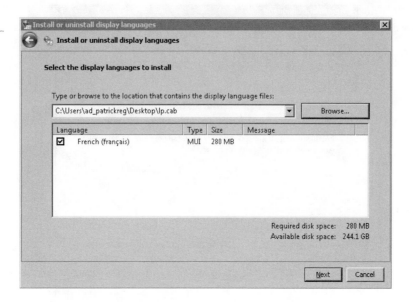

5. Click the I accept the license terms option (see Figure 2-53) and then click Next.

Figure 2-53

Viewing the language license agreement

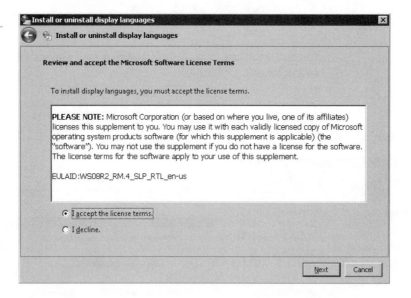

6. Click Install.

⚠ **WARNING** Use caution when installing multiple language packs. You might need to rename the downloaded files and save them in separate folders to prevent the newer from overwriting the older files.

After the operating system and Windows Server language packs are loaded, you can then install SharePoint and run the SharePoint Products Configuration Wizard. For SharePoint to support the additional language, you must download the appropriate language pack for SharePoint 2010. Some of the languages include Chinese (Simplified), English, French, German, Japanese, Russian, and Spanish. There is no single package of all languages.

 INSTALL THE SHAREPOINT LANGUAGE PACK

GET READY. To install the SharePoint 2010 Language Pack, perform the following steps:

1. Run the setup program for the language pack that you downloaded from Microsoft.
2. Select the I accept the terms of this agreement check box and then click Continue. The setup wizard runs and installs the language pack.
3. When the Run Configuration Wizard page displays, make sure the Run the Share-Point Products Configuration Wizard now option is selected, and then click Close.
4. When the Welcome to SharePoint Products page displays, click Next.
5. When prompted to restart IIS and SharePoint services, click Yes.
6. When the configuration is complete, click Finish.

■ Troubleshooting SharePoint Installation Problems

↓
THE BOTTOM LINE

If you work with SharePoint long enough, you will eventually have to deal with problems. Since SharePoint is a complex program and platform that depends on components built in Windows server—components that you have to install in SharePoint itself—you might have to deal with a wide range of problems.

As a server administrator, when you troubleshoot any problem, use a standard troubleshooting methodology. The whole reason for using an effective troubleshooting methodology is to reduce the amount of guesswork needed to troubleshoot and fix the problem in a timely manner.

Remember, before you perform an installation, you must do some planning. A little planning will help avoid many problems in the future and make sure that your system can perform its jobs properly.

For a troubleshooting methodology, Microsoft Product Support Service engineers use the *detect method*, which consists of the following six steps:

1. **Discover the problem**: Identify and document problem symptoms, and search technical information resources including Microsoft Knowledge Base (KB) articles to determine whether the problem is a known condition.
2. **Evaluate system configuration**: Ask the client or customer and check the system's documentation to determine if any hardware, software, or network changes have been made, including any new additions. Also check any available logs including looking in the Event Viewer.
3. **List or track possible solutions and try to isolate the problem by removing or disabling hardware or software components**: You might also consider turning on additional logging or running diagnostic programs to gather more information and test certain components.
4. **Execute a plan**: Test potential solutions and have a contingency plan if these solutions do not work, or have a negative impact on the computer. Of course, you don't want to make the problem worse, so if possible, back up any critical system or application files.
5. **Check results**: If the problem is not fixed, go back to track possible solutions.
6. **Take a proactive approach**: Document changes that you made along the way while troubleshooting the problem. Also notify the customer or client and document internal symptoms of the problem in case it happens in the future, or in case those changes that fixed the problem affect other areas.

As you gather information, you need to first determine which step of the installation is showing the problem and record any error messages that are displayed.

Analyzing ULS Logs, Installation Error Logs, Event Logs

CERTIFICATION READY?
What PowerShell Cmdlt allows you to view the ULS trace-log files?
1.1.7

Next, you must go through the installation logs and the Event Viewer, particularly the system and application logs. By default, the installation logs are located in the C:\Program Files\Common Files\Microsoft Shared\Web Server Extensions\14\LOGS folder. The PSCDiagnostics*.log and PSConfig.exe*.log files are the logs for the SharePoint 2010 Products Configuration wizard. Of course, if you have not encountered the problem and the solution is not obvious, do not be afraid to do a little research using your favorite search engine and Microsoft's Knowledgebase.

Besides manually opening the Event Viewer or the text logs, you can use the following PowerShell commands to obtain detailed information from these logs:

- Get-SPLogEvents can be used to view and extract details from the SharePoint Unified Logging Service (ULS) trace-log files.
- Get-Eventlog can be used to retrieve the events in an event log, or a list of the event logs, on the local or remote computers.

For example, to get all warning entries from the log files in the d:\Logs directory, execute the following command:

- Get-SPLogEvent -Directory "D:\Logs" | Where-Object {$_.Level -eq "Warning"}

To get error entries between 08/04/2011 6:00 pm and 08/04/2011 7:00 pm., use the following command:

- Get-SPLogEvent -StartTime "08/04/2011 18:00" -EndTime "08/04/2011 19:00"

+ MORE INFORMATION

For more information about the get-SPLogEvent command, visit http://technet.microsoft.com/en-us/library/ff607589.aspx

X REF

Analyzing the log files will be discussed more in Lesson 10.

To list the event logs that are available, execute the following command:

- get-eventlog -list

To display the 20 most recent entries in the application event log, execute the following command:

- get-eventlog -newest 20 -logname application

+ MORE INFORMATION

For more information about the get-eventlog command, visit http://technet.microsoft.com/en-us/library/dd315250.aspx

 ANALYZE AN INSTALLATION ERROR LOG

GET READY. To analyze the Installation Error Log, perform the following steps:

1. On the SharePoint server, click Start > Computer.

2. Navigate to the C:\Program Files\Common Files\Microsoft Shared\Web Server Extensions\14\LOGS folder.

3. To open the latest PSCDiagnostics log file with Notepad, double-click the most recent PSCDiagnostics log file.

4. To open the latest PSConfig.exe.log file with Notepad, double-click the most recent PSConfig.exe.log file.

5. Browse through or search the log files for errors in both text files.

 ANALYZE A ULS LOG

GET READY. To analyze the ULS Log, perform the following steps:

1. Click Start > All Programs > Microsoft SharePoint 2010 Products > SharePoint 2010 Management Shell.

2. Execute the desired commands (such as Get-SPLogEvent -StartTime "08/04/2011 18:00" -EndTime "08/04/2011 19:00").

ANALYZE AN EVENT LOG

GET READY. To open an Event Log, perform the following steps:

1. Click Start > All Programs > Microsoft SharePoint 2010 Products > SharePoint 2010 Management Shell.

2. Execute the desired commands (such as get-eventlog -newest 20 -logname application).

Repairing Installation Errors

The following are common causes for SharePoint installation failures and tips on how to avoid them:

- Make sure you have the minimum requirements, including the correct operating system, service packs, and patches. Also, make sure your servers are 64-bit.

- Make sure prerequisites are installed.

- Make sure there aren't any network connectivity problems for a server (SharePoint Server or SQL Server).

- Make sure you use the proper version, service pack, and patches for the SQL server.

- If you have a server running SQL Server 2005, make sure you have local and remote connections enabled and configured to use the TCP/IP protocol. If you have a server running SQL Server 2008, make sure you have the TCP/IP protocol enabled for the network configuration.

- Make sure that the service accounts and installation accounts have the proper rights and permissions on the SharePoint and SQL servers.

- Make sure that you ran the SharePoint 2010 Products Configuration Wizard.

Therefore, as you go through the installation program and encounter failures, examine any error messages that are displayed on the screen, in the logs, and the event viewer. Although some errors might not clearly reveal the real cause, you will need to make sure you have the basics covered by checking this list.

■ Activating Enterprise Features

THE BOTTOM LINE

When installing SharePoint, the installation process is the same for both Standard and Enterprise editions of SharePoint 2010. The product key that you enter at setup determines which set of features is available for use. Some of the features that are available with the Enterprise edition include the Access Services, Excel Services, Visio Services, Forms Services, and Performance Point Services.

If you installed SharePoint Server 2010 by using a Standard Client Access License (CAL), and you need to convert the license type to the Enterprise CAL, you can enable and then push the Enterprise feature set to all sites in your server farm. To enable enterprise features, you must be a member of the Farm Administrators group on the computer that is running Central Administration.

➜ ENABLE ENTERPRISE FEATURES FOR THE SERVER FARM

GET READY. To enable Enterprise features for the server farm, perform the following steps:

1. Open the Central Administration Web site.
2. On the Central Administration Web site, click Upgrade and Migration.
3. In the Upgrade and Patch Management section, click Enable Enterprise Features.
4. Type the product key and then click OK.

After you have enabled the features for the farm, you can enable the features on existing sites in the farm.

➜ ENABLE ENTERPRISE FEATURES ON EXISTING SITES

GET READY. To enable Enterprise features on existing sites by using Central Administration, perform the following steps:

1. Open the Central Administration Web site.
2. On the Central Administration Web site, click Upgrade and Migration.
3. In the Upgrade and Patch Management section, click Enable Features on existing sites.
4. On the Enable Features on existing sites page (see Figure 2-54), select the Enable all sites in this installation to use the following set of features check box and then click OK.

Figure 2-54

Enabling Enterprise Features

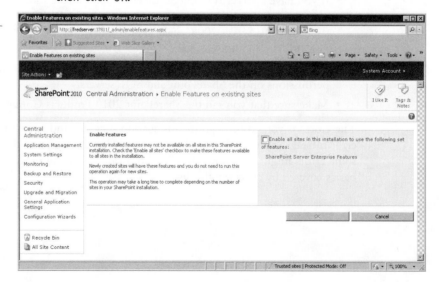

 VERIFY ENTERPRISE FEATURES FOR EXISTING SITES

GET READY. To enable Enterprise features on existing sites by using Central Administration, perform the following steps:

1. On the site collection root Web site, on the Site Actions menu, click Site Settings.
2. On the Site Settings page, in the Site Administration section, click Site features.
3. In the Status column for SharePoint Server Enterprise Site features, ensure that Active displays.

■ Applying and Managing Patches

THE BOTTOM LINE

To keep SharePoint secure and as reliable as possible, you need to upgrade (or *patch*) SharePoint server.

CERTIFICATION READY?
Why is it important to keep your SharePoint environment up-to-date with the newest security patches?
1.2.8

The ultimate goal of applying updates is to make sure your SharePoint environment is the latest and most stable version so that it is secure and reliable. A good place to start is to make sure that you load the standard updates/patches that are available through Windows updates, including updates/patches for Windows Server, SharePoint Server, and SQL Server.

Microsoft uses the following Web site to describe the SharePoint updates and includes a list of service packs and cumulative updates:

• http://technet.microsoft.com/en-us/sharepoint/ff800847

As with any update that you apply to a Windows Server, you should always:

• Take the time necessary to review the documentation that comes with each update.
• Test your update on a similar, if not duplicate, environment.
• Before applying any update, you should always make sure you have a good backup of your SharePoint systems, including the Web.config file and the SQL databases.
• When applying patches, you should schedule downtime within your organization, which is usually done during evenings or weekends.

Types of SharePoint Updates

Updates from Microsoft can be organized according to three categories:

• ***Individual updates*** resolve specific issues or vulnerabilities as they arise. Individual updates are as follows:

  • Standard updates are thoroughly tested and made available through the Windows Update site.
  • Hotfixes are aimed at a particular problem and are usually found when researching the encountered problem. Hotfixes have been tested but not as thoroughly as a standard update. Therefore, they are not made available through Windows Update site.

• ***Cumulative updates (CU)*** are relatively new to Microsoft but have become quite common for major applications. Cumulative updates group multiple updates (including hotfixes) since the last major update and are released every two months.

• ***Service packs*** are major updates to the platform and include updates as well as new functionality. Service packs are released very infrequently, but are thoroughly tested. When determining compatibility, you usually state the version/edition and the service pack.

➕ MORE INFORMATION

For more information about SharePoint 2010 Products, visit http://technet.microsoft.com/en-us/sharepoint/ff800847

> **TAKE NOTE** *
>
> When installing any individual update, cumulative update, or service pack, be sure to run the SharePoint 2010 Products Configuration Wizard to finalize the installation of the updates.

On June 28, 2011, Microsoft released SharePoint Service Pack 1 (SP1). It contains all SharePoint updates through April 2011 Cumulative Update in addition to other fixes that were applied specifically to SP1. SP1 also includes the following improvements:

- Improved support for Internet Explorer 9
- Support for Microsoft SQL Server 2011
- Ability to restore a site collection or a Web site that was deleted from the Recycle Bin
- Ability to recover deleted site collections and Web sites.

After you install SharePoint Foundation 2010 SP1 or SharePoint Server 2010 SP1, you must also install the corresponding June 2011 Cumulative Update (or newer) refresh package. As previously mentioned, you must run the SharePoint Products and Technologies Configuration Wizard to run the upgrade, which updates the farm to the latest version. In addition, you must restart the User Profile Synchronization service after installing the June 2011 cumulative update refresh.

> **+ MORE INFORMATION**
>
> For more information about SharePoint SP1 and to download SP1, visit http://support.microsoft.com/kb/2532120.

Identifying Your SharePoint Version

Sometimes it is useful to know which version of SharePoint you have, including the service pack and cumulative update. The numbering version of SharePoint uses the following format:

MMMM.mmmm.BBBB.rrrr

- MMMM indicates the major version for the product
- mmmm is the minor version
- BBBB is the build version number
- rrrr is the revision number

For example, consider 14.0.5136.5002:

- **14** represents SharePoint 2010
- **0** represents the initial main version of 14. Subsequent numbers — such as 1, 2, 3, and so on — represent minor upgrades to the main version. For example, the first minor upgrade would be 14.1.
- **5136** represents the Build version.
- **5002** represents the revision number.

Doing some searching on the Internet, this version of SharePoint 2010 includes the February 2011 Cumulative Update.

 IDENTIFY YOUR SHAREPOINT VERSION

GET READY. To see your version and build number of SharePoint 2010, perform the following steps:

1. Open Central Administration.
2. Click System Settings.
3. Click Manage servers in your farm.

Figure 2-55 shows the SharePoint Version and Build Number.

Figure 2-55

Verifying the SharePoint
Version and Build Number

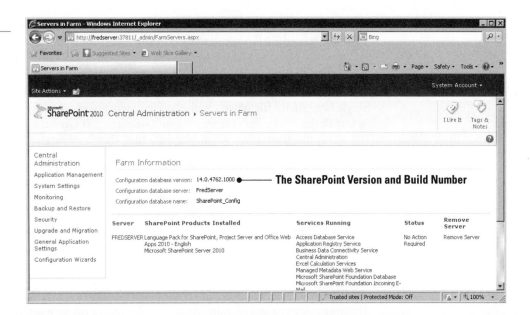

 **ANOTHER WAY**

Another way to look at the patch status is to open Central Administration, select Upgrade and Migration, and then select Manage Patch Status. This shows you the major components and language packs for each server and for the entire farm.

Configuring High Availability

 THE BOTTOM LINE

For many organizations, SharePoint is an essential tool. If SharePoint goes down, it could be quite costly to an organization. In these situations, you must use a variety of technologies to make SharePoint more fault-tolerant and highly available.

CERTIFICATION READY?
What components will help make SharePoint fault-tolerant?
1.2.3

As a server administrator, you need to minimize downtime by identifying potential failures and taking steps to avoid those failures and to reduce their effects. ***High availability*** is a system design protocol and associated implementation that ensures a certain degree of operational continuity during a given measurement period. When designing servers and the services they provide, servers and services are often assigned service-level agreements (SLAs), which state the level of availability those servers or services must maintain.

Introducing Fault-Tolerant Components

To make a server more fault-tolerant, you should first look at which components are most likely to fail, and then implement technology to make the system less likely to fail.

Some of the components that are made redundant within a system are usually:

- **Disks**: Use some form or RAID and hot spares.
- **Power supplies**: Use redundant power supplies.
- **Network cards**: Use redundant network cards.

DISKS

Because most drives are half-electronic, half-mechanical, you can connect multiple drives to special controllers to provide data production, system reliability, and better performance. A ***redundant array of independent disks (RAID)*** uses two or more drives in combination to create a fault-tolerant system that protects against physical hard-drive failure and increases hard-drive performance. RAID can be accomplished with either hardware or software and is usually used with network servers.

There are several levels of RAID available for use, based on your particular needs. The most commonly used RAIDs are described in the following sections.

Raid 0

RAID 0 stripes data across all drives. With striping, all available hard drives are combined into a single large virtual file system, with the file system's blocks arrayed so that they are spread evenly across all the drives. For example, if you have three 500 GB hard drives, RAID 0 provides for a 1.5 TB virtual hard drive. When you store files, they are written across all three of these drives.

For example, when a large file is written, one part of it might be written to the first drive, the next chunk to the second drive, more to the third drive, and perhaps more is wrapped back to the first drive to start the sequence again. Unfortunately, with RAID 0, there is no parity control or fault-tolerance; therefore, it is not a true form of RAID. Here, if one drive fails, you lose all data on the array. However, RAID 0 does have several advantages because it offers increased performance through load balancing.

Raid 1

RAID 1 is another common RAID that is used in networked PCs and servers. RAID 1 is sometimes known as disk mirroring. Disk mirroring copies a disk or partition onto a second hard drive. Specifically, as information is written, it is written to both hard drives simultaneously. This means that if one of the hard drives fails, the PC will still function because it can access the other hard drive. Then, should you later replace the failed drive, data will be copied from the remaining good drive to the new drive.

Raid 5

Another common RAID is RAID 5, which is similar to striping, except the space equivalent to one of the hard drives is used for parity (error correction) to provide fault-tolerance. To increase performance, the error correction function is spread across all hard drives in the array to avoid having one drive doing all the work in calculating the parity bits. Therefore if one drive fails, you can still continue working because parity calculations with the remaining drives will fill in any missing data. Later, when the failed drive is replaced, the missing information will be rebuilt. However, if two drives fail, you will lose all data on the array.

RAID 5 offers better performance than RAID 1. RAID 5 requires at least three drives, with more than three drives preferable. For instance, if you have just 3x500 GB drives, you will have only 2x500 GB or 1,000 GB of disk space because one of the three drives must be used for parity. Similarly, if you have 6x500 GB drives, you will have 5x500 GB or 2,500 GB of disk space available.

Spare Drives

Some RAID systems allow for spare drives. When one of the RAID drive fails, the system automatically replaces the failed drive with the spare drive so that you are running at 100% redundancy. You then replace the failed drive so that it will be available for the next failed drive.

Backups and Disaster Recovery

As a server or system administrator, you need to understand that backups are the best method for disaster recovery. While RAID and spare drives allow for limited failure, RAID and spare drives are not a replacement for backups. In addition, you should have a recovery plan if the SharePoint servers have to be rebuilt or restored. Therefore, you should create documentation detailing what it takes to build or restore a system and how the system is configured.

POWER SUPPLIES

A power supply is a mechanical device that converts AC power into clean DC power and includes fans for cooling. For systems that cannot afford to be down, these systems should have redundant power supplies (two or more power supplies). If a power supply fails or does not receive electricity, the remaining power supplies can power the system.

NETWORK CARDS

Network Interface Card (NIC) teaming is the process of grouping together two or more physical NICs into one single logical NIC, which can be used for network fault-tolerance and increased bandwidth through load balancing. *Network fault-tolerance* allows for a network card or cable to fail while still allowing for the system to function. Load balancing takes the traffic over multiple network cards, allowing for larger bandwidth. To make a system truly fault-tolerant, you should also have redundant switches where one network card of a team is connected to one switch and the other network card of the team is connected to another switch. This way, if the switch fails, you can still communicate over the network.

To support NIC teaming, the network card, network card driver, and switch must support the same teaming technology such as 802.3ad link aggregation. You will then most likely have to install and configure specialized software to activate the team.

Understanding Power

Without electricity, the server will not run. Even if you have redundant power supplies, they cannot protect against a power outage or other forms of power fluctuations. In these situations, your company should look at uninterruptible power supplies and power generators to provide power when no power is available from the power company.

An *uninterruptible power supply (UPS)* is an electrical device consisting of one or more batteries to provide backup power when a power outage occurs. UPS units range in size from those designed to protect a single computer without a video monitor (around 200 VA rating) to large units powering entire data centers or buildings. For server rooms that contain many servers, you will most likely install one or more racks full of batteries or UPS devices. For smaller deployments, you might have a single UPS connected to an individual server or essential computer. You also need the UPS to protect other key systems and devices such as primary routers, switches, and telecommunication devices.

What most people new to IT do not realize is that UPSs are not usually designed to provide power for lengthy periods of time. Instead, they are usually designed to provide power for momentary power outages and to allow adequate time to perform a proper shutdown on a server or to switch over to a power generator.

A power generator or a standby power generator is a backup electrical system that operates automatically within seconds of a power outage. Automatic standby generator systems might also be required by building codes for critical safety systems such as elevators in high-rise buildings, fire protection systems, standby lighting, or medical and life support equipment.

Using Fault-Tolerance Systems

Depending on the function or service that a SharePoint Server is providing, multi-server farms can use various technologies to make these server or services fault-tolerant.

Load balancing/*network load balancing (NLB)* is when multiple computers are configured as one virtual server to share the workload among multiple computers. Therefore, instead of providing fault-tolerance, it also provides increased performance. As far as users are concerned, they are accessing the virtual machine and the requests are distributed among the nodes within the cluster. Therefore, the Web front-end servers and applications can be protected with NLB. NLB is usually provided by dedicated software or a hardware-based device (such as a multilayer switch or a DNS server).

Since SharePoint centers around the SQL databases, there are several different technologies that can be used to make the SQL services fault-tolerant. They include:

- Failover clustering
- Database mirroring

FAILOVER CLUSTERING

A *failover cluster* is a set of independent computers that work together to increase the availability of services and applications. The clustered servers (called nodes) are connected by physical cables and by software. If one of the nodes fails, another node begins to provide services (a process known as failover). Failover clusters can be used for a wide range of network services including database applications such as Exchange Server or SQL Server, file servers, print services, or network services such as DHCP services.

The most common failover cluster is the *active-passive cluster*. In an active-passive cluster, both servers are configured to work as one, but only one at a time. The active node provides the network services while the passive node waits for something to happen to the active node where it cannot provide network services. If the active node goes down, the passive node becomes the active node and resumes providing the network services.

Another type of failover cluster is the active-active node that is designed to provide fault-tolerance and load balancing. Network services are split into two groups. One cluster node runs one set of network services while the other cluster node runs the other set of network services. Both nodes are active. If one of the nodes fails, the remaining node will take over providing all of the network services. Therefore, for SQL Server, you can have one node run some databases while a second SQL server runs other databases.

DATABASE MIRRORING

Database mirroring—introduced with SQL Server 2005—allows database transactions to be duplicated to a second SQL server. SharePoint 2010 can use mirroring databases where you specify the name of a secondary SQL server. If the primary server becomes unavailable, the SharePoint server will communicate with the secondary server.

TAKE NOTE *

You would typically use network load balancing for the front end and failover clustering for the back end (SQL server).

SKILL SUMMARY

IN THIS LESSON YOU LEARNED:

- When installing SharePoint, SharePoint can be installed on a single server with its own internal database or on a single server with a separate installation of SQL Server to a farm consisting of multiple servers.

- Planning is essential for every part of implementing SharePoint 2010 and it's a crucial part of preparing for the installation.

- SharePoint 2010 can be installed only on the 64-bit editions of Windows Server 2008 or Windows Server 2008 R2 and 64-bit editions of Microsoft SQL Server.

- SharePoint 2010 requires dedicated Active Directory user accounts, called service accounts, to run services and applications.

- To simplify the installation process, the SharePoint installation disk includes a SharePoint preparation tool that you can use to install all necessary prerequisites required for SharePoint 2010.

- When you install SharePoint as a stand-alone server, the installation program simplifies the installation process by installing the SharePoint program (sometimes referred to as SharePoint binaries) and enabling common SharePoint services.

- You should always run the SharePoint Products Configuration Wizard to complete a SharePoint 2010 installation, to complete a SharePoint 2010 upgrade, or after you apply patches.

- Similar to scripting an installation of Windows, you can also script the installation of SharePoint to simplify the installation and reduce the time it takes you to install a SharePoint server.

- Language packs are site templates that contain various languages.

- To keep SharePoint secure and as reliable as possible, you need to update SharePoint server.

- For many organizations, SharePoint is an essential tool. If SharePoint is down, an organization can lose money and their work can be hampered. In these situations, you can use various technologies to make SharePoint more fault-tolerant and highly available.

- To provide server fault-tolerance, you typically use network load balancing for the front end and failover clustering for the back end (SQL server). You can also use disk mirroring for the SQL server.

■ Knowledge Assessment

Fill in the Blank

Complete the following sentences by writing the correct word or words in the blanks provided.

1. When installing SharePoint 2010, all servers must be the _____-bit version of Windows Server 2008 or Windows Server 2008 R2.

2. A _____ account is used to install (or for SharePoint to use to access) the required resources needed to operate.

3. After installing SharePoint and after patching SharePoint, you should always run the _____.

4. After installing SharePoint 2010, the quickest way to perform the initial SharePoint configuration, create the home site, and make SharePoint available to users is to run the _____.

5. To run the SharePoint Product Configuration Wizard at the command prompt, use _____.

6. The command to install the SharePoint 2010 prerequisites for a scripted installation is _____.

7. The minimum amount of memory for a front-end SharePoint server used for production is _____ GB.

8. The minimum amount of memory for a SQL server used for medium deployments is _____ GB.

9. To make sure you load the necessary prerequisites, use the _____.

10. To provide redundancy for the SQL server, you should use a _____ cluster.

Multiple Choice

Circle the letter that corresponds to the best answer.

1. Which version of Windows Server does SharePoint 2010 run on?
   a. Windows Server 2003 R2 – 32-bit
   b. Windows Server 2003 R2 – 64-bit
   c. Windows Server 2008 – 32-bit
   d. Windows Server 2008 R2

2. Which version of SQL Server will not support SharePoint 2010?
   a. 64-bit edition of Microsoft SQL Server 2008 R2
   b. 64-bit edition of Microsoft SQL Server 2008 with SP1 and CU2
   c. 64-bit edition of Microsoft SQL Server 2005 with SP3
   d. 64-bit edition of Microsoft SQL Server 2005 with SP3 and CU3

3. Which of the following is *not* loaded by the SharePoint preparation tool?
   a. IIS
   b. .NET Framework version 3.5 SP1
   c. SQL Server Express
   d. Windows Identity Foundation (WIF)

4. By default, which port does the SQL server use?
   a. TCP port 80
   b. TCP port 443
   c. TCP port 1433
   d. TCP port 1500

5. Which SQL permissions does the Server Farm account need in order to function properly? (Choose two)
   a. dbcreator fixed server role
   b. dbsecurityadmin fixed server role
   c. Sysadmin fixed server role
   d. db_owner fixed database role for all SharePoint databases.

6. Which of the following is not loaded by the SharePoint preparation tool?
   a. Adobe Acrobat
   b. Microsoft .NET Framework 3.5 SP1
   c. Windows PowerShell 2.0
   d. Web Server (IIS) role

7. The largest database that the built-in SQL server supports is _____ GB.
   a. 1 GB
   b. 4 GB
   c. 10 GB
   d. 20 GB

8. What is a set of patches and hotfixes bundled together and released every two months?
   a. Ultimate patch
   b. Cumulative updates
   c. Patch bundle
   d. Fix bundle

9. What protects against disk failure for any SharePoint server, including the SQL server?
   a. RAID
   b. UPS
   c. NLB
   d. disk mirroring

10. What is needed to support the French language for SharePoint sites?
   a. Language Pack
   b. Language Translator
   c. Language Service Pack
   d. Language CU

True / False

Circle T if the statement is true or F if the statement is false.

T | F 1. If you installed SharePoint 2010 Language Pack for Russian and you forgot to load the Russian language pack for Windows, you just need to go back and install the Windows language pack.

T | F 2. The command to start the SharePoint 2010 Products Configuration Wizard is psconfig.exe.

T | F 3. RAID is a good substitute for backups.

T | F 4. Installing language packs allows you to translate SharePoint sites and SharePoint content to different languages.

T | F 5. After installing Windows or SharePoint 2010, you should always check for updates.

■ Case Scenarios

Scenario 2-1: Supporting Languages

You have been hired as a SharePoint consultant to help revamp the corporate SharePoint environment. Since the corporation has offices in several countries (including the United States, Mexico, Canada, France, United Kingdom, and Germany), you need to make the SharePoint environment usable by all users. Therefore, what must you do to ensure SharePoint can fully support multiple languages?

Scenario 2-2: Making SharePoint Fault-Tolerant

The use of SharePoint has grown significantly within your company and is now an essential tool used by several departments. Management is concerned that a server failure will impact users' abilities to do their jobs. Therefore, you are tasked with minimizing the failure of the SharePoint server. What can you do?

3 LESSON

Upgrading SharePoint 2010

OBJECTIVE DOMAIN MATRIX

TECHNOLOGY SKILL	OBJECTIVE DOMAIN	OBJECTIVE DOMAIN NUMBER
Upgrading SharePoint 2010	Deploying New Installations and Upgrades	1.1
Using the Pre-Upgrade Check Report and Other Tools	Analyzing a PreUpgradeCheck Report	1.1.4
Performing an In-Place Upgrade	Performing an In-Place Upgrade	1.1.2
Performing a Database Attach Upgrade	Performing a Database Attach Upgrade	1.1.3
Troubleshooting a SharePoint 2010 Upgrade		
Running Visual Upgrade	Running Visual Upgrade	1.1.1

KEY TERMS

database attach upgrade

in-place upgrade

visual upgrade

You have been hired as a server and SharePoint administrator by a corporation that uses a SharePoint 2007 environment. For the past month, you have been trying to persuade your management team to upgrade to SharePoint 2010. Therefore, you need to analyze the SharePoint 2007 environment and determine the best way to upgrade the SharePoint 2010 environment.

■ Upgrading SharePoint 2010

THE BOTTOM LINE

Many organizations are using WSS 3.0 or SharePoint 2007 and often these organizations have put a lot of time and effort into developing their SharePoint environment. Therefore, it's important to know how to upgrade SharePoint environments.

Since many of the SharePoint 2007 implementations can become quite complicated, it is best to plan and test an upgrade or migration to SharePoint 2010. Of course, the first place to start is to make sure that you have the correct hardware and software. Remember that all server hardware must be running a 64-bit version Windows Server 2008 with SP1, or Windows Server 2008 R2, and the SQL server running SQL Server 2005 SP3 and Cumulative Update 3, or SQL Server 2008 with SP1, or SQL Server 2008 R2.

CERTIFICATION READY
What are the two methods to upgrade to SharePoint 2010, and when should they be used?
1.1

It is also recommended that you upgrade your Microsoft Office SharePoint Server (MOSS) 2007 environment to Service Pack 2 or newer with October 2009 Cumulative Update for Windows SharePoint Services 3.0 and Office SharePoint Server 2007. You will also need to make sure that you correct any issues with any applications that may not be working or not working well, and uninstall any software that is no longer being used. Lastly, before you perform any type of upgrade or migration, make sure you have a current backup of the working SharePoint servers and databases.

There are two methods to upgrade to SharePoint 2010:

- In-place upgrade
- Database attach upgrade

An in-place upgrade upgrades the content and settings in a server farm as part of a single process, similar to what you do when you install SharePoint. The advantage of performing an in-place upgrade is that it is the simplest method to upgrade a system and it allows you to use the same hardware. During an in-place upgrade, servers and farms are offline during the upgrade process. While farm settings are preserved and upgraded, and customizations are available in the environment after the upgrade, manual steps may be required to upgrade or rework them.

The database attach upgrade takes a copy of the database and upgrades the content of the SharePoint environment on a separate farm. The advantage of performing a database attach upgrade is that you can create a second farm, copy the databases over, reconfigure and thoroughly test SharePoint and the SharePoint Customizations. When you are ready to go live, you will then have to copy and upgrade the database one more time and make changes to the SharePoint environment that were discovered during the testing phase. Of course, copying databases over a network takes time and bandwidth and you will need direct access to the database servers.

No matter which upgrade method you choose, make sure to document in detail each step and configuration change that you had to complete, identify the required components and their configuration, and determine how long the upgrade takes to complete. Therefore, when you decide to go into production, you will know exactly what needs to be done to make your SharePoint sites fully functional, and how long it will take, so that you can inform the users before you do the upgrade.

➕ MORE INFORMATION

For more information about the SharePoint 2010 upgrades, visit http://technet.microsoft.com/en-us/library/cc303420.aspx

■ Using the Pre-Upgrade Check Report and Other Tools

THE BOTTOM LINE

Most organizations that have embraced SharePoint 2007 will require a good deal of testing to make sure it is fully functional when you upgrade 2010. Microsoft provides multiple tools to evaluate your current system so that you can take the appropriate steps, which will allow for a smooth upgrade.

Similar to installing SharePoint, you will have to plan your upgrade. For a successful upgrade, you should first ensure that the servers you are upgrading have the minimum requirements and prerequisites. Remember, you need to have a 64-bit version of Windows Server 2008 or 2008 R2, and you need to have 64-bit of SQL Server 2005 with SP3, SQL Server 2008 with SP1 or SQL Server 2008 R2.

To evaluate your current system, Microsoft offers several tools to evaluate your SharePoint 2007 farm for upgradeability to SharePoint 2010. These tools include:

CERTIFICATION READY
What command is used to run the Pre-UpgradeCheck report?
1.1.4

- The `stsadm –o PreUpgradeCheck` command
- The `stsadm –o EnumAllWebs` command
- The SharePoint `2010 Test-SPContentDatabase` cmdlet

REF

The `stsadm` command will be explained more in Lesson 4.

WSS 3.0 and SharePoint Server 2007 include the Stsadm tool (stsadm.exe) for command-line administration of Office SharePoint Server 2007 servers and sites. SharePoint 2010 still includes the `stsadm` tool, but it has been depreciated in SharePoint 2010. It is located in the %COMMONPROGRAMFILES%\microsoft shared\Web server extensions\12\bin. You must be an administrator on the local computer to use `stsadm`.

The most common cause of upgrade failures is that the environment is missing customized features, solutions, or other elements. Therefore, you will need to ensure that if you install plug-ins, add-ons, or other SharePoint components that were provided by Microsoft, a third-party vendor, or from an internal developer.

For WSS 3.0 and SharePoint 2007, Microsoft provided the Fab 40, application templates created as out-of-the-box custom scenarios tailored to address the needs and requirements of specific business processes or sets of tasks in organizations of any size. Some of these templates include Absence Request and Vacation Schedule Management, Call Center, Change Request Management, Event Planning, Inventory Tracking, Knowledge Base, Sales Lead Pipeline, and so on. These templates were created to provide a starting point to build deeper SharePoint-based solutions. These application templates can be found at http://technet.microsoft.com/en-us/windowsserver/sharepoint/bb407286.

REF

For more information about customized features and solutions, refer to Lesson 6.

Microsoft is not releasing new versions of these templates for SharePoint 2010 Products. Also, .stp files are deprecated and cannot be used to create new sites when you upgrade to SharePoint Server 2010 or SharePoint Foundation 2010. Unfortunately, Microsoft has not created new templates for SharePoint 2010. Therefore, if your WSS 3.0 or SharePoint 2007 environment is using any of these templates, you should read the information from the http://blogs.technet.com/b/tothesharepoint/archive/2010/08/18/sharepoint-2010-products-upgrade-and-the-fabulous-40-application-templates.aspx. Fortunately, some of these templates have been recreated by third parties and are available at http://techsolutions.net/Blog/tabid/65/EntryId/17/Fab-40-Templates-for-MOSS-2010.aspx.

Starting with SharePoint 2007 Service Pack 2, `stsadm` includes the `preupgradecheck` option. By executing the `stsadm –o preupgradecheck` command, `stsadm` will perform a pre-upgrade check on your SharePoint 2007 environment to find any potential issues for upgrade and offer recommendations before upgrading to SharePoint 2010. The pre-upgrade

checker reports information about the status of your environment and the SharePoint sites in that environment, including:

- Upgrade readiness and supported paths including a list of all servers and components in the farm and information about whether the servers meet requirements for upgrading.
- Alternate access mapping settings used in the farm.
- A list of all site definitions, site templates, features, and language packs that are installed in the farm.
- A list of unsupported customizations including database schema modifications.
- A list of database or site objects (list items, lists, documents, Web sites, or collections) that are orphans in the farm, meaning they not associated with a particular site.
- Reports any missing or invalid configuration settings (such as a missing Web.config file, invalid host names, or invalid service accounts) that exist in the farm.
- Reports whether the databases meet the requirements for upgrade.

TAKE NOTE *

The `stsadm` command has been updated in the October 2009 Cumulative Update for Windows SharePoint Services 3.0 and Office SharePoint Server 2007. You can download and install the October 2009 Cumulative Update from October 2009 Cumulative Update Packages for SharePoint Server 2007 and Windows SharePoint Services 3.0 (http://go.microsoft.com/fwlink/?LinkID=169179).

By running the `stsadm -o preupgradecheck`, you can determine:

- Whether to perform an in-place upgrade or a database attach upgrade.
- Whether to upgrade some or all site collections that contain customized sites.
- Which sites need to have customizations reapplied or redone after upgrade, and therefore might take longer than others in the review stage.
- Whether you need to repair orphaned items before the upgrade, by following the steps in Knowledge Base article 918744, "Description of a new command-line operation that you can use to repair content databases in Windows SharePoint Services" (http://support.microsoft.com/kb/918744).

TAKE NOTE *

Since SharePoint has a tendency to change as users perform more actions, it is often recommended to run the pre-upgrade checker more than once, including right before you perform the upgrade, to ensure there are no additional issues.

 RUN THE PRE-UPGRADE CHECKER

GET READY. To run the pre-upgrade checker, you must be a member of the local Administrators group on the server running MOSS 2007. Then perform the following steps:

1. Click Start, right-click Command Prompt, and then select Run As Administrator. If prompted by the security dialog box, click Yes.
2. When the command prompt window opens, navigate to the following directory:
   `%COMMONPROGRAMFILES%\Microsoft Shared\Web Server Extensions\12\bin`
3. Execute the following command at the command prompt:
   `STSADM.EXE -o preupgradecheck`

Figure 3-1 shows running the `stsadm.exe -o preupgradecheck` command. Figure 3-2 shows the report that it generated.

Figure 3-1

Running the `stsadm.exe -o preupgradecheck` command

Figure 3-2

The SharePoint Products and Technologies Pre-Upgrade Check Report page

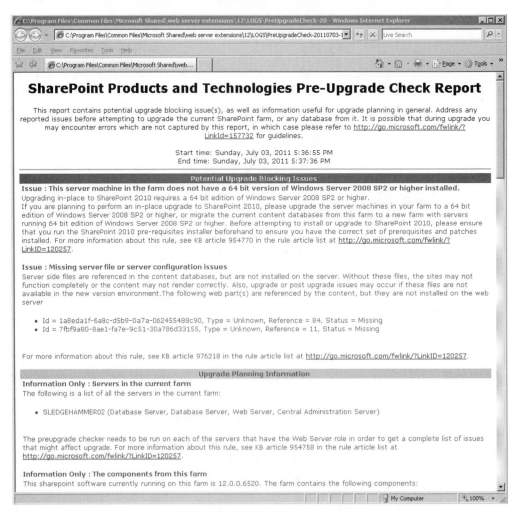

The pre-upgrade checker runs on the local server and examines your server farm settings. Once finished, the report will open in your Web browser. The report is also located in the `%COMMONPROGRAMFILES%\Microsoft Shared\Web Server Extensions\12\LOGS` folder.

Another useful option with the `stsadm` command is the `enumallwebs` option, which displays the IDs and site map status for all site collections and subsites in the content database. It can also be used to identify any orphaned sites in your environment, which must be repaired or deleted prior to an upgrade.

The syntax for the `enumallwebs` option is:

```
stsadm -o enumallwebs -databasename <database name>
```

Before moving on to the next section, one other tool should be mentioned. The `Test-SPContentDatabase` PowerShell command can be used to identify missing customizations and files, which are especially important for database attach upgrades.

■ Performing An In-Place Upgrade

THE BOTTOM LINE

As mentioned earlier, an *in-place upgrade* is when you upgrade the current SharePoint 2007 system to SharePoint 2010. While this is typically the easiest upgrade to perform, there are times when this method is not feasible. For example, if the current hardware cannot support SharePoint 2010 or you want to upgrade from one topology to another topology and the upgrade path is not supported.

CERTIFICATION READY
In what situations can you perform an in-place upgrade?
1.1.2

To upgrade SharePoint Server 2007 to SharePoint 2010, using an in-place upgrade, you must be a member of the local Administrators group on the server running MOSS 2007. An in-place upgrade upgrades the SharePoint 2007 farm's binaries and database to SharePoint 2010 functionality and settings. To perform an in-place upgrade, only the following upgrade topology paths are supported:

- MOSS 2007 stand-alone server with SQL Server 2005 Express Edition to SharePoint Server 2010 stand-alone server with Microsoft SQL Server 2008 Express. It cannot be upgraded to any farm topology.
- MOSS 2007 single server with SQL Server can only be upgraded to a SharePoint Server 2010 single server with SQL Server but not to a stand-alone server with SQL Server 2008 Express.
- Any MOSS 2007 Farm Topology can be upgraded to any size SharePoint Server 2010 farm topology but not to any stand-alone deployment.

If you are not performing one of these paths, you will have to choose the database-attach method.

In addition, you must upgrade to similar editions. For example, you can upgrade from SharePoint 2007 Standard Edition to SharePoint 2010 Standard Edition, and you can upgrade SharePoint 2007 Enterprise Edition to SharePoint 2010 Enterprise Edition. However, after you upgrade from SharePoint 2007 Standard Edition to SharePoint 2010 Standard Edition, you can then upgrade to Enterprise Edition.

The steps in performing an in-place upgrade include:

1. Making sure you have a backup of all servers and the databases.
2. Running the SharePoint Products and Technologies 2010 Preparations utility to install all prerequisites on all SharePoint servers similar to when you installed SharePoint 2010.

3. Running the SharePoint installation program to install upgrades for the SharePoint 2010 binaries on all SharePoint servers.

4. Running The SharePoint Products and Technologies Configuration Wizard on all SharePoint servers after you have upgraded the binaries of all SharePoint servers.

5. Reviewing and validating SharePoint functionality.

6. During the upgrade to SharePoint 2010, you will have the option to perform a visual upgrade, which will upgrade the SharePoint 2007 interface with the SharePoint 2010 interface.

   To perform this upgrade, you will need to perform a visual upgrade to the SharePoint site collections and then upgrade each site to the SharePoint 2010 interface. Fortunately, this upgrade does not have to be done during the SharePoint 2010 upgrade and can be done at a later time. Visual upgrade will be discussed later in this lesson.

7. Lastly, before you attempt an upgrade to a production environment, you should test the process in a staging or testing environment that mirrors the content and configuration of your production servers so that you can identify and fix problems before they go live. This can only increase your chances of success.

 UPGRADE THE SHAREPOINT BINARIES

GET READY. To upgrade SharePoint Server 2007 Binaries to SharePoint 2010, perform the following steps:

1. Log on to the server as an administrator.

2. Double-click the SharePoint executable file.

3. When the Microsoft Windows SharePoint 2010 splash screen displays, click the Install SharePoint Server option.

4. When prompted for the Product Key, type the appropriate key.

5. When the License Agreement displays, select the I accept the terms of this License Agreement checkbox and then click Continue.

6. When the Upgrade Earlier Versions page displays, click Install Now.

7. After the installation is complete, on the completion page, clear the Run The SharePoint Products And Technologies Configuration Wizard Now check box and then click Close.

If you are upgrading a single server, you can proceed immediately from running the prerequisite installer to Setup.exe to the Products And Technologies Configuration Wizard without interruption.

 RUN THE SHAREPOINT PRODUCTS CONFIGURATION AFTER AN UPGRADE

GET READY. After you have upgraded SharePoint, you need to run the SharePoint Product Configuration on each server. Therefore, perform the following steps:

1. Click Start > All Programs > Administrative Tools > SharePoint Products Configuration Wizard.

2. In the SharePoint Products Configuration Wizard, on the Welcome to SharePoint Products page, click Next.

3. When a message displays notifying you that Internet Information Services (IIS), the SharePoint Administration Services v4, and the SharePoint Timer Service v4 may need to be restarted or reset during configuration, click Yes to continue with the wizard.

4. On the Specify Farm Settings page, in the Passphrase box, type a passphrase. In the Confirm passphrase box, type the same passphrase.

5. On the Visual Upgrade page (see Figure 3-3), select one of the following options:

- Change existing SharePoint sites to use the new user experience. Administrators control the user experience for end users. You then choose the Preserve customized pages, but update template and application pages to use the new UI option or the Reset all customized pages to their original templates option.

- Preserve the look and feel of existing SharePoint sites, and allow end users to update their sites' user experience. This is the default option.

Figure 3-3

The Visual Upgrade page

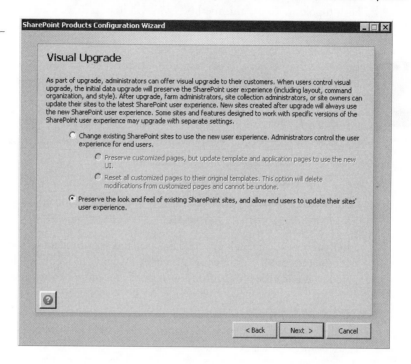

6. On the Completing the SharePoint Products Configuration Wizard page, verify the settings, and then click Next.

7. When a message displays, notifying you that if you have a server farm with multiple servers, you must run Setup on each server to install new binary files before you continue the SharePoint Products Configuration Wizard. If you have only one server, or you have executed the setup program on all servers, click OK to continue with the wizard.

8. When the Configuration Successful, Upgrade in Progress page displays, review the settings that have been configured, and then click Finish.

9. Then, run the SharePoint Products Configuration Wizard on the SharePoint servers in the farm.

After SharePoint has been upgraded and each site is tested, you might still need to configure new and upgraded services, start a crawl so that you have new updated indexes used for searches, and configure the use of forms-based authentication or Web single sign-on (Web SSO) authentication. These will be discussed in later lessons.

 **+ MORE INFORMATION**

Microsoft provides a thorough checklist for in-place upgrade located at http://technet.microsoft.com/en-us/library/ff608117.aspx

■ Performing A Database Attach Upgrade

THE BOTTOM LINE

To upgrade WSS 3.0 or Microsoft Office SharePoint Server 2007 to Microsoft SharePoint Server 2010 using the *database attach upgrade* approach, you are only upgrading the content contained in the content databases and not the configuration settings. You have to use this method if you are changing hardware, or if you want to reconfigure the server farm topology. To use this method, you will have to have direct access to the SQL server.

CERTIFICATION READY
What are the basic steps in performing a database attach upgrade?
1.1.3

Before you can begin this process, you must first set up your new SharePoint environment, including installing and configuring SharePoint. When you are ready to perform the database attached upgrade, perform the following steps:

1. Back up the previous version databases by using SQL Server tools
2. Detach the previous version databases (standard database attach)
3. Restore a backup copy of the database
4. Verify custom components
5. Attach a content database to a Web application and verify upgrade for the first database
6. Upgrade the shared services databases and My Sites

Alternately, you can back up the databases and restore them to the same SQL server with different names or on a different SQL server. As you can see, it is a bit more complicated compared to the in-place migration, but it gives you more control and flexibility.

+ MORE INFORMATION
For more information about the database-attach upgrade, visit the following Web site: http://technet.microsoft.com/en-us/library/cc303436.aspx

+ MORE INFORMATION
Microsoft provides a thorough checklist for database attach upgrade, located at http://technet.microsoft.com/en-us/library/ff607663.aspx

Before you begin the process:

- Make sure the account you use to attach the databases is a member of the db_owner fixed database role for the content databases on the SQL server.
- Check for and repair any database consistency errors. Unfortunately, this is out of the scope of this book.

 BACK UP THE SHAREPOINT 2007 CONTENT DATABASES USING SQL SERVER 2008/SQL SERVER 2008 R2

GET READY. To back up the SharePoint databases, perform the following steps:

1. Log on to the SQL server.
2. Click Start, click All Programs, click Microsoft SQL Server 2008 or Microsoft SQL Server 2008 R2, and then click SQL Server Management Studio.
3. Make sure the SQL Server 2008 Database Engine is selected. In the Connect to Server box, type in the name of the SQL Server and instance. If you are using the default instance, you just specify the SQL Server (see Figure 3-4). Then click Connect.
4. In Object Explorer, expand the server name and expand Databases. Figure 3-5 shows the SQL Server Management Studio console.

Figure 3-4

Connecting to a SQL Server database

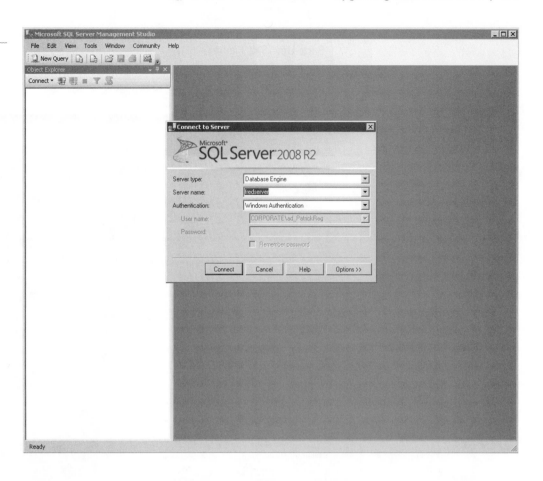

Figure 3-5

The SQL Server Management Studio console

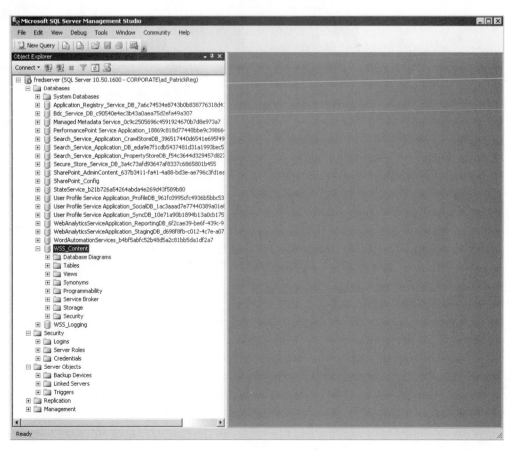

5. Right-click the database that you want to back up, point to Tasks, and then click Back Up. (See Figure 3-6.)

6. When the Back Up Database dialog box displays, verify the database name. In the Backup type box, select Full. (See Figure 3-7.)

Figure 3-6

Running the Back Up task

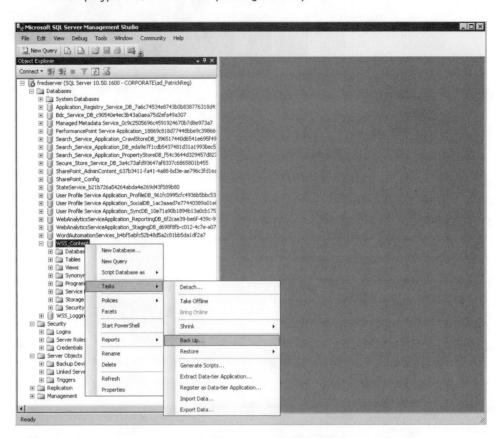

Figure 3-7

The Back Up Database dialog

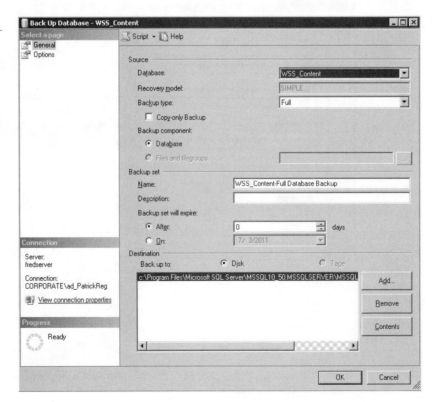

7. In the Destination section, specify the Disk for backup destination and then click Add to create a different destination. Specify a path and name of the backup file (such as J:\SPContentDB.BAK). (See Figure 3-8.)

Figure 3-8

Selecting the database destination

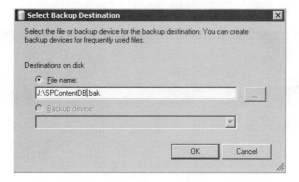

8. Click OK to start the backup process.

Repeat the previous procedure to back up all the content and shared services databases that are used by Office SharePoint Server 2007 in your environment.

Before you can attach your databases to the new environment and upgrade the data, you need to detach them from the current SharePoint environment. You can then move them to a new database server, or leave them on the existing database server and attach them to Web applications. For testing purposes, you can also restore the database to a new SQL server or even restore the database to the same SQL server but rename it to a different name so that you can have the old and new environments running at the same time.

 DETACH A CONTENT DATABASE FROM A WEB APPLICATION

GET READY. Removing the content database does not delete the database; it only removes the association of the database with the Web application. To detach a content database from a Web application, perform the following steps:

1. Log on to a SharePoint server and open Central Administration.

2. In Central Administration, on the Application Management page, in the SharePoint Web Application Management section, click Manage Content databases. (See Figure 3-9.)

Figure 3-9

Clicking the Manage content databases option

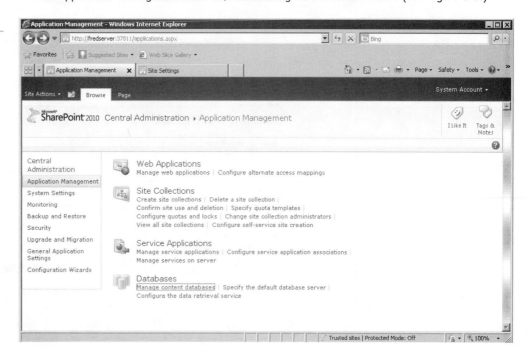

3. On the Manage Content Databases page (see Figure 3-10), click the content database you want to detach. If the content database does not appear, it might be associated with another Web application. To select another Web application, click Change Web Application on the Web Application menu.

Figure 3-10

Selecting the content database

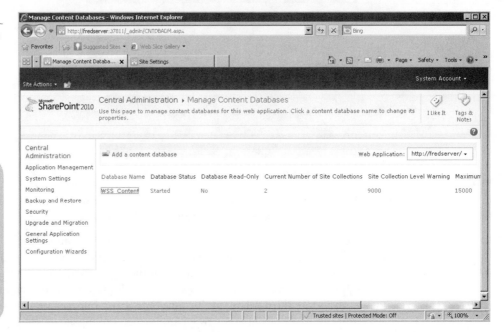

4. On the Manage Content Database Settings page, in the Remove Content Database section, select the Remove content database check box (see Figure 3-11), and then click OK.

Figure 3-11

Detaching a content database

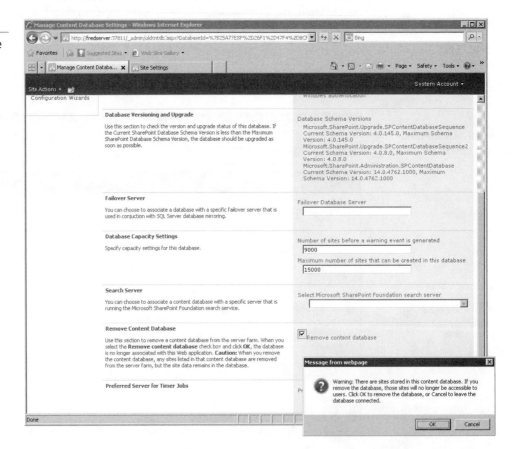

5. When the warning displays, click OK.

6. Repeat the previous steps for each content database that you want to detach.

If you are moving the databases to a different database server, you must also detach the databases from the instance of SQL Server before you move them and attach them to the new instance of SQL Server.

 DETACH AN SQL DATABASE FROM AN SQL SERVER INSTANCE

GET READY. To detach an SQL database, perform the following steps:

1. Within the SQL Server Management Console, expand the name of the server and expand the Databases node.

2. Right-click the content database, select Tasks, and then click Detach. (See Figure 3-12.)

Figure 3-12

Using the Detach task

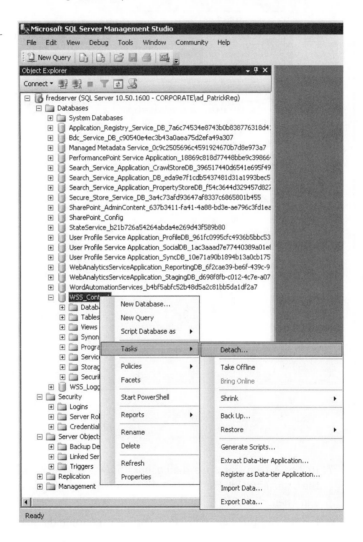

3. Repeat this step for each content database that you want to detach and move.

TAKE NOTE ★ Detach only the content databases. Do not detach any other SharePoint databases.

4. Using Windows Explorer, browse to the location of the .mdf and .ldf files for the content databases and copy them to the new server and/or destination directory.

5. On the new server, open SQL Server Management Console.

6. Right-click the Databases node, select Tasks, and then click Attach. (See Figure 3-13.)

Figure 3-13

Attaching a database

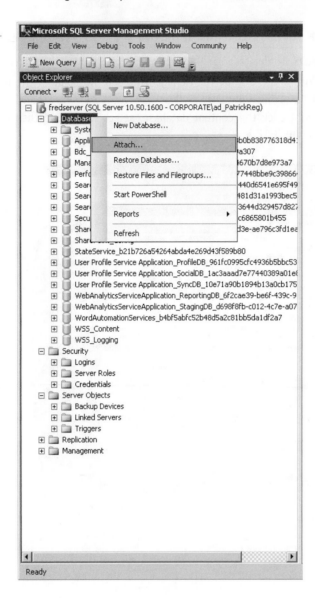

7. In the Attach Database dialog box, browse to the location to which you transferred the .mdf and .ldf files, select the .mdf file for the database you want to attach, and then click OK.

8. Repeat the previous two steps for each content database that you are moving.

 RESTORE A BACKUP COPY OF THE DATABASE TO ANOTHER SQL SERVER

GET READY. If you need to restore a backup copy of the database to another server, copy the backup files to the SQL server and perform the following steps:

1. Connect to the appropriate instance in the SQL Server 2008 Database Engine of the SQL Server using the SQL Server Management Console.

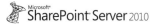

2. In Object Explorer, expand the server name, right-click Databases, and then click Restore Database. (See Figure 3-14.)

3. When the Restore Database dialog box displays on the General page, type the name of the database to be restored in the To database list. (See Figure 3-15.)

Figure 3-14

Restoring a database

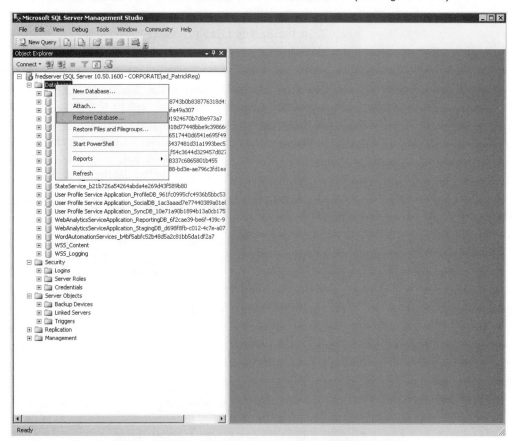

Figure 3-15

The Restore Database dialog

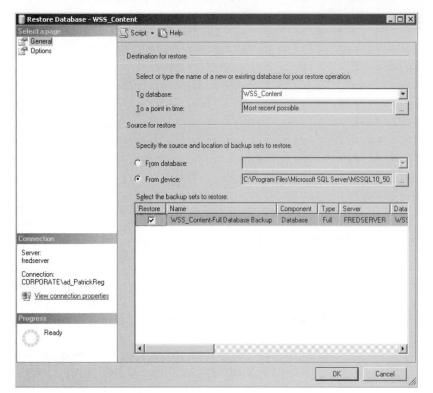

4. In the To a point in time text box, retain the default (Most recent possible).

5. To specify the source and location of the backup sets to restore, click From device, and then click Browse to select the backup file.

6. In the Specify Backup dialog box, in the Backup media box, make sure File is selected.

7. In the Backup location area, click Add.

8. In the Locate Backup File dialog box, select the file that you want to restore, click OK, and then, in the Specify Backup dialog box, click OK.

9. In the Restore Database dialog box, under Select the backup sets to restore grid, select the Restore check box next to the most recent full backup.

10. If you want to restore a database with the same name as an existing database, you need to tell the SQL Server to overwrite the previous database. Therefore, in the Restore Database dialog box, on the Options page, under Restore options, select the Overwrite the existing database check box. (See Figure 3-16.)

Figure 3-16

The Options page

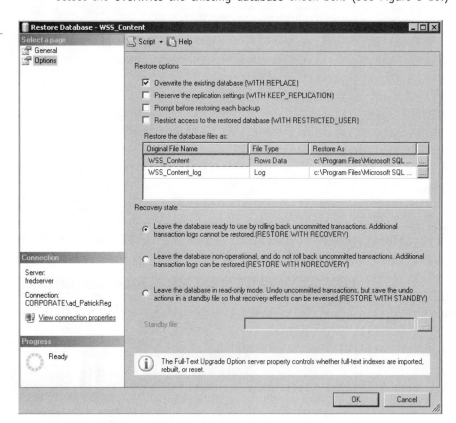

11. Click OK to start the restore process.

Next, you want to verify that you have installed all of the custom components on the SharePoint server. Therefore, you should use the Test-SPContentDatabaseWindows PowerShell cmdlet to verify that you have all the custom components that you need for that database.

 VERIFY INSTALLATION OF CUSTOM COMPONENTS

GET READY. To verify that all custom components are installed on the SharePoint server, perform the following steps:

1. On the SharePoint server, click Start > All Programs > Microsoft SharePoint 2010 Products > SharePoint 2010 Management Shell. (See Figure 3-17.)

Figure 3-17

Opening PowerShell

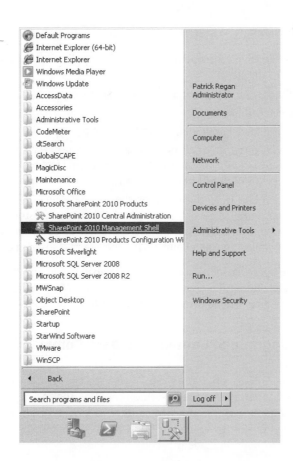

2. At the Windows PowerShell command prompt, type:

Test-SPContentDatabase -Name <DatabaseName> -WebApplication <URL>

<DatabaseName> is the name of the database you want to test and <URL> is the URL for the Web application that will host the sites. (See Figure 3-18.)

Figure 3-18

Running the Test-SPContentDatabase command with PowerShell

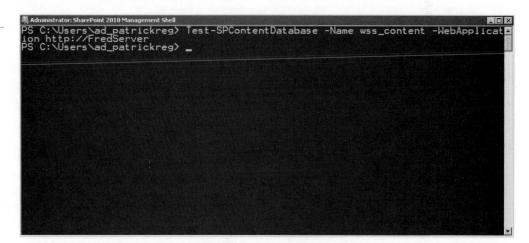

TAKE NOTE＊   When you attach a content database, make sure that the root site for the Web application is included in the first content database that you attach.

To attach an existing content database to the farm, use the Mount-SPContentDatabase PowerShell command. If the database being mounted requires an upgrade (such as when you are mounting a database from a MOSS 2007 system to a SharePoint 2010 system), Mount-SPContentDatabase cmdlet upgrades the database.

ATTACH A CONTENT DATABASE TO A WEB APPLICATION

GET READY. To attach a content database to a Web application by using Windows PowerShell, perform the following steps:

1. Click Start > All Programs > Microsoft SharePoint 2010 Products > SharePoint 2010 Management Shell.

2. At the Windows PowerShell command prompt, type the following command:

```
Mount-SPContentDatabase -Name <DatabaseName>
-DatabaseServer <ServerName> -WebApplication
<URL> [-Updateuserexperience]
```

<DatabaseName> is the name of the database you want to upgrade and <ServerName> is server on which the database is stored. <URL> is the URL for the Web application that will host the sites. If you want your site visual interface to be upgraded to SharePoint 2010, include the –Updateuserexperience option.

Once you have upgraded all of your content databases, you will then upgrade the shared services databases including the User Profile Services and My Sites. Upgrading the User Profile Services and My Sites will be discussed in Lesson 8.

Using the Upgrade-SPContentDatabase Command

The Upgrade-SPContentDatabase PowerShell cmdlet upgrades a SharePoint content database. When the Upgrade-SPContentDatabase cmdlet is run, an upgrade of an existing content database attached to the current farm is initiated. It can be used to resume a failed version-to-version or build-to-build upgrade of a content database, or to begin a build-to-build upgrade of a content database.

■ Troubleshooting A SharePoint 2010 Upgrade

THE BOTTOM LINE

When upgrading to SharePoint 2010, you can still have the same problems that you have when installing SharePoint 2010. Therefore, you need to verify that you have the proper permissions for the service accounts and that you meet the minimum requirements for hardware and software. However, the most common problem with upgrading a SharePoint environment is usually caused by missing components that existed on the SharePoint 2007 environment, but that have not been migrated or installed on the SharePoint 2010 environment.

After you have attached a database, you can use the Upgrade Status page in Central Administration to check the status of upgrade on your site collections. In addition, you can review the upgrade log file to see whether there were any issues during the upgrade. If the upgrade fails, you may need to install any missing components or fix any other problem, and then try attaching the database.

 VIEW THE UPGRADE STATUS PAGE

GET READY. To view the Upgrade Status page, perform the following steps:

1. In Central Administration, click Upgrade and Migration.

2. Click Check upgrade status. (See Figure 3-19.)

Figure 3-19

Checking the upgrade status

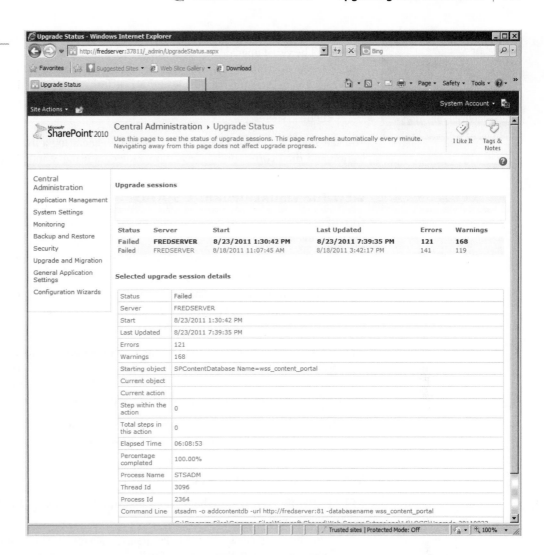

To help you identify errors during the upgrade, you should also look at the upgrade error log and upgrade log files. The upgrade error log upgrade log files are located at %COMMONPROGRAMFILES%\Microsoft Shared\Web server extensions\14\LOGS. The logs are named in the following format: Upgrade-*YYYYMMDD-HHMMSS-SSS*-error.log and Upgrade-*YYYYMMDD-HHMMSS-SSS*.log, where *YYYYMMDD* is the date and *HHMMSS-SSS* is the time (hours in 24-hour clock format, minutes, seconds, and milliseconds). Therefore, if you have done multiple upgrades, you will be able to find the appropriate upgrade error log and upgrade log files. The upgrade log file includes the name of the content database being upgraded.

■ Running Visual Upgrade

THE BOTTOM LINE

As discussed in the previous lesson, SharePoint 2010 offers a newer interface that includes the use of ribbons. However, to ease a new interface to users, you can manage if upgraded sites use the older interface or the newer SharePoint 2010 interface.

Therefore, when you perform an Upgrade for SharePoint 2010, you can choose to use *visual upgrade*. The visual upgrade feature is not available in the SharePoint Products Configuration Wizard if you are performing an upgrade on a stand-alone server with a built-in database. However, the Visual Upgrade feature is available in this case from the `psconfig` command-line tool:

```
psconfig.exe -cmd upgrade [-preserveolduserexperience
<true|false>]
```

You can view the current user interface status by generating a list of all Web sites in a site collection and their corresponding visual upgrade data using Windows PowerShell.

 VIEW THE VISUAL UPGRADE STATUS

GET READY. To view the status of current user interface by using Windows PowerShell, perform the following steps:

1. Click Start > All Programs > Microsoft SharePoint 2010 Products > SharePoint 2010 Management Shell.
2. At the Windows PowerShell command prompt, type the following command:

```
$sc = Get-SPSite http://machinename/sites/collectionname; $sc.
GetVisualReport() | Format-Table
```

Site owners can toggle between the **Use the previous user interface** (WSS 3.0/SharePoint 2007 interface) and **Preview the updated user interface** (SharePoint 2010 interface) options. Once the owner determines that there are no problems with the new user interface, the site owner can finalize the new user interface by selecting the Update the user interface option.

If a site is finalized by a user by mistake, or has encountered a problem that cannot be solved, you can use PowerShell to revert to the previous user interface.

 REVERT A USER INTERFACE

GET READY. To revert sites to the previous user interface by using Windows PowerShell, perform the following steps:

1. On the Start menu, click All Programs > Microsoft SharePoint 2010 Products > SharePoint 2010 Management Shell.
2. To revert a specific site in a site collection to the previous UI, at the Windows PowerShell command prompt, type the following command:

```
Get-SPSite http://machinename/sites/V3UI | Get-SPWeb "webname" |
Foreach{$_.UIVersionConfigurationEnabled=1;
$_.UIVersion=3;$_.Update();}
```

3. To revert all sites in a site collection to the previous user interface, at the Windows PowerShell command prompt, type the following command:

```
Get-SPSite http://machinename/sites/V3UI |
Foreach{$_.UIVersionConfigurationEnabled=1;
$_.UIVersion=3;$_.Update();}
```

SKILL SUMMARY

IN THIS LESSON, YOU LEARNED:

- There are two methods to upgrade to SharePoint 2010: an in-place upgrade and a database attach upgrade.

- Microsoft provides multiple tools to evaluate your current system so that you can take the appropriate steps to ensure a smooth upgrade, including the `stsadm -o preupgradecheck` command.

- To upgrade WSS 3.0 or Microsoft Office SharePoint Server 2007 to Microsoft SharePoint Server 2010 using the database attach upgrade approach, you are upgrading only the content contained in the content databases; you are not upgrading the configuration settings.

- To change a SharePoint site that was upgraded from SharePoint 2007 to SharePoint 2010 so that it will have the SharePoint 2010 interface, you must perform a Visual Upgrade.

■ Knowledge Assessment

Fill in the Blank

Complete the following sentences by writing the correct word or words in the blanks provided.

1. If you want to upgrade your MOSS 2007 environment, you should install Service Pack _____ or newer, and _____ Cumulative Update for Windows.

2. When you install SharePoint 2010 on a system running SharePoint 2007, you are performing a(n) _____ upgrade.

3. The `stsadm -o` _____ command displays the IDs and site map status for all site collections and subnets in the content database.

4. Before performing an upgrade, you must make sure you have a _____ of all SharePoint systems and databases.

5. The _____ cmdlet upgrades a SharePoint content database that is attached to the current farm.

6. The `stsadm.exe` command is located in the %COMMONPROGRAMFILES%\ microsoft shared\Web server extensions\12_____ folder on a SharePoint 2007 system.

7. Before upgrading SharePoint, you should always run the _____ report.

8. If the current hardware that you have for SharePoint 2007 does not support SharePoint 2010, you must perform a(n) _____ upgrade.

9. The _____ command can be used to identify missing customizations and files.

10. Use the _____ upgrade if you want to also upgrade the hardware while upgrading SharePoint 2007 to SharePoint 2010.

Multiple Choice

Circle the letter that corresponds to the best answer.

1. Which upgrade method allows you to copy the database to a new SharePoint farm and upgrade the content database?
   a. In-place upgrade
   b. Scan and copy upgrade
   c. Database attach upgrade
   d. Test and Copy upgrade

2. Which PowerShell command identifies missing customizations and files?
   a. `Test-SPContentDatabase`
   b. `Check-Customs`
   c. `Check-Files`
   d. `Test-ContentFiles`

3. Which of the following is the simplest upgrade that you can perform on a MOSS 2007 single server with SQL Server to SharePoint Server 2010 single server with SQL Server?
   a. in-place upgrade
   b. scan and copy upgrade
   c. database attach upgrade
   d. test and copy upgrade

4. Which command adds a database to a SharePoint Web site and upgrades the database to SharePoint 2010 if necessary?
   a. `Upgrade-SPContentDatabase`
   b. `Mount-SPContentDatabase`
   c. `Test-SPContentDatabase`
   d. `New-SPContentDatabase`

5. Which of the following is the simplest upgrade that you can perform if you are upgrading a MOSS 2007 stand-alone server with SQL Server 2005 Express Edition to a multi-farm SharePoint 2010 environment?
   a. in-place upgrade
   b. scan and copy upgrade
   c. database attach upgrade
   d. test and copy upgrade

6. Which of the following are considered upgrade methods for SharePoint 2010? (Choose two)
   a. in-place upgrade
   b. scan and copy upgrade
   c. database attach upgrade
   d. test and copy upgrade

7. Which of the following upgrades the SharePoint interface to SharePoint 2010 after an upgrade to SharePoint 2010 for a site?
   a. `psconfig` upgrade
   b. interface upgrade
   c. preview upgrade
   d. visual upgrade

8. Which of the following reverts a SharePoint site that has the user interface upgraded to SharePoint 2010?
   a. PowerShell
   b. `stsadm`
   c. `psconfig.exe`
   d. `vbupgrade.exe`

9. When you attach a database to the SQL server, you must have the _____ fixed database role for the content databases on the SQL server.
   a. security_admin
   b. disk_admin
   c. SQL_admin
   d. db_owner

10. After you perform a SharePoint upgrade, you should open the upgrade error _____.
   a. logs
   b. XML files
   c. config files
   d. customizations

True / False

Circle T if the statement is true or F if the statement is false.

T | F 1. You can perform an upgrade to SharePoint 2007 Standard edition to SharePoint 2010 Enterprise Edition.

T | F 2. The `stsadm preupgradecheck` command runs the SharePoint Pre-upgrade Check report.

T | F 3. If you installed a single-server deployment with built-in SQL Server, you can upgrade to a farm by using the SharePoint 2010 Products Configuration Wizard.

T | F 4. The most common failure when upgrading to SharePoint 2010 while using the database attach upgrade is missing customizations.

T | F 5. After installing Windows or SharePoint 2010, you should always check for updates.

■ Case Scenario

Scenario 3-1: Upgrading to SharePoint 2010

Your organization has SharePoint 2007 installation with SP1. Your boss wants to upgrade to SharePoint 2010 but is nervous that something will not be working after the upgrade. What methods can you use to determine what must be included in the upgrade so that SharePoint will be functioning properly?

Scenario 3-2: Expanding SharePoint 2010

You were just hired as a new network administrator. Your boss is complaining that SharePoint is running too slowly. In addition, your boss also decides that it is time to expand the use of SharePoint for the rest of the company. Therefore, it will need to be able to grow. When you are looking at the current installation of SharePoint 2010, you find out that SharePoint was installed as a single server deployment with the built-in SQL Server. What do you need to do make SharePoint faster and to allow for substantial growth?

Configuring SharePoint

OBJECTIVE DOMAIN MATRIX

TECHNOLOGY SKILL	OBJECTIVE DOMAIN	OBJECTIVE DOMAIN NUMBER
Using Central Administration		
Configuring SharePoint Farms	Configuring SharePoint Farms	1.2
Configuring Server Roles	Configuring Server Roles	1.2.2
	Managing Computer Accounts	2.2.4
Managing Databases	Managing Databases	3.1.1
Configuring Inter-Server Communications	Configuring Inter-Server Communications	1.2.1
Configuring Security	Configuring Security Settings	2.1.5
Managing SharePoint with Commands		
Managing SharePoint Online	Configuring SharePoint Farms	1.2

KEY TERMS

Administration Center

Central Administration

cmdlets

configuration database

content database

Get-Command

Microsoft SharePoint Designer 2010

SharePoint services

Simple Mail Transfer Protocol (SMTP)

stsadm

Windows PowerShell

Windows service

You just installed a SharePoint farm and you verified that you can access a SharePoint site on the farm. Therefore, you decided to hand SharePoint off to your test team so that they can start creating content and test to see what SharePoint can do. By the next day, the team leader comes back and says the SharePoint site is lacking some basic functionality, including the ability to send e-mails. You tell the team leader that you will determine what needs to be done, and will make the necessary adjustments.

■ Using Central Administration

As mentioned in Lesson 1 and Lesson 2, the primary tool used to configure SharePoint is Central Administration, which is a separate Web site created during the initial installation and configuration of SharePoint. Therefore, after you install SharePoint, you must use the SharePoint Central Administration to create and configure sites, and to enable and configure the many settings available within SharePoint.

Different from most other Microsoft Products, SharePoint 2010 is actually managed from a Web-based management tool called *Central Administration*. The advantage of using a Web-based management interface is that you do not need to install extra software and it can be accessed remotely (assuming it is not blocked by a firewall). The disadvantage of using a Web-based management tool is that you need to take additional steps to make sure that it is secure. While SharePoint sites can be found on the intranet and the Internet, you would not typically access the Central Administration site over the Internet.

After you have created and configured the Central Administration site, the simplest way to access this site is to log on to any SharePoint server and open it by clicking **Start > Microsoft SharePoint 2010 Products > SharePoint Central Administration**. Alternatively, you can open a browser and enter the server name and port (for example, http://spportal:45234).

If you recall from Lesson 1, Central Administration is divided into the following areas:

- **Application Management**: Allows you to manage Web applications, site collections, manage service applications, and manage content databases. This will be discussed in detail in Lesson 5.
- **System Settings**: Allows you to manage the SharePoint servers, including the SQL server and SMTP server. It also allows you to manage features, solutions, and farm-wide settings.
- **Monitoring**: Allows you to track, view, and report the health and status of your SharePoint farms. This will be discussed in detail in Lesson 10.
- **Backup and Restore**: Allows you to perform backups and restores. This will be discussed in detail in Lesson 12.
- **Security**: Allows you to configure security setting for users and the entire SharePoint environment. This will be discussed in detail in Lesson 7.
- **Upgrade and Migration**: Allows you to upgrade SharePoint, add licenses, and enable Enterprise Features. This was discussed in Lessons 2 and 3.
- **General Application Settings**: Allows you to configure external service connections, SharePoint Designer settings, and settings to integrate Reporting Services.

After SharePoint is installed, several tasks must be performed to give SharePoint basic functionality. Some of these tasks include:

- **Add servers to farm**: By adding servers to the farm, you can provide redundancy.
- **Create application Web sites**: Defines Web sites and creates a root SharePoint site to the Web site. This will be discussed in Lesson 5.
- **Configure outgoing e-mail server**: Required for users to receive alerts and notifications (such as an invitation to a site).
- **Configure incoming e-mail server**: Required if you want your lists to receive e-mail directly with their own e-mail address.

- **Add antivirus protection**: Be sure to configure prior to documents being uploaded into SharePoint.
- **Enabling and configuring logging**: Provides logs and reports, which can be used to identify and troubleshoot problems. While this is usually done during the initial configuration, monitoring will be discussed in Lesson 10.

■ Configuring SharePoint Farms

 THE BOTTOM LINE

The Central Administration's System Settings contains some of the core configuration requirements for the entire SharePoint farm. It includes managing and configuring your SharePoint farm servers and services. It can be used to remove a server from the farm if necessary.

CERTIFICATION READY
Where would you look to see what systems make up your farm if you were creating documentation for your SharePoint farm?
1.2

As you recall from Lesson 1, a SharePoint farm is a collection of one or more SharePoint servers and one or more SQL Server databases that come together to provide a set of basic SharePoint services bound together by a single configuration database in SQL. A farm can be a simple deployment with a single server with its own built-in database server, or it can consist of multiple servers.

If you are new to a SharePoint environment and need to figure out what makes up the current SharePoint environment, a good place to start is to open the Central Administration, click System Settings, and click Manage servers in this farm (see Figure 4-1).

Figure 4-1

Servers in a farm

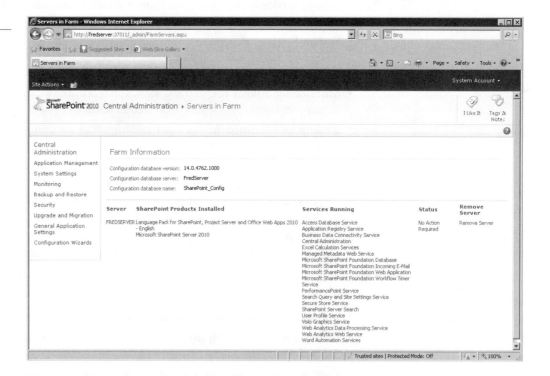

The top of the screen, below Farm Information, shows the Configuration database version, the Configuration database server, and the Configuration database name. This information

includes every server that is part of the farm and the services that each server is running. To remove the server from the farm, just click the **Remove Server** link.

The services shown are only the services that are currently running on the specific server. To see all of the services available on a server, you must use **System Settings > Manage servers in the farm**.

Understanding Windows Services

A ***Windows service*** is a long-running executable that performs specific functions. These services are designed to run in the background and are usually designed not to require user intervention.

As you recall from Lesson 1, SharePoint will run on top of Windows and the services provided by Windows, including Microsoft's Web services (Internet Information Services), .NET Framework, and SMTP. In addition, when installing SharePoint, SharePoint will install its own Windows services. You should know those services so that you can understand how SharePoint operates and use that information when troubleshooting,. The services that SharePoint uses include the following:

- **IIS Admin Service**: Enables the server to administer the IIS meta-database, which stores configurations for the SMTP and FTP services. If the service is stopped, you will not be able to configure SMTP or FTP. If the service is disabled, any services that depend on it will fail to start.
- **World Wide Web Publishing Service**: Provides Web connectivity and administration through the Internet Information Services (IIS) Manager. Without this service, SharePoint Web sites would not be available.
- **SharePoint 2010 Administration**: Performs administrative tasks for SharePoint.
- **SharePoint 2010 Timer**: Sends notifications and performs scheduled tasks for SharePoint.
- **SharePoint 2010 Tracing**: Manages trace output, which can be used for troubleshooting.
- **SharePoint 2010 User Code Host**: Executes user code in a sandbox so that the programming code is kept isolated.
- **SharePoint 2010 VSS Writer**: Allows backups of SharePoint while SharePoint is running.
- **SharePoint Foundation Search V4**: Provides full-text indexing and search capabilities of SharePoint content and users. This service is typically disabled on SharePoint Server 2010 since it is replaced by the SharePoint Server Search 14.
- **SharePoint Server Search 14:** Provides enhanced full-text indexing and search capabilities.

If the World Wide Web Publishing Service is down, the SharePoint sites will not be available. If any of the other services are down, the SharePoint site will be available but some functionality will not be available.

■ Configuring Server Roles

SharePoint is a complex system that consists of many **SharePoint services** (services built within SharePoint, not to be confused with Windows services) to provide its functionality. These services provide granular pieces of functionality to other Web and service applications in the farm, such as User Profile Sync service and the Search Indexing service. SharePoint services can be turned off, exist on one server, or be load-balanced across many servers in a farm. In addition, these services are designed to be as independent as possible, so that restarting a service or having a service misconfigured will not prevent the entire farm from functioning properly.

To view the list of SharePoint services, use **Central Administration > System Settings > Manage services on server**. You can also access them in the Service Applications group by using **Central Administration > Application Management > Manage services on server**. Figure 4-2 shows the Services on Server page.

On this page, you can choose any server in the farm to view its services. At the upper-left of the page, simply click the Server drop-down and choose your server of choice. At first, it

Figure 4-2

The Services on Server page

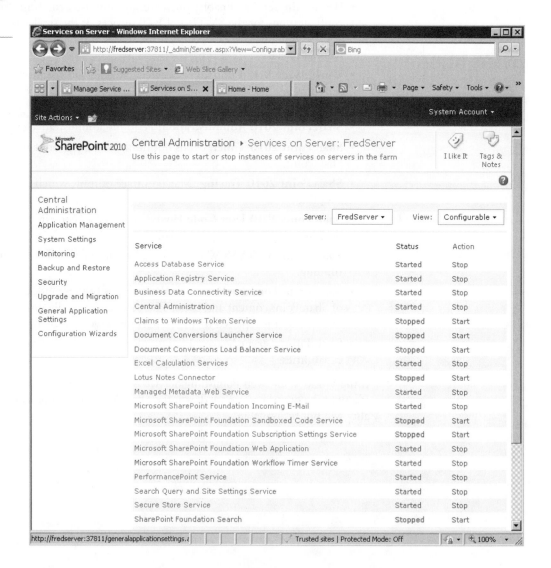

will display only the configurable services. You can click the **Configuration** option and select **All** to show all services running on the specific server. The Status column shows if the services are Started or Stopped. The Action column allows you to Start or Stop the service.

Some of the services listed will be links that indicate that additional configuration is necessary either before or after the service starts running. The hyperlink takes you to the services management page for that service so that you can perform the necessary configuration. For example, if you click the Microsoft SharePoint Foundation Workflow Timer Service, you will go to the Workflow Timer Settings page (see Figure 4-3), which allows you to configure Workflow Timer Batch Size and the number of workflow events that can be processed at every timer interval on this server.

Figure 4-3

The Workflow Timer Settings page

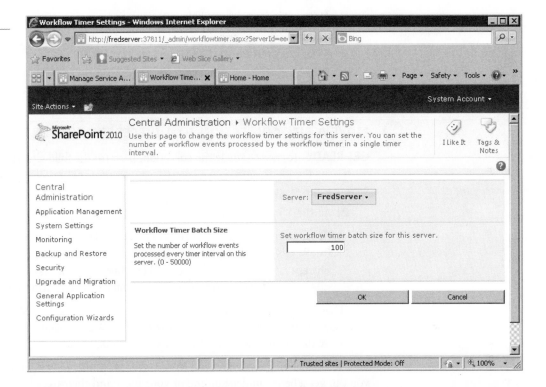

■ Managing Databases

THE BOTTOM LINE

SharePoint 2010 uses multiple databases for it to function. The most commonly known database is the content database because it holds the SharePoint data. However, you should also understand what the other databases are used for.

The *configuration database* handles all administration of deployment, directing requests to the appropriate database and managing load-balancing for the back-end databases for a farm. When a SharePoint Web site is accessed, it checks the configuration database to determine which content database holds the site's data.

The largest databases used in SharePoint are the content databases. The *content database* stores all site content, including site documents or files in document libraries, list data, and Web Part properties. Content databases also store user names and permissions. Content databases are usually created when you create a Web application within SharePoint.

Microsoft recommends that you limit the size of content databases to 200 GB to help ensure system performance. In some instances, the databases can go up to 1 terabyte for large, single-site repositories and archives where the data remains relatively static. In addition, a site collection should not exceed 100 GB unless it is the only site collection in the database. The SharePoint_Admin_Content database is the content database for Central Administration. If you need to move a collection because it has grown too large or you need to combine several collections into a single database, you would use the Windows PowerShell command Move-SPSite.

 DETERMINE THE SIZE OF A SITE COLLECTION

GET READY. To determine the size of a site collection, perform the following steps:

1. Click Start > All Programs > SharePoint 2010 Products > SharePoint 2010 Management Shell.

2. At the Windows PowerShell 2.0 command prompt, type the following commands:

   ```
   $used = (Get-SPSiteAdministration -Identity <http://ServerName/
   Sites/SiteName>).DiskUsed
   $used
   ```

   `<http://ServerName/Sites/SiteName>` is the name of the site collection.

 MOVE A SITE COLLECTION TO A DIFFERENT CONTENT DATABASE

GET READY. To move a single site collection, perform the following steps:

1. Click Start > All Programs > SharePoint 2010 Products > SharePoint 2010 Management Shell.

2. At the Windows PowerShell command prompt, type the following command:

   ```
   Move-SPSite <http://ServerName/Sites/SiteName> -DestinationData-
   base <DestinationContentDb>
   ```

   `<http://ServerName/Sites/SiteName>` is the name of the site collection and `<DestinationContentDb>` is the name of the destination content database.

The Usage and Health Data Collection Service collects and logs SharePoint Health indicators and usage metrics for analysis and reporting. The WSS_Logging holds the health monitoring and usage data temporarily; it can be used for reporting and diagnostics.

The Web Analytics Service is used to record Web traffic, search, and SharePoint assets so that you can get a better understanding of your users and their use of SharePoint. The databases used by the Web Analytics Service are the WebAnalyticsServiceApplication_ReportingDB_ *GUID* and WebAnalyticsServiceApplication_StagingDB_*GUID*.

+ MORE INFORMATION

Most database names used within SharePoint have a globally unique identifier (GUID) at the end of each database name. The purpose and benefit of the GUID is to uniquely identify a database, especially if your SQL server hosts multiple SharePoint servers. However, when creating SharePoint applications and when you enable certain services, you might choose to remove the GUID when the database is being created to simplify the naming convention. It is not recommended to change the rest of the name; if you do change the rest of the name, the databases might not be as easily identified.

The user profile database stores and manages user and associated information. It consists of multiple databases, including User Profile Service Application_Profile DB_*GUID*, User profile Service Application_SocialDB_*GUID*, and User Profile ServiceApplication_ StagingDB_*GUID*.

When you want to search SharePoint, you must first configure a crawl so that SharePoint will open each Web site and index the content of each page. When you search for something in SharePoint, SharePoint will search an index database. The Property Database stores crawled

properties associated with the crawled data to include properties, history data, crawl queues, and so on. The Crawl Databases host the crawled data and drives crawl.

Other databases may include the Managed Metadata Service_*GUID*, PerformancePoint Service Application _*GUID*, StateService_*GUID*, WordAutomationServices_*GUID*, and Secure_Store_ Service_DB_*GUID*.

To view the content databases, use **Central Administration > Application Management > Manage content databases**. If you click the name of the content database, you will open the Manage Content Database Settings page, in which you can do the following:

- Take a content database offline
- Determine the status of the database (if it is online or offline and if is read-only or not)
- Check the database schema version
- Specify a failover server if you are using database mirroring
- Specify the maximum number of sites used for a database
- Specify the search server
- Remove the content database
- Specify the preferred server from which Timer Jobs run

See Figure 4-4 for an illustration of the Manage Content Database Setting page.

Figure 4-4

The Manage Content Database Settings page

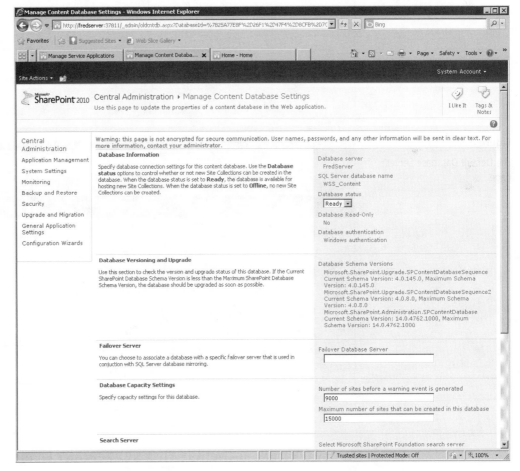

To see all of the databases, use **Central Administration > Upgrade and Migration > Review database status** (see Figure 4-5). To specify the default database server for content database, open **Central Administration** and click **Specify the default database server**. Then specify the name of the server and the username and password for the database server (see Figure 4-6).

There may be times where you will have to add a content database to an application/ SharePoint Web site. For example, if you are moving or want to have a copy of content database from another SQL server, you would use Central Administration's Manage Content Databases option to add the database to a site collection.

Figure 4-5

The Manage Databases Upgrade Status page

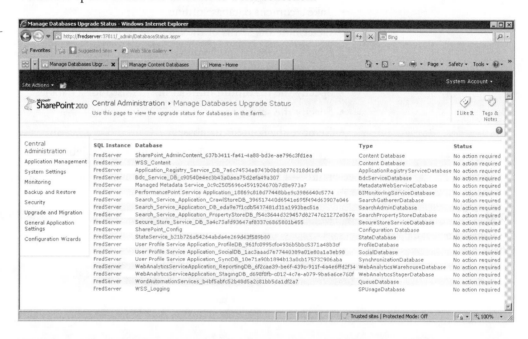

Figure 4-6

The Default Database Server page

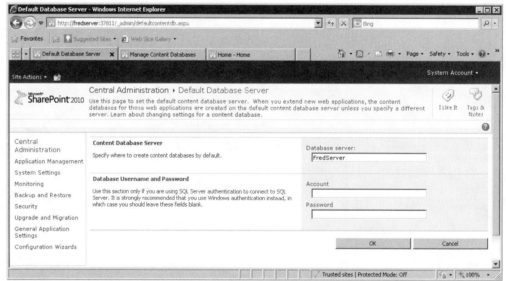

 ADD A CONTENT DATABASE TO A SHAREPOINT WEB SITE

GET READY. To add a content database to an application/SharePoint Web site, perform the following steps:

1. Open Central Administration and click Application Management.

2. In the Databases section, click Manage Content Databases.

3. At the top of the page, click Add a Content Database.

4. Use the Web Application menu to select the desired Web application for the new database (see Figure 4-7).

Figure 4-7

The Add Content Database page

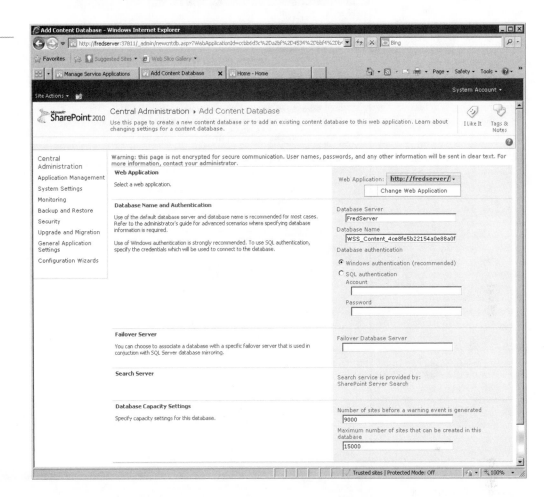

5. In the Database Server text box, type the name of the database server.

6. In the Database Name text box, type the name of the content database.

7. In the Database authentication section, select either Windows authentication (recommended) or SQL authentication.

8. If you have an SQL mirror server, specify the name of the failover server in the Failover Database Server text box.

9. Specify the Number of sites before a warning event is generated and the Maximum number of sites that can be created in this database. You can use the default values.

10. Click OK.

From time to time, you might have reason to make a database read-only so users can access the content database but not make any changes.

 MAKE A CONTENT DATABASE READ-ONLY

GET READY. To make a SharePoint Content database read-only, perform the following steps:

1. Open SQL Server Management Studio on the SQL server.

2. Right-click the content database and then click Properties (see Figure 4-8).

3. Click Options (see Figure 4-9).

Figure 4-8

Selecting the properties of a database

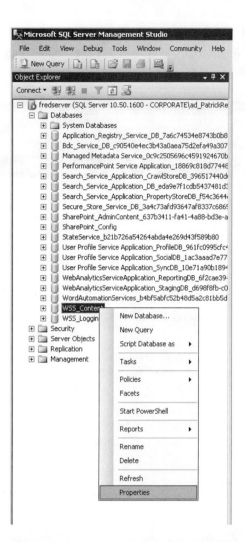

Figure 4-9

Selecting the Options page

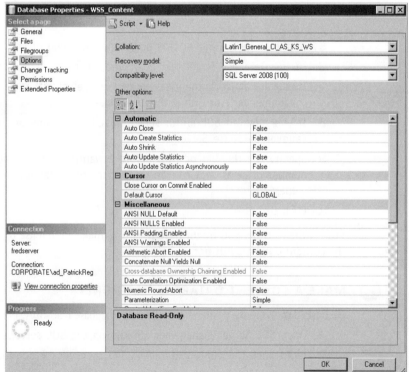

4. Scroll down to the bottom of the list and change the Database Read-Only state from False to True (see Figure 4-10).

Figure 4-10

Changing the Database Read-Only state

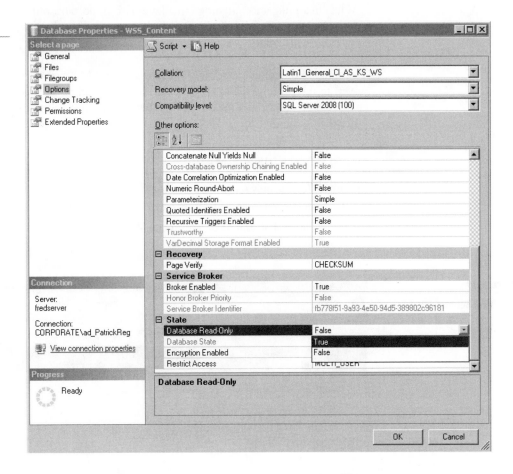

5. Click OK.

When you no longer need the database to be read-only, simply change the state back to True.

■ Configuring Inter-Server Communications

THE BOTTOM LINE

E-mail is a critical communication tool for most organizations. To allow SharePoint to communicate with its users, you must configure outgoing e-mail. To allow SharePoint to receive e-mails, you need to configure incoming e-mail.

CERTIFICATION READY
What service must be installed in Windows for your SharePoint farm to receive e-mails?
1.2.1

Simple Mail Transfer Protocol (SMTP) is an Internet standard for electronic mail (e-mail) transmission across Internet Protocol (IP) networks. It is the outgoing mail transport and is used to relay e-mails over the Internet using TCP port 25. SharePoint 2010 can be configured to communicate directly and automatically with its users and administrators by e-mail via Simple Mail Transfer Protocol (SMTP). By using e-mails, users can receive important notifications quickly, such as being notified when a task needs to be completed by the user or notified when a list item or document has been added to a list or library.

Outgoing E-mail

While incoming and outgoing e-mail are both important, outgoing e-mail is most likely more important because it allows SharePoint to communicate with your users.

To configure outgoing e-mail, you must specify an SMTP server (such as Microsoft Exchange server) to relay through, and an e-mail address for sending and receiving. In addition, to enable e-mail access, you must be a member of the Farm Administrators group on the computer that is running the SharePoint Central Administration Web site.

 ENABLE OUTGOING E-MAIL

GET READY. To enable outgoing e-mail, perform the following steps:

1. Open Central Administration and click System Settings.
2. In the E-Mail and Text Messages (SMS) section, click Configure outgoing e-mail settings (see Figure 4-11).

Figure 4-11

The System Settings page

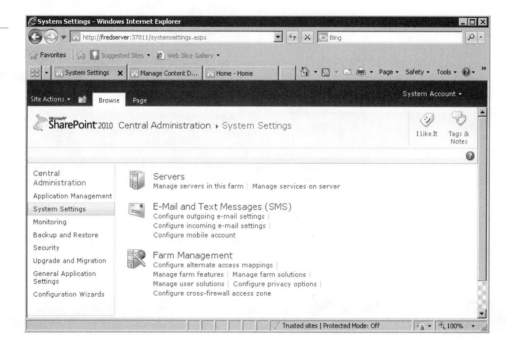

3. In the Outbound SMTP server text box (see Figure 4-12), type the SMTP server name.
4. In the From address text box, type the e-mail address that will be used as the sender of e-mail.
5. In the Reply-to address text box, type the e-mail address to which you want e-mail recipients to reply.
6. In the Character set drop-down list, select the character set that is appropriate for your language.
7. Click OK.

Figure 4-12

Configuring outgoing e-mail settings

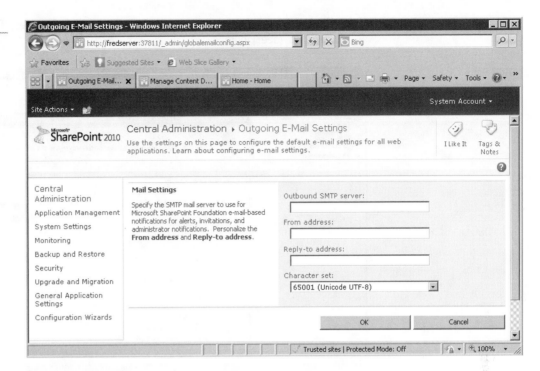

Incoming E-mail

By enabling incoming e-mail for SharePoint, you can have users send messages to an e-mail address that is assigned to a list on a SharePoint site, and those e-mails (or the content of those e-mails) can automatically be posted to a list (including a calendar), a document library, or a discussion board.

You can enable incoming e-mail by installing the SMTP service on the server running SharePoint 2010 and using the Automatic setting mode with all default settings. E-mail will be delivered directly to the SMTP server and SharePoint will check for e-mail in the default e-mail drop folder.

 INSTALL THE SMTP SERVER

GET READY. To install the SMTP server, you must be a member of the local administrator on the local computer. Then perform the following steps:

1. Click Start > Administrative Tools > Server Manager (see Figure 4-13).

Figure 4-13

The Server Manager page

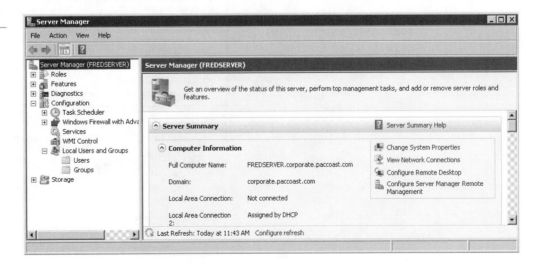

2. In the Server Manager list in the left pane, click Features. The Add Features Wizard displays (see Figure 4-14).

Figure 4-14

Using the Add Features Wizard

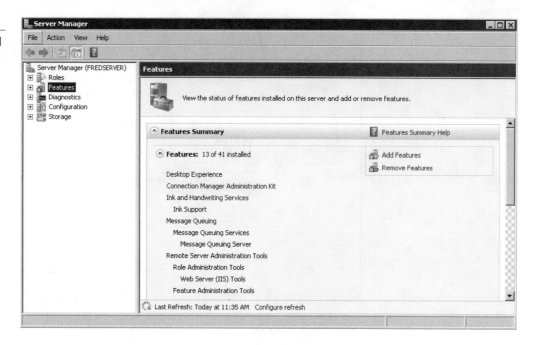

3. Click Add Features to open the Add Features Wizard.
4. Select SMTP Server and then click Next (see Figure 4-15).

Figure 4-15

Selecting the SMTP Server feature

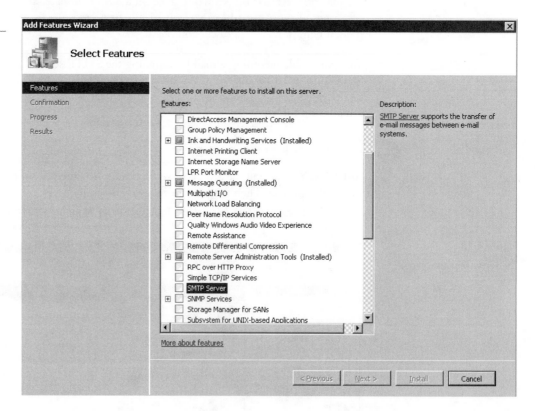

5. When the Add Features Wizard dialog box displays, click Add Required Role Services (see Figure 4-16), and then click Next.

Figure 4-16

Adding required features

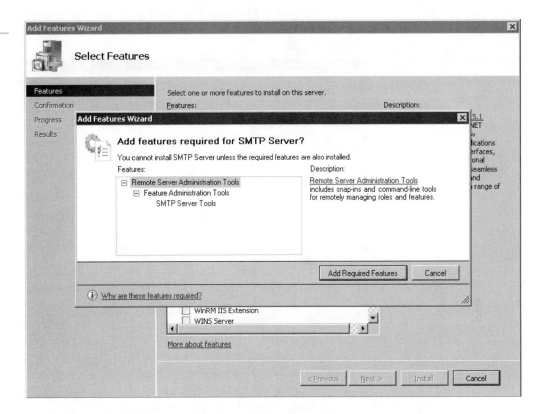

6. If the Web Server (IIS) page displays, click Next.
7. If the Select Roles Services page displays, click Next.
8. When the Confirm Installation Selections page displays, click Install.
9. On the Installation Results page, ensure that the installation finished successfully, and then click Close.

As a new added service, you need to configure SMTP to start automatically.

 CONFIGURE SMTP TO START AUTOMATICALLY

GET READY. To configure the SMTP service to start automatically, perform the following steps:

1. Click Start > Administrative Tools > Services.
2. In the Services section, right-click Simple Mail Transfer Protocol (SMTP), and then select Properties.
3. In the Simple Mail Transfer Protocol (SMTP) Properties dialog box, on the General tab, in the Startup type list, select Automatic.
4. Click OK.

After you have SMTP, you are ready to configure SharePoint to receive e-mail. You can configure the server to accept relayed e-mail from any e-mail server, or those that you specify.

→ CONFIGURE THE SMTP SERVER

GET READY. To configure the SMTP server, perform the following steps:

1. Click Start > Administrative Tools > Internet Information Services (IIS) 6.0 Manager (see Figure 4-17).

Figure 4-17

Internet Information Services (IIS) 6.0 Manager

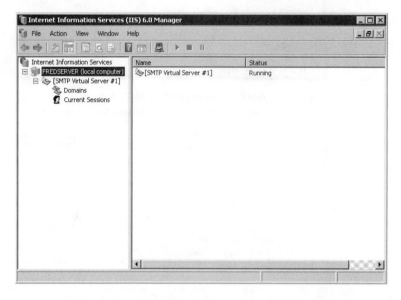

2. In IIS Manager, expand the server name that contains the SMTP server that you want to configure.

3. Right-click the SMTP virtual server that you want to configure, and then click Start. If Start is greyed out, proceed to Step 4.

4. Right-click the SMTP virtual server that you want to configure, and then click Properties. The SMTP Properties dialog box opens (see Figure 4-18).

Figure 4-18

The SMTP Properties dialog box

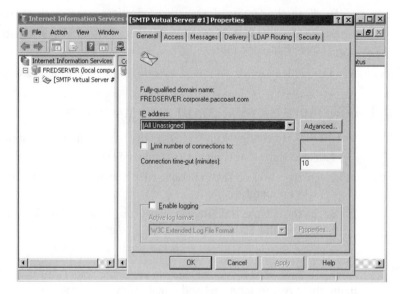

5. Click the Access tab, and in the Access control area, click Authentication (see Figure 4-19).

Figure 4-19

The Access tab

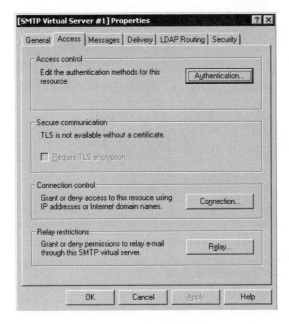

6. In the Authentication dialog box that displays (see Figure 4-20), verify that Anonymous access is selected.

Figure 4-20

The Authentication dialog box

7. Click OK.

8. On the Access tab, in the Relay restrictions area, click Relay to open the Relay Restrictions dialog box (see Figure 4-21).

9. To enable relaying from any server, click All except the list below. To accept relaying from one or more specific servers, click Only the list below. Then click Add, and then add servers one at a time by IP address or in groups by using a subnet or domain. Click OK to accept your changes and close the Computer dialog box.

10. Click OK to accept your changes and close the Relay Restrictions dialog box.

11. Click OK to accept your changes and close the Properties dialog box.

Figure 4-21

The Relay Restrictions dialog box

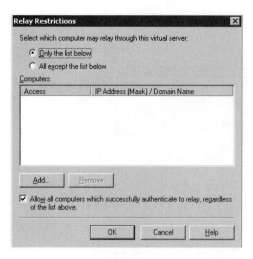

Now that SMTP is configured on the server, you are ready to configure SharePoint to use it. Microsoft describes two methods (basic and advanced) to accomplish this. For most cases, you can use the basic scenario, in which you select the Automatic setting mode and accept the defaults when configuring SharePoint.

 CONFIGURE SHAREPOINT TO USE INCOMING E-MAIL

GET READY. To quickly enable SharePoint to receive e-mails, perform the following steps:

1. Open Central Administration and then click System Settings (see Figure 4-22).

Figure 4-22

System Settings

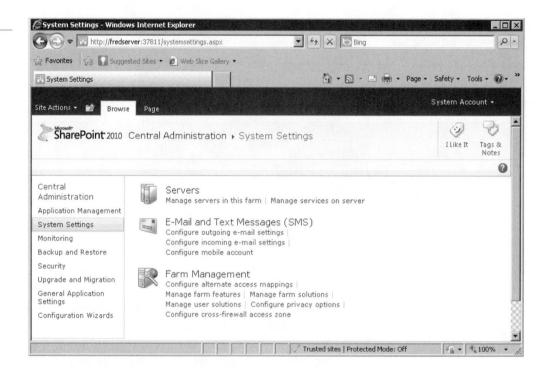

2. In the E-Mail and Text Messages (SMS) section, click Configure incoming e-mail settings. The Configure Incoming E-Mail Settings page displays (see Figure 4-23).
3. In the Enable Incoming E-Mail section, select Yes.
4. For the Settings mode, select Automatic.

Figure 4-23

The Configure Incoming E-Mail Settings page

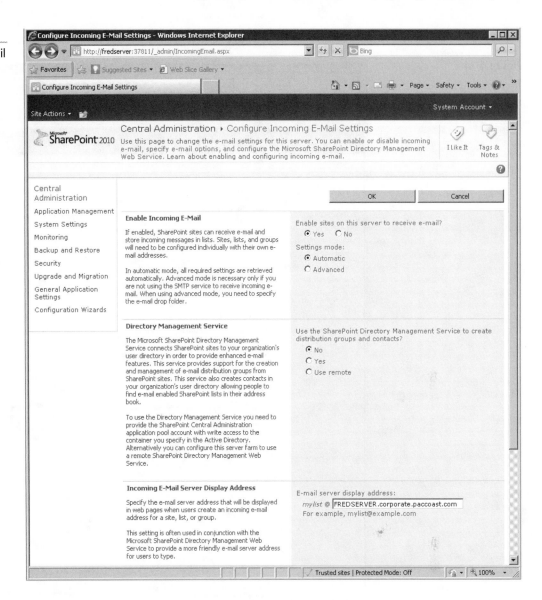

5. In the Incoming E-Mail Server Display Address section, in the E-mail server display address box, type a display name for the e-mail server.

6. Use the default settings for all other sections, and then click OK.

For more control, you can manually configure SharePoint to use SMTP by selecting Advanced as a Settings mode in Step 4. By using Advanced settings, you can specify a drop folder instead of using an SMTP server. In addition, you can configure SharePoint's Directory Management Service to automatically create contact addresses for document libraries to be created in Active Directory Users and Computers in the organizational unit (OU) that you specify.

 CONFIGURE SHAREPOINT TO USE INCOMING E-MAIL (ADVANCED)

GET READY. To configure SharePoint to use SMTP with Advanced settings, perform the following steps:

1. Open Central Administration and then click System Settings.

2. In the E-Mail and Text Messages (SMS) section, click Configure incoming e-mail settings to display the Configure Incoming E-Mail Settings dialog box (see Figure 4-24).

3. In the Enable Incoming E-Mail section, select Yes.

4. For the Settings mode, select Advanced.

Figure 4-24

The Advanced settings mode

5. If you want to connect to Directory Management Service, in the Directory Management Service section, select Yes (see Figure 4-25) and then follow these steps:

a. In the Active Directory container where new distribution groups and contacts will be created box, type the name of the container in the format OU=ContainerName, DC=domain, DC=com, where ContainerName is the name of the OU in AD DS, domain is the second-level domain, and com is the top-level domain.

b. In the SMTP mail server for incoming mail box, type the name of the SMTP mail server. The server name must match the FQDN in the A resource record entry for the mail server in DNS Manager.

c. To accept only messages from authenticated users, click Yes for Accept messages from authenticated users only?. Otherwise, click No.

d. To enable users to create distribution groups from SharePoint sites, click Yes for Allow creation of distribution groups from SharePoint sites?. Otherwise, click No.

e. Under Distribution group request approval settings, select the actions that will require approval.

Figure 4-25

Enabling the Directory
Management Service

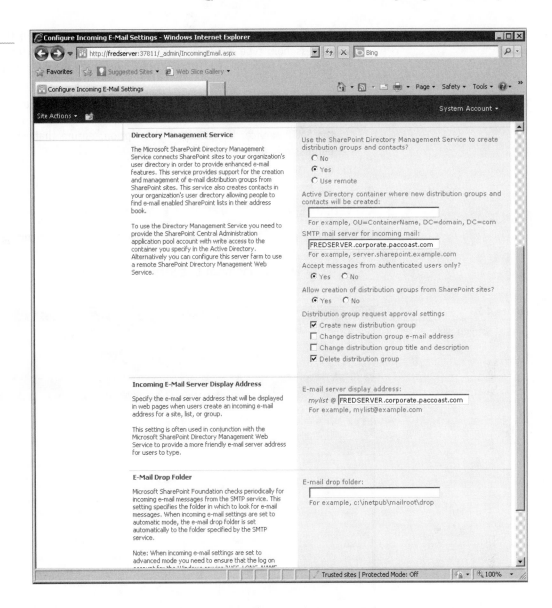

6. If you want to use a remote Directory Management Service, in the Directory Management Service section, select Use remote. However, if you use this method, you need to add an SMTP connector for your Exchange Server by following these steps.

   a. In the Directory Management Service URL box, type the URL of the Directory Management Service that you want to use. The URL is typically in the following format:

      http://server:adminport/_vti_bin/SharePointEmailWS.asmx.

   b. In the SMTP mail server for incoming mail box, type the name of the SMTP mail server. The server name must match the FQDN in the A resource record entry for the mail server in DNS Manager on the domain server.

   c. To accept messages from authenticated users only, click Yes for Accept messages from authenticated users only?. Otherwise, click No.

   d. To allow creation of distribution groups from SharePoint sites, click Yes for Allow creation of distribution groups from SharePoint sites?. Otherwise, click No.

7. If you do not want to use Directory Management Service, in the Directory Management Service section, click No.

8. In the Incoming E-Mail Server Display Address section, in the E-mail server display address box, type a display name for the e-mail server (for example, mail.fabrikam. com). You typically use this option together with the Directory Management Service.

9. In the E-Mail Drop Folder section, in the E-mail drop folder box, type the name of the folder from which SharePoint 2010 Timer service retrieves incoming e-mail from the SMTP service. If you select this option, ensure that you configure the necessary permissions to the e-mail drop folder.

10. Click OK.

CONFIGURE A LIST TO RECEIVE E-MAILS

GET READY. To configure a list including a calendar to receive e-mails, perform the following steps:

1. Go to any list and open List Settings (see Figure 4-26).

Figure 4-26

The List Settings page

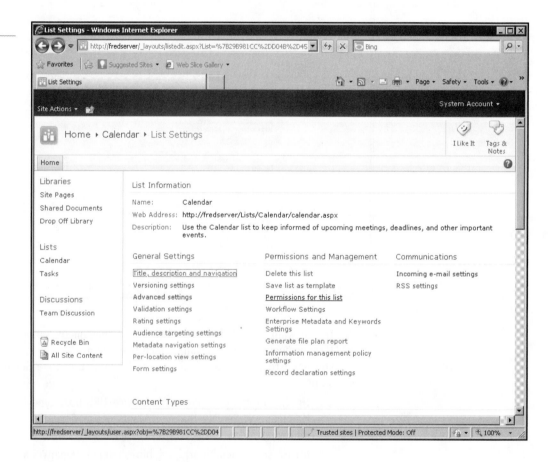

2. Click Incoming e-mail settings.

3. In the Incoming E-Mail section, select Yes so this list is allowed to receive e-mails (see Figure 4-27).

Figure 4-27

Configuring incoming e-mail for a list

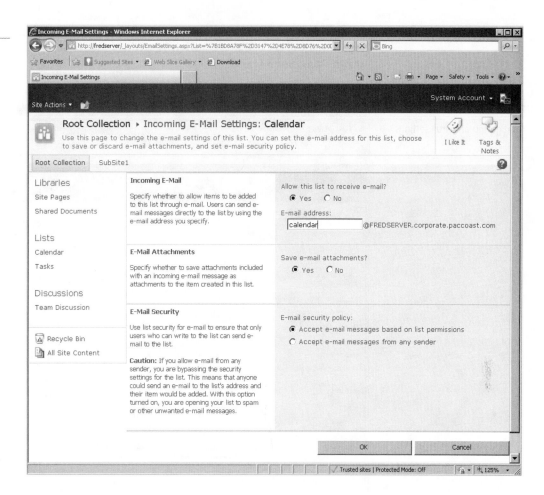

4. In the E-mail address text box, specify an e-mail address by typing a name that represents the list.

5. Click OK.

■ Configuring Security

THE BOTTOM LINE

There are many security settings configured in Central Administration including farm administration group, configuring managed accounts, and service account. Therefore, while many of these are covered in detail in later lessons, a few settings should be discussed in this lesson.

CERTIFICATION READY
How do you prevent malware from being uploaded to SharePoint?
2.1.5

Since SharePoint is used as a document repository, SharePoint can be easily turned against its users by storing and propagating malicious software. Malicious software or malware can be programs with viruses or programs that are used to collect sensitive information or bypass security systems. Therefore, to protect your network, to protect your users, and to protect your SharePoint environment, you need to protect yourself from malware.

Although it is recommended that all users have an anti-virus software package loaded on their computer, you can also install an anti-virus software package on SharePoint to provide a second layer of defense against viruses and other forms of malware. SharePoint can work with anti-virus software to scan files before they are uploaded to SharePoint. However, for this feature to work, you must first install a SharePoint 2010–compatible antivirus software package such as Microsoft Forefront. By installing one of these compatible antivirus software packages, you will automatically enable SharePoint protection, or you will have to open Central Administration, click **Manage antivirus settings** (under Security), and manually enable antivirus protection (see Figure 4-28).

Figure 4-28

Configuring antivirus settings

The four scanning options include:

- **Scan documents on upload**: Checks for malware on every document that is added to a document library or list.
- **Scan documents on download**: Checks for malware on every document accessed from SharePoint.
- **Allow users to download infected documents**: If malware is within a document, it allows users to download the infected document. Of course, this option is not recommended.
- **Attempt to clean infected documents**: If malware is found, it tries to remove the malware.

You can also configure how long the virus scanner should run before it times out; the default is 300 seconds.

Since SharePoint can be used as a repository for files, there are many file types that are blocked because they may be problematic, or have the potential of carrying a virus or being malware. Therefore, for security purposes, you might want to block specific file types from being saved or retrieved by any Web application on a SharePoint server.

By default, SharePoint blocks executable files such as .exe files and installation files such as .msi files. If you choose to unblock these files so that they can be stored within SharePoint, most of these cannot be installed directly from a SharePoint site. Instead, users will have to copy the file or files to their own computers and then install the program from their own computers.

 MANAGE BLOCKED FILE TYPES

GET READY. To specify which files are blocked, perform the following steps:

1. Click Central Administration > Security.

2. In the General Security settings, click Define Blocked File Types.

3. To block a specific file type, scroll to the bottom of the Type each file extension on a separate line text box, and then type the file extension you want to block (see Figure 4-29).

Figure 4-29

The Blocked File Types page

4. To stop blocking a file type, select the file type from the available list, and then press the Delete key on your keyboard.

5. Click OK.

Using SharePoint Designer

> ***Microsoft SharePoint Designer 2010*** is a Web and application design program used to design, build, and customize Web sites running on SharePoint 2010. With SharePoint Designer 2010, you can create data-rich Web pages, build powerful workflow-enabled solutions, and design the look and feel of your site.

SharePoint Designer is a powerful program that can be used to easily create customized applications and to modify the Master Page or site templates. While knowing how to use SharePoint Designer is beyond this course, as a SharePoint administrator you will need to understand that users could use SharePoint Designer, which causes sites to not function properly. Therefore, you can disable the use of SharePoint Designer with your SharePoint environment by opening Central Administration, clicking **General Application Settings** (see Figure 4-30), and then clicking **Configure SharePoint Designer** settings. The SharePoint Designer Settings page displays (see Figure 4-31).

You can then determine what SharePoint Designer can do with the following options:

- **Enable SharePoint Designer**: Allows SharePoint Designer to be used with the SharePoint sites.

Figure 4-30

The General Application Settings page

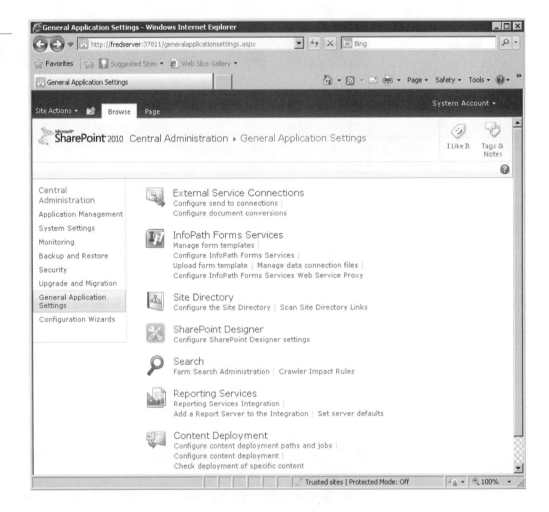

Figure 4-31

The SharePoint Designer
Settings page

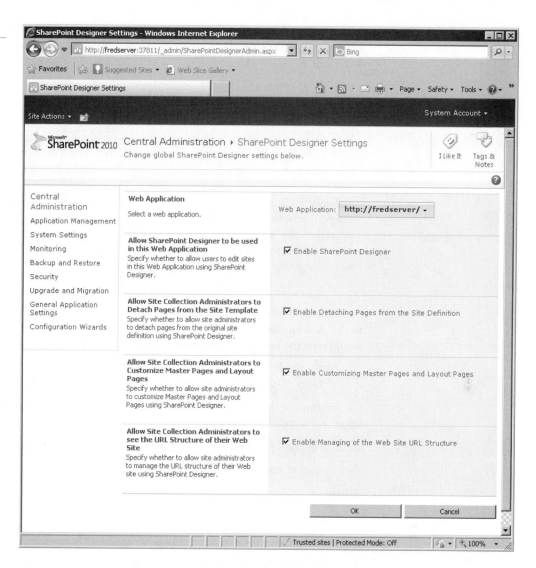

- **Enable Detaching Pages from the Site Definition**: Allows SharePoint Designer to detach pages from the site definition, which means deleting the page from the site.
- **Enable Customizing Master Pages and Layout Pages:** Allows SharePoint designer to customize or change the Master Pages and Layout Pages.
- **Enable Managing of the Web Site URL Structure**: Allows SharePoint Designer to modify or move sites, pages, libraries, and lists.

■ Managing SharePoint with Commands

THE BOTTOM LINE

In Lessons 2 and 3, you had a brief look at using stsadm and PowerShell to execute commands. With stsadm and PowerShell, you can script actions that need to be repeated often and sometimes you will find that certain activities can only be done by executing a command.

As Windows became popular over the years, most tasks were done using a graphical user interface (GUI). While scripting has been used with Windows since Windows Server 2008, there has been a push for some server administration to be completed through commands or scripting. Therefore, to administrate SharePoint 2010, you will need to learn the stsadm command and Windows PowerShell.

Using the stsadm Command

Stsadm.exe is an executable file located in the folder C:\Program Files\Common Files\ Microsoft Shared\Web server extensions\14\BIN. The `stsadm` command is used to configure certain SharePoint settings using commands. It was introduced in SharePoint 2007 and includes 182 commands. Since the introduction of SharePoint 2010 and its use of PowerShell, `stsadm` has been deprecated, but is included to support compatibility with previous product versions. There are, however, a small number of rarely used `stsadm` operations for which no Windows PowerShell equivalent exists. It should be noted that because of feature or architecture changes between SharePoint 2007 and SharePoint 2010, not all `stsadm` operations are supported.

Since the path to the stsadm.exe command is lengthy, it is sometimes better to add the path to the path environmental variable. For example, to add the path to the BIN folder, you would type the following command to add the BIN folder to your current path:

```
set path=%path%;C:\Program Files\Common
Files\Microsoft Shared\Web server extensions\14\BIN
```

Or you can use the SharePoint 2010 Management Shell, which includes the path to the \BIN folder in its path variable.

`stsadm` exposes functionality through operations. Each operation is invoked with this syntax:

```
stsadm -o <OperationName> [-parameter <Value> ...]
```

Where:

    `<OperationName>` is the name of an `stsadm` operation.

    `<Value>` is the value for a parameter used by the operation.

To discover the operations that are supported, type the following command:

```
stsadm -?
```

The following code shows the help screen for the stsadm command, including the general syntax and several examples of the stsadm command.

```
C:\Program Files\Common Files\Microsoft Shared\Web Server
Extensions\14\BIN>stsadm /?
```

Usage:

```
stsadm.exe -o <operation> [<parameters>]
stsadm.exe -help [<operation>]
```

Operations:

```
activatefeature
activateformtemplate
addalternatedomain
addcontentdb
adddataconnectionfile
add-ecsfiletrustedlocation
add-ecssafedataprovider
```

```
add-ecstrusteddataconnectionlibrary
add-ecsuserdefinedfunction
    .
    .
    .
uploadformtemplate
userrole
variationsfixuptool
verifyformtemplate
```

Examples:

```
stsadm.exe -o addpath -url http://server/sites -type wildcardinclusion
stsadm.exe -o adduser
    -url http://server/site
    -userlogin DOMAIN\name
    -useremail someone@example.com
    -role reader
    -username "Your Name"
    -siteadmin
stsadm.exe -o backup -url http://server/site -filename backup.dat
-overwrite
stsadm.exe -o backup -directory c:\backup -backupmethod full
stsadm.exe -o createsite -url http://server/site
    -ownerlogin DOMAIN\name
    -owneremail someone@example.com
stsadm.exe -o createweb -url http://server/site/web
stsadm.exe -o deletesite -url http://server/site
stsadm.exe -o deleteweb -url http://server/site/web
stsadm.exe -o enumsites -url http://server
stsadm.exe -o enumsubwebs -url http://server/site/web
stsadm.exe -o enumusers -url http://server/site/web
stsadm.exe -o extendvs -url http://server:80
    -ownerlogin DOMAIN\name
    -owneremail someone@example.com
stsadm.exe -o renameweb -url http://server/site/web1 -newname web2
stsadm.exe -o restore -url http://server/site -filename backup.dat
stsadm.exe -o restore -directory c:\backup -restoremethod overwrite
stsadm.exe -o setconfigdb -databaseserver server
stsadm.exe -o unextendvs -url http://server
```

For information about other operations and parameters, use "stsadm.exe -help" or "stsadm.exe -help <operation>".

Using Windows PowerShell

Windows PowerShell is a task-based command-line shell and scripting language used to control and automate the administration of multiple Microsoft technologies, including Windows, SharePoint 2010, Active Directory, and Exchange. Since PowerShell was added to SharePoint 2010, it is designed to replace the stsadm command.

Windows PowerShell commands are called **cmdlets**, which can be used to access data stores (such as the registry and certificate store) and the file system. While the capability of the stsadm command is duplicated in Windows PowerShell, there are some tasks that can only be done with Windows PowerShell. SharePoint 2010 provides more than 600 Windows PowerShell cmdlets to support the administration of the SharePoint farm, including providing the same access found in Central Administration.

The SharePoint 2010 Management shell is based on Windows PowerShell 2.0, which is installed by the Microsoft SharePoint Products Preparation Tool (PrerequisiteInstaller). To open the SharePoint 2010 Management Shell, click **Start > All Programs > Microsoft SharePoint 2010 Products > SharePoint 2010 Management Shell** (see Figure 4-32).

Figure 4-32

Opening the SharePoint 2010 Management Shell

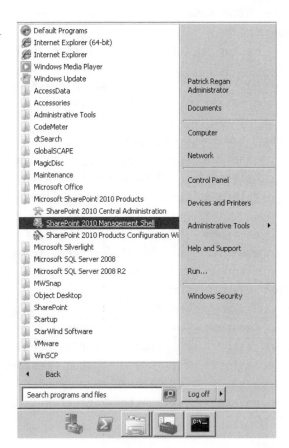

Get-Command is used to list the available cmdlets. (See Figure 4-33.)

Figure 4-33

Using the Get-Command cmdlet

USING POWERSHELL TO CHANGE THE PORT FOR SHAREPOINT CENTRAL ADMINISTRATION

The port number used by SharePoint Central Administration was specified when you initially ran the SharePoint Products Configuration Wizard. You can also change the port number using Windows PowerShell or using the stsadm command.

To change the power number using the Windows PowerShell, use the following command:

```
Set-SPCentralAdministration -Port <PortNumber>
```

<PortNumber> is an available port, greater than 1023 and less than 32767.

For the stsadm command, you can use the following command:

```
stsadm –o setadminport <PortNumber>
```

■ Managing SharePoint Online

↓ **THE BOTTOM LINE**

The SharePoint Online Administrator can use the Office 365 Admin Web site and the SharePoint Online Administration Center to create and manage users, and to create and manage settings for site collections. After a site collection is set up, the administrator can assign site collection administrators and site owners, allocate storage across site collections, determine whether to invite external users to sites, and set up a public site for the organization.

CERTIFICATION READY
What are the main tools to configure your SharePoint Online farm?

Managing SharePoint Online is not much different than managing SharePoint installed on local servers. The three primary methods for managing and administrating SharePoint Online are as follows:

- Use the SharePoint Site Settings option on the Site Actions menu
- Use the Admin Web site for Office 365
- Use the Administration Center for SharePoint Online

The Site Actions menu and Site Settings are exactly the same as SharePoint installed on local servers. However, instead of using Central Administration, SharePoint Online deploys a simpler version of Central Administration called **Administration Center**.

After you sign up for Microsoft Office 365, you will receive an email to sign in to the following admin Web site:

https://portal.microsoftonline.com/admin/default.aspx

The Office 365 Admin Web site (see Figure 4-34) allows you to add new users, reset user passwords, and assign user licenses, among other tasks. If you click the Setup overview option, you can also configure single sign-on and Active Directory synchronization.

Figure 4-34

Configuring Office 365

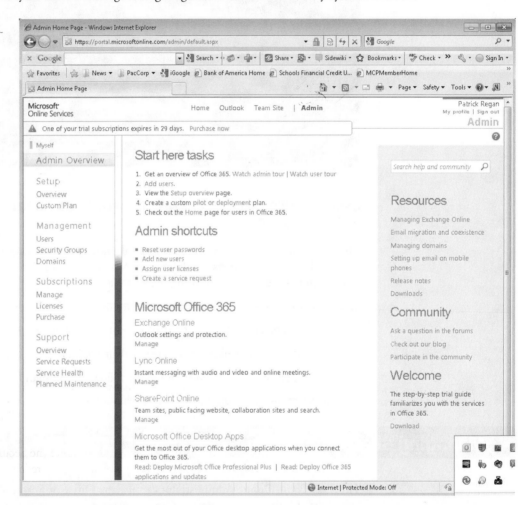

You can click the Manage link under SharePoint Online on the Admin page to go to the Administration Center (see Figure 4-35). The Administration Center can also be reached directly by going to the following URL:

https://<name>-admin.sharepoint.com/default.aspx

The Administration Center features the following options:

- **Manage site collections** allows you to create, delete, and manage site collections.
- **Configure InfoPath Forms Services** allows you to configure InfoPath Forms Services, which enables users to open and fill out InfoPath forms in a browser without requiring Microsoft InfoPath on their computers.
- **Configure InfoPath Forms Services Web service proxy** allows you to configure InfoPath Forms Services Web service proxy, which enables communication between InfoPath Forms and Web services.

Figure 4-35

The Administration Center

- **Manage User Profiles** allows you to configure the User Profile service, which provides a central location where administrators can configure user information, including user profiles, organization profiles, and My Site settings.

- **Manage Business Data Connectivity** allows you to connect SharePoint to other Web services, databases, and external business applications.

- **Manage Term Store** allows you to configure the Term Store, which contains a set of related keywords (called managed terms) organized into a hierarchy of information. As a result, a Term Store helps you improve the consistency, reliability, and discoverability of information within a site collection.

- **Manage Secure Store Service** allows you to configure the Secure Store, which contains credentials such as account names and passwords. The credentials are required to connect to external business applications.

SKILL SUMMARY

IN THIS LESSON YOU LEARNED:

- Different from most other Microsoft Products, SharePoint 2010 is actually managed from a Web-based management tool called Central Administration.

- SharePoint is a complex system that consists of many SharePoint services (services built within SharePoint—not to be confused with Windows services) to provide its functionality.

- SharePoint 2010 uses multiple databases for it to function. The most commonly known database is the content database because it holds the SharePoint data.

- To allow SharePoint to communicate with its users, you must configure outgoing e-mail. To allow SharePoint to receive e-mails, you need to configure incoming e-mail.

- SharePoint can work with anti-virus software to scan files before they are uploaded to SharePoint. However, for this feature to work, you must first install a SharePoint 2010-compatible antivirus software package such as Microsoft Forefront.

- Microsoft SharePoint Designer 2010 is a Web and application design program used to design, build, and customize Web sites running on SharePoint 2010.

- Since SharePoint Designer can be used to easily create customized applications or allow users to modify the Master Page or site templates, causing other sites to not function properly, you might want to disable the use of SharePoint Designer with your SharePoint deployment.

- Stsadm.exe is an executable that includes 182 commands.

- Windows PowerShell is a task-based command-line shell and scripting language used to control and automate the administration of multiple Microsoft technologies, including Windows, SharePoint 2010, Active Directory, and Exchange.

- The SharePoint Online Administrator can use the Office 365 Admin Web site and the SharePoint Online Administration Center to create and manage users and create and manage settings for site collections.

■ Knowledge Assessment

Fill in the Blank

Complete the following sentences by writing the correct word or words in the blanks provided.

1. The main tool used to configure SharePoint 2010 is _____.

2. An easy-to-use Web and application design program often used with SharePoint is _____.

3. _____ allows you to execute commands to configure SharePoint 2007 and SharePoint 2010.

4. Windows _____ provides a powerful command-line interface and scripting language.

5. When configuring incoming e-mail, you would typically use the _____ setting mode, which will deliver directly to the SMTP server and then SharePoint will check for e-mail in the default e-mail drop folder.

6. _____ is responsible for relaying e-mail toward its destination.

7. SharePoint can be configured to automatically check an e-mail _____ folder for incoming e-mail from the SMTP service.

8. stsadm is located in the C:\Program Files\Common Files\Microsoft Shared\Web server extensions\14_____ folder.

9. The _____ provides a Web connection to your Web sites in IIS.

10. To configure incoming e-mail to interface with Active Directory, you need to use the _____ settings.

Multiple Choice

Circle the letter that corresponds to the best answer.

1. Which section is used to configure incoming e-mail for SharePoint 2010 in Central Administration?
   a. Application Management
   b. System Settings
   c. Security
   d. General Application Settings

2. What does Microsoft recommend as the maximize size of the content database for SharePoint 2010?
   a. 100 GB
   b. 200 GB
   c. 500 GB
   d. 1 TB

3. Which application is used to make a database read-only?
   a. SharePoint 2010 Product Configuration Wizard
   b. Task Manager
   c. Central Administration
   d. SQL Server Management Studio

4. Which of the following actions are necessary to ensure that users can send messages to a SharePoint document library?
   a. Configure the incoming e-mail settings with Central Administration
   b. Configure the Web application outgoing e-mail settings with Central Administration
   c. Modify the Custom Send To Destination value from Document Library Settings
   d. Activate the E-mail Integration with Content Organizer feature from Site Settings

5. Which of the following actions prevents certain files from being uploaded to a SharePoint site?
   a. Define blocked file types
   b. Configure quarantined files
   c. Enable file quotas
   d. Enable Windows Defender

6. Which of the following actions determine if a service is running on a particular SharePoint Server?
   a. Open Server Manager on the SharePoint server
   b. Click Manage services on server in Central Administration
   c. Open Computer Management console
   d. Open the SharePoint Services MMC

7. Which database within SharePoint handles all of the administration of the deployment and directs other requests to the appropriate SharePoint database?
   a. configuration database
   b. content database
   c. SharePoint Admin Content
   d. Triage database

8. Which of the following actions disable the use of SharePoint designer with your SharePoint sites?
   a. Define blocked file types with Central Administration
   b. Configure quarantined files with Central Administration
   c. Enable file quotas with Central Administration
   d. Open General Application Settings within Central Administration

9. For users to receive e-mail notifications from SharePoint, you must configure
   _____.
   a. incoming e-mail
   b. outgoing e-mail
   c. file quotas with Central Administration
   d. General Application Settings within Central Administration

10. Which of the following is the maximum size of a site collection?
    a. 100 GB
    b. 200 GB
    c. 500 GB
    d. 1 TB

True / False

Circle T if the statement is true or F if the statement is false.

T | F **1.** To enable anti-virus protection within SharePoint, you need to have a SharePoint 2010 compatible antivirus software package.

T | F **2.** The configuration database is the largest database found on SharePoint.

T | F **3.** To simplify the use of the `stsadm.exe` command, add the BIN folder to the path statement.

T | F **4.** Most database names have the version of the database at the end of the name.

T | F **5.** The commands used in Windows PowerShell are known as applets.

■ Case Scenarios

Scenario 4-1: Troubleshooting Outgoing E-mail

You installed and configured SharePoint about a month ago and you are close to moving the server into production. Your test team realized that when a new document is added to the primary document library, the user is not getting notified by e-mail. What should you do to fix this problem?

Scenario 4-2: Scheduling Vacation

Your manager indicates there is a problem. When someone wants to go on vacation, he or she does not know who else will already be on vacation. When someone is on vacation, other team members might not know that person is on vacation. As a result, the members continue to put items in his or her inbox. What can you use in SharePoint to help keep track of vacations?

Deploying and Managing Web Applications and Collections

OBJECTIVE DOMAIN MATRIX

TECHNOLOGY SKILL	OBJECTIVE DOMAIN DESCRIPTION	OBJECTIVE DOMAIN NUMBER
Configuring and Managing Web Application Settings	Managing Web Applications	3.1
	Managing Web Application Settings	3.1.2
	Managing Security and Policies	3.1.3
	Configuring Alternate Access Mappings (AAM)	1.2.5
	Configuring External Sites	1.2.6
	Configuring Host Headers	1.2.7
Managing Site Collections	Managing Site Collections	3.2
Managing Site Collection Settings	Managing Site Collections	3.2
	Managing Site Collection Policies	3.2.1
	Managing Site Collection Features	3.2.2
	Managing Site Collection Caching	3.2.3
	Managing Site Collection Auditing	3.2.4
	Configuring Site Collection Security	3.2.5
Configuring Multi-Tenancy	Configuring Multi-Tenancy	3.2.6
Managing SharePoint Online Site Collections and Websites	Adding a Domain to Office 365	3.2.8
	SharePoint Online public websites	3.2.9

KEY TERMS

Alternate Access Mappings (AAM)

application pool

auditing

binding

branding

caching

claims-based authentication

classic-mode authentication

feature

information management policies

Kerberos

managed path

multi-tenancy

NTLM

site collection

Web applications

You just installed and completed the initial configuration of SharePoint. You just had a meeting with your management team and you have been given the task of creating multiple sites and related collections to be used by the major departments. You also need to keep each of these department sites separate from the other sites.

■ Configuring and Managing Web Application Settings

↓
THE BOTTOM LINE

When creating SharePoint sites, you will define Web applications, which are composed of an Internet Information Services (IIS) Web site. These Web applications act as a logical unit for the site collections.

CERTIFICATION READY
What is the underlining component on top of which all SharePoint content is built?
3.1

Since *Web applications* are linked to Web sites in IIS, Web applications are what you use to define the URLs that you use in your sites. They are also used to isolate content. When you create a new Web application, you also create a new content database and define the authentication method used to connect to the database.

Understanding Internet Information Services (IIS) Web Sites

As introduced in Lesson 1, IIS is Microsoft's Web server. IIS supports multiple Web sites on a single server. Therefore, instead of hosting three different servers to host three different Web sites, you can place all three Web sites on the same server.

CERTIFICATION READY
What do you call assigning an IP address, port, and host name to a Web site?
1.2.7

To ensure that users can reach a specific Web site, you must make each Web site unique based on IP address, TCP port number, and/or host header name. Of course, consolidating Web sites to one server saves hardware resources, conserves space, and reduces energy cost.

For example, you could do one of the following:

- You can configure each Web site to have its own IP address. Each Web site is still based on port 80 for HTTP and port 443 for HTTPS. The Web sites will be configured to respond to all names that point to the IP address and port 80/443.
- You can configure all of the Web sites to use the same IP address, but each Web site will use a different port (instead of the standard port 80 and 443). The Web sites will be configured to respond to all names that point to the IP address and the Web site's port number.
- You can configure all of the Web sites to use the same IP address and the standard port 80 and 443. Instead of having each Web site respond to any Web site name, you would use a host header name to specify what names each Web site will respond to. Therefore, while each of the three names will point to the same IP address and port, it will be directed to the correct Web site on the server based on the Web site name. Using host header names to identify unique sites on a server is recommended for most situations.

The process of assigning an IP address, port number, and host header is referred to as *binding* the Web site. A typical binding for Web sites are in the form of IP:Port:HostHeader. For IIS,

the default Web Site binding is set to *:80:*, which means that all requests to that server over port 80 will go to the site. Figure 5-1 shows the bindings for an IIS Web site.

Figure 5-1

Site bindings

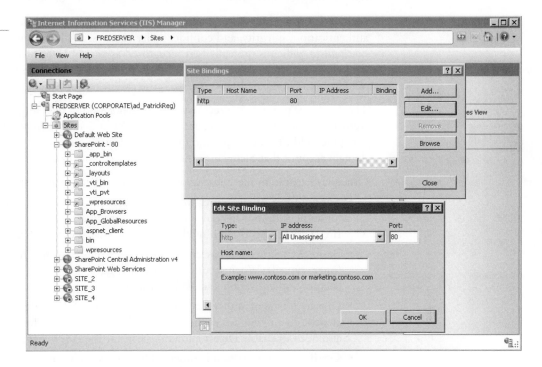

You cannot configure multiple running sites to use the same binding. You can have multiple sites configured with the same binding, but only one can be running at the one time.

UNDERSTANDING APPLICATION POOLS

Web sites can be configured to share the same application pool, or to have their own application pool. An *application pool* is one or more groupings of URLs or Web sites that are routed to one or more worker process. Process boundaries separate each worker process. Therefore, Web sites within one application pool will not affect Web sites in another application pool. As a result, application pools significantly increase both the reliability and manageability of a Web infrastructure.

UNDERSTANDING AUTHENTICATION METHODS

Authentication is the act of confirming the identity of a user and is an essential part used in authorization. In SharePoint Server 2010, there are two types of authentication:

- *Classic-mode authentication*: Classic-mode authentication is the same type of authentication used in Microsoft Office SharePoint Server 2007, which uses Microsoft Windows (which includes Anonymous, Basic, Digest, Certificates, NTML, and Negotiate (Kerberos or NTLM)).

- *Claims-based authentication*: Claims-based authentication is a new authentication mode, built on the Windows Identity Framework (WIF). It uses an identity system that allows users to present claims that include information about who the user is and what system and content the user can access. The claim must be validated against a trusted source such as Active Directory, LDAP, application specific databases, and user-centric identity models such as LiveID and OpenID. In addition to supporting Windows authentication, it also supports forms-based authentication (FBA) and Security Assertion Markup Language (SAML) token-based authentication.

SharePoint Web applications support both NTLM and Kerberos, which let clients seamlessly authenticate without being prompted for credentials (single sign-on). Typically, these credentials are the credentials that the user uses to log on to his or her computer.

NTLM (short for NT LAN Manager) is a suite of Microsoft security protocols that provides authentication, integrity, and confidentiality to users. NTLM is an integrated single sign-on mechanism, which is probably best recognized as part of Integrated Windows Authentication for HTTP authentication. It provides maximum compatibility with different versions of Windows and compared to Kerberos, is the easiest to implement.

The *Kerberos* protocol is a secure protocol that supports ticketing authentication. While Kerberos is considered more secure than NTLM, it is more complicated than NTLM in that it requires additional configuration (such as requiring a service principal name (SPN) for the domain account that SharePoint is using).

Configuring Kerberos will be discussed in Lesson 10.

Other authentication methods supported by SharePoint include the following:

- **Anonymous**: Allows a user to access SharePoint without providing any credentials for authentication. Instead, the computer-specific anonymous access account is used: IIS_IUSRS. This is often used with public Web sites where access is given to everyone.

- **Basic**: Authentication based on a user name and password that is transmitted clear-text (unencrypted). When security is necessary, Basic can be made secure by using SSL to encrypt authentication and Web traffic.

- **Digest**: A type of authentication that is similar to basic authentication except that the credentials are sent across the network encrypted. If you choose to use Digest, you will also need to enable Digest authentication for the IIS Web site.

- **Certificates**: Encryption is provided by SSL, which uses the exchange of public key certifications. Public key certificates are issued by a Certificate Authority (CA). If you choose to use Client Certificates, you will also need to configure the IIS Web site for certificate authentication.

XREF

Configuring and Managing authentication providers will be discussed in detail in Lesson 10, including configuring and managing Claims-based authentication and forms-based authentication.

Creating a Web Application

You can create a Web application by using the SharePoint Central Administration Web site or Windows PowerShell. After the Web site is created, you would then create one or several site collections on the Web application that you have created. You will not be able to access the SharePoint site until you create the collection.

To create a Web application, you must be a member of the Farm Administrators SharePoint group and member of the local Administrator group on the computer running Central Administration.

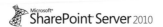

➡ **CREATE A WEB APPLICATION**

GET READY. To create a Web application in the SharePoint Central Administration Web site that uses classic-mode authentication, perform the following steps:

1. On the Central Administration Home page, in the **Application Management** section, click **Manage Web Applications** (see Figure 5-2).

Figure 5-2

Selecting Manage Web Applications in Central Administration

2. On the ribbon, click **New** (see Figure 5-3).

Figure 5-3

Clicking New to create a new Web application

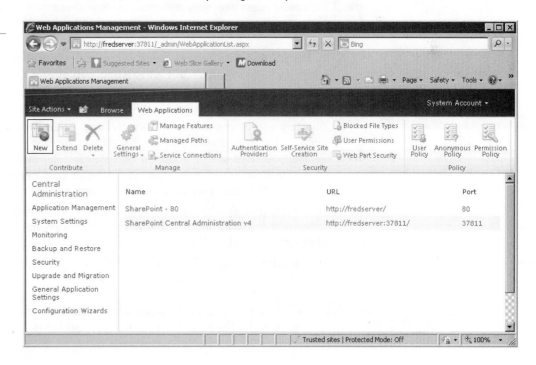

3. On the Create New Web Application page, in the **Authentication** section, click **Classic Mode Authentication** (see Figure 5-4).

Figure 5-4

Selecting the Authentication Mode

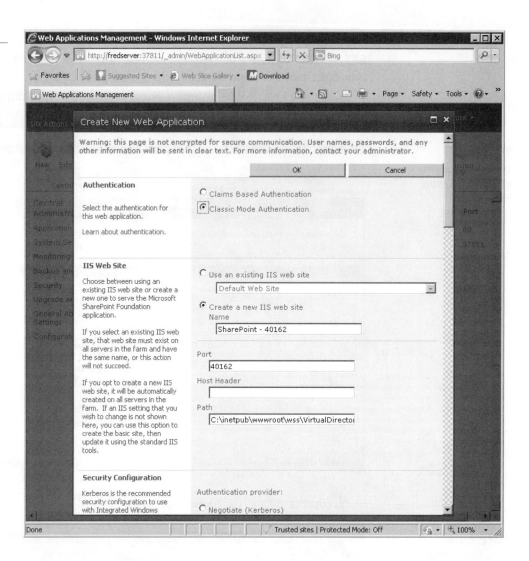

4. In the **IIS Web Site** section, you can configure the settings for your new Web application by selecting either **Use an existing web site** or **Create a new IIS Web site**.

   If you select **Create a new IIS web site**, it will ask for the name of the site, port number used by the site, the host header name and the path of where the Virtual Directory will be created. If you are creating a new Web site, this port field is populated with a random port number. If you are using an existing Web site, this field is populated with the current port number. Remember that you don't need to fill in the Host Header box unless you want to configure two or more IIS Web sites that share the same port number on the same server.

5. In the **Security Configuration** section, configure authentication and encryption for your Web application. For the Authentication Provider section, click **Negotiate (Kerberos)** or **NTLM**. The default value is NTLM authentication.

6. In the **Allow Anonymous** section, you can also choose whether or not to allow anonymous authentication by clicking **Yes** or **No**.

> **TAKE NOTE***
>
> If you want users to be able to access any site content anonymously, you must enable anonymous access for the entire Web application zone before you enable anonymous access at the SharePoint site level.

7. In the **Use Secure Sockets Layer (SSL)** section, if you require SSL, click **Yes** or **No**. If you choose to enable SSL for the Web site, you must configure SSL by requesting and installing an SSL certificate (see Figure 5-5).

Figure 5-23

Configuring site Bindings

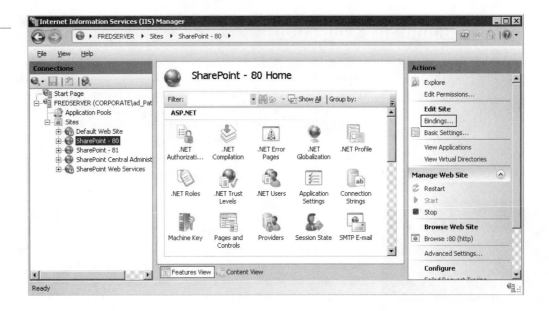

9. Click **Add**.

10. In the **Type** drop-down menu (see Figure 5-24), select **https** and then in the **SSL certificate** drop-down, select the certificate that was created earlier.

11. Click **OK**. The https binding should appear.

Figure 5-24

The Add Site Binding Dialog

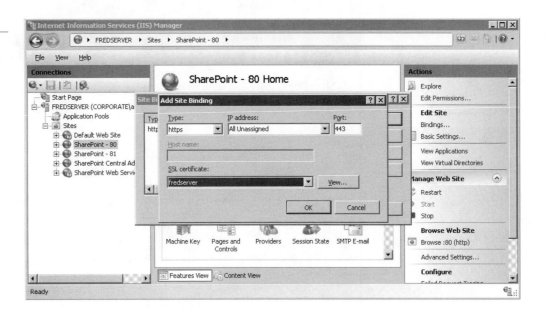

➕ MORE INFORMATION

For more information about configuring server certificates in IIS 7, visit http://technet.microsoft.com/en-us/library/cc732230(WS.10).aspx

■ Managing Site Collections

As discussed in Lesson 1, a *site collection* is grouping of sites. Every site collection has a single root site, which the other sites are built under. All sites within the site collection have the same site owners and share the same administrative settings. You can create a top-level site collection using either the root URL of an unextended Web application or a managed path such as /sites or any other wildcard inclusion path you have created. Site collections have a URL that is a managed path. Since the site collection includes the top-level site, you can then create subsites within the site collection.

All site collections you create must exist within a Web application. You can either create a site collection in an existing Web application or create a Web application specifically for the site collection. If your Web application is for a single project or for use by a single team, you should use a single site collection to avoid the overhead of managing multiple sites. However, many organizations will use multiple site collections because it is easier to organize content and manage permissions for each site collection. Figure 5-25 shows the Site Collections options for the Central Administration Web site.

Figure 5-25

The Site Collections section

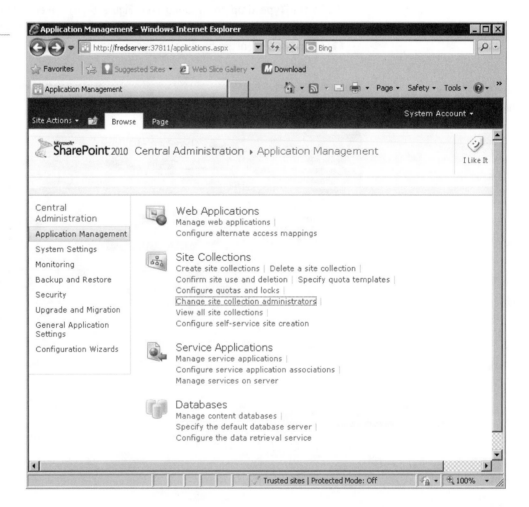

Creating and Deleting Site Collections

In Central Administration, the Site Collections section gives the farm administrator the ability to manage all aspects of a site collection, including creating and deleting site collections and changing site collection administrators.

Creating Site Collections

To create or delete a site collection, you must be a member of the Farm Administrators SharePoint group on the computer that is running the SharePoint Central Administration Web site.

CREATE A SITE COLLECTION

GET READY. To create a site collection, perform the following steps:

1. On the Central Administration Web site, in the **Application Management** section, click **Create site collections**.

2. On the Create Site Collection page (see Figure 5-26), in the **Web Application** section, if the Web application in which you want to create the site collection is not

Figure 5-26

The Create Site Collection page

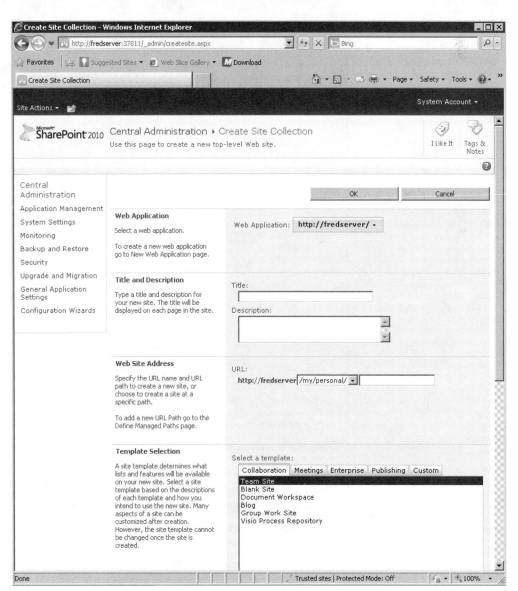

selected, on the **Web Application** menu, click **Change Web Application**, and then click the Web application in which you want to create the site collection.

3. In the **Title** and **Description** sections, type the title and description for the site collection.

4. In the **Web Site Address** section, select the path to use for your **URL** (for example, a wildcard inclusion path such as root directory (/), /my/personal/ or /sites/.

5. If you select a wildcard inclusion path, you must also type the site name to use in your site's URL.

6. In the **Template Selection** section, in the **Select a template** box, select a site that you want to use for the top-level site in the site collection (or click the **Custom** tab to create an empty site and apply a template later).

7. In the **Primary Site Collection Administrator** section and the **Secondary Site Collection Administrator** section, type the user names (in the form **DOMAIN\ username**) for the users who will be the site collection administrators. Figure 5-27 shows the site collection administrators and the quota template to be used by a collection.

Figure 5-27

Adding the site administrators

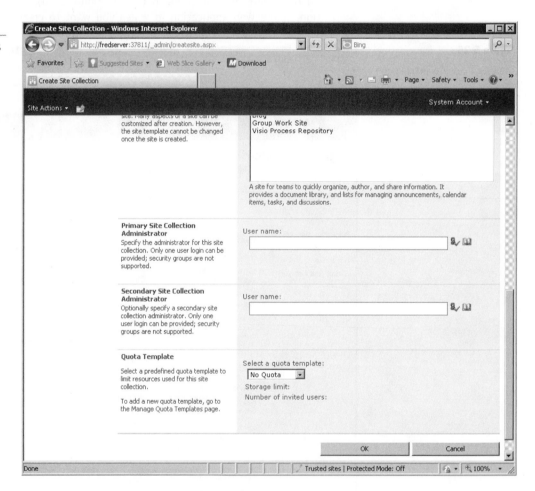

8. If you are using quotas to manage storage for site collections, in the **Quota Template** section, click a template in the **Select a quota template** list.

9. Click **OK**.

DELETING SITE COLLECTIONS

If you have multiple site collections, you will most likely have to eventually delete a site collection. When you delete a site collection, you are deleting a hierarchy of sites that make up the collection. When you delete a site collection, you permanently destroy all content and user information including documents and document libraries, lists and list data, site configuration settings, roles related to the Web site and subsites. Since site collections are not easily recreated, you should consider backing up the site collection before you delete it.

 ### DELETE A SITE COLLECTION

GET READY. To delete a site collection, perform the following steps:

1. On the Central Administration Web site, click **Application Management**.
2. On the Application Management page, in the **Site Collections** section, click **Delete a site collection**.
3. On the Delete Site Collection page (see Figure 5-28), in the **Site Collection** drop-down list, click the down arrow, and then click **Change Site Collection**. The Select Site Collection dialog box appears.

Figure 5-28

Selecting the site collection

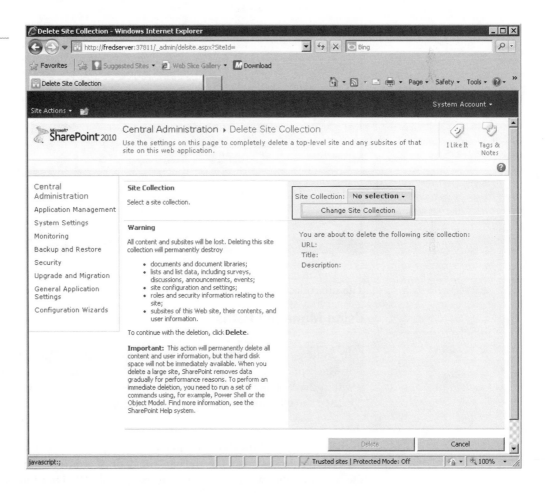

4. In the **Web Application** drop-down list, click the down arrow, and then click **Change Web Application**. The Select Web Application dialog box appears.
5. Click the name of the Web application that contains the site collection that you want to delete. Relative URLs of sites in the site collections of the Web application that you have selected appear in the Select Site Collection dialog box.

6. Click the relative URL of the site collection that you want to delete and then click **OK**.

7. Read the Warning section and verify that the site collection information is correct. On the Delete Site Collection page, click **Delete**. See Figure 5-29.

Figure 5-29

Deleting the site collection

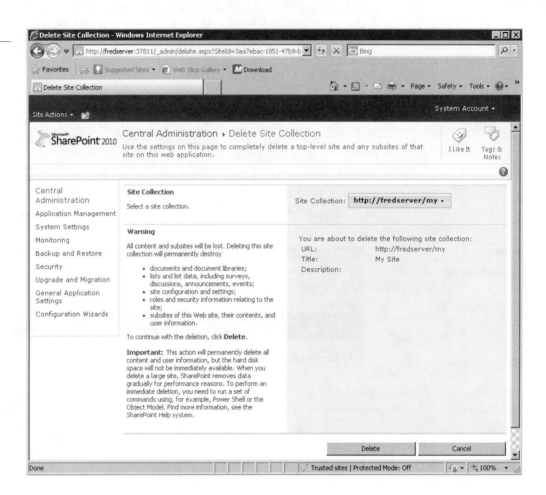

The site collection that you selected is deleted.

Using Managed Paths

To create a new site collection within a Web application, there must be a *managed path* at which to create the site collection. A managed path is not directly mapped to content within the Web application. Instead, it is used by SharePoint as a namespace (path) node where site collections can be created.

Explicit Managed Paths allow you to create a single SharePoint site with the specified URL. For example, let's say that a SharePoint site defined at http://portal and you want to create a site collection that will be assigned to http://portal/HR. Therefore, you will need to create an explicit managed path for HR.

A wildcard managed path such as /sites/ allows for an unlimited number of site collections to be created directly under the provided path. Since this is used to store an unlimited number of site collections, you cannot create a site at the top of the wildcard managed path. For example if you have defined http://portal/sites/ as a wildcard managed paths, you can create site collections for http://portal/sites/site1, http://portal/sites/site2, and http://portal/sites/site3, but you cannot create a site collection at http://portal/sites/.

It should be noted that exceeding twenty managed paths per Web application adds more load to the Web server for each request. If you plan to exceed twenty managed paths in a given Web application, you need to test for acceptable system performance.

DEFINE MANAGED PATHS

GET READY. To define managed paths, perform the following steps:

1. On the SharePoint Central Administration Web site, click **Application Management**.
2. On the Application Management page, click **Manage Web Applications**.
3. Select the Web application for which you want to manage paths and then on the ribbon, click **Managed Paths**. Figure 5-30 shows the Managed Paths button.

Figure 5-30

The Managed Paths button

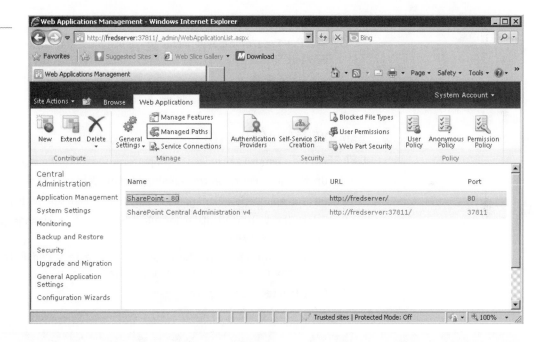

4. In the Define Managed Paths dialog, in the **Add a New Path** section, type the path to include (see Figure 5-31).

Figure 5-31

The Defined Managed Paths
page

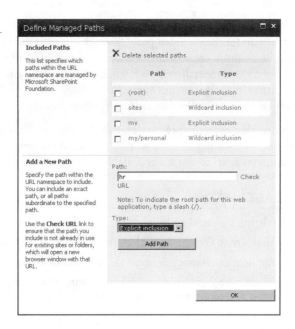

5. Click **Check URL** to confirm the path name.

6. Use the **Type** drop-down menu to identify the path as either **Wildcard inclusion** or **Explicit inclusion**.

7. Click **Add Path**.

8. When you have finished adding paths, click **OK**.

 REMOVE MANAGED PATHS

GET READY. To remove a managed path, perform the following steps:

1. On the SharePoint Central Administration Web site, click **Application Management**.

2. On the Application Management page, click **Manage Web Applications**.

3. Select the Web application for which you want to manage paths and then on the ribbon, click **Managed Paths**.

4. In the **Define Managed Paths** dialog, in the **Included Paths** section, select the check box next to the path that you want to remove.

5. Click Delete selected paths.

■ Managing Site Collection Settings

THE BOTTOM LINE

Now that you have created a site collection, you are ready to configure those settings related to a site collection. Instead of using the Central Administration Web site, these settings are modified within the Site Collection Administration list (see Figure 5-32) on the Site Settings page.

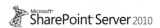

Figure 5-32

Site Collection Administration options

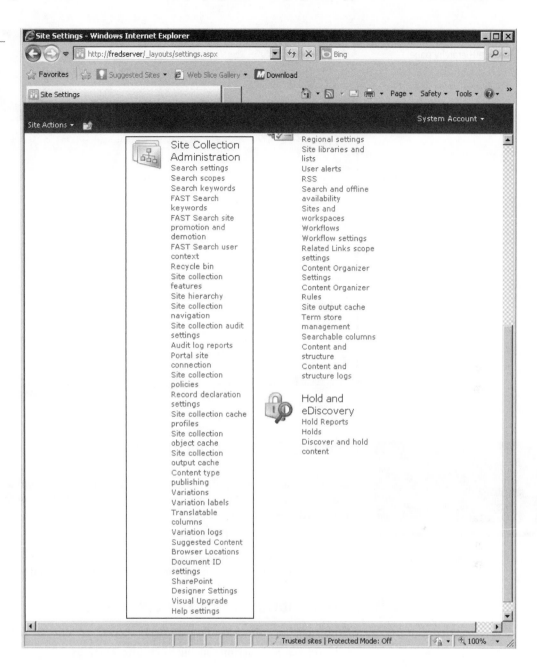

CERTIFICATION READY
What tools are available to secure a site collection?
3.2

To view all of the Web sites that have been created under the current site, you can click the **Site Hierarchy** option under Site Collection Administration. Figure 5-33 shows the Site Hierarchy page. You can also manage those sites and content with those sites by clicking **Content and Structure** under Site Collection Administration.

Figure 5-33

The Site Hierarchy page

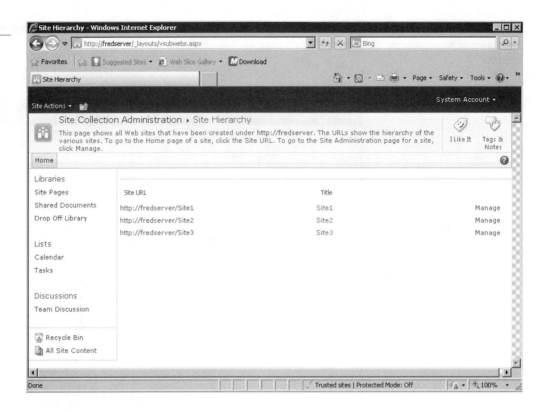

Managing Site Collection Auditing

Security of a system requires authentication, authorization, and auditing. *Auditing* is the measurable technical assessment of SharePoint to verify that users are only accessing what they need to and not accessing information that they should not be accessing.

The Site Collection Auditing Settings provides access to a number of settings pertaining to audit logs, including the automatic trimming of audit logs and what events are audited.

 ENABLE AUDITING FOR A SITE COLLECTION

GET READY. To enable auditing for a site collection, perform the following steps:

1. On the **Site actions** menu, click **Site settings**.

2. If you are not at the root of your site collection, on the Site Collection Administration page, click **Go to top level site settings**.

3. In the **Site Collection Administration** section, select **Site collection audit settings**. The Configure Audit Settings page displays, as shown in Figure 5-34.

Figure 5-34

The Configure Audit Settings page

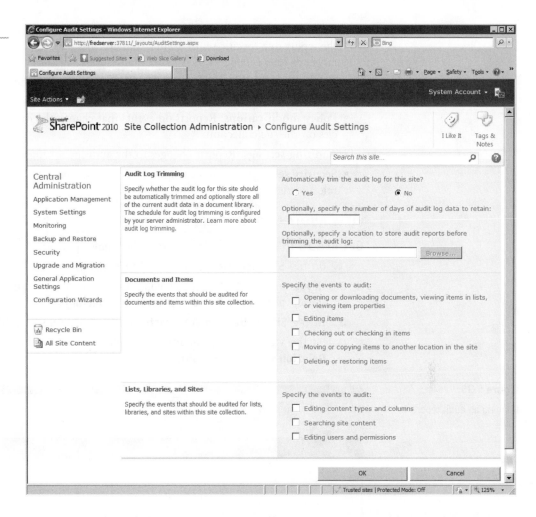

4. At the top of the screen, select **Yes** if you want to trim or delete older audit log entries.

5. In the **Optionally, specify the number of days of audit log data to retain** text box, specify the number of days before an audit log entry is deleted.

6. In the **Documents and Items** section, in the **Lists, Libraries, and Sites** section, specify the events that you want to audit.

7. Click **OK**.

By default, audit log trimming is disabled. If you do not enable audit log trimming but you enable auditing, the AuditData table within the content database keeps growing. By enabling audit log trimming, the actual trimming will be done by the Audit Log Trimming timer job, which is scheduled to execute once a month. Timer jobs will be discussed in Lesson 10.

After you have enabled auditing, you can use the audit log reports provided with SharePoint 2010 to view the data in the audit logs for a site collection, which helps you determine who is taking what actions with the content of a site collection. You can sort, filter, and analyze this data to determine who has done what with sites, lists, libraries, content types, list items, and library files in the site collection. The available reports include:

- **Content modifications**: Reports changes to content, such as modifying, deleting, and checking documents in and out.
- **Content type and list modifications**: Reports additions, edits, and deletions to content types.
- **Content viewing**: Reports users who have viewed content on a site.
- **Deletion**: Reports what content has been deleted.

- **Run a custom report**: You can specify the filters for a custom report, such as limiting the report to a specific set of events, to items in a particular list, to a particular date range, or to events performed by particular users.

- **Expiration and Disposition**: Reports all events related to how content is removed when it expires.

- **Policy modifications**: Reports on events that change the information management policies on the site collection.

- **Auditing settings**: Reports changes to the auditing settings.

- **Security settings**: Reports changes to security settings, such as user/group events, and role and rights events.

 VIEW AUDIT LOG REPORTS

GET READY. To view an audit log, perform the following steps:

1. On the **Site actions** menu, click **Site settings**.

2. If you are not at the root of your site collection, on the Site Collection Administration page, click **Go to top level site settings**.

3. In the **Site Collection Administration** section, select **Audit log reports**.

4. On the View Auditing Reports page, select the report that you want, such as **Deletion** (see Figure 5-35).

Figure 5-35

Running an audit report

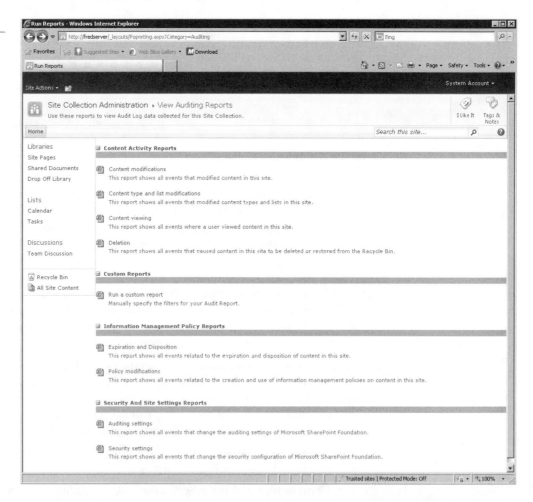

5. Type or Browse to the library where you want to save the report and then click **OK**.

6. On the Operation Completed Successfully page, click **Click here to view this report**. See Figure 5-36.

Figure 5-36

An audit report

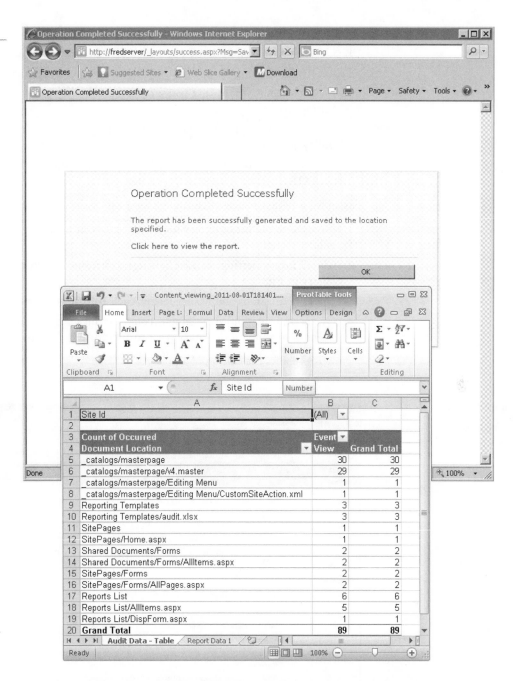

Creating and Applying Information Management Policies

Information management policies allow you to control who can access organization information stored within SharePoint, what they can do with it, and how long they can retain it. You can also enable auditing of opening or downloading documents, editing items, or deleting items. In addition, you can enable the user of barcodes and labels.

An information management policy can be created on a site in three different ways:

For multiple content types within a site collection, perform the following steps:

1. On the site collection home page, click **Site Actions** and then click **Site Settings**.
2. On the **Site Settings** page, in the **Site Collection Administration** list, click **Site collection policies.**
3. On the Site Collection Policies page, click **Create**.

For a site content type, perform the following steps:

1. On the site collection home page, click **Site Actions** and then click Site Settings.
2. On the Site Settings page, click **Site Content** types in the Galleries section.
3. Select the content type that you want to add a policy to on the Site Content Type Settings page.
4. On the Site Content Type page, in the **Settings** section, click **Information management policy settings**.
5. On the Information Management Policy Settings page, select **Define a policy** and then click **OK**.

For an information management policy for a list or library, perform the following steps:

1. Navigate to the list or library for which you want to specify an information management policy.
2. Click **Library Settings** or **List Settings** depending on whether you are working with a library or list.
3. Under Permissions and Management, click **Information management policy settings.**
4. On the Information Management Policy Settings page, make sure that the source of retention for the list or library is set to Library and Folders.

Figure 5-37 shows the editing of a policy.

Figure 5-37

Editing a Policy

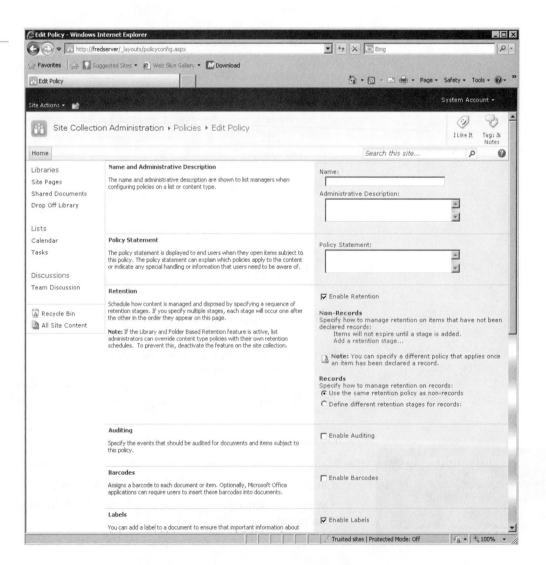

 CREATE AN INFORMATION POLICY

GET READY. To view an audit log, perform the following steps:

1. On the Edit Policy page (refer to Figure 5-37), type a **Name** and **Administrative Description** for the policy.

2. In the **Policy Statement** box, type a brief statement that explains to users what the policy is for. A description can be up to 512 characters long.

3. To specify a retention period for documents and items that are subject to this policy, select **Enable Retention** (see Figure 5-38).

Figure 5-38

Specifying a retention period

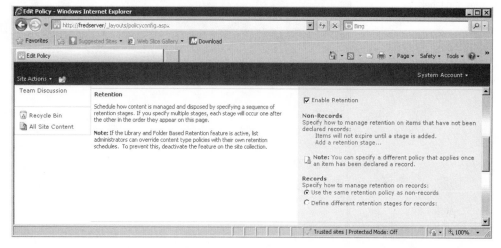

    a. Depending on the type of information policy being applied, you will select a **retention stage** to specify when documents or items are set to expire based on the date property. If you have no retention stages defined, click the **Add a retention stage** option.

4. To enable auditing for the documents and items that are subject to this policy, select **Enable Auditing**.

    a. On the Edit Policy page, in the **Auditing** section, select the **Enable Auditing** check box.

    b. In the **Specify the events to audit** list, select the check boxes next to the events you want to keep an audit trail for (see Figure 5-39).

Figure 5-39

Enabling Auditing of documents and Items

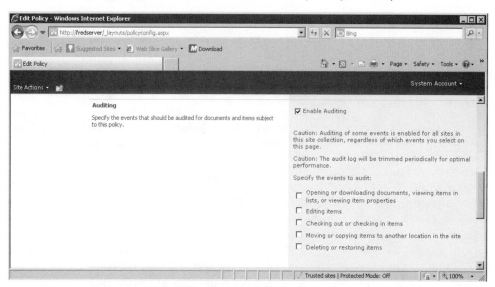

    c. To prompt users to insert these barcodes into documents, select the **Prompt users to insert a barcode before saving or printing** check box.

5. When barcodes are enabled as part of a policy, they are added to document properties and displayed in the header area of the document to which the barcode is applied. To enable barcodes, select the **Enable Barcodes** check box.

   a. To prompt users to insert these barcodes into documents, select the **Prompt users to insert a barcode before saving or printing check** box. Figure 5-40 shows the options for Barcodes and Labels.

Figure 5-40

Configuring options for barcodes and labels

6. To require that documents that are subject to this policy have labels, select the **Enable Labels** check box and then specify the settings that you want for the labels.

   a. To require users to add a label to a document, select the **Prompt users to insert a label before saving or printing** check box. If you want labels to be optional, do not select this check box.

   b. To lock a label so that it cannot be changed after it has been inserted, select the **Prevent changes to labels after they are added** check box.

   c. In the **Label format** box, type the text for the label as you want it to be displayed. Type the names of the columns in the order in which you want them to appear. Enclose the column names in curly brackets ({}). Type words to identify the columns outside the brackets. To add a line break, type **\n** where you want the line break to appear.

   d. Select the **Font**, **Size** and **Style** that you want, and in the **Justification** drop-down, specify whether you want the label positioned left, center, or right within the document.

> **e.** Type the **Height** and **Width** of the label. Label height can range from .25 inches to 20 inches and label width can range from .25 inches to 20 inches.
>
> **f.** Click **Refresh** to preview the label content.

7. Click **OK**.

➕ **MORE INFORMATION**

For more information about creating and applying information management policies, visit http://office.microsoft.com/en-us/sharepoint-server-help/create-and-apply-information-management-policies-HA101631505.aspx

Managing Site Collection Features

A *feature* is a container of various elements including Web parts, workflows, content type definitions, and event receivers that add functionality or apply customizations to a site, collection or Web site. It is composed of a set of XML files that are deployed to front-end Web servers and application servers. You can deploy a feature as part of a solution package, and you can individually activate a feature in SharePoint Server sites.

Features are defined in SharePoint based on scope (such as the farm), Web application, site collection, and site level. To activate or disable features for a site collection, open the Site Actions menu, choose site settings, and in the Site Collection Administration section, click **Manage Features**. Figure 5-41 shows the available features for a site collection.

CERTIFICATION READY
After a feature is installed for a collection, where do you go to enable that feature?
3.2.2

Figure 5-41

The site collection features page

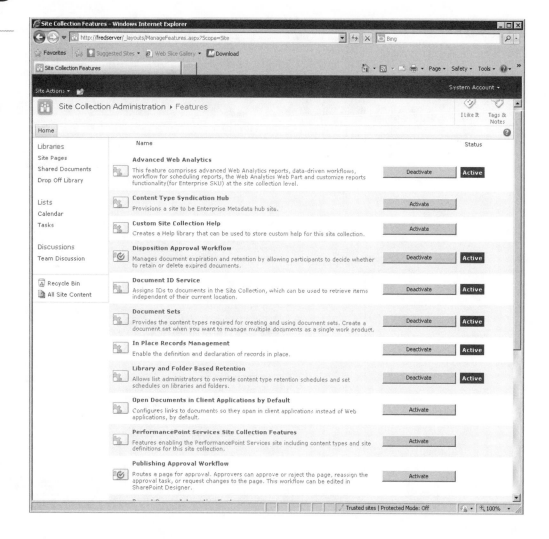

To activate a feature, click the **Activate** button and to deactivate a feature, click the **Deactivate** button. For example, if you need standard SharePoint features (such as user profiles or search), make sure that the SharePoint Server Standard Site Collection features is activated. If you need to use centralized libraries, content types, master pages, or page layouts, you must activate SharePoint Server Publishing Infrastructure.

Managing Site Collection Caching

Caching users a special high-speed storage mechanism that helps improve the speed at which Web pages load in the browser. The page output cache and object cache are usually configured in the user interface at the site collection level; however, certain settings for these caches can also be configured at the Web application level.

The object cache reduces the amount of traffic between the Web server and the SQL database by storing objects (such as lists, libraries, site settings, and page layouts) in the memory of the front-end Web server computer. By increasing the Object Cache Size (see Figure 5-42), you can speed up sending of navigation data and data accessed through cross-list questions because they are accessed from the RAM rather than always going back to the SQL server to acquire the necessary information. By default, the maximum cache size is 100 MB. However, for smaller site collections, this can be decreased. In addition, the object cache can be reset for troubleshooting purposes.

Figure 5-42

The Object cache settings page

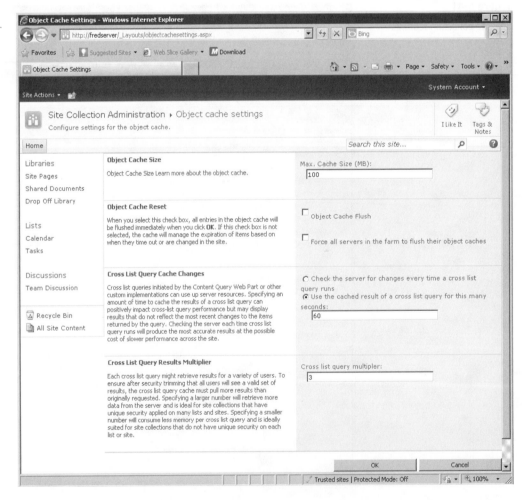

Page output cache settings can be configured at the site collection level, at the site level, and for page layouts. The page output cache stores the rendered output of a page and stores different versions of the cached page based on the permissions of the users who are requesting the page. By default, the page output cache is turned off. Figure 5-43 shows the site collection output cache settings.

Figure 5-43

The Output Cache Settings page

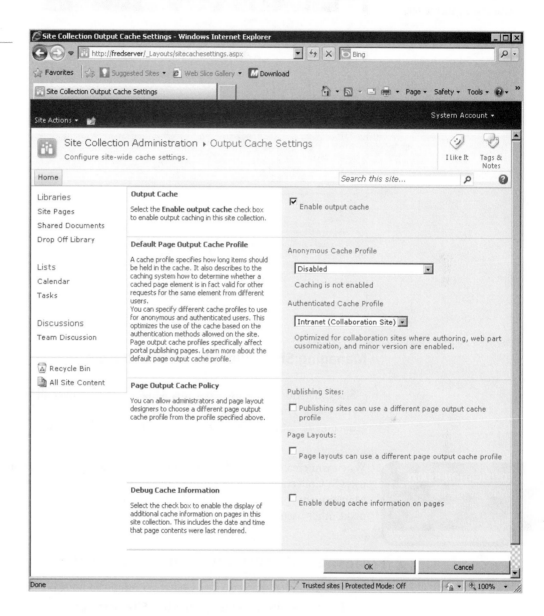

Site Collection Cache Profiles specifies how long items should be held in the cache based on the authentication method. It also describes to the caching system how to determine whether a cached page element is, in fact, valid for other requests for the same element from different users. By default, four cache profiles are provided, including:

- Disabled
- Public Internet (Purely Anonymous)
- Extranet (Published Site)
- Intranet (Collaboration Site)

Figure 5-44 shows the profile cache settings for Intranet (Collaboration Site).

Figure 5-44

The Cache Profiles—Intranet (Collaboration Site) settings

Managing Site Collection Administrators

Site Collection Administrators are giving full control over all Web sites in the site collection. Therefore, they can access and manage all sites, subsites, libraries, lists, and documents located within the site collection.

CERTIFICATION READY
How to you assign users as collection administrators?
3.2.5

When you create a site collection using Central Administration, you can define only two users as Collection Administrators. You can also use Central Administration Application Management to specify which two users are the initial Site Collection Administrators. You make other users Collection Administrators by using the Site settings.

MANAGE SITE COLLECTION ADMINISTRATORS

GET READY. To add users as Site Collection Administrators, perform the following steps:

1. On the **Site Actions** menu, click **Site Settings**.
2. In the **Users and Permissions** section, click **Site Collection Administrators**.
3. In the **Site Collection** Administrators box, type the user names. If you need more than one user, separate the users with semicolons (;). See Figure 5-45.
4. Click **OK**.

Figure 5-45

The Site Collection
Administrators page

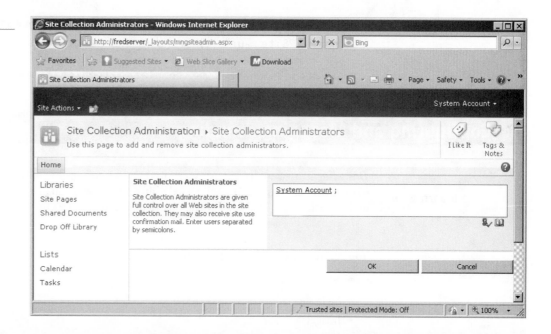

■ Configuring Multi-Tenancy

THE BOTTOM LINE

Multi-tenancy is the ability to partition data of shared services to meet the needs of multiple tenants, such as different subsidiaries or different customers, without having separate hardware platforms or running multiple instances of the service. As a result, site collections in a single Web application are grouped and the profile stores, search indexes, and other resources are isolated from other tenants. Each tenant is referred to as a subscriber who can host his own sandbox solutions, subscribe to one or more service applications, and manage his own usage quota and permissions.

CERTIFICATION READY
What is used to isolate SharePoint data of one company from users in another company, which are hosted on the same SharePoint server?
3.2.6

To support multi-tenancy, you need an existing Web application and a couple of Explicit Inclusion Managed Paths. You will then create an isolated collection by performing the three basic steps:

1. Create a subscription.
2. Create a Tenant Admin site.
3. Create a new member site.

 ENABLE MULTI-TENANCY

GET READY. To support multi-tenancy, perform the following:

1. On the SharePoint server, click **Start > All Programs > Microsoft SharePoint 2010 products > SharePoint 2010 Management Shell**.

2. To create a new sub, execute the following command:

   ```
   $sub = New-SPSiteSubscription
   ```

3. To create a Tenant admin site, perform the following:

   ```
   New-SPSite -url http://<SharePointURL>
       -owneralias <domainname>\<siteownername>
       -owneremail noone@nowhere.com -template
       <templatename> -SiteSubscription $sub
       -AdministrationSiteType TenantAdministration
   ```

4. To create a new member site, execute the following command:

```
New-SPSite -url <SharePointURL> -owneralias
    <domainname>\<siteownername> -owneremail
    noone@nowhere.com -template <templatename>
    -SiteSubscription $sub
```

■ Configuring and Managing Branding

THE BOTTOM LINE

Branding is used to distinguish your product, service, or organization with a specific identity. When you brand your SharePoint site, you will usually use logos, colors, fonts, and other imagery. It also achieves a particular look and feel for your SharePoint sites.

You can brand the following SharePoint components:

- Master pages
- Style sheets
- Images
- Page layouts
- Templates
- Themes

Master pages define the theme and general page template layout that generally provide the header, footer, and top and left navigation. They contain HTML, linked or embedded CSS, and SharePoint placeholders for specific SharePoint items such as logos.

Cascading Style Sheets (CSS) are separate files or are embedded in the master and/or page layouts. CSS rules define the visual properties for a specific element in your Web site. Style sheets can contain many rules, which make it easier to group large numbers of rules. Often a master page has an associated style sheet for its look and feel that overrides the out-of-the-box styles SharePoint provides for those elements in a master page.

To put a brand on a SharePoint site usually includes a logo and possibly other images. Typically, logos are not frequently changed after they have been defined.

Page layouts are defined layouts with specific content containers. Master pages work with page layouts to provide the look and feel of the publishing page. While the master contains the template branding elements, the page layouts provide the arrangement and type of content containers in the content area of the page.

Lastly, themes define SharePoint site color schemes, including those that are applied to menus, system pages, the ribbon, and so forth. Choosing a complementary color scheme completes the look and feel of the SharePoint sites.

Most of these settings are available by opening the Site Actions menu, selecting **Site Settings**, and then in the Look and Feel section, click the appropriate option (see Figure 5-46) (such as **Master page**, **Page layouts and site templates**, or **Site theme**, among other choices). In addition, you can also configure settings in the Galleries section (such as **Master pages and page layouts** and **Themes**).

It should be noted that while branding a Web site is easier than in previous versions of Windows, knowledge of creating Web pages might be required and additional Web publishing tools (such as SharePoint Designer) might be useful.

Figure 5-46

The Look and Feel settings

■ Managing SharePoint Online Site Collections and Websites

↓ **THE BOTTOM LINE**

SharePoint Online service administrators create organization-wide site collections and assign primary site collection administrators to each site collection. The administrator of each site collection has permission to set up sites and features within a site collection. Administrators can add or delete sites or change the settings for any site within a site collection. Creating and deleting site collections is done with SharePoint Online Administration Center.

 CREATE A SITE COLLECTION FOR ONLINE SHAREPOINT

GET READY. To create a site collection for Online SharePoint, perform the following steps:

1. Sign in to the SharePoint Online Administration Center.
2. On the home page, click Manage site collections.
3. On the Site Collections ribbon tab, click New in the Contribute section and select Private Site Collection (see Figure 5-47). The New Site Collection page displays (see Figure 5-48).
4. In the Title text box, type a title for the site collection.
5. In the Website Address section, select a domain name and a URL path from the list, and then type a URL name for the site collection.
6. In the Template Selection section, select a language from the language drop-down and choose a template for your site collection.

CERTIFICATION READY
What component or tool is used to add a domain to Office 365?
3.2.8

CERTIFICATION READY
What component or tool is used to create a site collection and external website for SharePoint Online?
3.2.9

Figure 5-47

Creating a New SharePoint
Online Site Collection

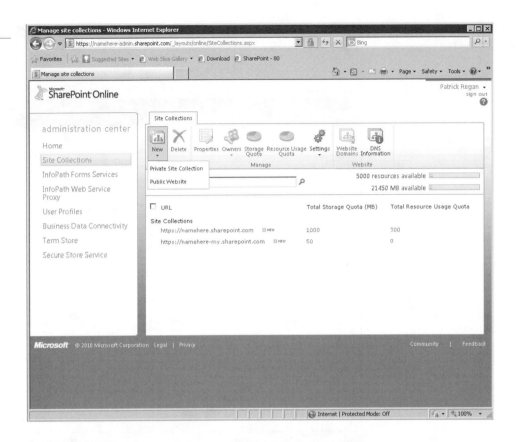

Figure 5-48

The New Site Collection page

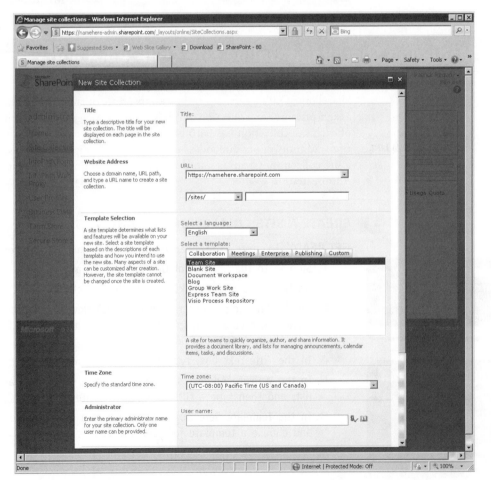

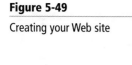 You must be
sure to select the appropriate language; once the language is chosen, it cannot be changed. While you can enable the SharePoint multiple language interface on your sites, the primary language for the site collection remains the same.

7. In the Time Zone section, select the standard time zone appropriate for the location of the site collection.

8. In the Administrator section, in the User name box, type the user name of your site collection administrator. Unlike using SharePoint on a local server, you can specify only one primary administrator.

9. In the Storage Quota section, in the Storage limit text box, type the number of MB to allocate to this site collection. The minimum is 50 megabytes (MB).

10. In the Resource Usage Quota section, in the Resource Usage limit text box, type the amount to allocate to the site collection.

11. Click OK. The new site collection will appear in the URL list.

The site collection administrator can now create and manage sites.

As a SharePoint Online Administrator, you can create a public-facing Web site that can be accessed by users outside your organization. When you set up the site, you are asked to provide a domain name (the URL that people will use to access your site). You can choose to use the default name (provided by Microsoft) or a custom name that your company owns.

 CREATE A PUBLIC WEBSITE WITH THE DEFAULT DOMAIN

GET READY. To create a public-facing Web site using the default domain specified in the Office 365 Administration Center, perform the following steps:

1. Sign in to the SharePoint Online Administration Center.

2. On the home page, click Manage site collections.

3. On the Site Collections tab, under Contribute, click New, and then click Public Website. The Create Your Web site page displays (see Figure 5-49).

Figure 5-49

Creating your Web site

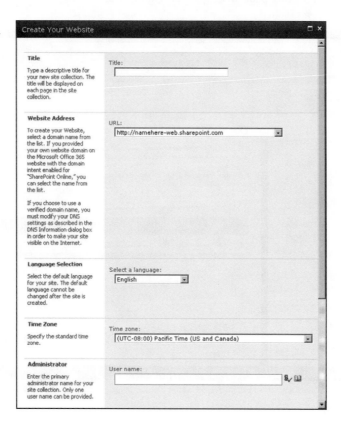

4. In the Title box, type the title that will appear at the top of each page on the website.

5. In the URL option, click the drop-down arrow and choose the default address provided to your organization.

6. In the Select a language option, click the drop-down arrow and select the primary language for the website. The language for the site cannot be changed after it is set.

7. In the Time zone option, click the drop-down arrow and select the appropriate time zone.

8. In the User name box, type the name of the person who will serve as the primary administrator for the Website. There can be only one administrator.

9. Type a number in the Storage Limit box. The minimum is 50 MB.

10. Type an optional number in the Resource Usage limit box.

11. Click OK.

A custom domain is a domain name that you purchase, and it can be used only by your organization. Before you can create a public Web site with a custom domain name in SharePoint Online, the custom domain name must be registered by the Global Administrator on the Office 365 Administration page. In addition, you will need to update your DNS settings with your domain registrar including A records and CNAME records,

 ADD A DOMAIN NAME

GET READY. To add a domain name to Office 365, perform the following steps:

1. On the Admin page, in the left pane, under Management, click Domains. The Domains page displays (see Figure 5-50).

Figure 5-50

The Domains page

2. Click Add a domain. The Specify Domain page displays (see Figure 5-51).

Figure 5-51

The Specify Domain page

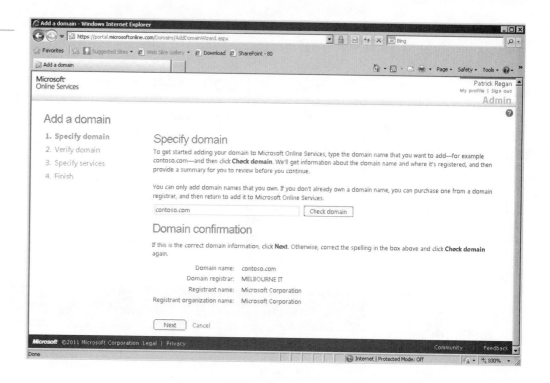

3. Type the name of the domain and click Check domain.

4. When it displays information about the domain, click Next.

5. You will then be shown instructions based on your domain registrar on how to verify the domain name.

Deleting a SharePoint Online site collection is very similar to deleting a site collection on a SharePoint server installed on a local server. Of course, before you delete a site collection, you should consider backing up the site collection. If you accidentally delete a site collection, it can be restored within seven days by contacting Microsoft.

 DELETE A SITE COLLECTION FOR ONLINE SHAREPOINT

GET READY. To delete a site collection for Online SharePoint, perform the following steps:

1. Sign in to the SharePoint Online Administration Center.

2. On the home page, click Manage site collections.

3. Select the check box next to one or more site collections that you want to delete. On the Site Collections tab, click Delete (see Figure 5-52).

4. When prompted to confirm to delete the Site Collection, click Delete.

Figure 5-52

Deleting a Site Collection

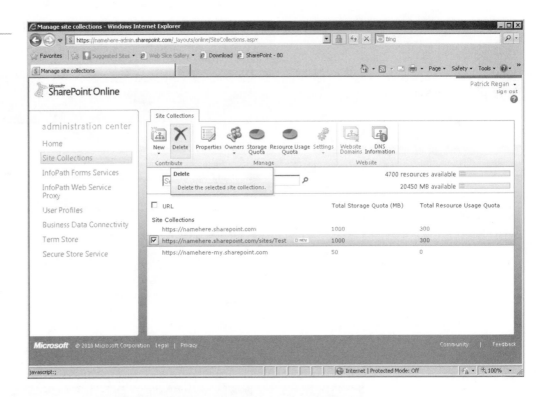

SKILL SUMMARY

IN THIS LESSON YOU LEARNED:

- The process of assigning an IP address, port number, and host header is referred to as binding the Web site.

- An application pool is one or more groupings of URLs or Web sites that are routed to one or more worker processes.

- Authentication is the act of confirming the identity of a user and is an essential part used in authorization. In SharePoint Server 2010, there are two types of authentication: Classic-mode authentication and Claims-based authentication.

- NTLM (short for NT LAN Manager) is a suite of Microsoft security protocols that provides authentication, integrity, and confidentiality to users and is the default protocol used by SharePoint 2010.

- Kerberos protocol is a secure protocol that supports ticketing authentication, however it is more complicated than NTLM, which requires additional configuration (such as requiring a service principal name (SPN) for the domain account that SharePoint is using).

- To provide some separation and control, you can use a different URL or authentication method by extending an existing Web application into a new zone, which are related to the zones available in Internet Explorer that a user is using to access the site.

- Alternate Access Mappings (AAM) are available to help SharePoint determine how to map a request that comes into a Web application to the correct URL, and then serve the correct URL back to the client that requested the content.

- A Site collection is a grouping of sites. Every site collection has a single root site, which the other sites are built under. All sites within the site collection have the same site owners and share the same administrative settings.

- To create a new site collection within a Web application, there must be a managed path at which to create the site collection. A managed path is not directly mapped to content within the Web application. Instead, it is used by SharePoint as a namespace (path) node where site collections can be created.

- Security of a system requires authentication, authorization, and auditing. Auditing is the measurable technical assessment of SharePoint to verify that users are only accessing what they need to and not accessing information that they should not be accessing.

- Information management policies allow you to control who can access organization information stored within SharePoint, what they can do with it, and how long they can retain it. You can also enable auditing of opening or downloading documents, editing items, or deleting items.

- A feature is a collection of elements that are grouped together and are often composed of logically related elements including Web parts, workflows, content type definitions, and event receivers.

- Caching uses a special high-speed storage mechanism that helps improve the speed at which Web pages load in the browser.

- Multi-tenancy is the ability to partition data of shared services to meet the needs of multiple tenants, such as different subsidiaries or different customers, without having separate hardware platforms or running multiple instances of the service.

- Branding is used to distinguish your product, service, or organization with a specific identity. When you brand your SharePoint site, you will usually use logos, colors, fonts, and other imagery. It also achieves a particular look and feel for your SharePoint sites.

- SharePoint Online service administrators create organization-wide site collections and assign primary site collection administrators to each site collection.

■ Knowledge Assessment

Fill in the Blank

Complete the following sentences by writing the correct word or words in the blanks provided.

1. _____ is the process of assigning an IP address, port number, and host header to a Web site.

2. The default ports for HTTP and HTTPS are TCP port _____ and port _____, respectively.

3. _____ a Web application into a new zone allows you to define a separate Web site so that it can serve the same content as another SharePoint Web application but with a unique URL or authentication.

4. _____ is used by SharePoint to determine how to map a request that comes into a Web application to the correct URL, and then serve the correct URL back to the client that requested the content.

5. A _____ is a grouping of sites that have a single root site and have the same site owners and share the same administrative settings.

6. _____ is the measurable technical assessment of SharePoint to verify that users are only accessing what they need to, and not information that they should not be accessing.

7. _____ allow you to control who can access organization information stored within SharePoint.

8. A _____ is a collection of elements that are grouped together, including Web parts, workflows, content type definitions, and event receivers.

9. _____ is the ability to partition data of shared services to meet the needs of multiple customers or subsidiaries within a company while keeping them isolated from each other.

10. _____ define SharePoint site color schemes.

Multiple Choice

Circle the letter that corresponds to the best answer.

1. Which authentication mode is the same as that which was used in SharePoint 2007 and supports Anonymous, Basic, NTLM, and Negotiate methods of authentication?
   a. Kerberos
   b. FBA
   c. Claims-based authentication
   d. Classic-mode authentication

2. Which method of authentication has the user name and password transmitted in clear text?
   a. Anonymous
   b. Basic
   c. Digest
   d. Certificates

3. Which option in Central Administration is used to create or delete a Web site?
   a. Application Management
   b. System Settings
   c. Security
   d. Upgrade and Migration

4. Which of the following permissions can be assigned as a permissions policy? (Choose all that apply.)
   a. Full Control
   b. Full Read
   c. Deny Read
   d. Deny All

5. To create a new site collection, it must be assigned to a _____.
   a. linked path
   b. managed path
   c. defined URL
   d. closed URL

6. What reduces the amount of traffic between the Web server and the SQL database by storing objects (such as lists, libraries, site settings, and page layouts) in the memory of the front-end Web server computer?
   a. object cache
   b. page output cache
   c. Site Collection Cache Profiles
   d. BLOB cache

7. Which cache stores the rendered output of a page and stores different versions of the cached page, based on the permissions of the users who are requesting the page?
   a. object cache
   b. page output cache
   c. Site Collection Cache Profiles
   d. BLOB cache

8. Which of the following are default Site Collection Cache Profiles?
   a. Disabled
   b. Public Internet
   c. Extranet
   d. Private Internet

9. What defines the theme and general page template layout that define the header, footer, and top and left navigation?
   a. master pages
   b. page layout
   c. theme
   d. page correction

10. Which of the following can an information management policy be applied to? (Choose all that apply.)
    a. Multiple content types
    b. Site content type
    c. Wikis
    d. list or library

True / False

Circle T if the statement is true or F if the statement is false.

T | F 1. Since NTLM is a mature protocol developed by Microsoft, NTLM is more secure than Kerberos when used with Microsoft products.

T | F 2. Since Basic authentication is considered insecure, you should use SSL to encrypt data transmissions.

T | F 3. If you have a SharePoint site that is available internally and externally, when SharePoint appears to send back incorrect links, it is most likely a problem is with managed paths.

T | F 4. When you want to create multiple sites under a particular URL, you should use wildcard managed paths.

T | F 5. If you want to support multi-tenancy, you need only to create separate collections.

■ Case Scenarios

Scenario 5-1: Keeping a Site Collection Secure

Your manager is concerned with the security of the SharePoint collections. He wants to ensure that each collection has only the users that need access to each collection and that no one has additional permissions that they do not need. He also wants to make sure that the documents within the Sales sites are kept secure, and that they are not blindly copied off the Web site to a USB drive. What can you use to help secure the collection?

Scenario 5-2: Supporting Multiple Clients

You and your team have done wonders with your SharePoint server. Your entire department has become more productive and SharePoint has become a valuable repository and business tool. Now your manager wants you to support other departments while keeping each department isolated so that they cannot access each other's SharePoint site. What do you need to enable and what are the basic steps to accomplish this?

Deploying and Managing SharePoint Features and Solution Packages

OBJECTIVE DOMAIN MATRIX

TECHNOLOGY SKILL	OBJECTIVE DOMAIN	OBJECTIVE DOMAIN NUMBER
Using SharePoint 2010 Features	Managing Site Collection Features	3.2.2
Managing SharePoint Solutions	Deploying and Managing SharePoint Solutions	3.3
	Deploying and Managing SharePoint Solution Packages	3.3.1
Deploying and Managing Sandbox Solutions	Managing Sandbox Solutions	3.3.2
	Managing User Solutions	3.3.3
	Configuring Site Collection Quotas and Locks	3.2.7

KEY TERMS

assembly

Developer Dashboard

farm solution

global assembly cache (GAC)

sandbox

sandbox solution

solution

solution affinity

user solution

You have been working with your SharePoint development team, which has created a couple of solutions that management wants to implement. These solutions will provide some added functionality and customizations to SharePoint. Since they have been newly created, you determine that these solutions must be thoroughly tested so that they do not negatively affect your SharePoint environment. Therefore, you need to determine the best way to test and deploy these solutions.

■ Using SharePoint 2010 Features

THE BOTTOM LINE

As discussed in Lesson 5, a feature is a container of various elements (including Web Parts, workflows, content type definitions, and event receivers) that add functionality or apply customizations to a site, collection, or Web site. It is composed of a set of XML files that are deployed to front-end Web servers and application servers. You can deploy a feature as part of a solution package, and you can individually activate or deactivate a feature in SharePoint Server sites. Features are defined in SharePoint based on scope, such as the farm, Web application, site collection and site level.

Features are stored on the front-end Web server in the %*ProgramFiles*%\Common Files\ Microsoft Shared\Web server extensions\14\TEMPLATE\FEATURES directory. Each feature has its own directory (see Figure 6-1), which will contain a minimum of a feature.xml file. The feature.xml file defines the base properties of the feature and the elements (Web Parts, workflows, menus, content type, lists, and so on) bound to it.

Figure 6-1

The Features folder

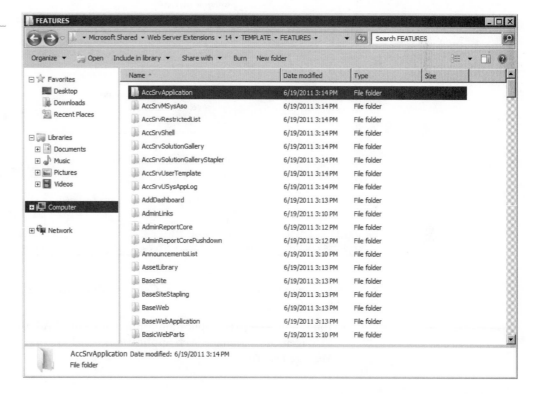

To give you control over how those features are applied, you can apply features based on scope (farm, Web application, site collection, and site level). To manage features, perform one of the following based on the desired scope:

- As shown in Lesson 5, you can manage Site Collection features at **Site Actions** > **Site Settings** > **Site collection features**.
- To manage site features, access the Site Actions menu and then choose **Site Settings** > **Manage site features**. (See Figure 6-2.)

Figure 6-2

Site features

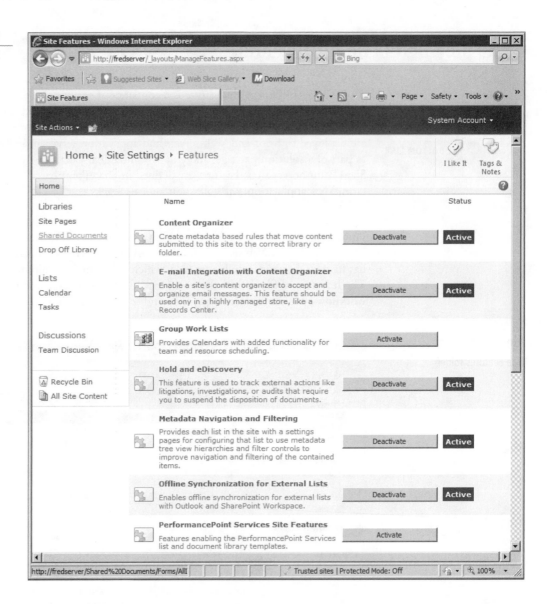

- You can manage farm features at **Central Administration** > **System Settings** > **Manage farm features**.
- You can manage Web application features at **Central Administration**> **Application Management** > **Manage Web applications**. Click the Web application and then click **Manage Features**.

Managing Site Collection Features

SharePoint allows you to manage features through Central Administration, Site Settings, PowerShell, or the stsadm command.

CERTIFICATION READY
What scopes can you
enable a feature for?
3.2.2

Each feature management page allows you to activate and deactivate features for the given scope, and also shows you the status of each feature (for instance, if it is active). You can use PowerShell and the stsadm command to view information, install/uninstall features, and activate/deactivate features. PowerShell cmdlets for feature include:

- Get-SPFeature
- Enable-SPFeature

- Disable-SPFeature
- Install-SPFeature
- Uninstall-Feature

INSTALL A FEATURE USING WINDOWS POWERSHELL

GET READY. To install a feature using Windows PowerShell, perform the following steps:

1. On the Start menu, click All Programs, click Microsoft SharePoint 2010 Products, and then click SharePoint 2010 Management Shell.

2. At the Windows PowerShell command prompt, type the following command:
   ```
   Install-SPFeature -path <Path>
   [-force]
   ```

   `<Path>` is a valid file path, which is a literal path to the 14\Template\Features folder name. The feature.xml file name is implied and does not need to be provided.

ACTIVATE A FEATURE USING WINDOWS POWERSHELL

GET READY. To install a feature by using Windows PowerShell, perform the following steps:

1. On the Start menu, click All Programs, click Microsoft SharePoint 2010 Products, and then click SharePoint 2010 Management Shell.

2. At the Windows PowerShell command prompt, type the following command:
   ```
   Enable-SPFeature -Identity <FeatureID> [-url] <URLname> [-force]
   ```
   <FeatureID> is the name of the feature folder located in the 14\Template\ Features folder and *<URLname>* is the feature parent URL of the Web application, site collection, or Web site for which the feature is being activated.

To uninstall a feature so that its definition is no longer available within a server farm, you first must deactivate the feature by using the Windows PowerShellDisable-SPFeature cmdlet, unless the feature is scoped for Web applications or farms. After you deactivate the feature, you can use the Uninstall-SPFeature cmdlet to uninstall it.

To prevent users from activating or deactivating a feature or to reduce the clutter associated with many features, a feature can be hidden. To hide a feature, update the Hidden attribute of the feature element to "TRUE" as shown here:

```
<Feature Id="A32144D-22DB-2311-BBC1-3E187DE50084" Title="Sample
Feature" Hidden="TRUE" .../>
```

For Features that are marked as hidden, your only option for managing them is the command line, using either PowerShell cmdlets or the stsadm command.

Managing Feature Dependency

> Some services in Windows Servers depend on other services. That means some services must be started before other services can be started. In SharePoint, some features might depend on other features.

A feature activation dependency specifies a requirement in the relationship between two features. You can express activation dependencies either for features of the same scope or for features at a higher scope. In addition, activation dependencies follow these rules:

- If a feature is dependent on another feature at the same scope, and the second feature is not activated when the first one is activated, Microsoft SharePoint activates the second feature.

- In turn, SharePoint will also deactivate a same-scope dependent hidden feature when the last visible feature that has an activation dependency on that hidden feature is deactivated.

If you try to activate features that are dependent on other features that have not been started, you might get a message similar to:

The feature being activated is a Site scoped feature, which has a dependency on a Site Collection scoped feature, which has not been activated. Please activate the following feature before trying again: SharePoint Server Publishing Infrastructure f6924d36-2fa8-4f0b-b16d-06b7250180fa

The SharePoint Server Publishing Infrastructure feature provides centralized libraries, content types, master pages, and page layouts, and enables page scheduling and other publishing functionality for a site collection. The SharePoint Server Publishing Infrastructure feature creates a Web page library as well as supporting libraries to create and publish pages based on page layouts.

To use the Web content management features, you need to activate the Publishing feature for a site by first enabling the Publishing Infrastructure for the top-level site in your site collection, and then enabling the Publishing feature for a subsite.

 ENABLE PUBLISHING SERVICES

GET READY. To deploy a solution, perform the following steps:

1. Open your SharePoint site and select Site Actions > Site Settings.
2. To enable publishing at the site level, in the Site Actions section, click Manage site features, and then next to SharePoint Server Publishing, click Activate.
3. To enable publishing at the site collection level, you must be at the root of your site. If you are not at the root of your site, under Site Collection Administration, click Go to top level site settings.
4. In the Site Collection Administration section, click Site collection features and then, next to SharePoint Server Publishing Infrastructure, click Activate.

■ Managing SharePoint Solutions

The Bottom Line

While a SharePoint feature is a defined functionality that administrators can enable or disable in a single operation, a SharePoint *solution* package is a set of functionality that administrators install in a single operation. While features will have to be installed on each front-end SharePoint server, solutions can be applied in a single operation to the entire farm, making customizations done with solutions easier than customizations done with features.

CERTIFICATION READY
How do solutions differ from features?
3.3

Solutions provide the following advantages:

- A unified infrastructure for deploying solutions makes it easier for developers to change site functionality.
- Solutions enable administrators to easily install files on all front-end Web servers in a server farm instead of separately installing to each server on the farm.
- Resource files and other localization components can be included in a solution package.

You can use solution packages to deploy new solutions and upgrade existing solutions across the farm. You can package all your SharePoint Server entities as one file, add the file to the

solution store, and deploy it to the front-end Web servers in the farm. Use solution packages to synchronize a front-end Web server so that its state is consistent with the state of other Web servers in the farm.

A solution package is a distribution package consisting of a single file with a .wsp filename extension used to deploy custom features, site definitions, templates, layout pages, Web Parts, cascading style sheets, and assemblies. While the file has the .wsp filename extension, in reality, it is a .cab file. Developers can create .wsp files by using the solution package designer tool in Visual Studio 2010 or other tools (such as MAKECAB) when they are ready to distribute their custom projects.

There are two types of solutions:

- Farm solutions
- Sandbox solutions

A ***farm solution*** is stored in the farm's solution store while a sandbox solution is deployed to the solution store of a site collection. A farm solution is also known as a full trust solution because it has full trust access to all resources and functionality in SharePoint; a sandbox solution is restricted.

Deploying and Managing SharePoint Solution Packages

> SharePoint Foundation has its own system for installing solutions on a SharePoint Foundation farm. Unlike other Windows applications and platforms, you do not use MSI file or executable files. To use a farm solution, you must first install the solution and then deploy it.

CERTIFICATION READY
What are the steps needed to deploy a SharePoint Solution?
3.3.1

To install a farm solution, you must be a farm administrator. Generally, the farm solution runs with full trust, although it is possible to deploy an assembly in a farm solution with a custom CAS policy that gives it less than full trust.

There are three major steps to installing a farm solution:

1. **Adding**: You add the solution package to the farm's solution store (which is stored in the farm's configuration database) with the SharePoint Management Shell.
2. **Deploying**: When you deploy the solution package, you unpack the package and copy the solution elements to the appropriate places.
3. **Feature Activating**: If the solution contains features, the features have to be activated. Features can contain content types, controls, custom actions, custom fields, files, workflows, list instances, list templates, event receivers, and document converters—however, some of these cannot be included in certain scopes.

Applying an add or update solution can only be done from the command prompt. To add a solution use the following command in PowerShell:

```
Add-SPSolution -LiteralPath <SolutionPath>
```

For example, to add a solution stored in the d:\customsolution.wsp file, execute the following command:

```
Add-SPSolution -LiteralPath "d:\customsolution.wsp"
```

If you have spaces in your path, it is best to add the quotes.

Or you can use the `stsadm` command:

```
stsadm -o addsolution -filename "d:\customsolution.wsp"
```

Once you have added the solution to the farm, you then need to deploy the solution using either Central Administration or using the PowerShell `Install-SPSolution` cmdlet.

When developers create a solution, they will often use assemblies. Assemblies are the building blocks of the .NET framework that allow for deployment, version control, reuse, activation scoping, and security permissions. An *assembly* is a collection of types and resources that are built to work together and form a logical unit of functionality. To the runtime, a type does not exist outside the context of an assembly.

To support a modular approach that allows developers to share assemblies across multiple applications, assemblies can be placed in the *global assembly cache (GAC)*, which is typically saved in the C:\Windows Assembly folder.

If you intend to share an assembly among several applications, you can install it into the global assembly cache. Each computer where the common language runtime is installed has this machine-wide code cache. The global assembly cache stores assemblies specifically designated to be shared by several applications on the computer.

When you deploy a solution, you install all of the necessary features, objects, and necessary files for the solution to function. Once a solution package has been added, you can view and deploy to your SharePoint applications using Central Administration or using PowerShell.

 DEPLOY A FARM SOLUTION

GET READY. To deploy a farm solution, perform the following steps:

1. Open Central Administration.
2. On the Central Administration page, click System Settings.
3. In the Farm Management section, click Manage farm solutions. The Solution Management page is displayed (see Figure 6-3).

Figure 6-3

The Solution Management page

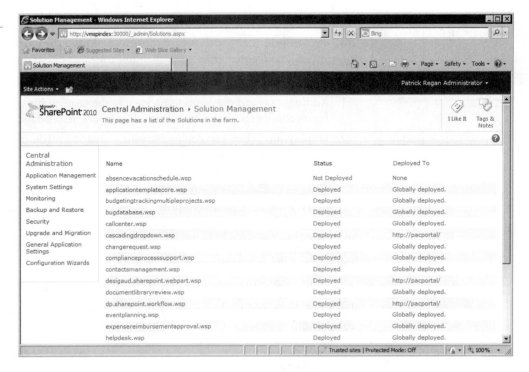

4. Click the solution that you want to deploy. The Solution Properties page is displayed (see Figure 6-4).

Figure 6-4

The Solution Properties page

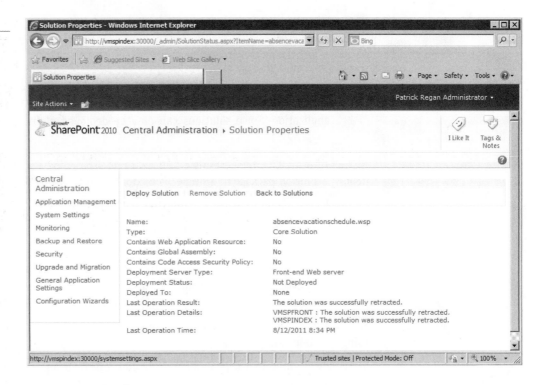

5. Click Deploy Solution. The Deploy Solution page is displayed (see Figure 6-5).

Figure 6-5

The Deploy Solution page

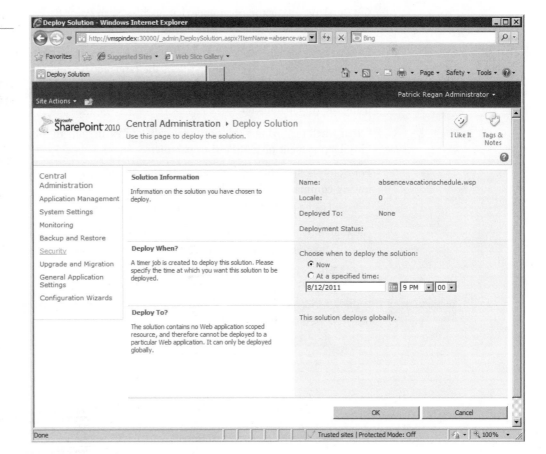

6. On the Deploy Solution page, in the Deploy When? section, in the Choose when to deploy the solution options, select either Now or At a specified time.

TAKE NOTE* If SharePoint performance is suffering, it is recommended to select a time when the load on the destination server is low.

7. In the Deploy To? section, click either All Web applications or select a specific Web application. Some solutions can only be deployed globally.
8. Click OK.

Instead of using Central Administration, you can also deploy a solution using PowerShell. To deploy a solution package to a single Web application by using Windows PowerShell:

```
Install-SPSolution -Identity <SolutionName> -WebApplication
<URLname>
```

Where:

<SolutionName> is the name of the solution.

<URLname> is the URL of the Web application to which you want to deploy the imported solution.

By default, the solution is immediately deployed. You can also schedule the deployment by using the time parameter.

To deploy a solution package to all Web applications by using Windows PowerShell:

```
Install-SPSolution -Identity <SolutionName> -AllWebApplications
-time <TimeToDeploy> -GACDeployment -CASPolicies
```

GACDeployment is the parameter that enables SharePoint Server 2010 to deploy the assemblies in the global assembly cache.

CASPolicies enables the creation of a custom code access security (CAS) policy file and the activation of it in the Web.config file of the targeted site collection.

The solution is immediately deployed by default. You can also schedule the deployment by using the time parameter.

Often when deploying a solution, you will get instructions to follow if you need to include the GACDeployment or CASPolicies parameter.

For example, to deploy customsolution to all Web applications, you would execute the following command in PowerShell:

```
Install-SPSolution -identity customsolution
```

Alternatively, you can deploy the solution using the stsadm command:

```
stsadm -o deploysolution -name customsolution
```

TAKE NOTE* If the solution is installing a feature, you still might need to enable the feature (as previously covered in this lesson).

Upgrading SharePoint Solution Packages

Sometimes, solutions will have to be upgraded to fix a bug or expand functionality. Assuming that the developer used the same solution ID as the original version, you can add and deploy the solution package. SharePoint will then automatically upgrade the solution instead of installing a new solution.

The upgrade solution syntax is similar to the previous commands, where you specify an `Identity` and a `LiteralPath` with the Update-SPSolution command. The identity is the name of the package on the server to upgrade and the `LiteralPath` is the full path to the new solution package on the file system.

```
Upgrade-SPSolution -Identity customsolution
-LiteralPath "d:\customsolution.wsp"-GACDeployment
```

Or you can use the `stsadm` command:

```
stsadm -o upgradesolution -name customsolution.wsp -filename cus-
tomsolution.wsp -immediate -allowCasPolicies
```

Removing a Solution

Since it took two steps to install and enable a solution, to remove a solution, you need only to first retract the solution and then remove it from the SharePoint solution store.

There are three major steps in uninstalling a farm solution:

1. **Feature deactivating**: If a farm solution includes one or more features, you should deactivate those features by using the Features Gallery where the feature was activated. Deactivation reverses the deployment of assemblies in the features.
2. **Retracting**: The deployment of the farm solution's components is reversed using Central Administration or the SharePoint Management Shell.
3. **Removing**: Delete the solution package from the solution store using the Central Administration, SharePoint Management Shell, or the object model.

To retract and remove a solution using PowerShell, run the following commands:

```
Uninstall-SPSolution -Identity customsolution
Remove-SPSolution -Identity customsolution
```

To uninstall and remove a solution package by using `stsadm`, run the following commands:

```
stsadm -o retractsolution -name costumsolution
stsadm -o deletesolution -name costumsolution
```

If you deactivate and remove a solution, and the Web Part associated with the solution still appears on the list of Web Parts that users can add to their pages, you must delete the Web Part descriptor from the Web Part Gallery.

 DELETE A WEB PART DESCRIPTOR

GET READY. To delete a Web Part descriptor, perform the following steps:

1. From root page in the site collection, click Site Actions, and then select Site Settings.

2. In the Galleries section, click Web parts.

3. Click the check box next to the Web Part you want to remove and click the Delete Document button in the Ribbon (see Figure 6-6).

Figure 6-6

Deleting a Web Part descriptor

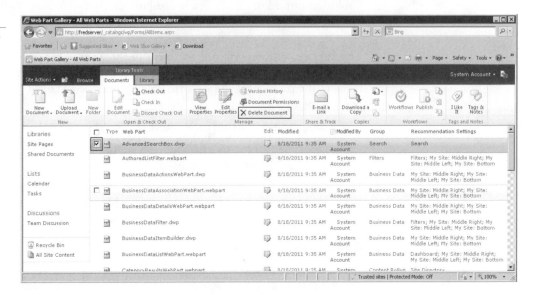

■ Deploying and Managing Sandbox Solutions

THE BOTTOM LINE

In computer security, a ***sandbox*** is a security mechanism for separating running programs that are used to isolate the execution of untested code, or untrusted programs from unverified third-parties, suppliers, and untrusted users. Starting with SharePoint 2010, SharePoint provides a sandbox that will separate code from other processes. As a result, a sandbox improves the security, helps control resources, and prevents performance problems.

CERTIFICATION READY
What are the limits of sandbox solutions?
3.3.2

As mentioned before, farm solutions have full trust access to all resources and functionality in SharePoint. Any time you add code or custom solutions to SharePoint, there is always a level of risk that may affect the stability of the farm. SharePoint 2010 introduced ***sandbox solutions*** (sometimes called ***user solutions***) that allow administrators to deploy thoroughly untested solutions while monitoring and restricting the sandbox solution. The sandboxed solution framework protects SharePoint farms by running solutions in a separate process that is restricted by .Net Code Access Security policy.

Sandboxed solutions are stored in the Solution Gallery in a site collection, which you can access from the Site Settings page. SharePoint solutions must contain a configuration file named manifest.xml, and may contain additional configuration files and assemblies. If the

solution will run in a sandbox, the assembly and configuration files are limited in what they can do. Sandbox solutions cannot do the following:

- They cannot connect to resources that are not located on the local farm
- They cannot access resources in a different site collection
- They cannot access a database
- They cannot change the threading model
- They cannot call unmanaged code
- They cannot write to disk

While farm solutions are deployed by farm administrators, if the sandbox solution contains an assembly, the solutions must be deployed by site collection administrators. If the solution does not contain an assembly, a user who has the Full Control permission level at the root of the site collection can deploy it.

Enabling a Sandbox

Installing a sandbox is similar to installing a solution. However, before you install a sandbox solution, you must first enable the sandbox.

To deploy a sandbox solution, you must first perform the following steps one time only:

1. Enable sandboxed solutions and start the sandboxed solutions service on each server that will run sandboxed solutions.
2. Determine the load-balancing scheme to use, which will be applied to all sandboxed solutions in all site collections on the farm.
3. Set the resource quotas that the combination of all sandboxed solutions in a site collection cannot exceed.

After the sandbox environment is configured, you will then need to upload and activate each sandbox solution.

If you have multiple front-end servers and you want a solution to have a sandbox environment on all servers, you will need to enable the sandbox service on all front-end servers. However, if you have multiple front-end servers and you want SharePoint user solutions to execute only on the designed servers, you need to enable the Microsoft SharePoint Foundation Sandbox Code Service on the server that you want to use and make sure that the Sandbox Code Service is stopped or not enabled on the other front-end servers.

 ENABLE SANDBOX SOLUTIONS AND START THE SANDBOX SOLUTIONS SERVICES

GET READY. To deploy a solution, perform the following steps on each SharePoint server that you want to enable sandboxed solutions:

1. Open Central Administration.
2. In the System Settings section, click Manage services on server. The Services on Server page is displayed (see Figure 6-7).

Figure 6-7

The Services on Server page

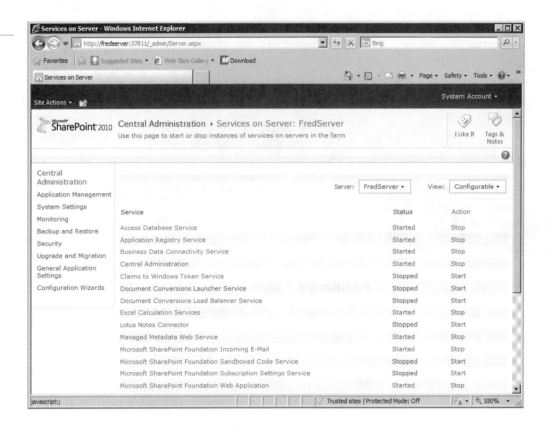

3. If necessary, in the Server box, select the server for which you want to enable sandboxed solutions.

4. In the Action column for the Microsoft SharePoint Foundation Sandboxed Code Service, click Start.

Or you can execute the following command to start the Microsoft SharePoint Foundation Sandboxed Code Service:

```
Start-Service -Name SPUserCodeV4
```

There are two load-balancing schemes available which determine which server to run the sandboxed solution on:

- **Local**: The solution runs on the same server that is servicing the request.
- **Remote**: The server that the solution runs on is selected based on the server that most recently ran the solution (this is known as *solution affinity*).

By default, SharePoint Foundation uses remote load balancing. You can increase isolation by using remote load balancing and by running the sandboxed solution service only on specific servers, which in turn will help protect the main part of your SharePoint 2010 site from code that might consume too many resources.

CONFIGURE LOAD BALANCING

GET READY. To change the load-balancing scheme used in the farm for a sandbox solution, perform the following steps on each SharePoint server that you want to enable sandboxed solutions:

1. Open Central Administration.

2. Click System Settings. The System Settings page is displayed (see Figure 6-8).

3. In the Farm Management section, click Manage user solutions. The Sandboxed Solution Management page is displayed (see Figure 6-9).

Figure 6-8

The System Settings page

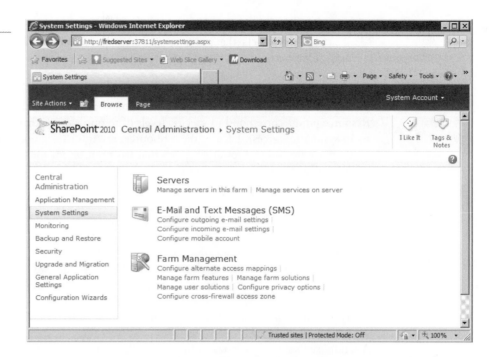

Figure 6-9

The Sandboxed Solution
Management page

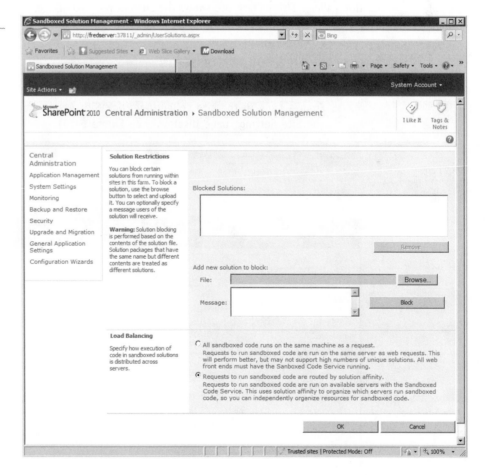

4. In the Load Balancing section, select one of the following options:

- **All sandboxed code runs on the same machine as a request.** This load-balancing scheme runs sandboxed code on the same server that handles the rest of the request.

- Requests to run sandboxed code are routed by solution affinity. This load-balancing scheme selects the server on which to run sandboxed code based on solution affinity.

   5. Click OK.

To set resource quotas that a sandboxed solution consumes, you define resource points. Resource points correspond to specific levels of resource usage that you want to monitor (up to 15 system resources). Each of these resources accumulates points used by a sandbox solution, which are counted toward a quota that has been set for the entire site collection. If the number of accrued resource points exceeds the quote set for the site collection, the sandboxed solution in the site collection is stopped.

Installing a Sandbox Solution

Similar to installing a farm solution, to install a sandbox solution, you must first upload the solution and then activate the solution. When you upload the sandbox solution, you are adding the solution to the solution gallery of a site collection (similar to the farm solution). Then when you activate the solution, the solution files are deployed, event receivers are registered, and the solution validation is performed.

A sandboxed solution is installed by a site collection administrator to the site collection's solution gallery. This gallery also shows the current resource usage, average resource usage over the past two weeks, and the status of each sandboxed solution.

 INSTALL A SANDBOX SOLUTION

GET READY. To install a Sandbox solution, perform the following steps:

   1. From a page in the site collection, click Site Actions, and then select Site Settings. The Site Settings page displays (see Figure 6-10).

Figure 6-10

The Site Settings page

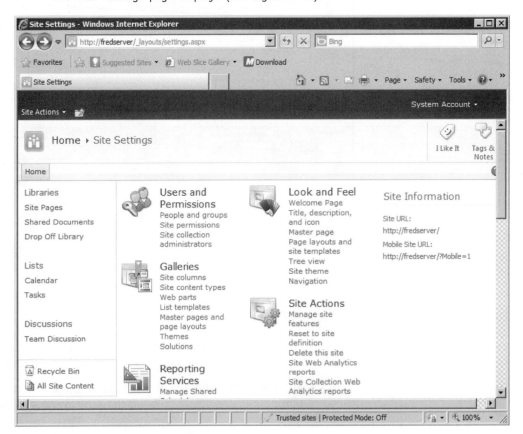

2. In the Galleries section, click Solutions. The Solutions tab displays (see Figure 6-11).

Figure 6-11

The Solutions tab

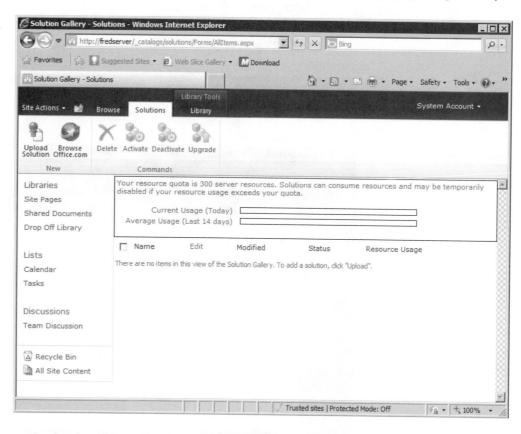

3. On the Ribbon, click Upload Solution. The Upload Document dialog displays (see Figure 6-12).

Figure 6-12

The Upload Document dialog

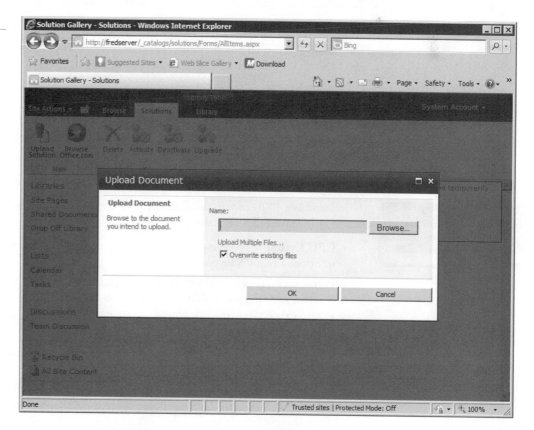

4. In the Upload Document dialog box, click Browse, and then browse to the sandboxed solution package (.wsp file).

5. Click Open.

6. On the Ribbon, click Activate to activate the solution (see Figure 6-13).

Figure 6-13

The Activate Solution dialog

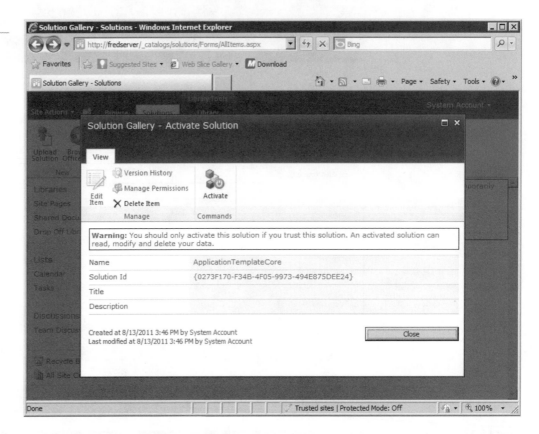

If the sandboxed solution package contains a feature that is scoped to the site collection level, the feature is activated automatically. Features that are scoped to the Web site level must be activated on the Manage site features page.

Configuring Site Collection Quotas and Locks

A sandbox can restrict the server resources that a solution can consume each day based on a point system that reflects the processor time, memory usage, database queries, and other resources that a solution uses.

CERTIFICATION READY?
How do quotas relate to sandbox solutions?
3.2.7

SharePoint uses 14 metrics to calculate points to determine the resources consumed by a solution. These include the following values:

- **CPU Cycles:** When the processor uses a predefined number of cycles on the sandboxed solution, a point is logged.

- **Percentage Processor Time**: When the sandboxed solution uses more than a predefined percentage of the processing time, a point is logged.

- **Critical Exception Count**: When a predefined number of exceptions occur in a sandboxed solution, a point is logged.

- **Thread Count**: When the solution exceeds a predefined number of threads in the SPUCWorkerProcess process, a point is logged.

- **SharePoint Database Queries**: When a solution initiates more than a predefined number of queries to the SharePoint content database, a point is logged.

To view the current consumption (current usage and average usage of the last 14 days) of a sandbox solution, open the site settings and, in the **Galleries** section, click **Solutions**. By default, the sandbox solutions resource quota is 300 points per day with warning emails sent after 100 points. The administrator can influence the algorithm by setting these numbers in PowerShell.

> **➕ MORE INFORMATION**
>
> For more information on configuring the resource points for sandboxed solutions, visit http://technet.microsoft.com/en-us/library/hh230316.aspx

 SET QUOTAS USED BY SOLUTIONS

GET READY. To set the quotas used for a site collection, perform the following steps:

1. Open Central Administration.
2. Click Application Management, and then click Configure quotas and locks. The Quotas and Locks page displays (see Figure 6-14).
3. Select the Site Collection you wish to administer.
4. In the Site Quota Information section, you can set the Limit maximum usage per day to settings based on a point total that you determine.

Figure 6-14

The Quotas and Locks page

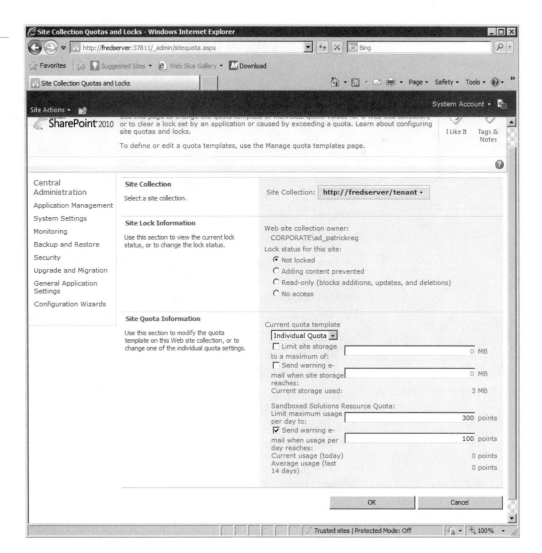

5. To specify a warning level, select the Send warning e-mail when usage per day reaches option and specify the number of points. Administrators receive e-mail alerts when a solution exceeds this limit.

If a solution consumes too many resources or poses a security issue, you can block the sandboxed solution. To block a solution, open Central Administration and access Manage user solutions.

 BLOCK A SOLUTION

GET READY. To block a user solution, perform the following steps on each SharePoint server that you want to enable sandboxed solutions.

1. Open Central Administration.
2. Click System Settings.
3. In the Farm Management section, click Manage user solutions.
4. In the Solution Restrictions section, in the File box, either type the full path of the file that contains the solution to block or click the Browse button to browse for the file to block.
5. If necessary, type a message in the Message box; this message is displayed when a user tries to use the solution.
6. Click Block and then click OK.

Using the Developer Dashboard

A new feature introduced with SharePoint 2010 is the ***Developer Dashboard***, which provides diagnostic information that can help a developer or system administrator troubleshoot problems with page components that would be difficult to isolate.

The Developer Dashboard is designed to provide detailed information about the execution of all the components on a SharePoint page. While it is mostly used by developers to trouble-shoot and optimize the speed of their code, administrators may also find the information helpful. In addition, as a SharePoint administrator, you might be asked to install or enable the Developer Dashboard.

The Developer Dashboard displays the following kinds of information:

- **Execution time**: This is the time in milliseconds that each component on the page took to complete. Slow components take many milliseconds and delay the page load.
- **Call stack**: This is the hierarchy of objects that were involved in page rendering.
- **Database query time**: This is the time in milliseconds that any request to the content database took.
- **Web Part execution time**: This is the time, in milliseconds, that each Web Part took to render its user interface.

The easiest way to enable the developer dashboard is to use stsadm. When you turn on the Developer Dashboard, it will always show up at the bottom of the Web page (see Figure 6-15). If you enable the on demand option, there will be a button next to the user menu to show the Developer Dashboard (see Figure 6-16).

To enable or disable the Developer Dashboard, open a command prompt and navigate to the C:\Program Files\Common Files\Microsoft Shared\Web Server Extensions\14\BIN folder.

To enable (always show):

```
stsadm -o setproperty -pn developer-dashboard -pv On
```

Figure 6-15

The Developer Dashboard

Figure 6-16

The Developer Dashboard
button

To enable (on demand):

```
stsadm -o setproperty -pn developer-dashboard -pv OnDemand
```

To disable:

```
stsadm -o setproperty -pn developer-dashboard -pv Off
```

To use PowerShell, you must use multiple commands to perform the same:

```
$srv = [Microsoft.SharePoint.Administration.
SPWebService]::ContentService

$setting =$srv.DeveloperDashboardSettings

$setting.DisplayLevel = [Microsoft.SharePoint.Administration.SPDev
eloperDashboardLevel]::OnDemand

$setting.Update()
```

SKILL SUMMARY

IN THIS LESSON YOU LEARNED:

- A feature is a container of various elements, including Web Parts, workflows, content type definitions, and event receivers. The feature adds functionality or applies customizations to a site, collection, or Web site.

- SharePoint allows you to manage features through Central Administration, Site Settings, PowerShell, or the `stsadm` command.

- Some services in Windows Servers depend on other services, which means that some services must be started before other services can be started. In SharePoint, some features might depend on other features.

- While a SharePoint feature is a defined functionality that administrators can enable or disable in a single operation, a SharePoint solution package is a functionality that administrators install in a single operation.

- To install a solution, you must first upload the solution and then activate the solution.

- You can use solution packages to deploy new solutions and upgrade existing solutions across the farm.

- To install a farm solution, you must be a farm administrator.

- To support a modular approach that allows developers to share assemblies across multiple applications, assemblies can be placed in the global assembly cache, which is typically saved in the C:\Windows Assembly folder.

- A sandbox is a security mechanism for separating running programs that are used to isolate the execution of untested code or untrusted programs that come from unverified third-parties, suppliers, and untrusted users.

- Starting with SharePoint 2010, SharePoint provides a sandbox that will separate code from other processes. As a result, a sandbox improves the security, helps control resources, and prevents performance problems.

- Before you install a sandbox solution, you must first enable the sandbox.

- A sandbox can restrict the server resources that a solution can consume each day based on a point system that reflects the processor time, memory usage, database queries, and other resources that a solution uses.

- A new feature introduced with SharePoint 2010 is the Developer Dashboard, which provides diagnostic information that can help a developer or system administrator troubleshoot problems with page components that would be difficult to isolate.

■ Knowledge Assessment

Fill in the Blank

Complete the following sentences by writing the correct word or words in the blanks provided.

1. The command to list installed features is _____.

2. If you activate a collection feature that requires a second feature within the same collection, the second feature will automatically be _____.

3. A farm solution is known as a(n) _____ trust solution.

4. The C:\Windows Assembly folder is used to store the _____.

5. If a solution does not remove a Web Part that is included with the solution, you will have to delete the Web Part _____ from the Web Part Gallery.

6. A _____ is a security mechanism to run programs in an isolated area.

7. Solutions that you install will have the _____ filename extension.

8. The default sandbox solutions resource quota is _____ points.

9. Sandbox solutions were introduced in _____.

10. Before you can remove a solution, you must first deactivate any _____ associated with the solution.

Multiple Choice

Circle the letter that corresponds to the best answer.

1. Which of the following is a scope where a feature can be applied? (Choose all that apply.)
   a. site collection
   b. Web Part
   c. farm
   d. Web application

2. Which command installs a SharePoint feature?
   a. `Get-SPFeature`
   b. `Enable-SPFeature`
   c. `Install-SPFeature`
   d. `Place-SPFeature`

3. Which of the following tasks hides a feature?
   a. Using the `Get-SPFeature` PowerShell command
   b. Using the `Hide-SPFeature` PowerShell command
   c. Using Central Administration
   d. Modifying the feature.xml file for the respective feature

4. Another name for sandbox solution is a(n) _____ solution.
   a. users
   b. test
   c. temporary
   d. unmanaged

5. Sandbox solutions are installed by _____ administrators.
   a. farm
   b. site collection
   c. server
   d. domain

6. Which of the following is a step in using a SharePoint sandbox? (Choose all that apply.)
   a. Set the quotas for all sandboxed solutions.
   b. Enable DPA.
   c. Enable sandboxed solutions and start the sandbox solutions service.
   d. Determine the load-balancing scheme to use.

7. Which of the following SharePoint components provides diagnostic information about a SharePoint page and its components?
   a. Developer Dashboard
   b. Collection Monitor
   c. Site Diag Program
   d. Application Query Analyzer

8. Which type of user has the ability to install a user solution?
   a. Users who are server administrators
   b. Users who are farm administrators
   c. Users who are DB administrators
   d. Users who have Full Control permission at the root of the site collection

9. Which of the following choices allows you to install features, Web Parts, and site customizations in one simple installation process?
   a. resource
   b. solution
   c. subfeature
   d. workflow

10. Which of the following choices is used to store assemblies that can be used by multiple applications in SharePoint?
    a. sandbox
    b. workflow gallery
    c. template
    d. GAC

True / False

Circle T if the statement is true or F if the statement is false.

T | F 1. To use a feature, you need only to install the feature.

T | F 2. To use the SharePoint Publishing feature, you must enable the Publishing Infrastructure for the top-level site in your site collection and then enable the Publishing feature for a subsite.

T | F 3. SharePoint 2010 Features are stored in the %ProgramFiles%\Common Files\ Microsoft Shared\Web server extensions\12\TEMPLATE\FEATURES.

T | F 4. When you need to remove a solution, you must first retract the solution and then uninstall the solution.

T | F 5. For a solution to be upgraded, the upgraded solution must use the same solution ID as the original solution.

■ Case Scenarios

Scenario 6-1: Looking at Solution Performance

You want to add a new solution but you are hesitant because you are afraid that the solution will affect performance. So if you decide to load the solution, how can you determine its impact on performance?

Scenario 6-2: Restricting a New Solution

You have just hired an inexperienced SharePoint developer. Over the past month, he has been developing several solutions that he says are ready to deploy in your SharePoint environment. These solutions consist of multiple front-end servers, multiple collections, and multiple sites. What should you do to deploy these solutions?

Managing Accounts and User Accounts

LESSON 7

OBJECTIVE DOMAIN MATRIX

Technology Skill	Objective Domain Description	Objective Domain Number
Introducing SharePoint Security	Manage Accounts and User Roles	2.2
	Managing Service Accounts	2.2.5
	Delegating Site Collection Administration	2.2.6
Managing User and Group Accounts	Managing User Accounts	2.2.1
	Managing Group Accounts	2.2.2
Managing Managed Accounts	Managing Managed Accounts	2.2.3
Managing Online SharePoint Users	External User Policy	2.2.7
	Supporting Single Sign-On for SharePoint Online	2.3.7

KEY TERMS

collection administrators
farm administrators
feature administrator
groups
inheritance

managed account
permission
permission levels
service account
service application administrators

site owners
Windows Administrators group

You have just completed the installation of SharePoint and you are ready to make SharePoint available to the different departments within your organization. Before you get final approval to make SharePoint available to the departments, your manager wants to know how you will control the security within the SharePoint environment.

227

■ Introducing SharePoint Security

| ↓ THE BOTTOM LINE | Since SharePoint can provide vital services for a company while storing confidential information, it is imperative that you plan and implement proper security. |

CERTIFICATION READY
What are the two main tools used to manage accounts and user roles ?
2.2

When securing a SharePoint site, you must perform three basic tasks:

- Manage administrative access
- Assign permissions to sites, lists, and libraries
- Manage group membership

When managing administrative access, you are defining (as well as limiting) your farm administrators, Windows administrators, Service application administrators, and site collection administrators. Modifying administrative access will be done when initially configuring a SharePoint environment. After SharePoint is installed and initially configured, the day-to-day tasks include managing the permissions/permission levels and managing the groups.

CERTIFICATION READY
Why should you use different accounts for the different SharePoint Service Accounts?
2.2.5

Understanding the Administration Hierarchy in SharePoint 2010

Several individuals can be involved in managing a SharePoint environment and as the number of users increases and the application grows, you can designate several administrators to manage security.

By using a hierarchical level in SharePoint, you can delegate the task and responsibility of security administration to others. At higher levels, administrators will most likely configure and manage security for services, features, and site collections. After site and site collections have been created, permissions can be granted to users and groups for managing Web pages, lists, and libraries.

High-level administrators include:

- Farm administrators
- Windows administrators
- Service application administrators
- Feature administrators
- Site collection administrators
- Site owners

Farm administrators have full access to all servers in the server farm, including performing all administrative tasks in Central Administration for the server or server farm and managing service applications. Users in this group can also use PowerShell cmdlets for various administrative activities and assign users administrative roles for service applications. Farm administrators do not have access to individual sites or their content, but can grant themselves access if needed through Web application policies that will grant them access to any site collection within that particular Web application. They can also take ownership of any content site.

 ADD USERS TO THE FARM ADMINISTRATORS GROUP

GET READY. To add users to the Farm Administrators group, perform the following steps:

1. Open Central Administration and click Security. The Security page displays (see Figure 7-1).
2. Click Manage the farm administrators group. The People and Groups—Farm Administrators page displays (see Figure 7-2).

Figure 7-1

The Security page

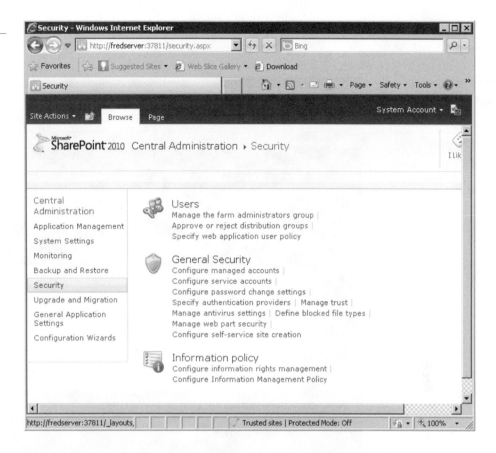

Figure 7-2

The People and Groups—Farm Administrators page

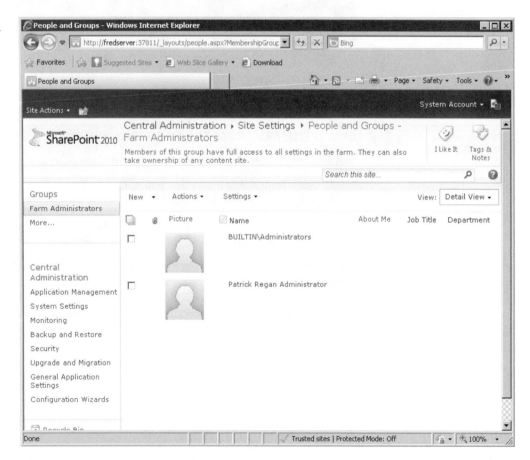

3. Click the New drop-down and select Add Users. The Select Users dialog box displays (see Figure 7-3).

Figure 7-3

The Select Users dialog box

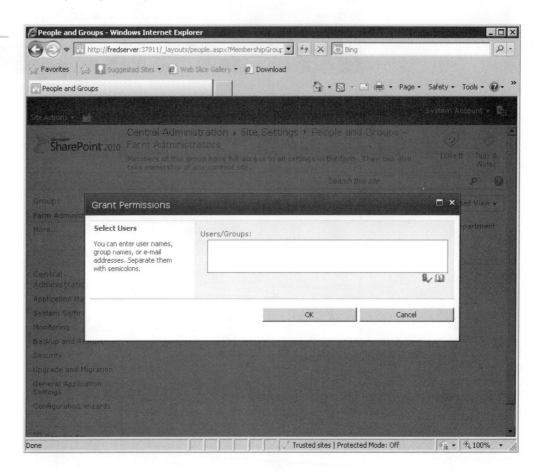

4. Type the username or usernames separated by semicolons and then click OK.

REMOVE USERS FROM THE FARM ADMINISTRATORS GROUP

GET READY. To remove users from the Farm Administrators group, perform the following steps:

1. Open Central Administration and click Security.

2. Click Manage the farm administrators group.

3. To remove a user, click the check box next to his or her name, click the Actions menu, and then click Remove Users from Group (see Figure 7-4).

The **Windows Administrators group** on the local server can perform all farm administrator actions and install new products or applications, deploy Web Parts and new features to the global assembly cache, create new Web applications and new Internet Information Services (IIS) Web sites, and start services. Like farm administrators, windows administrators do not have access to individual sites or their content.

Figure 7-4

Removing a user from the Farm Administrator group

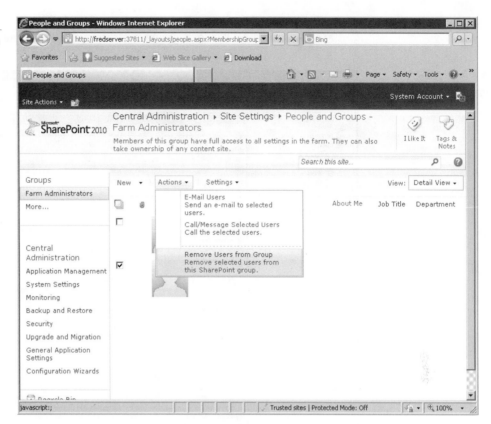

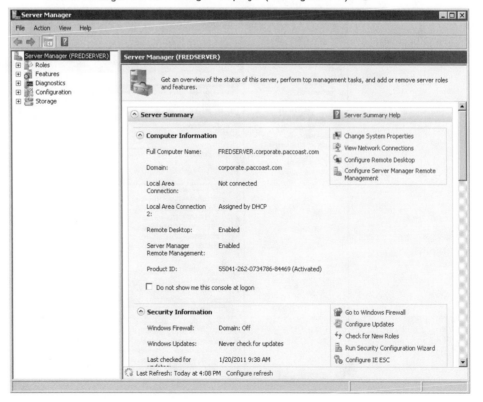

ADD USERS TO THE WINDOWS ADMINISTRATORS GROUP

GET READY. To add users to the Windows Administrators Group, perform the following steps:

1. To open Server Manager, click the Start button, right-click Computer, and then select Manage. Server Manager displays (see Figure 7-5).

Figure 7-5

The Server Manager settings

2. In the left pane, expand Configuration, expand Local Users and Groups, and then click Groups. All Windows groups are displayed (see Figure 7-6).

Figure 7-6

Local Windows groups

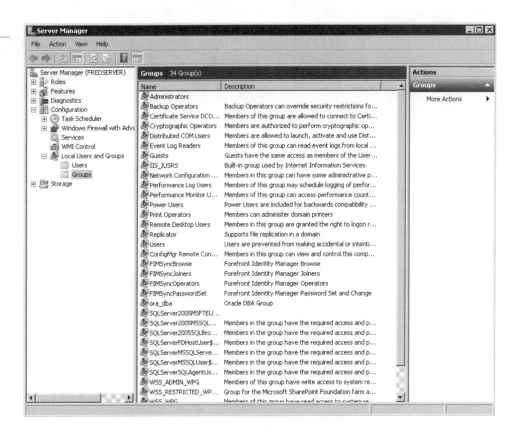

3. In the right pane, double-click the Administrators group. The Administrators Properties dialog box displays (see Figure 7-7).

Figure 7-7

The Administrators Properties dialog

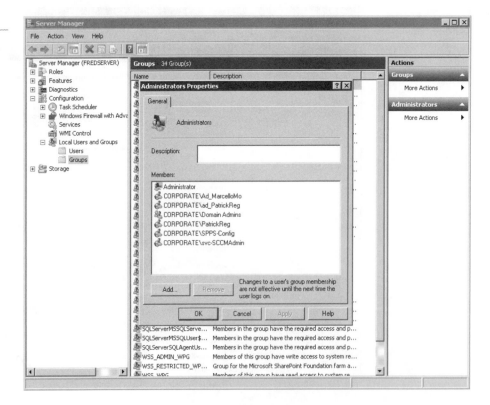

4. Click the Add button. The Select Users, Computers, Service Accounts, or Groups dialog box displays (see Figure 7-8).

Figure 7-8

The Select Users, Computers, Service Accounts, or Groups dialog

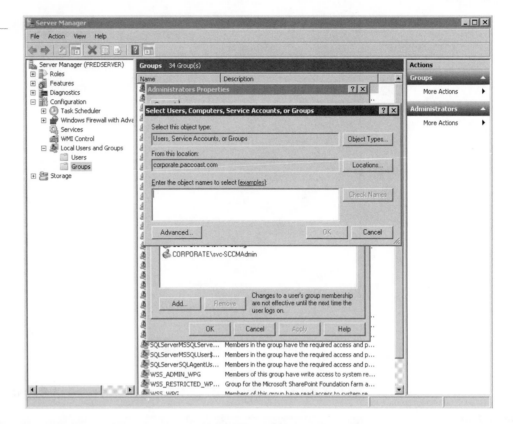

5. Type the name of the user and click OK to accept your change and close the dialog box.

6. Click OK to close the Administrators Properties dialog box.

Service application administrators can configure settings for a specific service application within a farm. However, they cannot create service applications, access any other service applications in the farm, or perform any farm-level operations.

 MANAGE SERVICE ADMINISTRATORS

GET READY. To grant service application administrator privileges, perform the following steps:

1. Open Central Administration and click Manage service applications in the Application Management section. The Manage Service Applications page displays (see Figure 7-9).

2. Select a service and then, on the Ribbon, click Administrators. The Administrators page displays (see Figure 7-10).

3. To add users, type the name in the first text box, click Add, and then select the appropriate permission. To remove an administrator, click the user, and then click the Remove button.

4. Click OK.

A ***feature administrator*** can manage a subset of service application settings and permissions, but not the entire service application. It should be noted that most service applications do not have this flexibility.

Figure 7-9

The Manage Service
Applications page

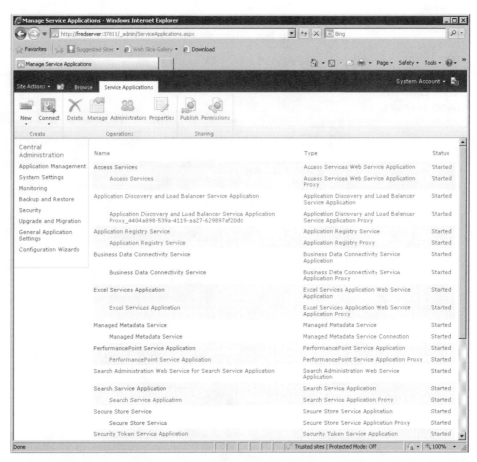

Figure 7-10

Configuring administrators for
a service

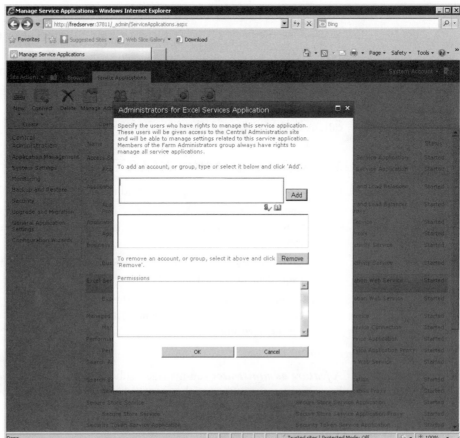

TO MANAGE PERMISSIONS FOR AN APPLICATION SERVICE

GET READY. To manage permissions for an application service, perform the following steps:

1. Open Central Administration, click Application Management, and then click Manage service applications.

2. Select a service, and then on the Ribbon, click Permissions (if available). The Permissions dialog box displays (see Figure 7-11).

Figure 7-11

Configuring connection permissions for a service

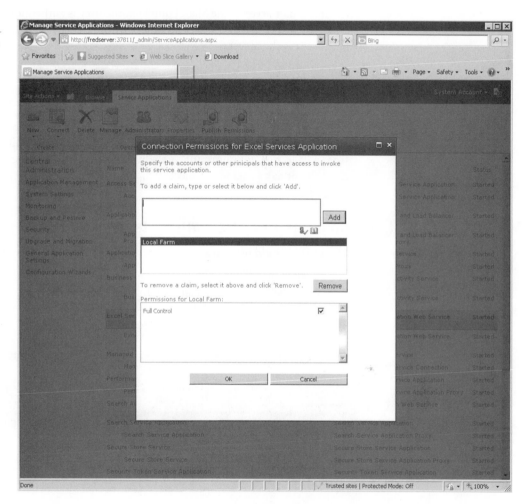

3. Type the name of the user and click Add. Then select the appropriate permission.
4. Click OK.

CERTIFICATION READY
What group has full control over all sites within a site collection and the lists and libraries within each site?
2.2.6

Collection administrators have the Full Control permission level on all Web sites within a site collection and are responsible for planning how the access is granted to the site collection. They have Full Control access to all site content in that site collection, even if they do not have explicit permissions on that site. They can audit all site content and receive any administrative alert. As mentioned in Lesson 5, you can use Central Administration Application Management to specify which two users are initial Site Collection Administrators. Use Site Settings to make other users collection administrators.

Understanding Site Permissions and Permission Inheritance

The administrative roles discussed earlier in this lesson are focused on the roles that are used to manage and configure the SharePoint server, services, and the entire environment as a whole. However, most day-to-day tasks will be done at the site level or within items within the site.

Any time a user accesses the SharePoint site, the user is authenticated. After a user is authenticated, every time a user accesses an object within a SharePoint site, the user must be authorized to access the object.

Managing Site Owners

Site owners have full control of content on the site. They can perform administrative tasks on the site, including tasks that affect any list or library within that site. Different from a collection administrator, site administrator permissions can be overridden on a child site or at a lower level object such as a list or library.

 ADD USERS TO A SITE OWNERS GROUP

GET READY. To add users to a site owners group, perform the following steps:

1. Open a SharePoint site.
2. Click the Site Actions menu and select Site Permissions. The Permissions page displays (see Figure 7-12).

Figure 7-12

The Permissions page

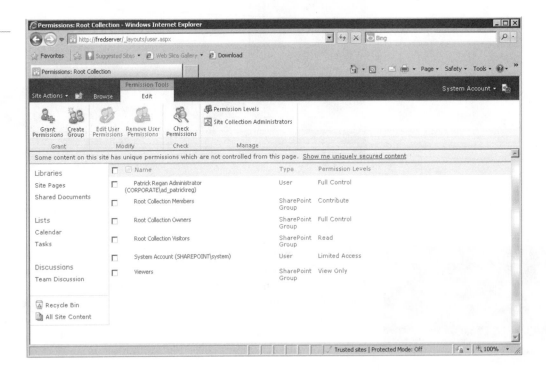

3. On the Ribbon, click the Grant Permissions button. The Grant Permissions dialog box displays (see Figure 7-13).

Figure 7-13

The Grant Permissions dialog

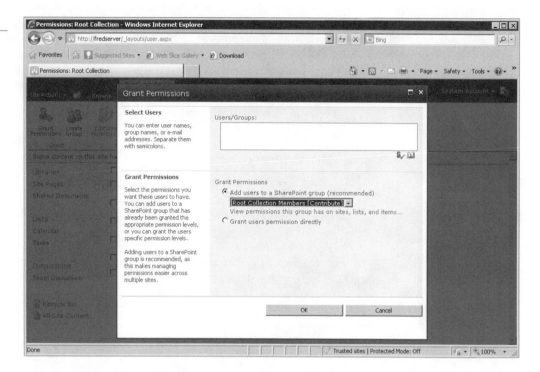

4. In the Users/Groups text box, type the name of the user or group.

5. For the Add users to a SharePoint group option, select the appropriate group. Options include the following:

<collection name> Viewers (with View Only permission)

<collection name> Owners (with Full Control level permission)

<collection name> Visitors (with Read level permission)

<collection name> Members (with Contribute permission)

TAKE NOTE*

The default groups are based on the name of the site collection. Therefore, if the site collection is Root Collection, your groups will be Root Collection Viewers, Root Collection Owner, Root Collection Visitor, and Root Collection Member.

6. Click OK.

Understanding Permission Levels

Web sites, lists, libraries, folders, and list items are all securable in SharePoint. A *permission* grants access to the securable object and specifies what kind of access a user (or group of users) has to the specified object.

Permissions are contained within a site collection. Therefore, all of the groups and permission levels defined for a site collection are available to every site, list, and library within the collection. Similar to NTFS permissions, SharePoint permissions are divided into *permission levels* that consist of several permissions that allow users to perform a set of related tasks. Table 7-1 shows the default permissions for a team site.

Table 7-1

Permission Levels

PERMISSION LEVEL	DESCRIPTION	DEFAULT PERMISSIONS
Limited Access	Allows access to shared resources in the Web site so that the users can access an item within the site. Usually is combined with fine-granted permissions without giving users access to the entire site. Limited Access cannot be customized or deleted.	• View Application Pages • Browse User Information • Use Remote Interfaces • Use Client Integration Features • Open
Read	Allows users to view pages, list items, and download documents. However, users cannot add or change content.	• Limited Access permissions, plus: • View Items • Open Items • View Versions • Create Alerts • Use Self-Service Site Creation • View Pages
Contribute	Allows users to view, add, update, and delete items in the existing lists and document libraries.	• Read permissions, plus: • Add Items • Edit Items • Delete Items • Delete Versions • Browse Directories • Edit Personal User Information • Manage Personal Views • Add/Remove Personal Web Parts • Update Personal Web Parts
Design	Allows users to view, add, update, delete, approve, and customize items or pages in the Web site.	• Approve permissions, plus: • Manage Lists • Add and Customize Pages • Apply Themes and Borders • Apply Style Sheets
Full Control—	Allows full control to the sites, pages lists, libraries and items.	• All permissions

 ASSIGN PERMISSION LEVELS

GET READY. To assign site permission levels, perform the following steps:

1. Open a SharePoint site.
2. Click the Site Actions menu and select Site Permissions.
3. On the Ribbon, click the Grant Permissions button.
4. In the Users/Groups text box, type the name of the user or group.

5. Select the Grant users permission directly option. The Grant Users Permissions Directly option displays (see Figure 7-14).

Figure 7-14

The Grant Users Permissions Directly option

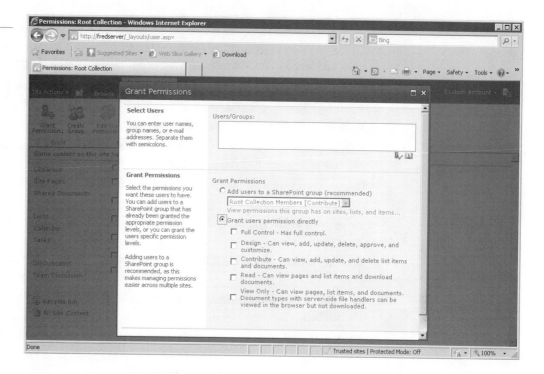

6. Select your preferred permission level.

7. Click OK.

UNDERSTANDING USER PERMISSIONS

The five default permission levels are built from 33 permissions, which are categorized into list permissions (see Table 7-2 and Table 7-3), site permissions (see Table 7-4 and Table 7-5), and personal permissions (see Table 7-6 and Table 7-7). List permissions are applied to a list, site permissions are applied to a particular site, and list permissions apply to lists and libraries. Personal permissions apply to personal views, private Web Parts, and more. You can change which permissions are included in a particular permission level (except for the Limited Access and Full Control permission levels), or you can create a new permission level to contain specific permissions.

Many of these permissions are dependent on other permissions. Therefore, when you select a permission that is dependent on another permission, you are also selecting the dependent permission. When you clear a permission on which it is dependent, you also clear the depending permissions. For example, the Manage Personal View depends on the View Items, View Pages, and open permissions.

Table 7-2

List Permissions

Permission Level	Description	Dependent Permissions
Manage Lists	Creates or deletes lists, adds or removes columns in a list, and adds or removes public views of a list.	View Items, View Pages, Open, Manage Personal Views
Override Check Out	Discards or checks in a document that is checked out to another user without saving the current changes.	View Items, View Pages, Open
Add Items	Adds items to lists and adds documents to document libraries.	View Items, View Pages, Open
Edit Items	Edits items in lists, edits documents in document libraries, and customizes Web Part Pages in document libraries.	View Items, View Pages, Open
Delete Items	Deletes items from a list and deletes documents from a document library.	View Items, View Pages, Open
View Items	Views items in lists and views documents in document libraries.	View Pages, Open
Approve Items	Approves minor versions of list items or documents.	Edit Items, View Items, View Pages, Open
Open Items	Views the source of documents with server-side file handlers.	View Items, View Pages, Open
View Versions	Views past versions of list items or documents.	View Items, Open Items, View Pages, Open
Delete Versions	Deletes past versions of list items or documents.	View Items, View Versions, View Pages, Open
Create Alerts	Creates e-mail alerts.	View Items, View Pages, Open
View Application Pages	Views forms, views, and application pages. Enumerates lists.	Open

Table 7-3

List Permissions as they Relate to Permission Level

Permission	Full Control	Design	Contribute	Read	Limited Access
Manage Lists	X	X			
Override Check-Out	X	X			
Add Items	X	X	X		
Edit Items	X	X	X		
Delete Items	X	X	X		
View Items	X	X	X	X	
Approve Items	X	X			
Open Items	X	X	X	X	
View Versions	X	X	X	X	
Delete Versions	X	X	X		
Create Alerts	X	X	X	X	
View Application Pages	X	X	X	X	X

Table 7-4

Site Permissions

PERMISSION	DESCRIPTION	DEPENDENT PERMISSIONS
Manage Permissions	Creates or changes permission levels on the Web site and assigns permissions to users and groups.	View Items, Open Items, View Versions, Browse Directories, View Pages, Enumerate Permissions, Browse User Information, Open
View Usage Data	Views reports on Web site usage.	View Pages, Open
Create Subsites	Creates subsites such as team sites, Meeting Workspace sites, and Document Workspace sites.	View Pages, Browse User Information, Open
Manage Web Site	Performs all administration tasks for the Web site and manages content.	View Items, Add and Customize Pages, Browse Directories, View Pages, Enumerate Permissions, Browse User Information, Open
Add and Customize Pages	Adds, changes, or deletes HTML pages or Web Part pages; edits the Web site by using a Windows SharePoint Services-compatible editor.	View Items, Browse Directories, View Pages, Open
Apply Themes and Borders	Applies a theme or borders to the entire Web site.	View Pages, Open
Apply Style Sheets	Applies a style sheet (.css file) to the Web site.	View Pages, Open
Create Groups	Creates a group of users that can be used anywhere within the site collection.	View Pages, Browse User Information, Open
Browse Directories	Enumerates files and folders in a Web site by using Microsoft SharePoint Designer 2010 and Web DAV interfaces.	View Pages, Open
Use Self-Service Site Creation	Creates a Web site by using Self-Service Site Creation.	View Pages, Browse User Information, Open
View Pages	Views pages in a Web site.	Open
Enumerate Permissions	Enumerates permissions on the Web site, list, folder, document, or list item.	Browse Directories, View Pages, Browse User Information, Open
Browse User Information	Views information about users of the Web site.	Open
Manage Alerts	Manages alerts for all users of the Web site.	View Items, View Pages, Open
Use Remote Interfaces	Uses SOAP, Web DAV, or SharePoint Designer 2010 interfaces to access the Web site.	Open
Use Client Integration Features	Uses features that start client applications. Without this permission, users must work on documents locally and then upload their changes.	Use Remote Interfaces, Open
Open	Opens a Web site, list, or folder to access items inside that container.	None
Edit Personal User Information	Allows users to change their own user information, such as adding a picture.	Browse User Information, Open

Table 7-5

Site Permissions as they Relate
to Permission Level

Permission	Full Control	Design	Contribute	Read	Limited Access
Manage Permissions	X				
View Usage Data	X				
Create Sub-sites	X				
Manage Web Site	X				
Add and Customize Pages	X	X			
Apply Themes and Borders	X	X			
Apply Style Sheets	X	X			
Create Groups	X				
Browse Directories	X	X	X		
Use Self-Service Site Creation	X	X	X	X	
View Pages	X	X	X	X	
Enumerate Permissions	X				
Browse User Information	X	X	X	X	X
Manage Alerts	X				
Use Remote Interfaces	X	X	X	X	X
Use Client Integration Features	X	X	X	X	X
Open	X	X	X	X	X
Edit Personal User Information	X	X	X		

Table 7-6

Personal Permissions

Permission	Description	Dependent Permissions
Manage Personal Views	Creates, changes, or deletes personal views of lists.	View Items, View Pages, Open
Add/Remove Personal Web Parts	Adds or removes personal Web Parts on a Web Part page.	View Items, View Pages, Open
Update Personal Web Parts	Updates Web Parts to display personalized information.	View Items, View Pages, Open

Table 7-7

Personal Permissions as they
Relate to Permission Level

Permission	Full Control	Design	Contribute	Read	Limited Access
Manage Personal Views	X	X	X		
Add/Remove Private Web Parts	X	X	X		
Update Personal Web Parts	X	X	X		

MANAGING PERMISSION LEVELS

Depending on your environment, you might need to either change the default permission levels or create your own default permission levels. Rather than build a new permission from scratch, you can base your new permission levels on other permissions levels.

 CREATE A NEW PERMISSION LEVEL BASED ON ANOTHER PERMISSION LEVEL

GET READY. To create a new permission level based on existing site permission level, perform the following steps:

1. Open your top-level site.
2. Click the Site Actions menu and select Site Permissions.
3. On the Ribbon, click the Permission Levels button. The Permissions Levels page displays (see Figure 7-15).

Figure 7-15

The Permissions Levels page

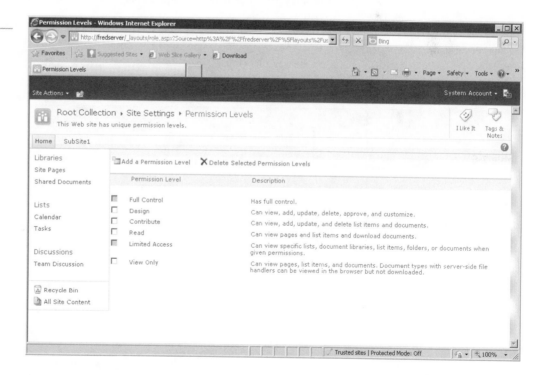

4. Select the permission level link (not the check box) that you want to use as the basis for your new permission level. The Edit Permission Level page displays (see Figure 7-16).

Figure 7-16

The Edit Permission Level page

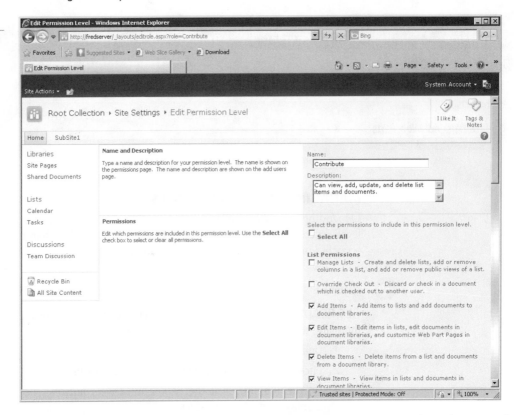

5. Scroll to the bottom of the page and click Copy Permission Level (see Figure 7-17). The Copy Permission Level page displays (see Figure 7-18).

Figure 7-17

The Copy Permission Level page

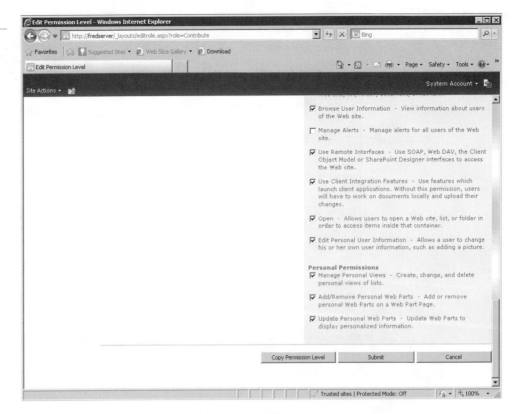

Figure 7-18

The Copy Permission
Level page

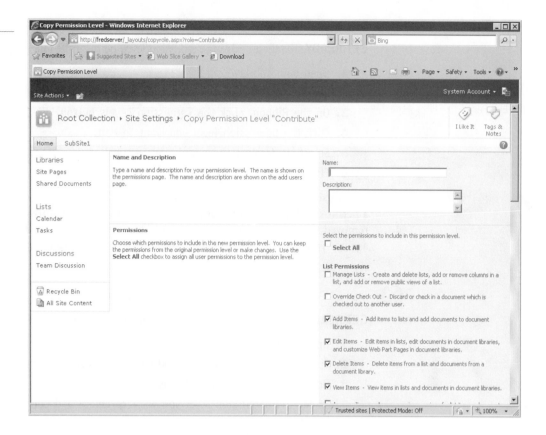

6. Type a Name and Description for the permission level.

7. Modify the permissions by selecting or deselecting the permissions as needed.

8. Click Create at the bottom of the page.

If you want a fresh start when creating a permission level, you have the option to create a permission level from scratch. You start with a blank permission level and select the desired permissions that you need.

 CREATE A NEW PERMISSION LEVEL FROM SCRATCH

GET READY. To create a new permission level from scratch, perform the following steps:

1. Open your top-level site.

2. Click the Site Actions menu and select Site Permissions.

3. On the Ribbon, click the Permission Levels button.

4. Click the Add a Permission Level button.

5. Type a Name and Description for the new permission level.

6. Modify the permissions by selecting or deselecting the permissions as desired.

7. Click Create at the bottom of the page.

If you can create permission levels, it will also make sense that you can edit the existing permission levels (except the Full Control and Limited Access Permissions). It should be noted that it is not recommended to edit the default permission levels. Instead, you should only edit the custom permission levels that were created.

EDIT AN EXISTING PERMISSION LEVEL

GET READY. To edit an existing permission level, perform the following steps:

1. Open your top-level site.
2. Click the Site Actions menu and select Site Permissions.
3. On the Ribbon, click the Permission Levels button.
4. Click the permission level you want to edit.
5. Select or deselect the permissions as desired.
6. Click the Submit button.

Of course, there may be a time when you want to delete a permission level. When you delete a permission level, any users or groups that are using the permission level for access will be removed from the Site Permissions page. Therefore, you will need to grant them permissions again if you wish for them to have access to the site or objects in the site.

 DELETE AN EXISTING PERMISSION LEVEL

GET READY. To delete an existing permission level, perform the following steps:

1. Open your top-level site.
2. Click the Site Actions menu and select Site Permissions.
3. On the Ribbon, click the Permission Levels button.
4. Select the permission level you want to delete and click Delete Selected Permission Levels.
5. When the warning appears asking if you want to confirm deletion of the selected permission, click OK.

MANAGING PERMISSION INHERITANCE

By default, permissions within a site collection are inherited from the root site to subsites and all lists and pages, which means that those permissions cascade down to the lower sites and objects from the parent site. The mechanism of permissions cascading down to lower objects is called *inheritance*. Permissions can be overridden or broken at the site or list level so that unique permissions can be set at either level.

 STOP INHERITING PERMISSIONS FROM THE PARENT SITE TO A SUBSITE

GET READY. To stop permissions from inheriting from a parent site to a subsite, perform the following steps:

1. Open a SharePoint subsite.
2. Click the Site Actions menu and select Site Permissions. The Permissions page displays (see Figure 7-19).
3. On the Ribbon, click the Stop Inheriting Permissions button in the ribbon.
4. When a warning appears that you are about to create unique permission for this Web site, click OK.

If you need to have a site inherit its permission from the parent, you would click the **Inherit Permissions** button instead of the **Stop Inheriting Permissions** button. If you are creating a site using a site template (as detailed in Lesson 1), you would click the **More Options** button, which gives you the option to select **Use unique permission** or **Use same permissions as parent site**.

Figure 7-19

The Permissions page

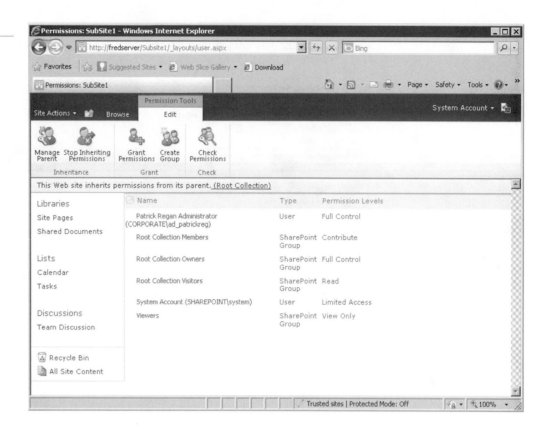

ASSIGN PERMISSION LEVELS FOR A LIST

GET READY. To assign permission levels for a list, perform the following steps:

1. Open a list in SharePoint.

2. In the List Tools section on the Ribbon, click List, and then click the List Permissions button (see Figure 7-20). Alternatively, you can click List Settings and then click Permissions. If the list inherited permissions from the parent site, a yellow bar displays, stating This list inherits permissions from its parent.

Figure 7-20

The List Permissions button

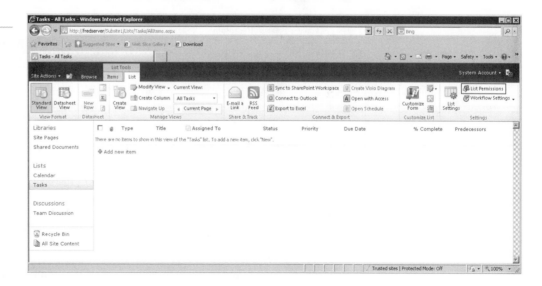

3. To stop inheritance, click the Stop Inheriting Permissions button (see Figure 7-21). If the list has unique permissions, click the Inherit Permissions button.

Figure 7-21

The List Permissions page

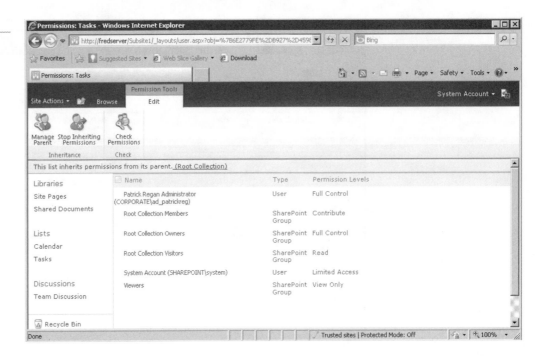

4. When a warning appears indicating that you are about to create unique permissions for this list, click OK. Notice the yellow bar that indicates This list has unique permissions (see Figure 7-22).

Figure 7-22

The unique permissions warning

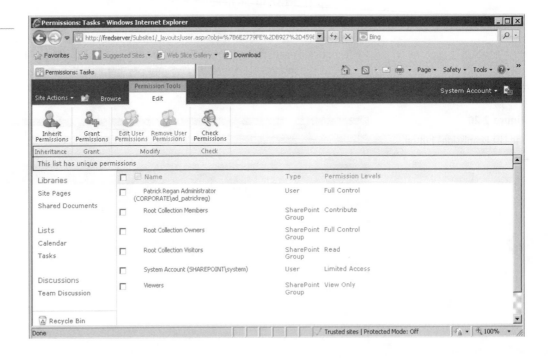

5. To grant permission to a group or user, click the Grant Permissions button.
6. In the User/Group text box, type the user or group.

7. Select one of the following:

Select Add users to a SharePoint group and select the appropriate group.

Select Grant users permission directly and select the specific permission level.

8. Click OK.

Anytime you want to check the permissions for a site, list, or library, click the **Check Permissions** button on the Permissions page. Then select the user or group using what is known as the "people picker" input box and click **Check Now**. SharePoint then shows you all of the permissions for the user as well as how the user's permissions were obtained.

Any time permissions are explicitly applied, you will see an icon labeled **Check Permissions**. Clicking this icon presents the "people picker" input box, into which you enter a user or group name and then click **Check Now**. SharePoint then shows you, for the local site, all of the permissions for that user as well as how that user's permissions were obtained (see Figure 7-23).

Figure 7-23

The Check Permissions page

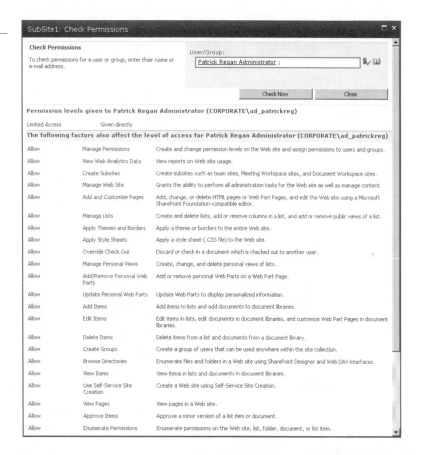

■ Managing User and Group Accounts

THE BOTTOM LINE

SharePoint is tightly integrated with Microsoft's Active Directory. Therefore, users and groups can be accessed from SharePoint. As a SharePoint administrator, you must determine who needs access to your SharePoint environment and then grant access as needed.

CERTIFICATION READY
What methods can
you use to add users
to SharePoint?
2.2.1

CERTIFICATION READY
Why do you use groups
in SharePoint?
2.2.2

Using *groups* is similar to managing folders and files on a Windows server or managing Active Directory. The idea behind groups is to group users together so that when you assign permissions, you assign them once to a group and all users in the group receive those permissions. As a result, permission management is simplified.

When you assign permissions, you typically assign a permission level to a group and then add users to the group as needed. You cannot assign base SharePoint permissions to a user or group; it must be a permission level.

SharePoint supports Active Directory groups and SharePoint groups. In Active Directory, there are two types of groups:

- Security groups
- Distribution groups

Both of these groups can be used to send a single email to multiple people. However, security groups can be used to assign rights and permissions to multiple users.

TAKE NOTE * If you try to assign permissions to an Active Directory and the group does not appear so that you can select it, make sure that the group is a security group (and not a distribution group).

If you choose to use Active Directory groups, Active Directory groups must be managed using Active Directory Users and Computers. Of course, the IT department must maintain the Active Directory structure and groups. Active Directory groups can contain other Active Directory groups, but they cannot contain SharePoint groups. Since groups are managed using Active Directory tools, you cannot see the membership of Active Directory groups with SharePoint.

SharePoint groups are managed with SharePoint. Different from Active Directory, the managing of SharePoint groups can be delegated to other SharePoint users. In addition, SharePoint users can see who the members are of each SharePoint group. Lastly, SharePoint groups cannot contain another SharePoint group.

By default, SharePoint creates a single set of three groups. Each group maps to a set of permissions that defines the tasks that a user can perform. Most of your users fall into one of SharePoint's three default groups:

- **Site Members**: Grants the Contribute permission level for users, which allows them to add, edit, and modify site content. Since most members on team sites need to read, add, and modify content, most team members are assigned to the Site Members group.
- **Site Owners**: Grants full control. Besides adding, editing, and modifying site content, a site owner can delegate administrative and design tasks to others.
- **Site Visitors**: Grants read-only access to a site, list, or library; allows the user to create alerts.

The actual names of the groups are determined by the name of the site. Of course, these groups—as well as any other groups—can be managed by the site collection administrators.

TAKE NOTE * If you need to give access to all users within your organization, you can assign the Active Directory authenticated users group to the appropriate group. Of course, you should only provide access that is required for them to do their job.

SharePoint also provides the following set of specialized administrative groups for publishing sites:

- **Approvers**: Gives the user the Approve permission, which allows users to approve items and override document check-outs.
- **Designers**: Grants permission to change the look and feel of sites with style sheets and themes.
- **Hierarchy Managers**: Allows the user to manipulate the site's hierarchy and customize lists and libraries.

⊕ **ADD A USER TO A GROUP**

GET READY. To add a user to a group, perform the following steps:

1. Click the Site Actions menu and select Site Permissions. The permissions page displays.
2. Click the link for the security group to which you want to add users. The People and Groups page displays (see Figure 7-24).

Figure 7-24

The People and Groups page

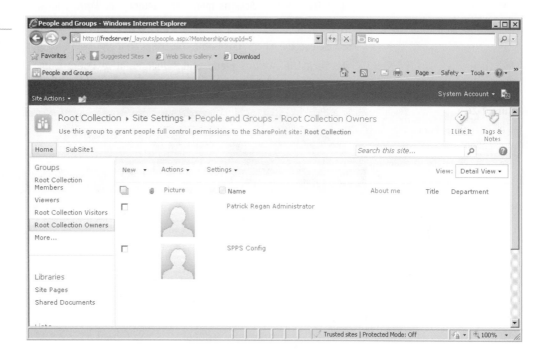

3. Click the New menu and select Add Users. The Grant Permissions dialog box displays (see Figure 7-25).

Figure 7-25

The Grant Permissions dialog box

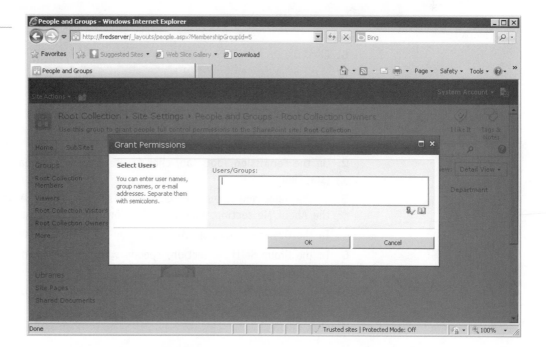

4. In the Users/Groups section, click the Browse button (the book icon) to select the users that you want to add to this security group.

5. Click OK.

 REMOVE A USER FROM A GROUP

GET READY. To remove the users from a group, perform the following steps:

1. Click the Site Actions menu and select Site Permissions. The permissions page displays.

2. Click the link (not the check box) for the group from which you want to remove users.

3. Select the check boxes for the users that you want to remove from this security group.

4. Click the Actions menu and select Remove Users from Group (see Figure 7-26).

Figure 7-26

The Remove Users from Group option

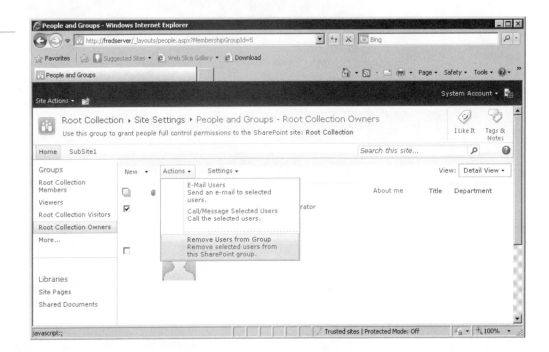

5. Click OK.

 CREATE A NEW SHAREPOINT GROUP

GET READY. To create a new group, perform the following steps:

1. Click the Site Actions menu and select Site Permissions. The permissions page displays.

2. On the Permission Tools tab, click Create Group. The Create Group page displays (see Figure 7-27).

3. In the Name and About Me Description section, type the Name. If you'd like, in the About Me section, type a description for this security group.

4. In the Owner section, specify the Group owner of this security group.

5. In the Group Settings section, specify who can view and edit the membership of this group.

6. In the Membership Requests section, specify the settings that you want for requests to join or leave the group.

7. Click Create.

Figure 7-27

The Create Group page

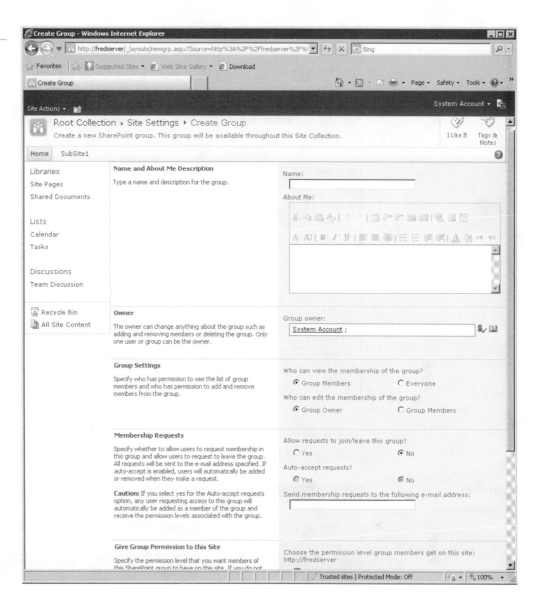

![arrow icon] **DELETE A SHAREPOINT GROUP**

GET READY. To delete a SharePoint group, perform the following steps:

1. Click the Site Actions menu and select Settings.
2. On the Site Settings page, in the Users and Permissions column, click People and groups. The Peoples and Groups page displays (see Figure 7-28).
3. In the Quick Launch bar (displayed at the left of the screen), click Groups. The All Groups: All Groups page displays (see Figure 7-29).
4. On the People and Groups: All Groups page, in the Group column, click the Edit icon for the group that you want to delete. The Change Group Settings page displays.
5. At the bottom of the page, click Delete.
6. Click OK to confirm the action.

There may be a time when you will have to remove an account from the site collection. To remove a user from a site collection, you must remove the user from the All People group, which is a hidden group.

Figure 7-28

The People and Groups page

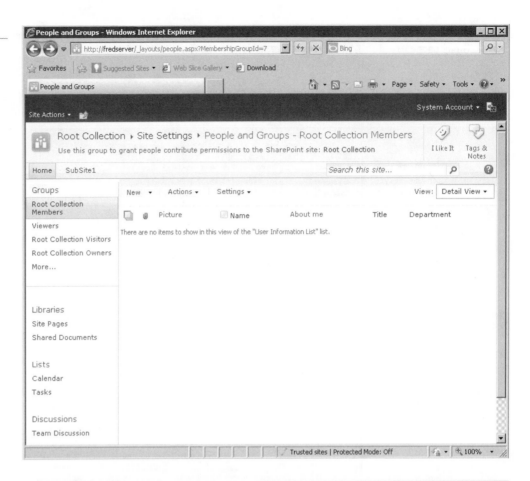

Figure 7-29

The All Groups page

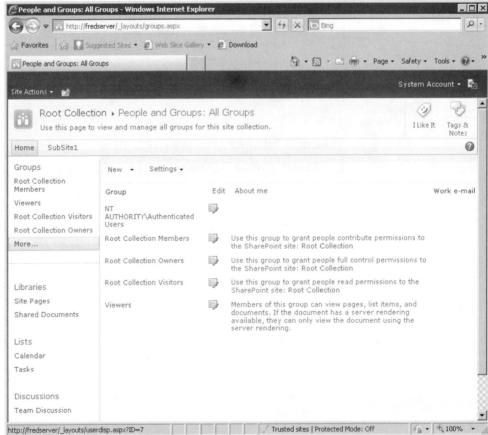

 DELETE USERS FROM A SITE COLLECTION

GET READY. To delete users from the site collection, perform the following steps:

1. Click the Site Actions menu and select Settings. The permissions page displays.

2. Click into any existing group (for example, site Owners). The URL will be something like http://server/_layouts/people.aspx?MembershipGroupI=511.

3. To show the All People group, change the Group ID to 0 (http://server/_layouts/ people.aspx?MembershipGroupID=0). The list should now show you All People (see Figure 7-30).

Figure 7-30

The All People group

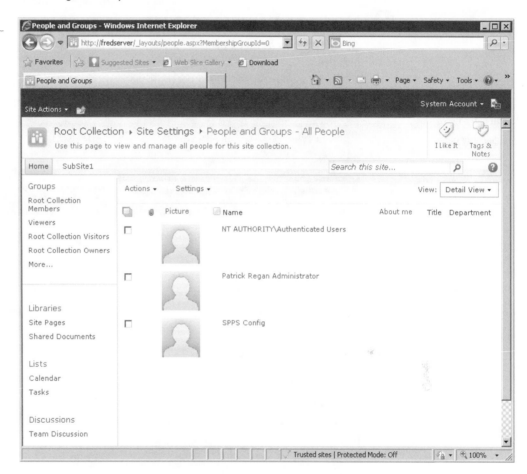

4. Find the user who isn't updating and click the check box by their name. Click Actions and then click Delete Users from Site Collection.

■ Managing Managed Accounts

A **service account** is an account that an operating system, process, or service runs under. A service account can allow the application or service specific rights and permissions to function properly while minimizing the permissions required for the users using the application server.

CERTIFICATION READY
What mechanism allows SharePoint to manage a service account password?
2.2.3

When managing service accounts, you need to maintain security. Like any other user account, you should change the password on a regular basis and you should use strong passwords. A strong password is a password that cannot be easily guessed and is usually eight or more characters with a combination of upper case, lower case, digits, and special characters (for example, T1g3rRoar5! or TTm#AS53). Because service accounts are often used all of the time, you must coordinate password changes with the service or application that is using them so that there is no downtime.

A ***managed account*** is an Active Directory user account whose credentials are managed by and contained in SharePoint. If combined with a group policy that is assigned to the domain, you can configure SharePoint so that these password are automatically reset. You do not have to know the password for an account to assign it to service applications in SharePoint.

You can manage these accounts from Central Administration, where you can view the existing managed accounts, register a new managed account, or change a password. Once you have established these accounts, you can assign them to a service application from Central Administration.

 REGISTER A MANAGED ACCOUNT

GET READY. To register a managed account to be used as a service account, perform the following steps:

1. Open the Central Administration Web site and click Security (see Figure 7-31).

Figure 7-31

The Security page

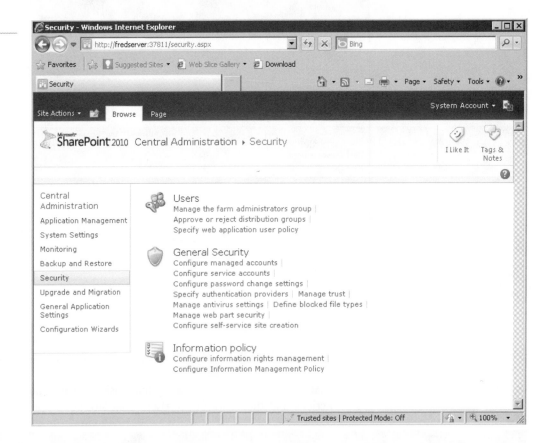

2. In the General Security section, click Configure managed accounts. The Managed Accounts page displays (see Figure 7-32).
3. Click Register Managed Account. The Registered Managed Account page displays (see Figure 7-33).
4. In the Account Registration section, type the User name and Password.
5. In the Automatic Password Change section, select the Enable automatic password change check box to allow SharePoint Server 2010 to manage the password for the selected account. Then type a numeric value that indicates the number of days prior to password expiration that the automatic password change process will be initiated.

Figure 7-32

The Managed Accounts page

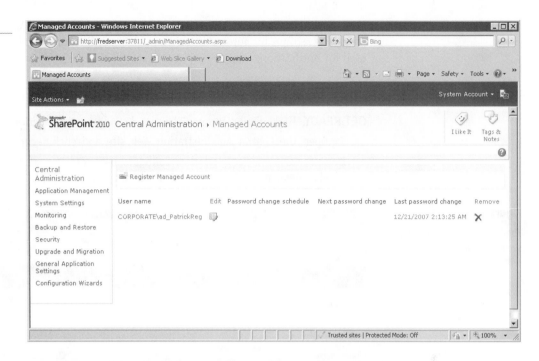

Figure 7-33

The Registered Managed
Account page

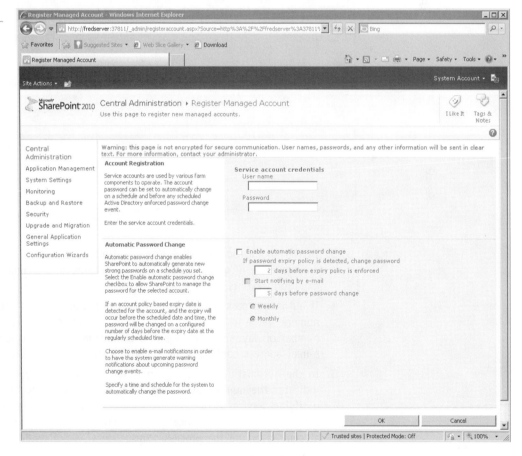

6. In the Automatic Password Change section, select the Start notifying by e-mail check box, and then enter a numeric value that indicates the number of days prior to the initiation of the automatic password change process that an e-mail notification will be sent. You can then configure a Weekly or Monthly e-mail notification schedule.

7. Click OK.

You can use the Password Management Settings page of Central Administration to configure farm-level settings for automatic password changes, including configuring the email address used for notifications. You can also configure monitoring and scheduling options.

 CONFIGURE AUTOMATIC PASSWORD CHANGE SETTINGS

GET READY. To configure automatic password change settings, perform the following steps:

1. Open the Central Administration Web site and click Security.
2. Under General Security, click Configure password change settings. The Password Management Settings page displays (see Figure 7-34).

Figure 7-34

The Password Management settings page

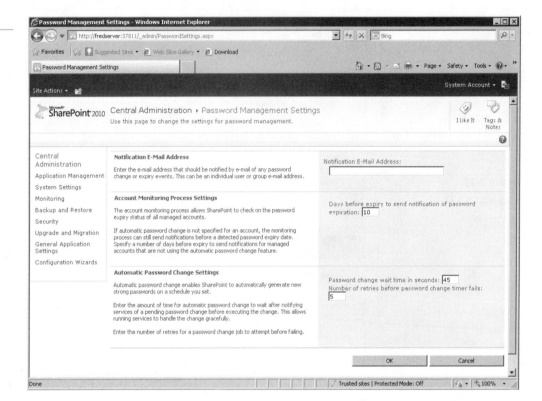

3. In the Notification E-Mail Address section, type the Notification E-Mail Address of an individual or group that should be notified of any imminent password change or expiration events.

4. If automatic password change is not configured for a managed account, type a numeric value in the Account Monitoring Process Settings section that indicates the number of days prior to password expiration that a notification will be sent to the e-mail address configured in the Notification E-Mail Address section.

5. In the Automatic Password Change Settings section, type a numeric value that indicates the number of seconds that automatic password change will wait (after notifying services of a pending password change) before initiating the change. Type a numeric value that indicates the number of times a password change will be attempted before the process stops.

6. Click OK.

Once you have your Managed Accounts created, you can use them for Service Instances and Service and Content Application Pools. To associate a managed account with a specific Service Instance using Central Administration, you can go to Security and then select Configure service accounts. On the Service Accounts page you can set the account used for the Farm Account, Service Instances, Web Content Application Pools, and Service Application Pools.

If, for some reason, the automatic password change process fails and SharePoint gets an access denial at login or account lockout, you can use `Set-SPManagedAccount` PowerShell command to fix the password mismatch and then resume the password change process.

 CORRECT A PASSWORD MISMATCH

GET READY. To correct a password mismatch, perform the following steps:

1. Click Start > All Programs > Microsoft SharePoint 2010 Products > SharePoint 2010 Management Shell.

2. From the Windows PowerShell command prompt, type the following and then press Enter:

   Set-SPManagedAccount [-Identity] <SPManagedAccountPipeBind> -ExistingPassword <SecureString> -UseExistingPassword $true

Managing Online SharePoint Users

THE BOTTOM LINE

After Office 365 and SharePoint Online is configured, assigning permissions to a site, list, or library is the same as assigning user permissions in a server installation of SharePoint. However, before you get there, you have to adding users to Office 365 and define collection administrators.

As covered in Lesson 1 and Lesson 4, SharePoint Online is part of Office 365. Therefore, to manage users in SharePoint Online, you have to first add users to Office 365. You can then configure a user as a collection administrator or assign permissions for a user to a site, list, or library.

Adding Users to Office 365

To add users to SharePoint Online, use Office 365's Admin overview page. When you add users, you must create user names and email addresses for them. After you have added users to your service, you can assign suite licenses to those users.

The licenses available for each user include:

- An Office 365 mailbox that users can access from their Outlook desktop app or Outlook Web App.
- Access to the Downloads page to download desktop apps (such as Microsoft Office 2010 and Lync for instant messaging) and to set up and configure their computers to work with Office 365.

When you create a user, you can specify an administrative role to a user. The three administrative roles available:

- **Global administrator**: The administrator of the Microsoft Online Services Portal, with permissions to manage service licenses, users and groups, domains, and subscribed services.
- **SharePoint Online service administrator**: The administrator of the SharePoint Online Administration Center, with permissions to create and manage site collections. In the Microsoft Office 365, the Microsoft Online Services administrator is also the SharePoint Online service administrator.
- **Site collection administrator**: A user with administrative permissions to manage a site collection. There can be only one primary administrator and several administrators for a site collection.

ADD A NEW USER IN OFFICE 365

GET READY. To add a new user in Office 365, perform the following steps:

1. Go to the Admin page for Office 365.
2. In the left pane, in the Management section, click Users. The Users page displays (see Figure 7-35).

Figure 7-35

The Office 365 Users page

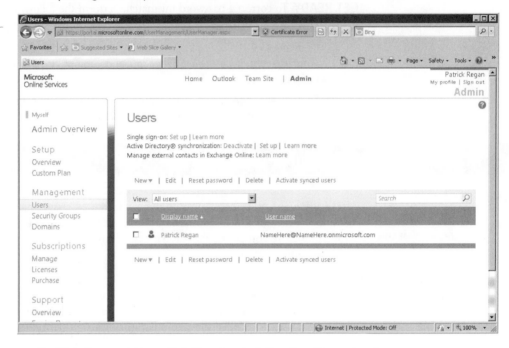

3. Click New and then click User to start the New User wizard.
4. On the Details page, type the First name, Last name, Display name, and User name (see Figure 7-36). If you want to include the job title, department, office number, office phone, mobile number, or fax number address, expand Additional details.
5. Click Next.

Figure 7-36

The Details page

6. On the Settings page (see Figure 7-37), in the Assign role permissions section, specify administrator permissions for the user. You can also specify an Alternate email address for password recovery.

7. Click Next.

Figure 7-37

The Settings page

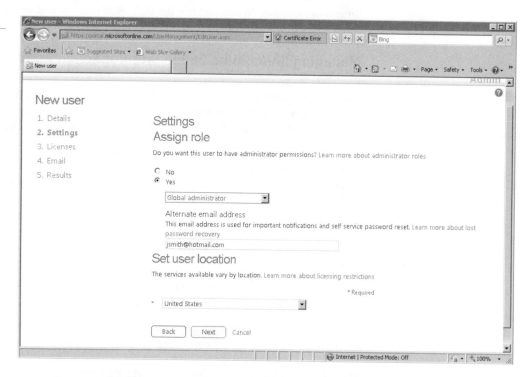

8. On the Assign licenses page (see Figure 7-38), select the license for the user, including SharePoint Online.

9. Click Next.

Figure 7-38

Assigning licenses

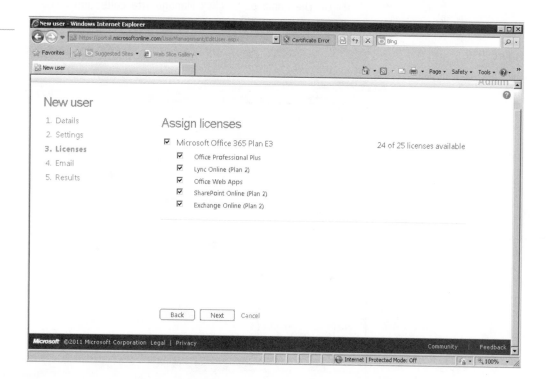

10. On the Send results in email page, specify the email address where you want to send the username and temporary passwords. Click Create.

11. On the Results page, review the information and then click Finish.

If you want to add more than one user at a time, you can alternatively select Bulk Add instead of Add user. When you use the Bulk Add option, you will use a CSV text file that contains a list of all of the users that you want to add.

Managing SharePoint Online Site Collection Administrators

> While SharePoint Online does not have Central Administration, you can still assign collection administrators via the Administration Center. Instead of having a primary and secondary collection administrator, SharePoint Online only has a primary collection administrator.

SharePoint Online permissions and user groups are managed separately from Office 365 settings. If you want a user to be a site collection administrator or a site owner, you'll need to add yourself as a site collection administrator and/or site owner on your SharePoint Online team sites. In addition, new user accounts that you create in Office 365 are not automatically added to your team sites' respective user lists. You must manually add users to your organization's team sites so that you can control access to them. You can also set user account permissions that are specific to each team site.

Once you set the primary administrator when creating a site collection, you should set a second or third site collection administrator as a backup.

The SharePoint Online service administrator can use the following procedure to change the primary administrator for a site collection or to add or remove administrators for a site collection.

MANAGE SHAREPOINT ONLINE COLLECTION ADMINISTRATORS

GET READY. To manage SharePoint Online collection administrators, perform the following steps:

1. Sign in to the SharePoint Online Administration Center.

2. On the home page, click Manage site collections. The Site Collections page displays (see Figure 7-39).

Figure 7-39

The Site Collections page

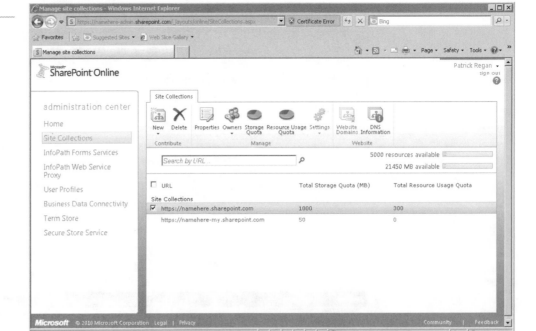

3. Select the check box next to the appropriate site collection.

4. On the Site Collections ribbon tab, in the Manage group, click Owners, and then click Manage Administrators. The Manage Administrators dialog displays (see Figure 7-40).

Figure 7-40

The Manage Administrators dialog

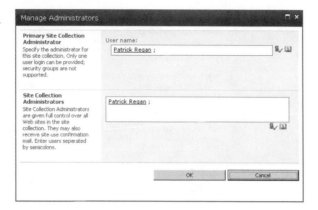

5. In the Primary Site Collection Administrator section, change the User name.

6. To validate user names, click the Check Names button.

7. Click OK.

Implementing Active Directory Synchronization

Organizations using Active Directory can use the Microsoft Online Directory Synchronization tool to synchronize existing Active Directory users to an Office 365 directory and keep it synchronized. In addition, Directory Synchronization can be combined with Single Sign-on to create a true Identity Management solution.

Before you install the Active Directory Synchronization tool, you must first activate the Office 365 directory synchronization feature by running the Microsoft Office 365 Deployment Readiness tool. This tool inspects your Active Directory environment and then provides a report that includes a prerequisite check and an attribute assessment that are specific to the directory synchronization tool requirements. If your environment doesn't meet the minimum requirements, the tool lists the changes you must make before you can begin directory synchronization.

 IMPLEMENT DIRECTORY SYNCHRONIZATION

GET READY. To activate Office 365 directory synchronization and install the Active Directory Synchronization tool, perform the following steps:

1. In the Office 365 header, click Admin.

2. On the Admin page, in the left pane, click Users.

3. At the top of the page, next to Active Directory synchronization, click the Setup link. The Set up and manage Active Directory synchronization page displays (see Figure 7-41).

Figure 7-41

The Manage Administrators page

4. In the Activate Active Directory synchronization section, click Activate.

5. When prompted to activate Active Directory synchronization, click Activate.

6. In Step 4, select the Windows 32-bit version or the Windows 64-bit version and click Download. Save and run the dirsync.exe file on your Windows computer that is part of the domain.

7. If prompted to run or save the file, click Run.

8. When the Welcome screen displays, click Next.

9. When the setup program displays the software license terms, select I accept and then click Next.

10. When prompted to select an installation folder, click Next.

11. On the last page of the installation program, select Start Configuration Wizard now, and then click Finish.

12. The Microsoft Online Services Directory Synchronization Configuration Wizard starts.

TAKE NOTE *

For more information, visit http://onlinehelp.microsoft.com/en-us/office365-enterprises/ff652545.aspx and http://onlinehelp.microsoft.com/en-us/office365-enterprises/ff652557.aspx

Managing External Users

CERTIFICATION READY
What steps have to be performed before you can invite external users?
2.2.7

While most think of SharePoint as an organizational tool that is meant to be used by an organization, often the organization needs to interface with external users such as vendors and customers. Therefore, you will need to know how manage external users.

By default, SharePoint Online does not allow external users. The SharePoint Online administrator can enable or disable the Manage External Users feature. If you enable external users, any site collection administrator can turn on the External user invitations feature for her site collection. You will then finish by inviting the external user to the SharePoint site by sending them an email.

 ENABLE EXTERNAL SHARING FOR SHAREPOINT ONLINE

GET READY. To enable external users for SharePoint Online, perform the following steps:

1. Sign in to the SharePoint Online Administration Center.
2. On the home page, click Manage Site Collections. The Site Collections page displays.
3. Click Settings and then click Manage External Users. The External Users dialog box displays.
4. Click Allow.
5. Click Save.

 ACTIVATE EXTERNAL SHARING FOR A SITE COLLECTION

GET READY. To activate external sharing for a site collection, perform the following steps:

1. Sign in to the site collection for which you want to enable external users.
2. Click Site Actions > Site Settings. The Site Settings page displays.
3. In the Site Collection Administration section, click Site collection features. The Site Collection Administration Features page displays.
4. In the list of features, for External user invitations, click Activate.

 SHARE A SITE WITH EXTERNAL USERS

GET READY. To share a site with external users, perform the following steps:

1. From any page in the site, click Site Actions > Share Site.
2. In either the <site name> Visitors box or the <site name> Members box, type the e-mail address of the external user you want invite.
3. In the Message box, type a message to the user explaining that they are receiving permission to the site.
4. Click Share.

The invited person receives an email that includes a link to accept the invitation. To accept the invitation, the user must provide a Windows Live ID or, if he's an existing Office 365 customer, he can provide his Microsoft Online Services ID. If he doesn't have an existing Windows Live ID, he can create an account at https://accountservices.passport.net/ppnetworkhome.srf. He will use the Windows Live ID or the Microsoft Online Services ID to log in to your SharePoint site.

SKILL SUMMARY

IN THIS LESSON YOU LEARNED:

- Since SharePoint can provide vital services for a company while storing confidential information, it is imperative that you plan and implement proper security.
- When securing a SharePoint site, you will need to perform three basic tasks. They include managing administrative access, assigning permissions to sites, lists and libraries and managing group membership.

- By using a hierarchical level in SharePoint, you can break up the task and responsibility of security administration.

- Farm Administrators have full access to all servers in the server farm including performing all administrative tasks in Central Administration for the server or server farm, and managing service applications.

- The Windows Administrators group on the local server can perform all farm administrator actions such as installing new products or applications, deploying Web Parts and new features to the global assembly cache, creating new Web applications and new Internet Information Services (IIS) Web sites, and starting services.

- Service application administrators can configure settings for a specific service application within a farm.

- A feature administrator can manage a subset of service application settings, but not the entire service application

- Collection administrators have the Full Control permission level on all Web sites within a site collection and are responsible for planning how the access is granted to the site collection.

- Site owners have full control of content on the site. They can perform administrative tasks on the site including any list or library within that site.

- Web sites, lists, libraries, folders, and list items are all securable in SharePoint.

- A permission grants access to the securable object and specifies what kind of access a user (or group of users) has to the specified object.

- Similar to NTFS permissions, SharePoint permissions are divided into permission levels that consist of several permissions that allow users to perform a set of related tasks.

- By default, permissions within a site collection are inherited from the root site to subsites and all lists and pages, which means that those permissions cascade down to the lower sites and objects from the parent site.

- The idea behind groups is to group users together so that when you assign permissions, you assign them once to a group and all users in the groups receive those permissions. As a result, permission management is simplified.

- A service account is an account that an operating system, process or service runs under. A service account can allow the application or service specific rights and permissions to function properly while minimizing the permissions required for the users using the application server.

- A managed account is an Active Directory user account whose credentials are managed by and contained in SharePoint.

■ Knowledge Assessment

Fill in the Blank

Complete the following sentences by writing the correct word or words in the blanks provided.

1. The _____ has full access to all servers in the server farm including performing all administrative tasks in Central Administration.

2. A _____ grants access to the securable object and specifies what kind of access a user or group of users has to the specified object.

3. _____ have full control of content on a site.

4. The mechanism whereby permissions generally flow from the parent object to a child object is known as _____.

5. _____ are used to combine multiple users into a single collective so that you can assign permissions to all users within the collective quickly and easily.

6. _____ assigns the Contribute permission level for users.

7. The _____ group assigns read-only access to a site, list, or library.

8. A _____ is an account that the SharePoint Timer service runs under.

9. Only _____ collection Administrators can be assigned within SharePoint Administration Web site.

10. Use _____ to manage Active Directory groups.

Multiple Choice

Circle the letter that corresponds to the best answer.

1. Which administrator can configure settings for a specific service application but cannot assign Farm Administrators?
   a. service application administrator
   b. feature administrator
   c. site administrator
   d. collection administrator

2. What role has Full Control permission level on all Web sites within a site collection, including all lists and libraries?
   a. service application administrator
   b. feature administrator
   c. site owner
   d. collection administrator

3. What are permissions grouped into?
   a. permission group
   b. permission level
   c. permission frame
   d. permission right

4. What is the minimum SharePoint permission level used to assign permissions to a list or library?
   a. Full Control
   b. Contribute
   c. Read
   d. Limited Access

5. What is the minimum permission level needed to add content to a list?
   a. Full Control
   b. Contribute
   c. Read
   d. Limited Access

6. What permission level can be given to Web developers who need to apply style sheets, themes, and borders to the various SharePoint sites without giving them Full Control?
   a. Design
   b. Contribute
   c. Read
   d. Limited Access

7. Which account can have SharePoint automatically manage and change the password when necessary?
   a. full access account
   b. administrative account
   c. local server account
   d. managed account

8. In Windows Server 2008, Windows Administrators are managed through _____.
   a. SharePoint Central Administration
   b. SharePoint Site Settings
   c. Server Manager
   d. SharePoint Control Panel

9. Which group should you assign to Web developers and SharePoint users who need to control the look feel of SharePoint?
   a. Contributor
   b. site member
   c. site owner
   d. designer

10. Which administrator will usually perform the day-to-day security tasks?
    a. farm administrator
    b. windows administrator
    c. feature administrator
    d. site owner

True / False

Circle T if the statement is true or F if the statement is false.

T | F **1.** Permissions within a site always cascade down to its lower objects.

T | F **2.** You can see the members of an Active Directory group in SharePoint.

T | F **3.** You can manage SharePoint groups with Active Directory Users and Computers.

T | F **4.** When creating service accounts, it is recommended to use strong passwords that are changed on a regular basis.

T | F **5.** If you use the no-override permission, you can ensure that permissions are always inherited downward.

■ Case Scenario

Scenario 7-1: Management SharePoint 2010 Security

You have a large organization with multiple departments. You just installed and implemented a SharePoint 2010 environment with multiple servers. Your manager wants to know how you are going to plan the security for SharePoint and its content. Explain your security plan.

Scenario 7-2: Configuring Access Across Networks

Within your large organization, you have an IT department. Within your large SharePoint environment, you have a site for each department within your organization. The Help Desk usually handles creating and managing users and groups within Active Directory. What is the best way to assign permissions to the various users within your organization to the various SharePoint sites?

Configuring Service Applications

OBJECTIVE DOMAIN MATRIX

TECHNOLOGY SKILL	OBJECTIVE DOMAIN DESCRIPTION	OBJECTIVE DOMAIN NUMBER
Configuring Service Applications	Configuring Service Applications	1.3
Managing Office 2010 Applications	Configuring Access Services	1.3.2
	Configuring Visio Services	1.3.3
	Configuring Microsoft Office Excel Services	1.3.6
	Configuring InfoPath Forms Services (IPFS)	1.2.4
	Configuring IPFS	1.3.8
Configuring PerformancePoint Services	Configuring Microsoft Office PerformancePoint Server 2007	1.3.4
Configuring Business Connectivity Services	Configuring Business Connectivity Services (BCS)	1.3.1
Managing Metadata Services	Configuring Managed Metadata Services (MMS)	1.3.7
Configuring and Managing User Profiles	Configuring User Profiles	1.3.5
	Configuring SharePoint Online Store	1.3.9

KEY TERMS

Access services

Audiences

Business Connectivity Services (BCS)

Business Data Connectivity (BDC)

Excel Services

Forefront Identity Manager (FIM)

InfoPath Forms Services (IPFS)

managed metadata

metadata

My Sites

Organization profiles

PerformancePoint

Service Application Proxy

Service Applications (SAs)

term store

Term Store Management Tool

User profile

User Profile Service Application

User Profile Synchronization Service

Visio Graphics Service

Your manager approaches you and is very impressed with what SharePoint has to offer. Now, he would like to see SharePoint taken to the next level by using some more advanced tools, so that SharePoint can be used as a business intelligence tool that will harbor collaboration between your users. You respond by saying that there are several Service Applications that can be configured to provide what he is asking for.

■ Configuring Service Applications

THE BOTTOM LINE

Microsoft Office SharePoint Server 2007 introduced Shared Services Providers (SSPs) to provide common services to Web applications. In SharePoint 2010, SSPs have been replaced by Service Applications (SAs). Different from SSP, SAs provide granular pieces of functionality to other Web and Service Applications in the farm. An SA can be turned off, exist on one server to break up the workload of the servers, or be load-balanced across multiple servers in the farm.

Service Applications are designed to be as independent as possible. Therefore, if a Service Application is having problems such as a failure or is misconfigured, its effect will be minimized. As a result, each SA enabled on the farm typically runs in its own process and typically has its own configuration database and Active Directory (AD) service account. In fact, some Service Applications can be published across farms and can be made available to other farms over remote connections. SharePoint 2010 Enterprise edition contains more SAs than SharePoint 2010 Standard edition, which contains more SAs than SharePoint Foundation.

Some of the popular services include:

- **Access Services**: Lets users view, edit, and interact with Microsoft Access 2010 databases in a Web browser.
- **Business Data Connectivity Service**: Gives access to line-of-business data systems.
- **Excel Services Application**: Lets users view and interact with Microsoft Excel 2010 files in a Web browser.
- **InfoPath Forms Services (IPFS)**: Gives users the ability to deploy your organization's forms to Microsoft SharePoint Server and enables users to fill out these forms using a Web browser.
- **Managed Metadata Service**: Manages taxonomy hierarchies, keywords, and social tagging infrastructure; publishes content types across site collections.
- **PerformancePoint Service Application**: Provides the capabilities of PerformancePoint, which allows you to monitor and analyze your business.
- **Search Service**: Crawls content, produces index partitions, and serves search queries. Search services are discussed in Lesson 9.
- **Secure Store Service**: Provides single sign-on authentication to access multiple applications or services.
- **State Service**: Provides temporary storage of user session data for SharePoint Server components.
- **Usage and Health Data Collection Service**: Collects farm-wide usage and health data and provides the ability to view various usage and health reports. Usage and Health Data Collection services are discussed in Lesson 10.
- **User Profile Service**: Adds support for My Sites, profile pages, social tagging, and other social computing features.

- **Visio Graphics Service**: Lets users view and refresh published Visio 2010 diagrams in a Web browser.
- **Web Analytics Service**: Collects, reports, and analyzes the usage and effectiveness of SharePoint Server 2010 sites. Web Analytics Service is discussed in Lesson 10.
- **Word Automation Services**: Performs automated bulk document conversions.

Some of these Service Applications have a service connection referred to as a ***Service Application Proxy***. A Service Application Proxy is a virtual link between the Service Application or Web application that also coordinates with any related SharePoint load-balancing mechanisms. Some also enable inter-farm services.

To configure the SAs, open Central Administration and, located under Application Management, click **Manage Service Applications**. Figure 8-1 shows the Service Applications page. To configure an installed Service Application, click the **Service Application**. To add or install a Service Application, click the **New** button and select the Service Application that you want to install or add.

Figure 8-1

The Service Applications page

■ Managing Office 2010 Applications

The Bottom Line

For many organizations, Microsoft Office is the primary software suite used by users to create documents and manage data. Microsoft Office 2010 is more tightly integrated with SharePoint than previous versions of SharePoint. As a result, Office integrates with collaboration tasks while improving communications.

With early network technology, the two common methods of sharing documents were using a shared folder or sending an email with attachments. When using a shared folder, only one user can open a document at one time. Sending emails simply puts multiple copies of the document in each user's email inbox and can create confusion regarding which version is current and which user made which change to the document. SharePoint can overcome these shortcomings and provide a collaborative environment.

When combined with Office 2010, SharePoint 2010 offers Live Co-Authoring, which allows multiple users to open, view, and change the same document at the same time. Different from previous versions of SharePoint 2010 and Office 2010, the familiar Save button at the top-left corner of the application is combined with the refresh symbol (see Figure 8-2). So when you click Save, the document is saved *and* refreshed at the same time, showing any changes that other users might have also made to the document while you've been working with it. As shown in Figure 8-2, if multiple users are editing the same document, the bottom of the screen shows the number of users working on the document. Clicking the number shows the list of users who are accessing the document.

Figure 8-2

The Live Co-Authoring application

By clicking the File menu, users can access the Backstage view (see Figure 8-3).

Figure 8-3

BackStage view

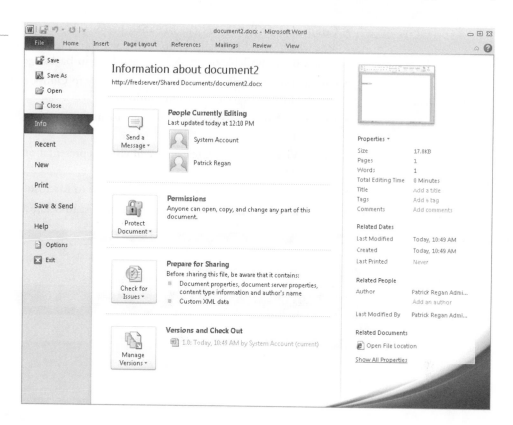

Backstage view allows you to manage permissions, prepare the document for sharing, and manage document versions, among other options:

- **Permissions**: Click the Protect Document button to access the following sub options:
  - **Mark the document as Final**: Indicates that editing is complete.
  - **Encrypt with Password**: Require a password to open this document.
  - **Restrict Editing**: Restrict editing to only certain parts of a document.
  - **Restrict Permission by People**: Used with Microsoft's Information Rights Management Service, this option restricts access to a document even if the file has been copied or saved away from the SharePoint environment.
  - **Add a Digital Signature**: Adds a digital signature box that acts as an official signature of approval.
- **Prepare for Sharing**: Prepares a document for sharing by checking for issues that may cause problems:
  - **Inspect Document**: Checks the document for items such as comments, personal information, or hidden text.
  - **Check Accessibility**: Inspects the document for any content that people with disabilities may find difficult to read.
  - **Check Compatibility**: Looks for compatibility issues that may exist with earlier versions of Office.
- **Versions and Check Out**: Click the Manage Versions button to check the file in or out, compare major versions, recover draft versions, or delete all draft versions.

If you open a list or library in SharePoint, you will find several options in the List or Library ribbon that allow you to connect Office to the site or library (see Figure 8-4). Depending on the current type of list or library, different options will appear in this area. The options include the following:

- **Sync to SharePoint Workspace**: Creates a synchronized copy of the current library on your local computer using SharePoint Workspace 2010. SharePoint Workspace can then be used offline.

- **Connect to Office**: Users can save their personal favorite SharePoint links to their own lists, which would be available no matter which computer a user logs into. These locations are also available on the Save & Send tab in Backstage view.
- **Connect to Outlook**: Connects a list or library to Outlook, allowing users to access and edit the list or library items from Outlook.
- **Export to Excel**: Copies data from a list to an Excel spreadsheet, allowing you to further analyze the data.
- **Create Visio Diagram**: Creates several visual representations of the task list in a new Visio diagram.
- **Open With Access**: Connects a SharePoint list to Microsoft Access.
- **Open Schedule**: Exports tasks in the current list to Microsoft Project.

Figure 8-4

Connecting to Office

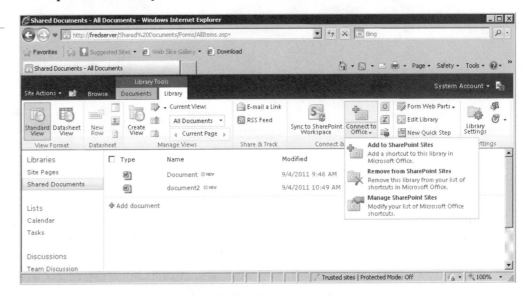

Microsoft Office Web Apps is the online version of Word, Excel, PowerPoint, and OneNote applications. It allows users to access and edit documents using their personal computers, mobile phones, and the Internet. Office Web Apps is available to users through Windows Live, and to business customers with Microsoft Office 2010 volume licensing and document management solutions based on Microsoft SharePoint 2010 Products.

When you install Office Web Apps, the Office Web Apps Services are added to the list of SharePoint Services and the Office Web Apps Feature is added to the available SharePoint Features. Office Web Apps services include the Word Viewing Service, PowerPoint Service, and Excel Calculation Services.

+ MORE INFORMATION

While installing Office Web Apps on SharePoint is beyond the contents of the 70-667 exam, information on deploying Office Web apps can be found at http://technet.microsoft.com/en-us/library/ff431687.aspx

Configuring Access Services

Microsoft Access is a relational database management system from Microsoft that combines the relational Microsoft Jet Database Engine with a graphical user interface and software-development tools. It is included within some editions of the Microsoft Office suite, including Office Professional and Office Enterprise. Access is a popular application that can be used to create custom database applications with sophisticated queries and reports, but it does have its shortcomings, including a lack of fault tolerance, load-balancing, and disaster recovery capabilities. *Access services* improves Access' capabilities within the SharePoint environment so that data remains secure and available.

Access Services is new to SharePoint 2010. It is a Service Application that allows users to host Access databases directly within SharePoint. It allows users to edit,update, and create linked Access 2010 databases that can be viewed and manipulated with Internet browsers, the Access client, or a linked HTML page. When an Access database is linked to SharePoint, any changes made to the database are automatically copied to the SharePoint site.

While you do not need Access in order to use the published Web database, Access is required to make any changes to the database structure. In addition, a user account is required to use the Web database on SharePoint Server 2010. Anonymous access is not supported.

 DEPLOY ACCESS SERVICES

To deploy Access Services, perform the following steps:

1. Install and configure Microsoft SQL Server 2008 R2 Reporting Services Add-in for SharePoint Technologies 2010 (SSRS).

> **TAKE NOTE** * To download the Microsoft SQL Server 2008 R2 Reporting Services Add-in for SharePoint Technologies 2010, visit http://www.microsoft.com/download/en/details. aspx?id=622

2. Create an account in the Active Directory to run the application pool for the Access Services Service Application.
3. Register that account as a managed account in SharePoint Server 2010.
4. Start Access Services.
5. Create an Access Services Service Application.

 **CREATE THE ACCESS SERVICES SERVICE APPLICATION**

GET READY. If your system is running the Enterprise edition of SharePoint 2010, you can add the Access Services Service Application by performing the following steps:

1. Open Central Administration and, under Application Management, click Manage Service Applications.
2. On the Manage Service Applications page, click New, and then click Access Services (see Figure 8-5). The Create New Access Services Application page displays (see Figure 8-6).

Figure 8-5

Adding a Service Application

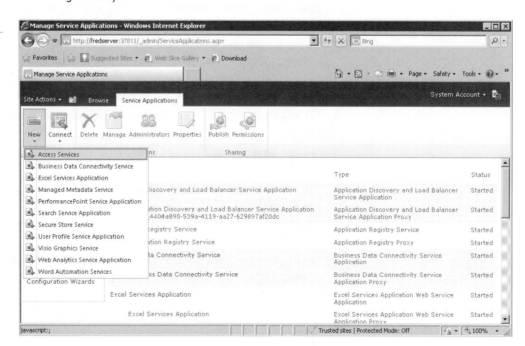

Figure 8-6

The Create New Access
Services Application page

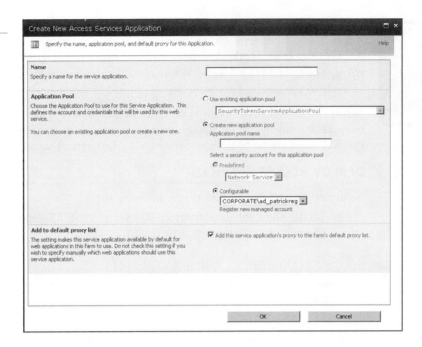

3. In the Specify a name for the service application text box, type Access Services.

4. Leave the Create new application pool option selected and, in the Application pool name text box, type AccessServicesAppPool.

5. Select the Configurable option and, from the drop-down list, select a service account.

6. Leave the Add this service application's proxy to the farm's default proxy list option selected.

7. Click OK.

 CONFIGURE ACCESS SERVICES

GET READY. To configure the access services, perform the following steps:

1. Open Central Administration and, under Application Management, click Manage Service Applications.

2. In the list on the Manage Service Applications page, select the desired Access service you want to configure. The Manage Access Services page displays (see Figure 8-7).

3. In the Lists and Queries section, in the Maximum Columns Per Query box, type a value from 1 to 255 (40 is the default).

4. Set the Maximum Rows Per Query to a value between 1 and 200000 (25000 is the default).

5. Set the Maximum Sources Per Query to a value between 1 and 20 (12 is the default).

6. Set the Maximum Calculated Columns Per Query to a value between 0 to 32 (10 is the default).

7. Set the Maximum Order By Clauses Per Query to a value between 1 and 8 (4 is the default).

8. Set Allow Outer Joins by selecting or de-selecting the check box Outer Joins Allowed (with inner joins always being allowed).

9. Set Allow Non Remote-able Queries by selecting or de-selecting the Remoteable Queries Allowed check box.

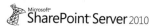

Figure 8-7

The Manage Access
Services page

10. Set Maximum Records Per Table to any positive integer (500000 is the default and -1 indicates that there is no limit).

11. Under Application Objects, set Maximum Application Log Size to any positive integer (3000 is the default and -1 indicates that there is no limit).

12. Under Session Management, set Maximum Request Duration in seconds to a value between 1 and 2007360 (24 days). The default value is 30 and -1 indicates there is no limit.

13. Set Maximum Sessions Per User to any positive integer (10 is the default and -1 indicates there is no limit).

14. Set Maximum Sessions Per Anonymous User to any positive integer (25 is the default and -1 indicates there is no limit).

15. Set Cache Timeout to a value in seconds between 1 and 2007360 (24 days). The default is 300 and -1 indicates there is no limit.

16. Set Maximum Session Memory to a value in megabytes between 0 (disable) and 4095 (64 is the default).

17. Under Memory Utilization, set Maximum Private Bytes (In MB) to any positive integer (the default of -1 indicates the use of 50 percent of the physical memory on the computer).

18. Under Templates, set Maximum Template Size (In MB) to any positive integer (the default is 30 and -1 indicates there is no limit).

19. Click OK.

DELETE THE ACCESS SERVICES SERVICE APPLICATION

GET READY. To delete the Access Services Service Application, perform the following steps:

1. Open Central Administration and, under Application Management, click Manage Service Applications.

2. On the Manage Service Applications page, select the Access Services Service Application you want to delete.

3. On the Ribbon, click Delete. The Delete Service Application page displays (see Figure 8-8).

4. Select Delete data associated with the Service Applications and click OK.

Figure 8-8

The Delete Service
Application page

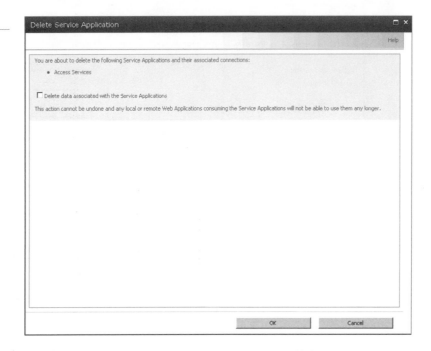

5. When the Service Application has been deleted, click OK.

Configuring Excel Services

> Microsoft Excel is a spreadsheet program that works with workbooks consisting of multiple sheets. Each sheet contains rows and columns to store data. Besides doing calculations within the spreadsheet, Excel can also perform powerful analysis of the data. *Excel Services* provides a secure method to exchange and analyze business data while providing a way to manage, monitor, and secure the sensitive data contained with the Excel spreadsheets.

Excel Services is a shared service that you can use to publish Excel workbooks to a SharePoint server. Once the workbook is in SharePoint, users can share the workbook and collaborate using the workbook.

Trusted data connection libraries are SharePoint Server 2010 document libraries that contain data connection files that Excel Calculation Services will trust to use to connect to databases. Excel Calculation Services does not use data connection files that are not stored in a trusted data connection library. However, data connection information can be embedded directly in a workbook that is trying to make a connection.

CERTIFICATION READY
What in SharePoint can be used to exchange and analyze business data found in Excel spreadsheets while making sure that sensitive data remains secure?
1.3.6

Excel Services loads data connection files if they are stored in a SharePoint Server 2010 library that is on the trusted data connection libraries list. Data connection libraries are a type of list in the SharePoint Server that contains data connection files that work well with external data connections. These files contain everything that Excel Services and Excel clients must have to connect to an external data source. Data connection libraries enable broad reuse and sharing of data connections. Data connections can be loaded using information from the workbook file, but using a data connection library provides an additional layer for data connections so that they can be managed separately from workbooks.

Data connections connect workbooks to data providers. Initially, there are no Excel Services trusted data connection libraries configured. To store data connection files, you must create at least one trusted data connection library.

ADD A TRUSTED DATA CONNECTION LIBRARY

GET READY. To add a trusted data connection library for Excel Services Service Application, perform the following steps:

1. Open Central Administration and, under Application Management, click Manage Service Applications.

2. Click Excel Services Application. The Manage Excel Services Application page displays (see Figure 8-9).

Figure 8-9

The Manage Excel Services Application page

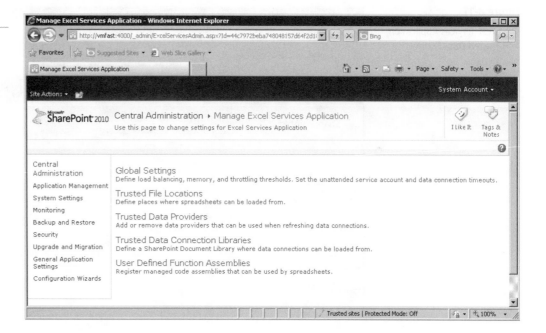

3. Click Trusted Data Connection Libraries. The Excel Services Application Trusted Data Connection Libraries page displays (see Figure 8-10).

4. Click Add Trusted Data Connection Library. The Excel Services Application Add Trusted Data Connection Library page displays (see Figure 8-11).

5. In the Location section, in the Address box, type the address of the trusted data connection library.

6. In the Description box, you can also type a description of the purpose for this trusted data connection library.

7. Click OK.

Figure 8-10

The Excel Services Application Trusted Data Connection Libraries page

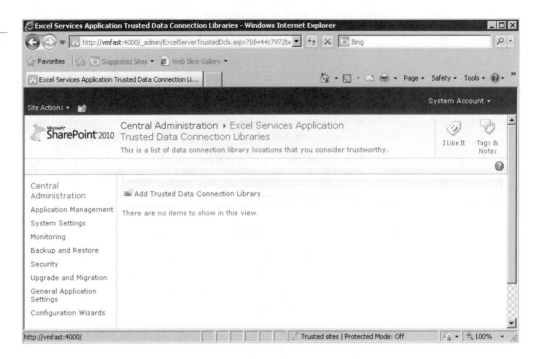

Figure 8-11

The Excel Services Application Add Trusted Data Connection Library page

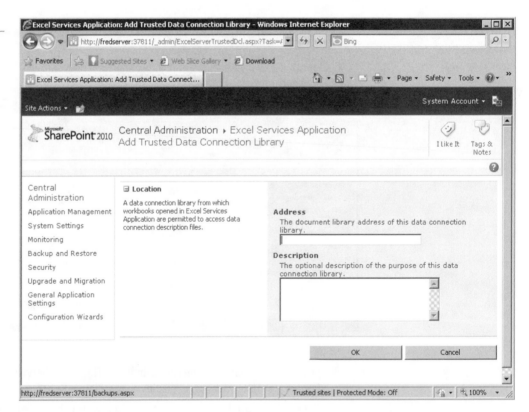

Microsoft SharePoint 2010 automatically creates a default trusted file location for Excel Services. The default trusted location site is http://, which represents the entire SharePoint farm. As a result, any Excel file loaded from the SharePoint farm can be loaded with Excel Services. Administrators can define new trusted file locations to expand workbook capabilities and tighten security. Trusted file locations are either SharePoint sites, UNC paths, or HTTP Web sites from which a server that is running Excel Calculation Services is permitted to access workbooks.

 ADD AN EXCEL SERVICES TRUSTED FILE LOCATION

GET READY. To add an Excel Services Trusted File Location, perform the following steps:

1. Open Central Administration and, under Application Management, click Manage Service Applications.

2. Click Excel Services Application. The Manage Excel Services Application page displays.

3. Click Trusted File Locations. The Excel Services Application Trusted File Locations page displays (see Figure 8-12).

Figure 8-12

The Excel Services Application Trusted File Locations page

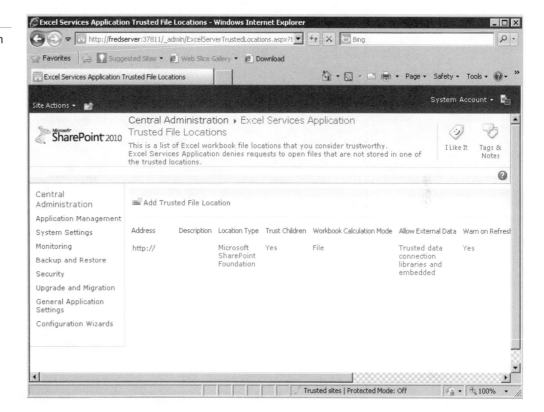

4. Click Add Trusted File Location. The Add Trusted File Location page displays (see Figure 8-13).

5. In the Address text box, type the SharePoint document library that you want to add as a trusted file location in Excel Services and choose the appropriate Location Type (Microsoft SharePoint Foundation, UNC, or HTTP).

6. In the Session Management section, you determine the behavior Excel Calculation Services sessions can have on your server. Therefore, type a value for the Session Timeout. While you should start with the default value (450 seconds), you can change the session timeout if desired.

7. In the Short Session Timeout box, type a value in seconds that an Excel Web Access session stays open and inactive (before any user interaction) before it is shut down. This is measured from the end of the original open request. The default is 450 seconds.

8. In the New Workbook Session Timeout box, type a value in seconds that an Excel Calculation Services session for a new workbook stays open and inactive before it is shut down, as measured from the end of each request. The default value is 1,800 seconds.

Figure 8-13

The Excel Services Application
Add Trusted File Location page

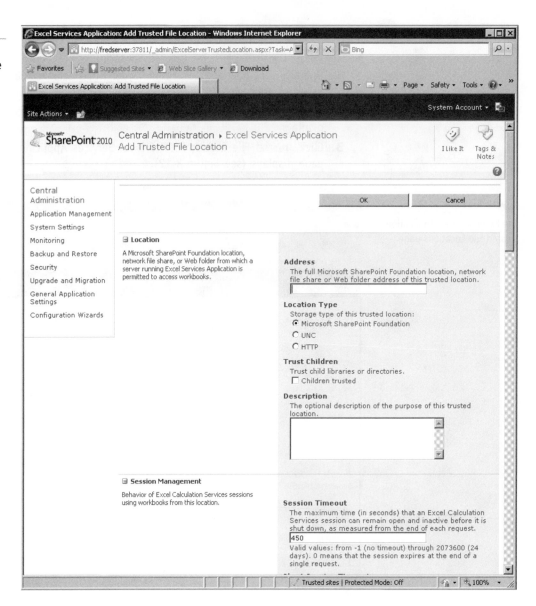

9. In the Maximum Request Duration box, type a value in seconds for the maximum duration of a single request in a session. The default is 300 seconds.

10. In the Maximum Chart Reader Duration box, type a value in seconds for the maximum time that is spent rendering any single chart. The default is 3 seconds.

11. In the Workbook Properties section, you determine the resource capacity for the server when Excel Services opens workbooks. In the Maximum Workbook Size box, type a value in megabytes (MB) for the maximum size of workbooks that Excel Calculation Services can open. The default size is 10 megabytes.

12. In the Maximum Chart or Image Size box, type a value in megabytes (MB) for the maximum size of charts or images that Excel Calculation Services can open. The default size is 1 megabyte.

13. In the Volatile Function Cache Lifetime box, type the value in seconds that a computed value for a volatile function is cached for automatic recalculations. The default is 300 seconds.

14. Under Workbook Calculation Mode (see Figure 8-14), select one of the following:

- File: Select this option to perform calculations as specified in the file.

- Manual: Select this option to recalculate only when a Calculate request is received.

- Automatic: Select this option if you want any change to a value to cause the recalculation of all other values dependent on that value.

- Automatic except data tables: Select this option if you want any change to a value to cause the recalculation of all other values dependent on that value (however, the values cannot be in a data table).

Figure 8-14

Choosing a Workbook
Calculation Mode

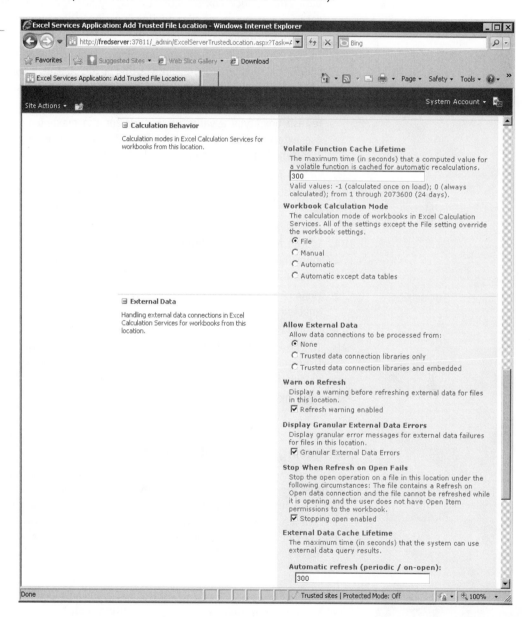

15. In the External Data section, you determine how Excel Calculation Services handles external data connections for workbooks from this location. Under Allow External Data, select one of the following:

- None: Select this option to disable all external data connections for the trusted file location.

- Trusted data connection libraries only: Select this option to only enable connections to data sources that are stored in a trusted data connection library. The server ignores settings embedded in the worksheet.

- Trusted data connection libraries and embedded: Select this option to enable connections that are embedded in the workbook file or connections that are stored in a trusted data connection library.

16. In the Warn on Refresh section, leave the Refresh warning enabled check box selected to display a warning before refreshing external data for files in this location. When you select this option, you ensure that external data is not automatically refreshed without user interaction.

17. In the Display Granular External Data Errors section, leave the Granular External Data Errors check box selected to display specific error messages when external data failures occur for files in this location. Displaying specific error messages can help troubleshoot data connectivity issues if they occur.

18. In the Stop When Refresh on Open Fails section, leave the Stopping open enabled check box selected to prevent viewing a file in this trusted file location.

19. In the External Data Cache Lifetime section, you can determine the maximum time, in seconds, that the system can use external data query results. In the Automatic refresh box, type a value in seconds for the maximum time that the system can use external data query results for automatically refreshed external query results. The default is 300 seconds.

20. In the Manual refresh box, type a value in seconds for the maximum time that the system can use external data query results for automatically refreshed external query results. To prevent data refresh after the first query, type -1. The default is 300 seconds.

21. In the Maximum Concurrent Queries Per Session box, type a value for the maximum number of queries that can run at the same time during a single session. The default is 5 queries.

22. Under Allow External Data Using REST section, select the Data refresh from REST enabled check box to all requests from the REST API to refresh external data connections.

23. In the User-Defined Functions section, under Allow User-Defined Functions, select User-defined functions allowed if you want to allow user-defined functions in Excel Calculation Services for workbooks from this location.

24. Click OK.

Configuring Visio Graphics Services

Microsoft Visio is a commercial diagramming program that is great in making flow charts, organizational charts, floor plans, and IT documentation. The Visio Graphics Service is a SharePoint 2010 Service Application that allows users to share and view Visio Web drawings using Visio Services. Similar to Excel Services, Microsoft Visio 2010 Web drawings can be refreshed and updated from a variety of data sources.

CERTIFICATION READY
What business intelligence tool can be used with SharePoint to analyze and present data?
1.3.3

While Visio is a powerful, easy-to-use diagraming tool, Visio combined with SharePoint acts as a business intelligence (BI) tool used to analyze and present data. It can be configured to show an organizational chart whereby each department can be clicked to show statistics for the department or a dashboard of metrics.

 CREATE A VISIO GRAPHICS SERVICE APPLICATION SERVICE

GET READY. To create a Visio Graphics Service Application Service, perform the following steps:

1. Open Central Administration and, under Application Management, click Manage Service Applications.
2. On the Ribbon, click New, and then click Visio Graphics Service.
3. Type a name for the new Service Application.
4. Choose an existing application pool or create a new one.
5. Choose Visio Graphics Service Application Proxy (recommended).
6. Click OK.

 CONFIGURE A VISIO GRAPHICS SERVICE APPLICATION SERVICE

GET READY. To configure a Visio Graphics Service Application Service, perform the following steps:

1. Open Central Administration and, under Application Management, click Manage Service Applications.
2. Click the Visio Graphics Service application service that you want to configure.
3. Click Global Settings to manage settings for performance, security, and refreshing data connections. The Visio Graphics Service Settings page displays (see Figure 8-15).

Figure 8-15

The Visio Graphics Service Settings page

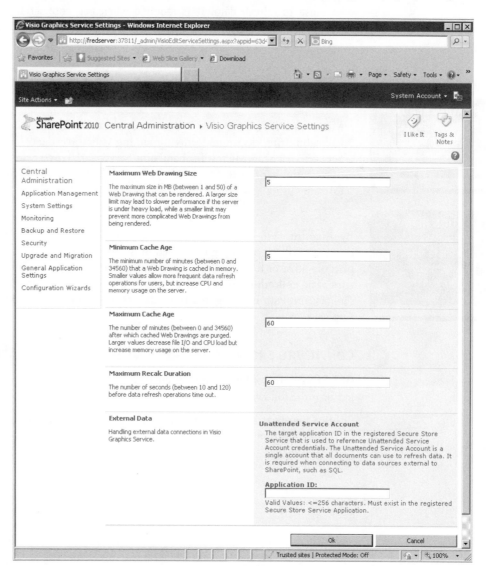

4. In the Maximum Web Drawing Size text box, type a value that specifies the maximum size in MB of a Web drawing that can be rendered. A larger size limit may lead to slower performance if the server is under heavy load; a smaller limit may prevent more complex Web drawings from being rendered. The default is 5 MB.

5. In the Minimum Cache Age text box, type a value that specifies the minimum number of minutes that a Web drawing is cached in memory. Smaller values allow for more frequent data refresh operations for users, but increase CPU and memory usage on the server.

6. In the Maximum Cache Age text box, type a value that specifies the number of minutes after which cached Web drawings are purged. Larger values decrease file I/O and CPU load but increase memory usage on the server.

7. In the Maximum Recalc Duration text box, type a value that specifies the number of seconds before data refresh operations time out. Longer timeouts allow for more complex data connected Web drawings to be recalculated, but longer timeouts also use more processing power. This applies only to data connected Web drawings.

8. In the Application ID text box, type the target application ID in the registered Secure Store Service that is used to reference Unattended Service Account credentials. The Unattended Service Account is a single account that all documents can use to refresh data. It is required when you connect to data sources external to SharePoint Server, such as the SQL Server.

9. Click OK.

Configuring InfoPath Forms Services

Microsoft Office InfoPath is a software application for designing, distributing, filling, and submitting electronic forms containing structured data. The InfoPath Forms Services (IPFS) in Microsoft SharePoint Server 2010 gives you the ability to deploy your organization's forms to Microsoft SharePoint Server and enable users to fill out these forms by using a Web browser.

CERTIFICATION READY
What application service allows you to implement electronic forms in SharePoint?
1.2.4

CERTIFICATION READY
What would you do when you want to delete a form to prevent any loss of data for current users using the forms?
1.3.8

By using InfoPath Forms Services, you can deploy forms within the SharePoint environment that users will fill out using their Web browsers. SharePoint users can publish form templates to a list or form library in a site collection. To deploy form templates that require full trust, data collections must be deployed by a farm administrator. Unlike other Office-related services, InfoPath is configured through General Application Settings instead of Service Applications.

→ **CONFIGURE BROWSER-ENABLED USER FORM TEMPLATES**

GET READY. To configure browser-enabled user form templates for InfoPath Forms Services, perform the following steps:

1. Open Central Administration and click General Application Settings. The General Application Settings page displays (see Figure 8-16).

Figure 8-16

The General Application
Settings page

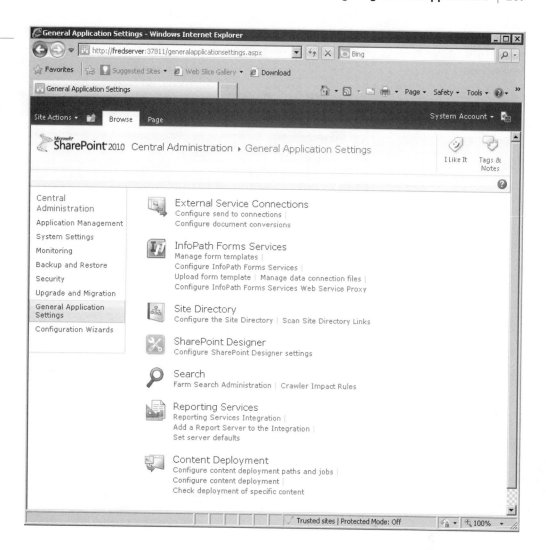

2. In the InfoPath Forms Services section, click Configure InfoPath Forms Services. The Configure InfoPath Forms Services page displays (see Figure 8-17).

3. In the User Browser-enabled Form Templates section, if you want to allow users to publish browser-enabled form templates, select the Allow users to browser-enable form templates check box.

4. If you want to allow browser-enabled form templates that users publish to be rendered in a Web browser, select the Render form templates that are browser-enabled by users check box.

5. In the Data Connection Timeouts section, set the connection timeout by typing the time in milliseconds that will elapse before timeout in the Default data connection timeout text box.

6. To set the maximum amount of time that can elapse before connection timeout, type the time in milliseconds in the Maximum data connection timeout text box.

7. To set the maximum size of responses that data connections are allowed to process, type the value in kilobytes in the Data Connection Response Size text box so that any responses that exceed the set size will throw an error message.

Figure 8-17

The Configure InfoPath Forms Services page

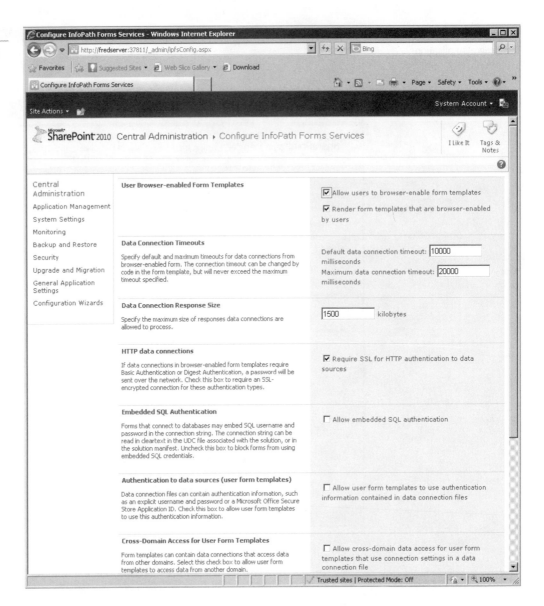

8. In the HTTP data connections section, select the Require SSL for HTTP authentication to data sources check box if you want to require SSL-encrypted connections for data connections using Basic or Digest authentication (see Figure 8-18).

9. In the Embedded SQL Authentication section, if you want to allow forms to use embedded SQL Server credentials, select the Allow embedded SQL authentication check box.

10. In the Authentication to data sources (user form templates) section, if you want to allow user form templates to use embedded authentication data, select the Allow user form templates to use authentication information contained in data connection files check box.

11. In the Cross-Domain Access for User Form Templates section, if you want to allow user form templates to access data from another domain, select the Allow cross-domain data access for user form templates that use connection settings in a data connection file check box.

12. In the Thresholds section, in the Number of postbacks per session text box, type the maximum number of postbacks you want to allow (75 is the default value).

Figure 8-18

Configuring the Require SSL for HTTP Authentication option

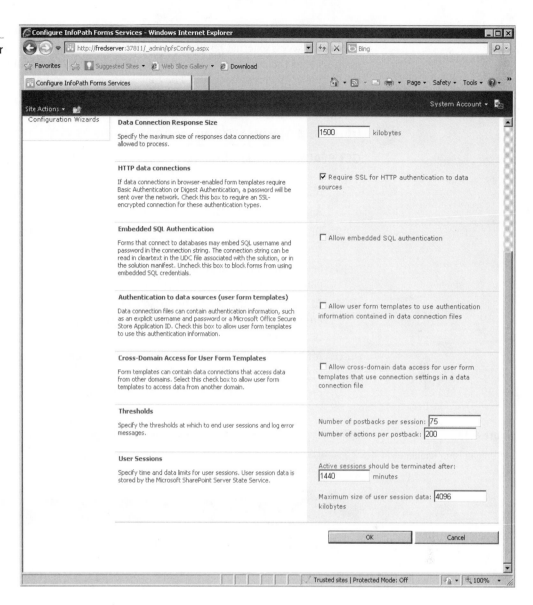

13. In the Number of actions per postback text box, type the value for the maximum number of actions per postback you want to allow (200 is the default value).

14. In the User Sessions section, in the Active Sessions Should Be Terminated After text box, type the value for the maximum session duration in minutes (1440 is the default value).

15. In the Maximum size of user session data text box, type the maximum session state size in kilobytes (4096 is the default value).

16. Click OK to apply your settings.

Most of the time, you need only to configure steps 1 through 4. If you clear the Allow users to browser-enable form templates check box, you disable browser-enabled form templates for the entire server farm. If you clear the Render form templates that are browser-enabled by users check box, users can still publish browser-enabled form templates to form libraries, but the templates that have been published to form libraries will be unable to be filled out in a Web browser. Templates published to lists will be unaffected. Lastly, if you need a form to use embedded SQL authentication, be sure to select the Allow embedded SQL authentication option.

As previously mentioned, if you need to upload a form that uses business logic using managed code, access external resources, or use administrator-managed data connection, you must grant trust to the executed code and accessed data. Therefore, you must have a farm administrator upload the form template. The following steps show you how to upload administrator-approved form templates using Central Administrator.

 UPLOAD ADMINISTRATOR-APPROVED INFOPATH FORM TEMPLATES

GET READY. To upload administrator-approved InfoPath form templates, perform the following steps:

1. Open Central Administration and click General Application Settings. The General Application Settings page displays.

2. In the InfoPath Forms Services section, click Upload Form Template. The Upload Form Template page displays (see Figure 8-19).

3. Select the form template by clicking the Browse button. When you locate the template to upload, click the Open button.

4. To make sure the template doesn't register any errors, click the Verify button; if errors exist, they will be displayed in the Report Details section of the Form Verification Report.

5. After the verification is complete and no errors display, click OK to return to the Upload Form Template page.

6. Browse to the location of the template again to choose and open the template.

Figure 8-19

The Upload Form Template page

7. In the Upgrade section, if the template does not already exist on the server or if it exists but you do not want to upgrade the template, clear the Upgrade the form template if it already exists check box.

8. If you want existing and new browser sessions to use the new form template, select the Terminate existing browser-based form filling sessions option. If not, leave the Allow existing browser-based form filling sessions to complete using the current version of the form template option selected.

9. Click Upload.

After the administrator-approved form template is uploaded, it must be activated before the form can be used by the users. To activate the form, you must activate it using Central Administration or from the site collection features page.

 ACTIVATE A FORM TEMPLATE

GET READY. To activate a form template, perform the following steps:

1. Open Central Administration and click General Application Settings. The General Application Settings page displays.

2. In the InfoPath Forms Services section, click Manage Form Templates. The Manage Form Templates page displays (see Figure 8-20).

3. Click the name of the form template you want to activate and then click Activate To a Site Collection (see Figure 8-21).

Figure 8-20

The Manage Form Templates page

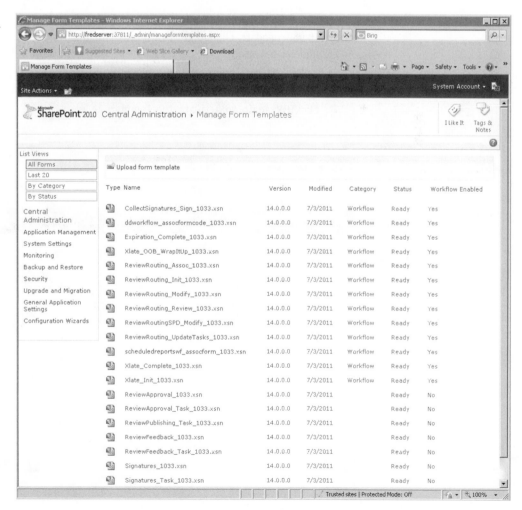

Figure 8-21

Choosing the Activate to a Site Collection option

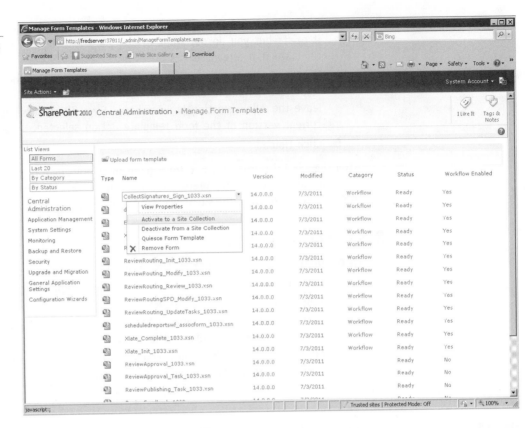

4. If you need to change to a different site location, click the Site Collection box under Activation Location (see Figure 8-22) and then click Change Site Collection. The Site Collection dialog box displays.

5. Click the URL of the desired site collection and then click OK.

6. Click OK again to activate the template.

Figure 8-22

Activating a location

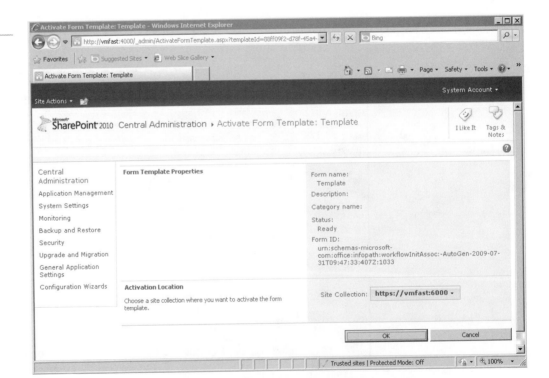

You can deactivate an administrator-approved form template for a site collection using Central Administration. Since any currently running form-filling sessions will be terminated at this time, causing all form data to be lost, you should quiesce the form template before deactivating the template to prevent data loss. You can also quiesce a form if you are uploading the new version of the form.

 QUIESCE A FORM TEMPLATE

GET READY. To quiesce a form template, perform the following steps:

1. Open Central Administration and click General Application Settings. The General Application Settings page displays.

2. In the under InfoPath Forms Services section, click Manage Form Templates. The Manage Form Templates page displays.

3. Click the name of the desired form template and then click Quiesce Form Template. The Quiesce Form Template page displays (see Figure 8-23).

Figure 8-23

The Quiesce Form Template page

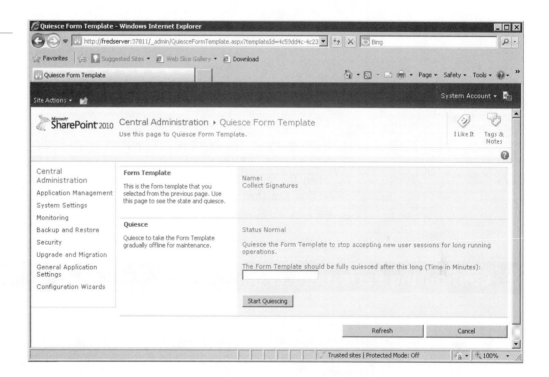

4. In the Quiesce section, type the number of minutes to quiesce form sessions prior to the form template becoming.

5. Click Start Quiescing, and verify that the status under Quiesce changes to Quiescing.

When the status changes to Quiesced, you can upload the new version of the form or deactivate the existing version of the form.

 DEACTIVATE A FORM TEMPLATE

GET READY. To deactivate a form template, perform the following steps:

1. Open Central Administration and click General Application Settings. The General Application Settings page displays.

2. In the InfoPath Forms Services section, click Manage Form Templates. The Manage Form Templates page displays.

3. Click the name of the desired form template and then click Deactivate from a Site Collection (see Figure 8-24).

Figure 8-24

Deactivating a location

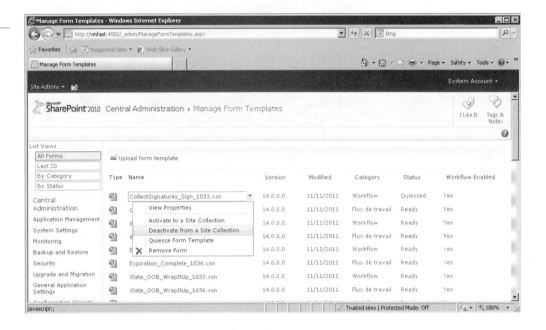

4. If necessary, in the Deactivation Location section, click Site Collection and then click Change Site Location.

5. When the Select Site Collection page displays, click the URL of the desired site collection and then click OK.

6. Click OK to deactivate the template for the site collection.

■ Configuring PerformancePoint Services

↓
THE BOTTOM LINE

PerformancePoint is a business intelligence tool integrated into SharePoint 2010 that provides dashboards, scorecards, and analytic components. While you will usually create the PerformancePoint Services site using the Farm Configuration Wizard, you can setup PerformancePoint manually.

CERTIFICATION READY
What Service Application in SharePoint allows you to create and use dashboards and scorecards?
1.3.4

If you install PerformancePoint manually, you can enable PerformancePoint manually by performing the following steps:

1. Configure the PerformancePoint Services application pool account
2. Start the PerformancePoint Services
3. Create a PerformancePoint Services Service Application
4. Configure Service Application associations

To configure the PerformancePoint Services application pool account, you must register a managed account in SharePoint 2010 and grant access to the content database that will contain the PerformancePoint data.

 CONFIGURE THE PERFORMANCEPOINT SERVICES APPLICATION POOL ACCOUNT

GET READY. To register a managed account, perform the following steps:

1. Open Central Administration and click Security. The security page displays.
2. In the General Security section, click Configure managed accounts.
3. Click Register Managed Account.
4. In the Service account credentials section, type the user name and password for the Active Directory account that you want to register.
5. Click OK.

 GRANT ACCESS TO THE CONTENT DATABASE

GET READY. To grant access to the content database for the Application Pool account, perform the following steps:

1. Click Start > All Programs > Microsoft SharePoint 2010 Products > SharePoint 2010 Management Shell.
2. At the Windows PowerShell command prompt, execute the following commands:

```
$w = Get-SPWebApplication -identity <Web application>
$w.GrantAccessToProcessIdentity("<service account>")
```

Starting the PerformancePoint Services is similar to starting other SharePoint services and creating the PerformancePoint Services Application is similar to creating Excel or Access Services Service Applications. You also need to make sure that the SharePoint Server Publishing Infrastructure is activated. Use the following procedure to start the PerformancePoint Service, to start the PerformancePoint Services Service Application, and to confirm that the association is configured between the Web application and the PerformancePoint Services proxy.

 START THE PERFORMANCEPOINT SERVICE

GET READY. To start the PerformancePoint Services manually, perform the following steps:

1. Open Central Administration and, under Application Management, click Manage Service Applications.
2. Next to PerformancePoint Service, click Start.

 CREATE THE PERFORMANCEPOINT SERVICES SERVICE APPLICATION

GET READY. To create the PerformancePoint Services Service Application, perform the following steps:

1. Open Central Administration and, under Application Management, click Manage Service Applications.
2. Click New, and then click PerformancePoint Service Application.
3. Type a name for the Service Application.
4. Select the Add this service application's proxy to the farm's default proxy list check box.
5. Select the Create new application pool option and type a name for the application pool.
6. Under the Configurable option, select the managed account to run the application pool.
7. Click Create.
8. Click OK.

CONFIGURE THE SERVICE APPLICATION ASSOCIATIONS

GET READY. To configure the PerformancePoint Services Service Application proxy, perform the following steps:

1. Open Central Administration and click Application Management.
2. In the Service Applications section, click Configure service application associations.
3. In the Application Proxy Group column, click default.
4. Ensure that the PerformancePoint Services box is selected.
5. Click OK.

To use the PerformancePoint Services, you can launch the PerformancePoint Dashboard Designer from a site, a site collection, or the Business Intelligence Center (see Figure 8-25) and start creating dashboards, key performance indicators (KPIs), and scorecards (a card for keeping score or status of an indicator, such as a service. See Figure 8-26). A Business Intelligence Center site can be created using the site Business Intelligence Center template. After creating the site, you can configure data access and data connections.

➕ **MORE INFORMATION**

For more information on creating a Performance Point Services Service Application including how to configure data access, data connections, and user permissions, visit the following Web site:
http://technet.microsoft.com/en-us/library/ee748644.aspx

Figure 8-25

The Business Intelligence Center

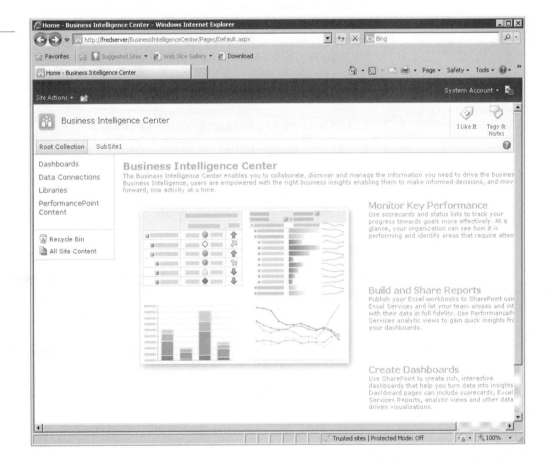

Figure 8-26

SharePoint Samples using
PerformancePoint Services

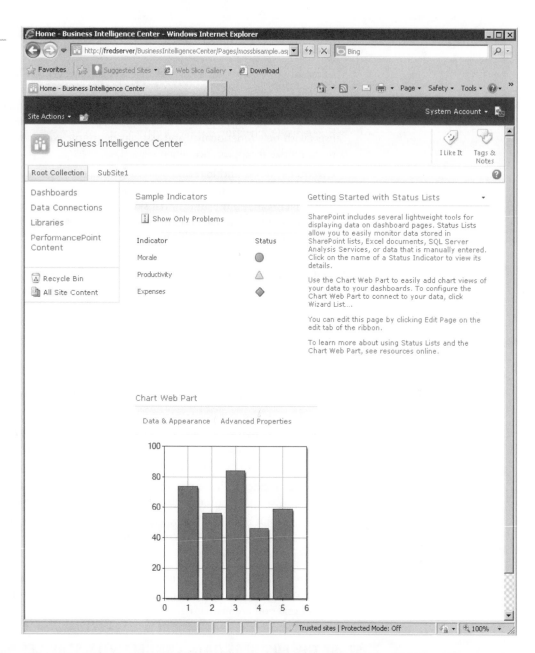

■ Configuring Business Connectivity Services

THE BOTTOM LINE

Microsoft Business Connectivity Services (BCS) are administered primarily by using the Business Data Connectivity service. Microsoft *Business Data Connectivity (BDC) Services* is a set of services and features that connect SharePoint-based solutions to sources of external data (such as a Web service, SAP application, or SQL Server database).

CERTIFICATION READY
What application services allow you to interface with an SAP system to import employee or customer information?
1.3.1

Microsoft Business Connectivity Services (BCS) Service Application is a collection of features and services used to connect SharePoint solutions to external data sources (including SQL Server databases, SAP applications, and Web services) and to define external content types based on external data. This data can be presented and interact with SharePoint lists and Web parts.

Using the Business Data Connectivity Service, administrators can manage the following types of objects:

- **External content types**: These are external content types with a set of fields (such as Customer, Order, or Contact) and include the method to create, read, update, or delete that object in its external data source. To use an external content type, you must set the external content type's permissions, adding actions to an external content type to provide users with new functionality and associating profile pages with an external content type to customize its appearance when viewed.

- **External systems and external system instances**: These are external systems based on supported sources of data, such as Web services, SQL Server databases, and other relational databases. To use an external system, you must set permissions on the external system, viewing the external content types that are associated with it and viewing instances of an external system. In addition, you must define the authentication mode and the type of the external system instance.

- **BDC models and resource files**: The Business Data Connectivity service supports two types of XML application definition files: application model files and resource files. An application model file contains the XML descriptions of one or more external content types. A resource file enables you to import or export only the localized names, properties, and permissions for one or more external content types. Typical tasks that administer a BDC model include importing and exporting models or resource files, setting permissions on them, and viewing the external content types associated with a model.

While adding external connections are beyond this course, the following information is useful:

- To add an external content type, use SharePoint Designer 2010 and select External Content Types in the left pane. For more information, visit http://technet.microsoft.com/en-us/library/ff607971.aspx.

- To create an external list, open the Site Actions menu and select **More Options**. Then select the External List template and click the **Create** button.

- To import BDC Models files, open Central Administration, click **Manage Services**, click the **Business Data Connectivity Service** instance, and then click the **Import** button in the BDC Models section on the ribbon.

To create Service Applications, you must be a farm administrator. To manage a Service Application, you must be a farm administrator or an administrator of the specific Service Application that you are managing.

 START THE BUSINESS DATA CONNECTIVITY SERVICES

GET READY. To start the BDC Service, perform the following steps:

1. Open Central Administration and, under Systems Settings, click Manage Services on Server. The Services on Server Web page displays.

2. In the Server drop-down list, choose the server on which you want to start the service.

3. In the Action column, next to the Business Data Connectivity Service, click the Start link.

CREATE THE BUSINESS DATA CONNECTIVITY SERVICES

GET READY. To create the Business Data Connectivity Services Service Application, perform the following steps:

1. Open Central Administration and, under Application Management, click Manage Service Applications.

2. On the Ribbon, click New and then click Business Data Connectivity Service. The Create New Business Data Connectivity Service Application page displays (see Figure 8-27).

Figure 8-27

Creating the Business Data Connectivity Services

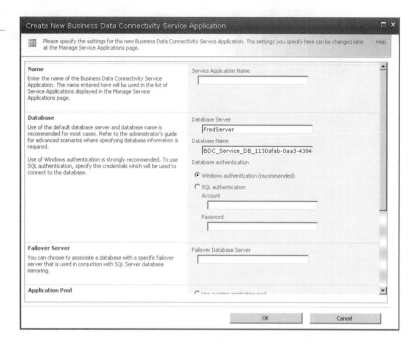

3. Provide values for each of the following BDC Service Application settings:
   - Service Application Name: Enter the name of the new BDC Service application (for example, FredServer).
   - Database Server, Database Name, and Database authentication: Type the name of the database server that will host the BDC Service application database, the name of the database that you want to give to the BDC metadata store, and the credentials that the BDC service will use to connect to the database.
   - Application Pool: Select the application pool that you want to use for the Service Application.
4. Click OK.

When you set permissions on an external system, you determine who can edit and execute operations in the system or on external content types stored on the system. You can also decide who can create external lists and who else can set permissions on the system.

 ASSIGN AN ADMINISTRATOR TO THE BDC SERVICE INSTANCE

GET READY. To assign an administrator to the BDC service instance, perform the following steps:

1. Open Central Administration and, under Application Management, click Manage Service Applications.
2. Click the Business Data Connectivity Service page instance. The View External Content Types page opens (see Figure 8-28).
3. If it is not already selected, click the Edit tab.

Figure 8-28

The View External Content
Types page.

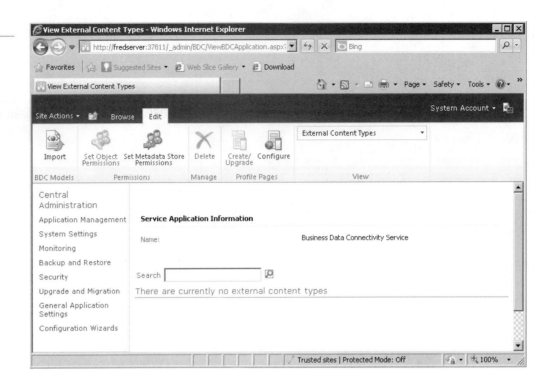

4. On the Ribbon, click Set Metadata Store Permissions. The Set Metadata Store
Permissions page displays(see Figure 8-29).

Figure 8-29

The Set Metadata Store
Permissions page

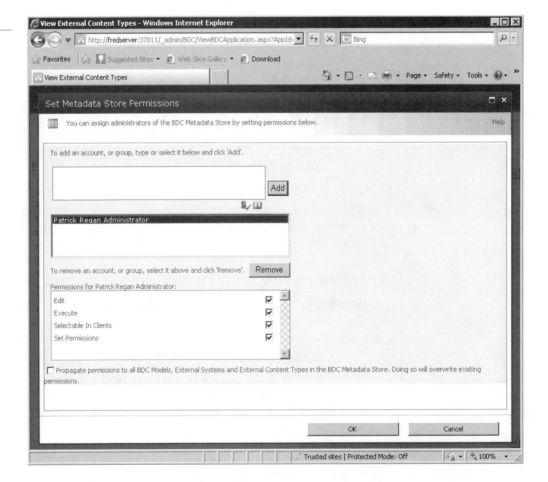

5. In the To add an account, or group, type or select it below and click 'Add' box, type the name for the user or account you want to make an administrator (as shown in the figure), and then click Add.

6. Click to select the check box for the permission that you want to assign.

7. If desired, click Propagate Permissions to all BDC Models, External Systems and External Content Types in the DBC Metadata Store. Doing so will overwrite existing permissions.

8. Click OK.

■ Managing Metadata Services

THE BOTTOM LINE

Metadata is a generic term that describes information about an information system. It is also sometimes referred to as data about data that describes the contents and context of data files. In SharePoint, metadata is used to label and identify SharePoint items so that they can be quickly and easily retrieved.

CERTIFICATION READY
What allows you to assign tags to SharePoint objects?
1.3.7

When you enabled *managed metadata* in SharePoint 2010, a managed metadata service and connection were created automatically, storing enterprise keywords in a database known as a *term store*. You can also publish a managed metadata service to an URL and this service can be accessed as a Web service. Lastly, you can share all content types in the site collection's content type gallery by specifying a content type hub.

The first step in administering managed metadata is to create the managed metadata Service Application. To create the managed metadata Service Application, you must be an administrator on the machine containing the SharePoint Central Administration site.

 CREATE A MANAGED METADATA SERVICE APPLICATION

GET READY. To create a managed metadata Service Application, perform the following steps:

1. Open Central Administration and, under Application Management, click Manage Service Applications.

2. On the Ribbon, click New and then click Managed Metadata Service. The Create New Managed Metadata Service page displays (see Figure 8-30).

3. In the Name field, type a name for the service.

4. In the Database Server field, type the name of the database server that is hosting the term store.

5. In the Database Name field, type the name of the database that you want to host the term store.

6. Select the Database authentication type to connect to the SQL Server instance, such as Windows authentication or SQL authentication.

7. In the Failover Server section, if you choose to use SQL server failover, type the name of the database server to be used for failover in the Failover Database Server field.

Figure 8-30

The Create New Managed Metadata Service page

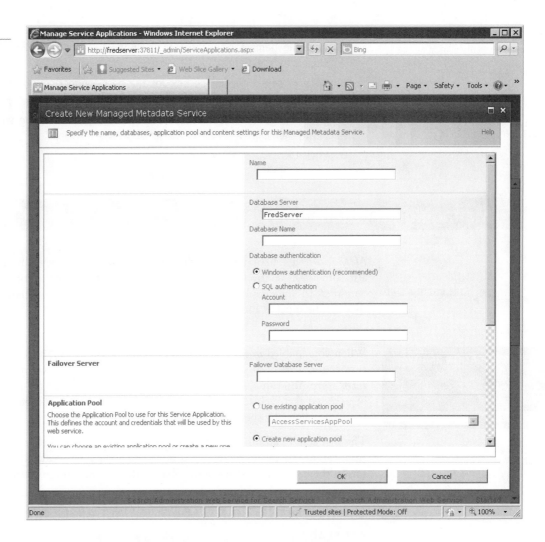

8. In the Application Pool section, select Use existing application pool and then select a pool from the drop-down list. Or select Create new application pool and then select an account under which to run the pool (see Figure 8-31).

9. If you optionally want the managed metadata service to access a content type library in addition to a term store, then in the Content Type hub field, type the URL to the site collection containing the content type library.

10. If you want to record any errors when using the content type hub, select Report syndication import errors from Site Collections using this service application. This option is enabled by default.

11. To create a connection to this service automatically when a new Web application is added to the farm, select Add this service application to the farm's default list.

12. Click OK.

The service becomes available in the Web application where the service was created, but you must publish the service if you want to share it with other Web applications.

Figure 8-31

Defining the Application Pool
and Content Type Hub

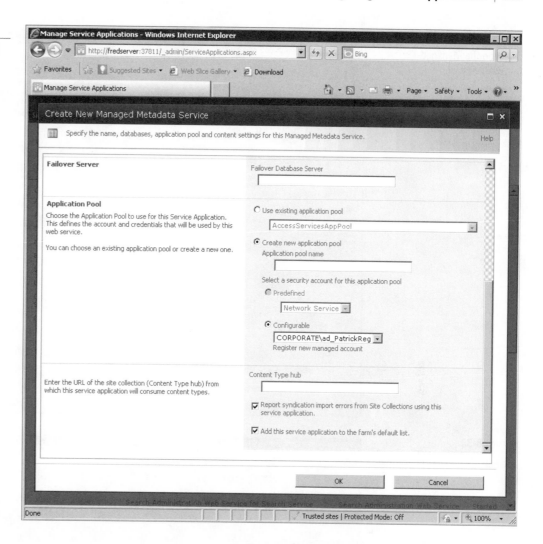

 PUBLISH A MANAGED METADATA SERVICE APPLICATION

GET READY. To publish a managed metadata Service Application, perform the following steps:

1. Open Central Administration and, under Application Management, click Manage Service Applications.

2. Select the row for the managed metadata Service Application that you want to publish without clicking the service name.

3. On the Ribbon, click Publish (see Figure 8-32).

4. When the Publish Service Application displays (see Figure 8-33), click the Connection Type drop-down menu to select a connection type (such as http or https).

5. In the Publish to other farms section, select the Publish this Service Application to other farms check box to make the service available to other server farms.

6. In the Trusted Farms section, click the Click here to add a trust relationship with another farm link. The Establish Trust Relationship page displays (see Figure 8-34).

Figure 8-32

Selecting the Managed
Metadata Service

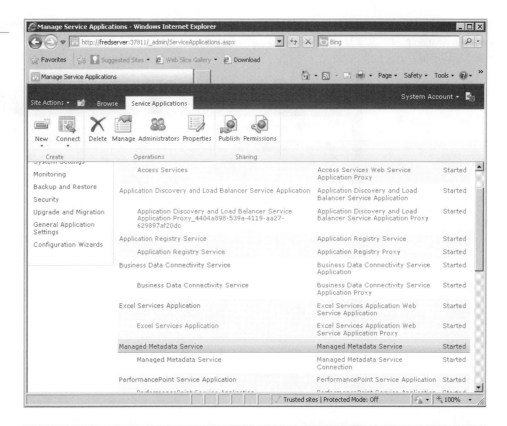

Figure 8-33

The Publish Service Application
page

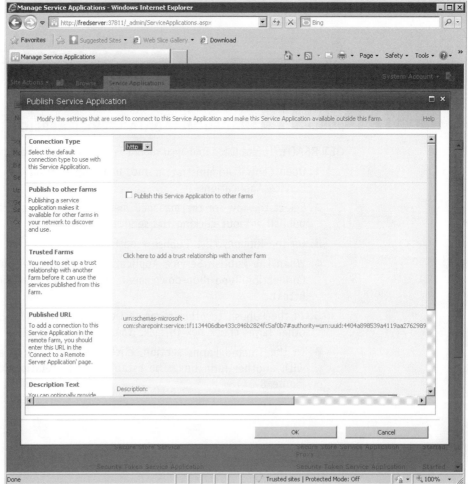

Figure 8-34

The Trust Relationship page

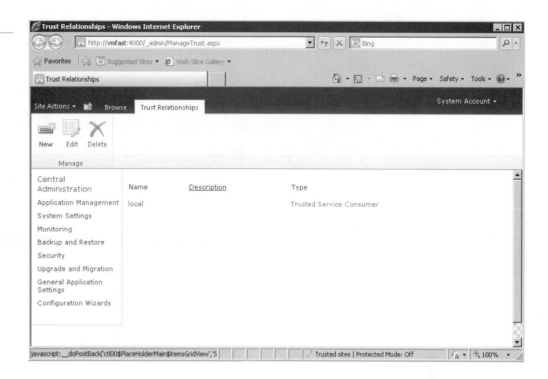

7. Select a farm in the list, click the New button (see Figure 8-35), and then use the Establish Farm Trust screen to create a name for the trust.

Figure 8-35

The Establish Trust Relationship page

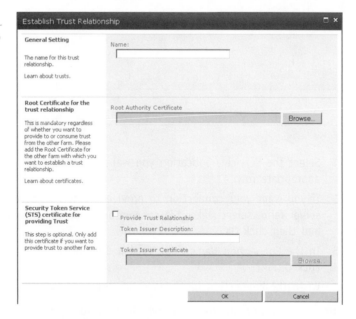

8. In the Root Certificate for the trust relationship section, click the Browse button to specify the STS certificate for the Root Authority for the Trust relationship. When finished, click OK.

9. In the Published URL section, make a note of the service URL so you can provide it to administrators who want to make a connection to the service.

10. In the Description Text section, in the Description field, type a description of the published service.

11. In the Help URL field, if you have created a Web page with information about this service, type the URL of the Web page.

12. Click OK.

CREATE A CONNECTION TO A MANAGED METADATA SERVICE APPLICATION

GET READY. To create a connection to a managed metadata Service Application, perform the following steps:

1. Open Central Administration and, under Application Management, click Manage Service Applications.

2. On the Ribbon, click Connect and then choose Managed Metadata Service Connection.

3. On the Connect to a Remote Service Application page (see Figure 8-36), in the Farm or Service Application address, type the URL to the managed metadata service (the administrator of the service must provide the URL) and then click OK.

Figure 8-36

The Connect to a Remote Service Application page

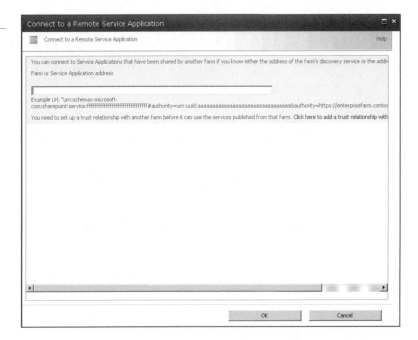

4. Select the Service Application you want to connect to by clicking its name in the appropriate row.

5. If you want your connection to provide the service to all Web applications in your server farm, select Make this connection to be the default for all sites in My Farm and then click OK.

6. In the Connection Name field, type a descriptive name for the connection and then click OK.

7. When the connection has been created, click OK.

A term store is a container for terms, which are words or phrases that are associated with a particular item in SharePoint. To organize these terms, terms can be collected in sets of related terms, and term sets can then be collected into groups. Eventually, you can organize them into a hierarchy, which users can select in a document library. Lastly, you can also use managed keywords with SharePoint items so that they can be tagged in order that users can find these items when searching for these tags.

Once the managed data services and service connection are available, you can use the ***Term Store Management Tool*** to create metadata terms for the SharePoint enterprise environment. This tool is a centralized database that allows term sets to be shared across the SharePoint farm. The following steps show you how to use this tool.

 USE THE TERM STORE MANAGEMENT TOOL

GET READY. To use the Term Store Management Tool, perform the following steps:

1. Open Central Administration and, under Application Management, click Manage Service Applications.

2. Click the desired managed metadata service that you want to access. The Term Store Management Tool page displays (see Figure 8-37).

Figure 8-37

The Term Store Management Tool page

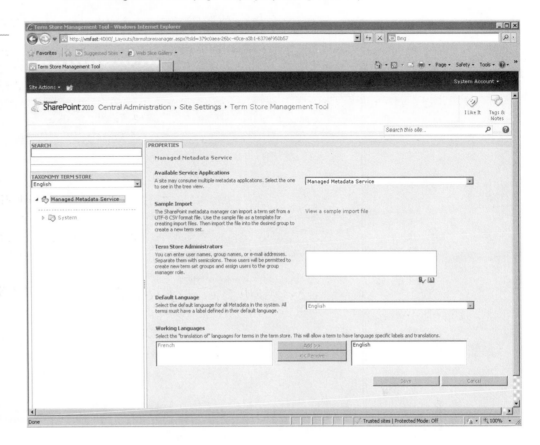

3. In the Properties tab, type the name of the user in the Term Store Administrators field or use the address book to add a user.

4. In the Taxonomy Term Store drop-down in the left pane, select your desired language and then expand Managed Metadata Service.

5. Expand System and then click Keywords.

6. Click OK.

You can also create terms for a document library in a site collection, which can be assigned to documents in the library.

 CREATE METADATA TERMS FOR A LIBRARY

GET READY. To create metadata terms for a library, perform the following steps:

1. Navigate to a document library.

2. On the Library Tools menu, click the Library tab.

3. On the Ribbon, click Create Column. The Create Column window displays (see Figure 8-38).

Figure 8-38

The Create Column page

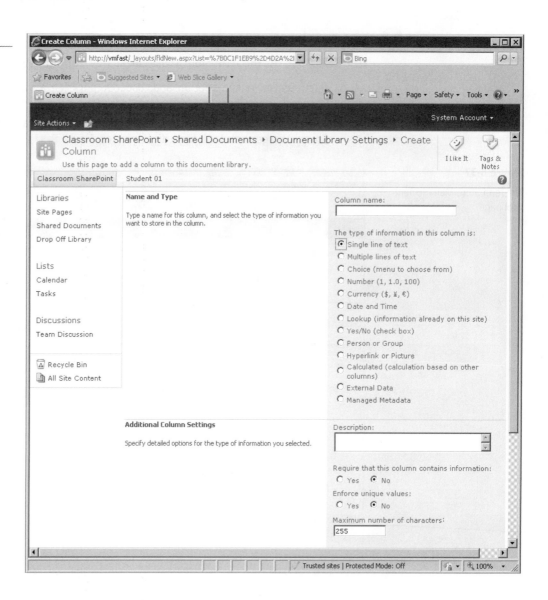

4. In the Column name box, type your column name.

5. In The type of information in this column is section, select Managed Metadata.

TAKE NOTE *

When you select Managed Metadata, the following message appears: "Earlier versions of client programs might not support this type of column. Adding this column might block those programs from saving documents to the library." While this does not affect uploading documents using the Web interface, you will not be able to load documents to a library using Office 2003 or 2007 since Managed Metadata did not exist when these applications were introduced.

---

6. Select Customize Your Term Set (see Figure 8-39).

7. In the Description field, type a descriptive name.

8. In the Additional Column Settings section, you can add more conditions for the column settings and, in the Description field, type a description of those conditions in the Description field.

9. In the Require that this column contains information setting and the Enforce unique values setting, select either Yes or No.

Figure 8-39

Customizing your term set

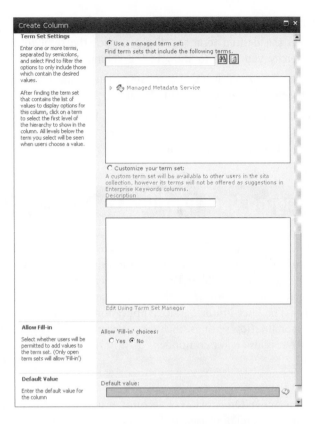

10. Select or deselect the Add to default view check box.

11. Select Use a managed term set (see Figure 8-40), and in the Find term sets that include the following terms field, type one or more terms separated by semicolons.

Figure 8-40

Selecting the Use a managed term set option

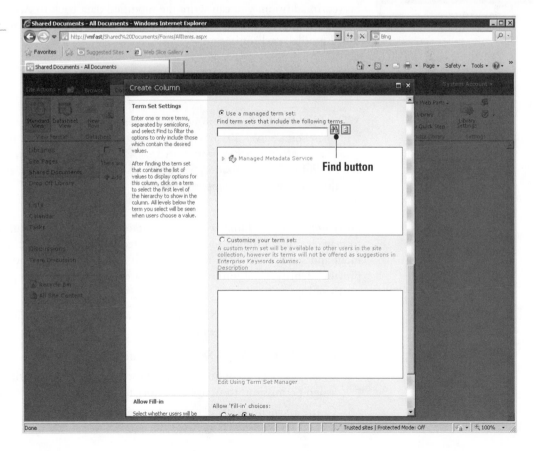

12. Click the Find button to locate the desired terms.

13. When the desired term set displays, click the term to select the first level of the hierarchy you want to show in the column.

14. If you are using an open term set, then in the Allow 'Fill-in choices' options, you can select Yes to enable this feature.

15. If necessary, in the Default value field, type or browse for a default value for the column.

16. Click OK to create the column.

■ Configuring and Managing User Profiles

THE BOTTOM LINE

SharePoint 2010 has many features that facilitate collaboration. The *User Profile Service Application* is the primary Service Application that controls many of the personal features and is the central point for SharePoint's social networking features. It lets you create and manage SharePoint *user profiles*, which can be accessed from sites, site collections, and server farms. The User Profile Service Application offers you a central place from which to manage personalization settings, including user profile settings, audience settings, and My Site settings. It is also a key component used in the social computing features found within SharePoint.

CERTIFICATION READY
What Service Application is used to synchronize user profiles with Active Directory?
1.3.5

Similar to an Active Directory user account, a user profile is a collection of properties that describes a SharePoint user. In fact, much of the information will come from Active Directory or a similar system. Information that can be stored with a SharePoint profile includes job titles, telephone numbers, and addresses, just to name a few. User profiles can be augmented by importing data from other systems, such as SAP or Microsoft SQL Server. In addition, you can write the modified data back to Active Directory. The process of importing profile data from Active Directory or other external systems to SharePoint is called profile synchronization.

Configuring the User Profile Synchronization

The *User Profile Synchronization Service* is the core of the synchronization architecture in SharePoint Server 2010, which uses the Microsoft Forefront Identity Manager (FIM) to participate in synchronization. A User Profile Service Application can have only one User Profile Synchronization Service. A User Profile Synchronization Service is associated with connections and mappings.

Forefront Identity Manager (FIM) is a state-based identity management component used to manage a user's digital identities and credentials. To support integrated user management and self-service, FIM integrates with Active Directory and Exchange Server to provide identity synchronization, certificate management, user password resets, and user provisioning.

To use User Profiles within SharePoint and synchronize the information with Active Directory, perform the following steps:

1. Create the User Profile Service Application.

2. Create a service account that will be used to synchronize with Active Directory and assign permissions to Active Directory using the Delegate Control Wizard.

3. Create a Synchronization connecting with Active Directory.

 CREATE A USER PROFILE SERVICE APPLICATION

GET READY. To create a User Profile Service Application, perform the following steps:

1. Open Central Administration and, under Application Management, click Manage Service Applications. The Manage Service Applications page displays).

2. On the Ribbon, click New, and then click User Profile Service Application. The Create New User Profile Service Application page displays (see Figure 8-41).

Figure 8-41

The Create New User Profile Service Application page

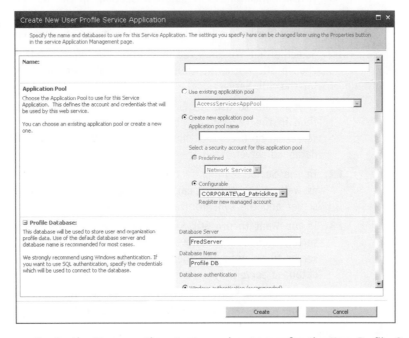

3. In the Name section, type a unique name for the User Profile Service Application.

4. In the Application Pool section, select Use existing application pool to choose an existing pool or select Create new application pool to create a new pool. If you choose to create a new security pool, select Predefined to choose an existing predefined security account or select Configurable to select an existing managed account.

5. In the Profile Database section (see Figure 8-42), type the name of the Database Server and the Database Name.

Figure 8-42

Defining the user profile database

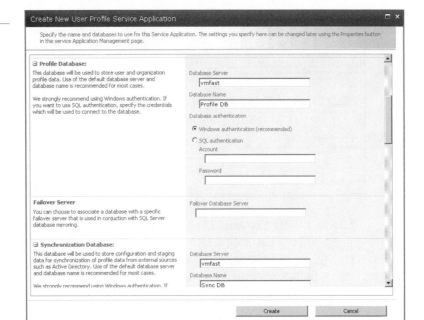

6. Select either Windows authentication (recommended) or SQL authentication. If you choose SQL authentication, type the Account username and Password for the SQL Server authentication method.

7. In the Failover Server section, if you want to use SQL Server database mirroring, then in the Failover Database Server text box, type the name of the database server to be used.

8. In the Synchronization Database section, in the Database Server text box, type the name of the server.

9. In the Database Name field, type the name of your synchronization database.

10. Select either Windows Authentication (Recommended) or SQL Authentication. If you choose SQL Authentication, you must to enter the Account username and Password for the SQL Server.

11. If you want to use SQL Server database mirroring for the synchronization server, then in the Failover Database Server text box, type the name of the database server to be used and then select an authentication method as you did for the database server.

12. In the Social Tagging section, type the name of the database server and database as well as the authentication method, just as you did for the failover database server and the synchronization database server.

13. If you want to use SQL Server database mirroring for the social tagging database server, then in the Failover Database Server field, type the name of the database server to be used and then select an authentication method as you did for the database server.

14. In the Profile Synchronization Instance section (see Figure 8-43), select a machine in the server farm on which you want to run the Profile Synchronization service.

Figure 8-43

Selecting the Profile Synchronization Instance

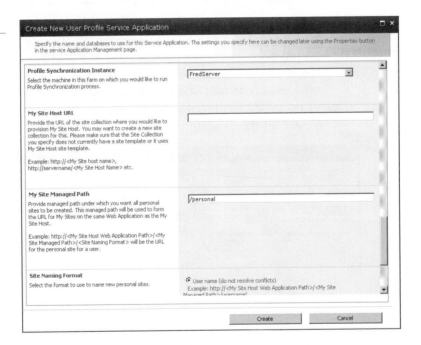

15. In the My Site Host URL section, type the URL of the site collection where the My Site host has been created.

16. In the My Site Managed Path section, type the managed path where individual My Site Web sites are to be created.

17. In the Site Naming Format section, select a format for naming personal sites (such as User name (do not resolve conflicts), User name (resolve conflicts by using domain username), or Domain and user name (will not have conflicts).

18. In the Default Proxy Group section, choose whether you want to make the proxy of the User Profile service part of the default proxy group.

19. Click Create.

When you provision a User Profile Service Application, the following three SQL databases are created:

- **ProfileDB**: Stores user and organization profile information.
- **SocialDB**: Stores social tags and notes that are created by users.
- **SyncDB**: Stores configuration and staging information for synchronizing profile data from external sources.

You can then manage user profiles by opening the User Profile Service Application and clicking Manage User Profiles.

After the User Profile Service Application is created, you must create a profile synchronization connection so that it can synchronize with Active Directory. If you are synchronizing with Active Directory, you must have the Replicate Directory Changes permissions in Active Directory. If you want to export properties (such as profile pictures) to Active Directory, you must create All Child Objects permissions.

 DELEGATE CONTROL TO ACTIVE DIRECTORY

GET READY. To delegate control to Active Directory, perform the following steps:

1. Open the Active Directory Users and Computers console for your domain. If you do not have Active Directory administrative tools loaded on your workstation, Active Directory Users and Computers can be accessed from Administrative Tools on any domain controller.

2. Right-click the domain and choose Delegate Control (see Figure 8-44).

Figure 8-44

Choosing the Delegate Control command

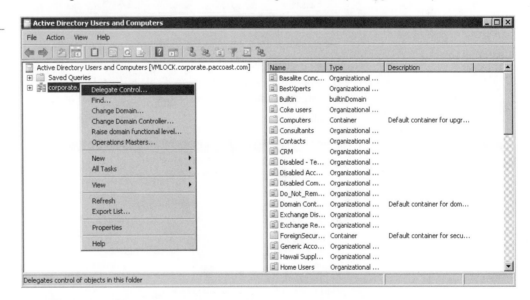

3. When the Welcome to the Delegation of Control Wizard displays, click Next.

4. On the Users or Groups page (see Figure 8-45), click the Add button, and in the Select Users, Computers, or Groups dialog box, type the name of the user.

5. Click OK and then click Next.

6. Select Create a custom task to delegate (see Figure 8-46) and then click Next.

Figure 8-45

The Users or Groups page

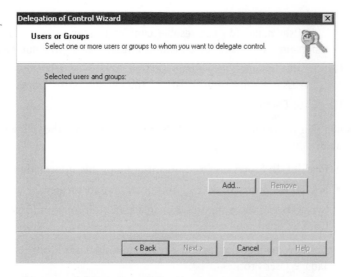

Figure 8-46

The Tasks to Delegate page

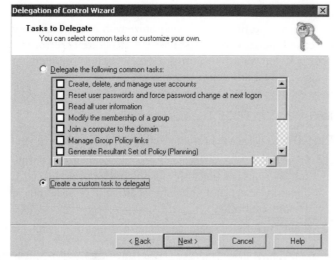

7. When prompted for the Active Directory Object Type, leave the default selection and then click Next.

8. When the Permissions page displays (see Figure 8-47), select the Replicating Directory Changes permission and then click Next.

9. Click Finish.

Figure 8-47

The Permissions page

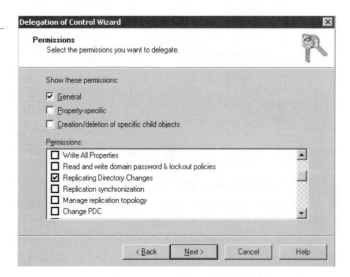

To create a profile synchronization connection, you must have the following prerequisites:

- You must have the User Profile Service Application created and started.
- You must be using either a Standard or Enterprise version of SharePoint Server 2010 and must run it as a server farm. You cannot perform profile synchronization using a stand-alone installation of SharePoint with a built-in database.
- If you are using SQL Server 2008, you must have SP1 with Cumulative Update 2 (CU2).
- If you are using Windows Server 2008 R2, hotfix KB976462 must be installed.
- You must be a member of the Farm Administrators group and a local administrator on the computer where the User Profile Synchronization service is deployed. In addition, the Farm Administrators account must also be a service administrator for the User Profile service you are configuring.

 CREATE A SYNCHRONIZATION CONNECTION

GET READY. To create a synchronization connection, perform the following steps:

1. Open Central Administration and, under System Settings, click Manage services on server.
2. Verify the User Profile Synchronization Services is started. If it is not, click the Start button. It will take 5-10 minutes for the Profile Synchronization Service to start. If the Central Administrator is on the same box as the User Profile Synchronization occurs on, you will need to reset IIS.
3. After the User Profile Synchronization Services is started, in the under Application Management section, click Manage Service Applications. The Manage Service Applications page displays.
4. Click the name of the User Profile Service Application. The User Profile Service Application page displays (see Figure 8-48).

Figure 8-48

The User Profile Service Application page

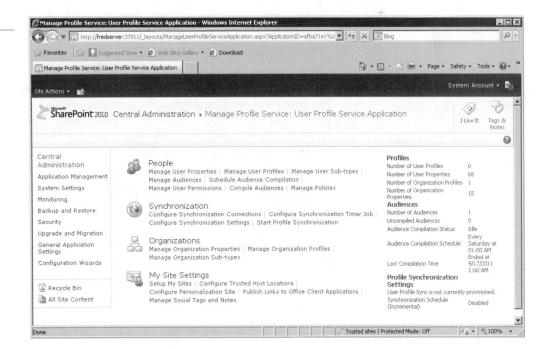

5. In the Synchronization section, click Configure Synchronization Connections. The Synchronization Connections page displays.

6. Click Create New Connection. The Add New Synchronization Connection page displays (see Figure 8-49).

Figure 8-49

The Add New Synchronization Connection page

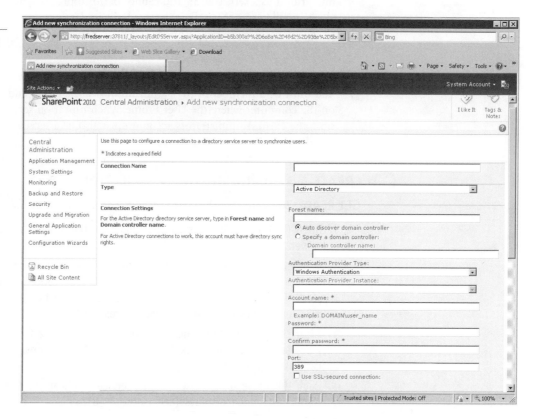

7. In the Connection Name text box, type the name of the new synchronization connection.

8. Click the Type down arrow to select the desired directory service (such as Active Directory).

9. In the Connection Settings section, type the Forest name of the directory service forest you want to connect to, type the account credentials for the directory service and the desired port, and then select Auto discover domain controller or select Specify a domain controller and then type the name of the domain controller in the Domain controller name text box.

10. If you want to use a Secure Sockets Layer connection to connect to the directory service, select the Use SSL-secured connection check box.

11. In the Containers section (see Figure 8-50), click Populate Containers.

12. Select the desired containers for which you want to create connections; otherwise, click Select All to make connections for all containers.

13. Click OK.

If you go back to the User Profile Service Application, click the Start Profile Synchronization option to start synchronizing with Active Directory. This may take some time depending on how big your Active Directory hierarchy is. To configure SharePoint to synchronize automatically, you must configure a Synchronization Timer Job. When done, you can search for and view user Profiles by using the Manage User Profiles option on the User Profile Service Application page.

Figure 8-50

Selecting a container

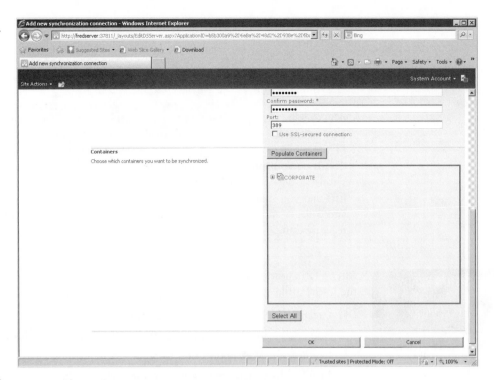

 CONFIGURE A SYNCHRONIZATION TIMER JOB

GET READY. To configure a synchronization timer job, perform the following steps:

1. Open Central Administration, and under Application Management, click Manage service applications. The Manage Service Application page displays.

2. Click User Profile Service Application. The Manage Profile Service: User Profile Service Application page displays.

3. Click Configure Synchronization Timer Job. The Edit Timer Job page displays (see Figure 8-51).

Figure 8-51

The Edit Timer Job page

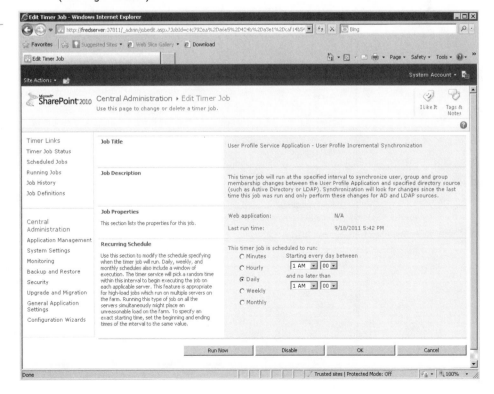

4. Specify how often you want the timer job to run.

5. Click OK.

Configuring My Sites

My Sites are personal sites that provide users in your organization with a rich set of social networking features. You can advertise details about yourself via the My Profile page (see Figure 8-52) to others using a public profile page while controlling who can see which details on your profile page (see Figure 8-53). In addition, you can create a personal site, known as My Content (see Figure 8-54) so that you can store personal documents and lists that you share with others. Lastly, you can use social features including social tagging and collages and an activity feed that shows the activities that your colleagues have recently done.

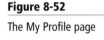

CERTIFICATION READY
What Service Application is required to configure My Sites?
1.3.5

After a farm administrator has created a User Profile Service application, an administrator for the User Profile application can configure My Sites by performing the following steps:

1. Create a site collection to host My Sites

2. Add a wildcard inclusion for the Web collection that will host My Sites

3. Connect the Web application to Service Applications

4. Enable self-service site creation for the Web application

5. Configure My Site settings

Figure 8-52

The My Profile page

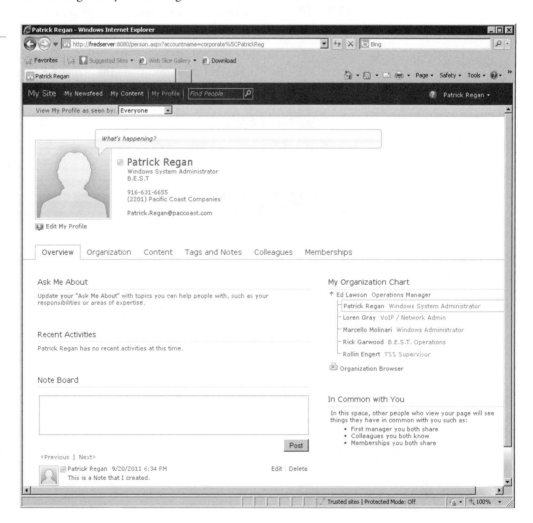

Figure 8-53

The Basic Information page

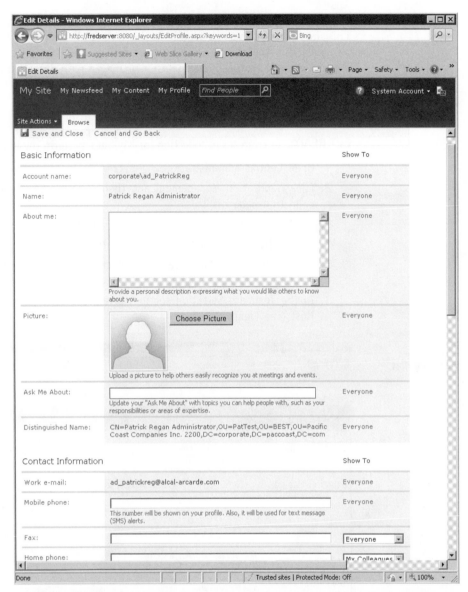

Figure 8-54

The My Content page

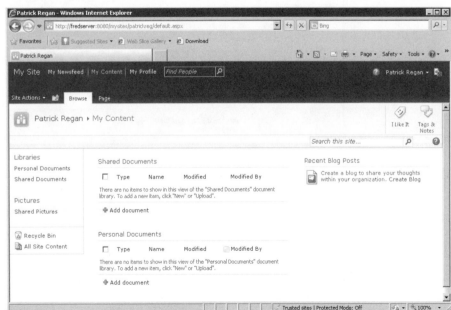

The first thing you should do to use My Sites is to create a site collection to host My Sites. This site collection must be created in the Web application that you want to host My Sites. Generally, this site collection can be created at the root path of the Web application, although it can be created as an explicit, inclusion-managed path deeper in the URL as long as there is a site collection created at the Web application root.

CREATE A SITE COLLECTION FOR MY SITES

GET READY. To create a site collection for My Sites, perform the following steps:

1. Open Central Administration.
2. Click Application Management and then click Create site collections. The Create Site Collection page displays.
3. If necessary, select the correct Web Application that you want to host My Sites.
4. Type a Title and Description for the site collection.
5. In the Web Site Address section, select the URL where you want this site collection created.
6. In the Template Selection section, select the Enterprise tab and then click My Site Host (see Figure 8-55).

Figure 8-55

Selecting the My Site Host template

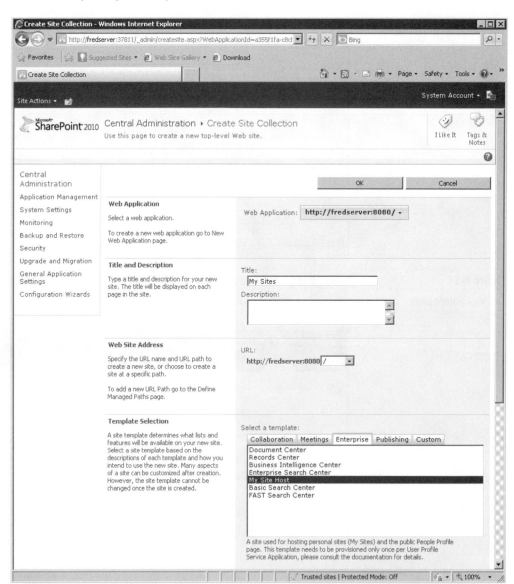

7. Type the names of the Primary Site Collection Administrator and Secondary Site Collection Administrator.

8. If desired, select a quota template for the My Site host site collection.

9. Click OK.

SharePoint Server includes a default Personal Site quota template, which has a storage limit of 100 MB and no user limit. This quota template is used for each user's individual site collection in his My Site. Of course, you can edit this template as needed.

The next thing to do is to add a wildcard inclusion managed path to the Web application. The wildcard inclusion managed path is the path under which separate site collections are created the first time each user clicks her My Content link.

 ### ADD A WILDCARD INCLUSION

GET READY. To add a wildcard inclusion, perform the following steps:

1. Open Central Administration.

2. Click Application Management and then click Manage Web applications. The Web Applications page displays.

3. Select the Web application that you created to host My Sites and then click Managed Paths. The Define Managed Paths dialog box displays.

4. In the Add a New Path box, type a value that you want to append to the URL namespace and select Wildcard inclusion, such as http://mysites.contoso.com/MySites or http://mysites.contoso.com/personal/.

5. Click Add Path.

6. Click OK.

To fully support features associated with My Sites, you should connect the following Service Applications:

- User Profile Service Application
- Managed Metadata Service Application
- Search Service Application

In addition, if you have other SharePoint sites for which you want users to be able to access their My Site and My Profile links from the upper-right corner menu, connect the Web applications of those sites to the User Profile Service Application.

 ### CONNECT THE WEB APPLICATION TO SERVICE APPLICATIONS

GET READY. To connect the Web application to Service Applications, perform the following steps:

1. Open Central Administration.

2. Click Application Management and then click Manage Web applications. The Web Applications page displays.

3. Select the Web application that you created to host My Sites.

4. In the Manage group, click Service Connections. The Configure Service Application Associations page displays (see Figure 8-56).

Figure 8-56

The Configure Service Application Associations page

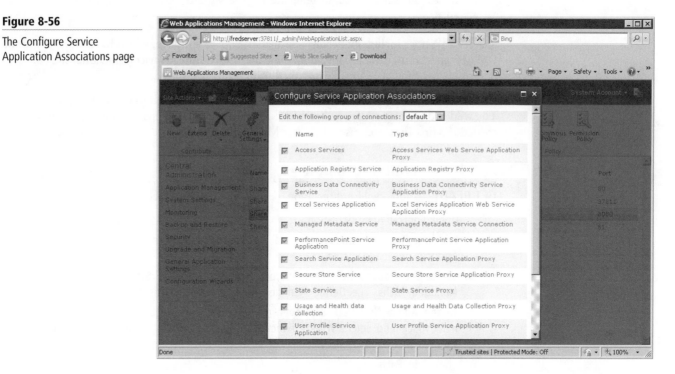

5. In the Edit the following group of connections list, leave default selected unless the default group does not already contain the Service Applications to which you want to connect the Web application. If you choose Custom, select any Service Applications to which you want to connect the Web application, including the User Profile Service Application, the Managed Metadata Service, and Search Service Application.

6. Click OK.

Self-service site creation enables the automatic creation of a separate site collection for each user when the user first clicks the My Content link. You will then update the My Sites settings in the User Profile Service Application.

 ENABLE SELF-SERVICE SITE CREATION FOR THE WEB APPLICATION

GET READY. To enable self-service site creation for the Web application, perform the following steps:

1. Open Central Administration.

2. Click Application Management and then click Manage Web applications. The Web Applications page displays.

3. Select the Web application that you created to host My Sites.

4. In the Security group, click Self-Service Site Creation. The Self-Service Site Collection Management dialog box displays.

5. Select On.

6. If you want to require users to supply a second contact name on the signup page, select the Require secondary contact option.

7. Click OK.

 CONFIGURE MY SITE SETTINGS FOR THE USER PROFILE SERVICE APPLICATION

GET READY. To configure My Site settings for the User profile Service Application, perform the following steps:

1. Open Central Administration.

2. Click Application Management and then click Manage Service Application.

3. Click the User Profile service application that you connected to the Web application hosting My Sites. The Manage Profile Service page displays (see Figure 8-57).

Figure 8-57

The Manage Profile Service page

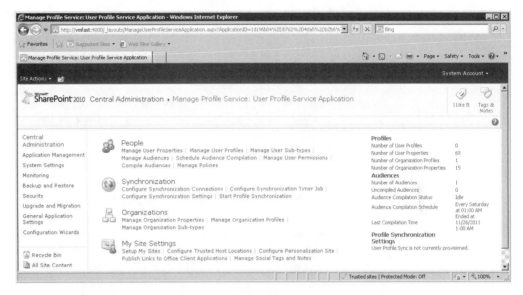

4. In the My Site Settings section, click Setup My Sites. My Site Settings page displays (see Figure 8-58).

Figure 8-58

The My Site Settings page

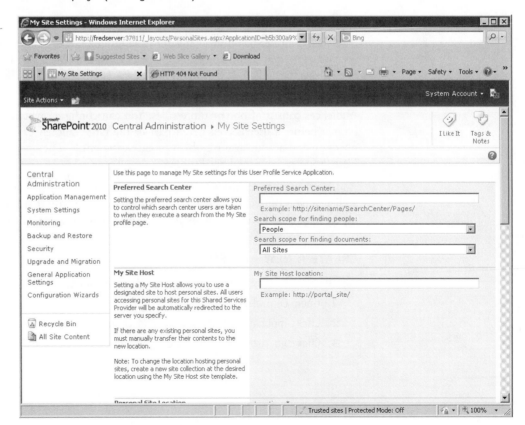

5. In the Preferred Search Centersection, specify settings for the Search Center to direct users to when they search for people or documents from their My Profile pages. If you do not have a search center set up yet, you can skip this step and complete it later.

6. In the My Site Host section, type the URL for the My Site Host location site collection you created earlier in this task (such as http://mysites.contoso.com).

7. In the Personal Site Location section, type the wildcard inclusion managed path you configured earlier (such as mysites or personal). By default, my/personal is pre-populated in the box.

8. In the Site Naming Format section, select a naming format for the My Sites site collections that will be created when users click My Content in their My Sites the first time.

9. In the Language Options section, specify whether users can select a preferred language for their My Site.

10. In the Read Permission Level section, specify the users or groups that can view other users' My Sites when they are created. By default, this includes all authenticated users.

11. Click OK.

Organization Profiles and Audiences

Besides managing the user profiles and My Sites, the User Profile Service Application also provides organization profiles and audiences. ***Audiences*** enables organizations to target content to users based on their jobs or tasks, as defined by their membership in a SharePoint Server group or distribution list, by the organizational reporting structure, or by the public properties in their user profiles. ***Organization profiles*** contain detailed information about an organization, such as a subsidiary, departments, teams, and so on.

Audience is a rules-based mechanism for defining a target group of people so you can aim specific content at them. For example, you can insert a Web Part that displays only to members of specific audiences. It should not be used to restrict access but instead should be used to display information selectively.

Audiences consist of one or more rules. You can configure whether one rule or all rules must be met before a user is considered part of the target audience. Each rule has an operand, an operator, and a value against which to check the result. The operand can either be a User or a User Property from the User Profiles.

Audiences must be compiled before they can be used. When you've successfully compiled an audience, you can view the names of its members to verify that it's picking up the people you expect it to. Audiences can be used to influence content, as detailed in the following steps.

 CREATE A NEW AUDIENCE

GET READY. To create a new audience, perform the following steps:

1. Open Central Administration.

2. Click Application Management and then click Manage Service Application.

3. Click the User Profile service application. The Manage Profile Service page displays.

4. Click Manage Audiences, which displays the View Audiences page (see Figure 8-59). By default, there is an All site users audience.

Figure 8-59

The View Audiences page

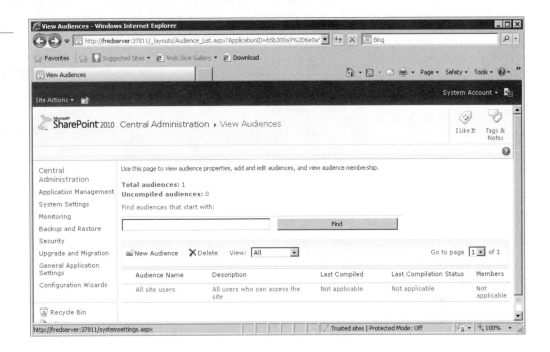

5. To create a new audience, click the New Audience button. The Create Audience page displays (see Figure 8-60).

Figure 8-60

The Create Audience page

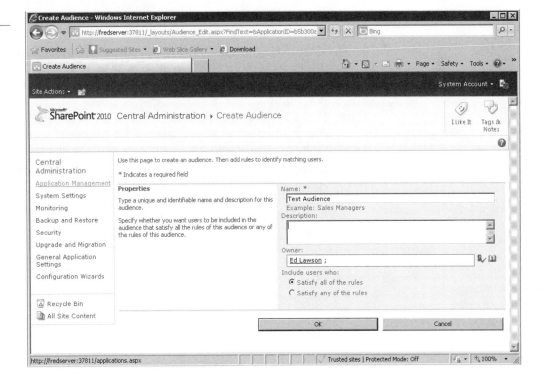

6. Specify a Name, Description, and Owner of the audience.

7. Specify if a user has to Satisfy any of the rules or Satisfy all of the rules defined to become a member of the audience and click OK. The Add Audience Rule page displays (see Figure 8-61).

Figure 8-61

The Add Audience Rule page

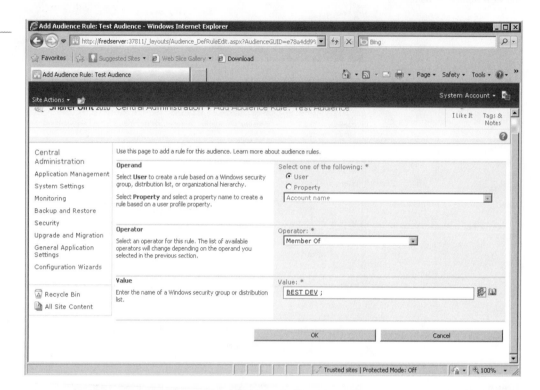

8. In the Operand section, select the User or Property. If you select User, the rule will be based on a Windows security group, distribution list, or organization hierarchy. If you select Property, you must select the Account name to create the rule on.

9. In the Operator section, click the down-arrow to select an Operator, which will change based on what you selected for the operator (for example, it will change for a user who reports to a certain person or member of a group).

10. In the Value section, select the Value that the rule is based on.

11. Click OK.

When the View Audience Properties page displays (see Figure 8-62), you can then add additional rules. You can also edit the audience, view membership, and compile an audience.

Figure 8-62

The View Audience Properties page

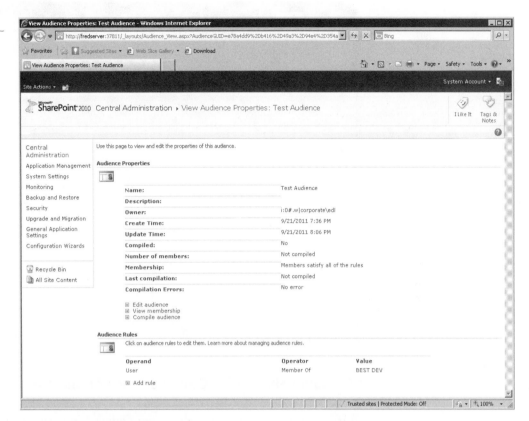

While Organization Profiles are introduced with SharePoint 2010, they are similar to User Profiles because they define a set of properties and allocate to Organization Sub-Types instead of users. Organization Profiles describes business teams so that SharePoint users can determine the purpose and function of each team. Each Organization Profile can be maintained by a named individual who can identify members of that organization (either manually or through a reporting structure or group).

To create and manage Organization Profiles, open User Profile Service Applications and click **Manage Organization Profiles**. When the Manage Organization Profiles page displays, you can create a new Organization Profile by clicking the **New Profile** button. You will then type basic information and specify the parent organization and its members (see Figure 8-63).

Figure 8-63

The Add Organization Profile page

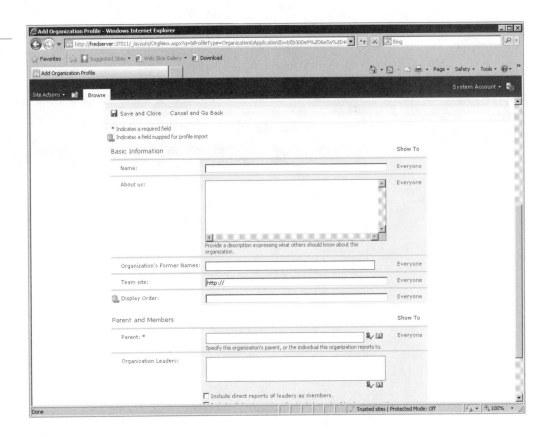

Managing SharePoint Online Service Applications

As described in Lesson 4, the SharePoint Online Administration Center is one of the primary tools to configure and manage SharePoint Online. While some of the Service Applications exist with SharePoint Online, the managing and configuring of Service Applications is simplified compared to an on-premise version of SharePoint.

CERTIFICATION READY
How do you configure the SharePoint Online term store?
1.3.9

With the Administration Center, you can configure and manage the following Service Applications:

- InfoPath Forms Services
- InfoPath Forms Services Web service proxy
- User Profiles
- Business Data Connectivity
- Term Store

Since SharePoint Online is installed and configured by Microsoft, you don't need to install these Service Applications or start related services.

When you configure InfoPath Forms Services, you can configure the following settings for browser-enabled user form templates (see Figure 8-64):

- Enable or disable publishing of browser-enabled user form templates
- Enable or disable rendering of browser-enabled user form templates

By default, browser-enabled user form templates can be published and rendered.

Figure 8-64

Configuring InfoPath Forms
Services

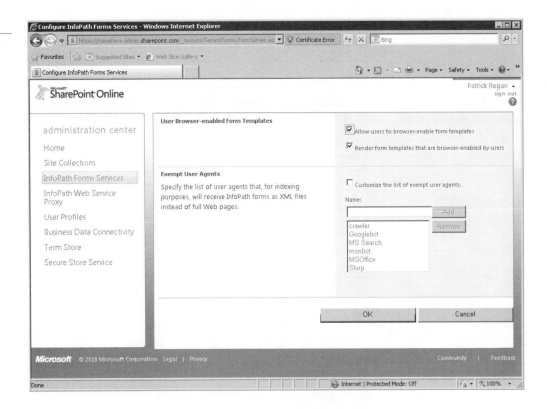

Configuring user profiles (including My Sites and audiences) with SharePoint Online is very similar to SharePoint installed locally on a server (see Figure 8-65). Since user profiles are derived from Active Directory, you should configure Active Directory Synchronization as described in Lesson 7.

Figure 8-65

Configuring User Profiles

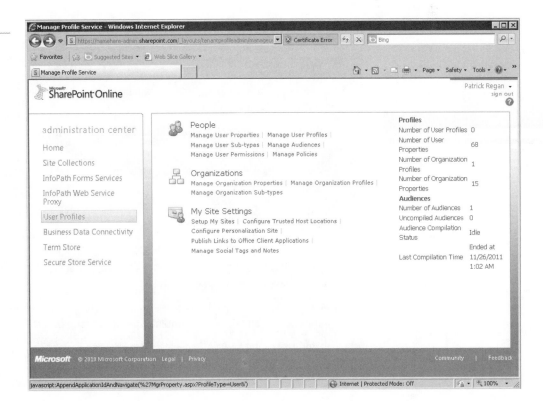

Finally, configuring the SharePoint Online Term Store is very similar to configuring SharePoint installed on an on-premise server. When you first configure the Term Store, be sure to define your Term Store Administrators and specify the languages you want to support (see Figure 8-66).

Figure 8-66

The SharePoint Online Term Store

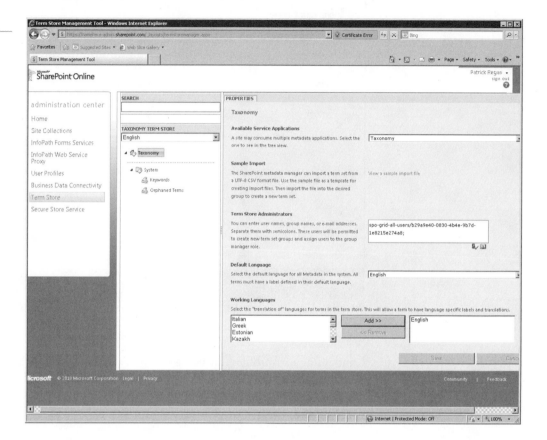

SKILL SUMMARY

IN THIS LESSON, YOU LEARNED:

- Service Applications (SAs) provide granular pieces of functionality to other Web and Service Applications in the farm.

- Access Services lets users view, edit, and interact with Microsoft Access 2010 databases in a Web browser.

- Excel Services Application lets users view and interact with Microsoft Excel 2010 files in a Web browser.

- Visio Graphics Service lets users view and refresh published Visio 2010 diagrams in a Web browser.

- The InfoPath Forms Services (IPFS) in Microsoft SharePoint Server 2010 gives you the ability to deploy your organization's forms to Microsoft SharePoint Server and enable users to fill out these forms by using a Web browser.

- Managed Metadata service manages taxonomy hierarchies, keywords, and social tagging infrastructure, and publishes content types across site collections.

- PerformancePoint Service Application provides the capabilities of PerformancePoint, which allows you to monitor and analyze your business.

- Microsoft Business Connectivity Services is a collection of features and services used to connect SharePoint solutions to external data sources (including SQL Server databases, SAP applications, and Web services) and to define external content types based on external data.

- A user profile is a collection of properties that describes a SharePoint user.

- User Profile service adds support for My Sites, profile pages, social tagging, and other social computing features.

- The User Profile Synchronization Service is the core of the synchronization architecture in SharePoint Server 2010, which uses the Microsoft Forefront Identity Manager (FIM) to participate in synchronization.

- Forefront Identity Manager (FIM) is a state-based identity management component used to manage user's digital identifies and credentials.

- My Sites are personal sites that provide users in your organization with a rich set of social networking features.

- Audiences enables organizations to target content to users based on their jobs or tasks, as defined by their membership in a SharePoint Server group or distribution list, by the organizational reporting structure, or by the public properties in their user profiles.

- Organization profiles contain detailed information about an organization, such as a subsidiary, departments, teams, and so on.

■ Knowledge Assessment

Fill in the Blank

Complete the following sentences by writing the correct word or words in the blanks provided.

1. The _____ provides a service or functionality accessed through one or more Web applications.

2. The Service Application that provides profile pages and social tagging is _____.

3. The _____ is combined with SharePoint to form a business intelligence tool to analyze and present data.

4. When upgrading a form, you should _____ the form to prevent data loss.

5. The _____ is a business intelligence tool that provides dashboards, scorecards, and analytic components.

6. _____ is data about data that describes the content and context of data files.

7. The _____ is a database that stores enterprise keywords.

8. _____ are personal sites that provide users in your organization with a rich set of social networking features.

9. The Personal Site quote templates has a _____ storage limit for a site.

10. _____ contains information about an organization or team.

Multiple Choice

Circle the letter that corresponds to the best answer.

1. What do many Service Applications use to provide a virtual link between the users or Web application and the service?
   a. Shared Services Provider
   b. SharePoint Service
   c. Service Application Proxy
   d. Windows Service

2. Which Service Application is used to link keywords to SharePoint items?
   a. Access Services
   b. Business Data Connectivity
   c. Managed Metadata service
   d. State service

3. Which service provides an infrastructure to support electronic forms?
   a. Excel Services Applications
   b. Word Automation Services
   c. Web Analytics Services
   d. InfoPath Forms Services

4. To use Excel documents with Excel Services, you must _____.
   a. add the library to the trusted data connection libraries
   b. add the SQL Server 2008 Report Add-in to SharePoint 2010
   c. execute the Excel Export function
   d. add the Excel Service to the SharePoint Library

5. What is used to connect an SQL database to SharePoint to display data from the non-SharePoint database?
   a. Business Connectivity Services
   b. InfoPath Forms Services
   c. Word Automation Services
   d. Web Analytics Services

6. Which tool is used to create metadata terms for the SharePoint enterprise environment?
   a. Term Store Management Tool
   b. Metadata Modify Tool
   c. Metadata List Tool
   d. Tax Store Tool

7. What is the primary service that synchronizes user profiles?
   a. AD Synchronization Tool
   b. Forefront Identity Manager
   c. Term Store Manager
   d. Audience Migrator

8. What enables organizations to target content to users based on their jobs or tasks?
   a. organization profile
   b. user profile
   c. Taxonomy terms
   d. audience

9. Which Service Application manages Organization Profiles?
   a. Access Services
   b. Business Data Connectivity
   c. User Profile
   d. State service

10. What is a collection of properties that describes a SharePoint user?
    a. organization profile
    b. user attribute collection
    c. user collection
    d. user profile

True / False

Circle T if the statement is true or F if the statement is false.

T | F **1.** SharePoint 2010 is designed to closely interact with Office 2010.

T | F **2.** By default, SharePoint automatically trusts the SharePoint farm for Excel Services Application.

T | F **3.** Profile Synchronization can retrieve information from only AD.

T | F **4.** When you create an audience, you create the audience and then select each user that you want to add the audience.

T | F **5.** The Business Intelligence Center allows you to use PerformancePoint Services.

■ Case Scenario

Scenario 8-1: Upgrading to SharePoint 2010

You are having a meeting with a group of managers. So far, they have been very impressed with the SharePoint services. Currently, there are many departments and teams that use a large number of Microsoft Office documents, many of which are quite large and/or complicated. They are curious what tools are available to make the management and collaboration of these documents more effective. What do you tell them?

Scenario 8-2: Expanding SharePoint 2010

You manager would like for users to create and manage their personal Web sites. What solution can you provide for your users and what steps are required to implement personal Web sites?

9 LESSON

Configuring Indexes and Searches

OBJECTIVE DOMAIN MATRIX

TECHNOLOGY SKILL	OBJECTIVE DOMAIN DESCRIPTION	OBJECTIVE DOMAIN NUMBER
Configuring and Managing Crawl Schedules	Configuring Indexing and Search	1.4
	Configuring Crawl Schedules	1.4.2
	Configuring iFilters	1.4.3
	Configuring Crawl Rules	1.4.4
	Configuring Content Sources	1.4.5
	Configuring Scopes	1.4.6
	Configuring Managed Properties	1.4.7
	Configuring Content Types	1.4.8
	Configuring Search Components	1.4.9
	Configuring Index Partitioning	1.4.10
	Configuring Federated Search Locations	1.4.11
Configuring FAST Search Server	Configuring FAST Search for SharePoint	1.4.1

KEY TERMS

authoritative
    pages

content source

content type

Crawl rules

Crawl Servers

crawler impact rules

crawling

Federated search
    connectors

full crawl

iFilters

incremental crawl

index partition

Metadata property
    mappings

Microsoft FAST Search
    Server 2010 for
    SharePoint

Query Servers

Search Box

Search scopes

Search Server
    2010 Express

Search Service
    Application

SharePoint 2010
    Search

Over the last several months, the use of your SharePoint sites has significantly grown as users have embraced the new technology, including adding thousands of documents for easy access. However, as SharePoint has grown, it has become more difficult for users to find documents. Therefore, management is asking you for help.

■ Configuring and Managing Crawl Schedules

↓
THE BOTTOM LINE

Since SharePoint can be a valuable tool for any company, it becomes more important to find items quickly with SharePoint. Unfortunately, as SharePoint environments grow in size, it becomes more difficult to find items. Therefore, SharePoint includes several enterprise search tools.

Depending on your needs, SharePoint has multiple production editions for searching. They include:

- *Microsoft SharePoint Foundation 2010:* Includes a search tool, which is limited to the local site.

- *Microsoft SharePoint Server 2010:* An Enterprise search solution that scales up to 100 million documents.

- *Search Server 2010 Express:* Used as a standalone system, it can scale up to 10 million items with subsecond response times and search 31 file types using the extensible iFilter platform, including Microsoft Office; Hypertext Markup Language (HTML); SharePoint 2003, SharePoint 2007, and SharePoint 2010 sites; Open Document format; and many others. SharePoint 2010 Search supports 51 languages, including compound handling, numbers, and dates in languages such as Thai, Russian, and Arabic. While it does not have advanced content management features, it is a good option as an enterprise search for non-SharePoint document management systems.

- *SharePoint 2010 Search:* SharePoint 2010 Search is like Search Server 2010 Express but can be scaled to several servers.

- *Microsoft FAST Search Server 2010 for SharePoint:* An Enterprise Search solution that can scale up to 500 million documents. It also adds increased performance and relevancy tuning algorithms, advanced sorting on any managed property, and advanced features such as scrolling preview and document thumbnails.

Understanding the SharePoint 2010 Search Architecture

When working with digital information, create a full-text index of content and properties and organize them in a way to quickly retrieve search results from the index.

CERTIFICATION READY
What are the search components that make it possible for users to find a SharePoint item using SharePoint search?
1.4.9

To provide the search capability in SharePoint 2010, start with content sources found in the content databases. SharePoint uses connectors to gather the content from the content sources so that it can be processed by an indexing engine. SharePoint includes connectors for different *content types* (including SharePoint data, file shares, Exchange public folders, and Business Connectivity Services).

To add content to the search databases, each item must be crawled and indexed. *Crawling* is the process of traversing the URL namespace associated with content sources, looking for links to content that should be indexed. During the crawl, each searchable item is opened, read, and analyzed; all of the content is consolidated into an index database (also known as a search catalog). While crawlers create the index, they do not actually store the index. The storage is actually done by the Query component.

A single Search server application contains several server roles. These roles can be placed on a single server or distributed among several servers for larger deployments. The roles include:

- *Crawl Servers* build and store the index file. They read each document on the Web front-end servers and index the content of each page.
- *Query Servers* are servers to which users submit queries to find content stored in the index.

Search consists of a Search Service Application, Search Service Application proxy, Web services, search service instance, and the following SQL databases:

- Search Service Application DB
- Search Service Application Crawl Store DB
- Search Service Application Property Store DB

The Search Center site provides a user interface that allows you to perform a query and to display the results. When you perform a query, you are asking a query server to search for something. After it searches through the index, it displays the results to the user.

Besides storing the data, the Query component is responsible for responding to search queries. Every time a query is executed, the query component searches the index and property database to come up with a list of items for the search. Before the results are displayed, security trimming removes items that the user cannot access. Therefore, when a user performs a search, he only sees items he can access.

Performing a search can be done from various locations within SharePoint. The Search box appears on all pages in the Team Site template. You can also create a dedicated search center. In any case, the search components consist of one or more Search Web Parts. Some of the popular Search Web parts include the following:

- *Search Box:* Users enter query terms, select the search scope, and then click the Search button.
- *Advanced Search Box:* Users can perform searches with the Search Box and perform queries based on managed properties and parameters.
- *People Search Box:* A Search box that searches only the People scope.
- *Refinement Panel:* A Web part that displays a range of links users can select to refine their searches rapidly.
- *Search Best Bets:* A Web part that the Best Bet results administrators have created for common search terms.
- *Search Statistics:* Displays the approximate total number of results and the time taken to return results.
- *Federated Results:* Displays results from federated locations, such as Internet Search engines or other SharePoint farms.

Creating and Configuring the Search Service Application

Before your users can search for content using Microsoft SharePoint Server 2010, you must create and configure the Search Service Application. The *Search Service Application* provides the mechanism to search and index content with SharePoint and other sources.

CERTIFICATION READY
What must you create to provide indexing and search capabilities?
1.4

While the Search Service application can be installed using the Farm Configuration Wizard, it can also be installed manually. Like other service applications, to create a Search Service Application, you must be a farm administrator.

 CREATE THE SEARCH SERVICE APPLICATION

GET READY. To create the Search Service Application, perform the following steps:

1. Open Central Administration.

2. In the Application Management section, click Manage service applications. The Manage Service Application page displays.

3. On the Ribbon, click New, and then click Search Service Application. The Create New Search Service Application page displays (see Figure 9-1).

Figure 9-1

The Create New Search Service Application page

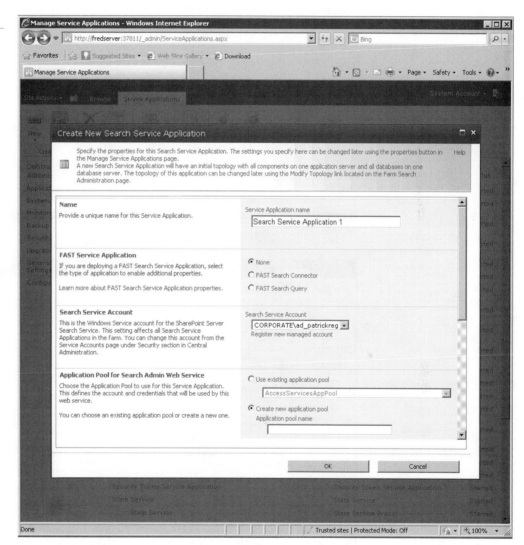

4. In the Name section, accept the default value for Search Application name or type a new name.

5. For the Search Service Account setting, accept the default for the farm or click Register new managed account to create a new account for the Search Service.

TAKE NOTE *

You should register a new user account for the SharePoint Server Search service. If you use the farm administrator account, the content access account has permission to crawl all the drafts and Help files in your SharePoint implementation, thus exposing all content in the search results.

6. In the Application Pool for Search Admin Web Service section, leave the default (Create new application pool) setting, and then type an Application pool name.

7. In the Application Pool for Search Query and Site Settings Web Service section, use the same application pool that you created for the Search Admin Web Service. Click Use existing application pool, and then select the pool name from the drop-down list.

8. Click OK.

The crawler uses a user account as the default content access account. This account must have read access to content that you want to crawl. Of course, you can change the default content access account at any time.

 SPECIFY THE DEFAULT CONTENT ACCESS ACCOUNT

GET READY. To specify the default content access account, perform the following steps:

1. Open Central Administration.

2. In the Application Management section, click Manage service applications. The Manage Service Application page displays.

3. Click Search Service Application. The Search Administration page displays (see Figure 9-2).

Figure 9-2

The Search Administration page

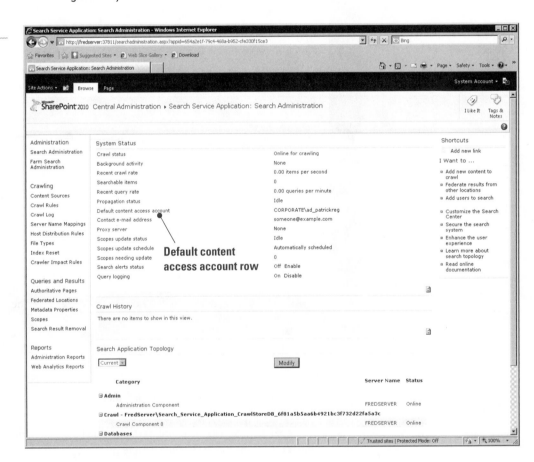

4. Click the link in the Default content access account row. The Default Content Access Account dialog displays (see Figure 9-3).

5. In the Account box, type a different user name in the form domain\user name.

6. In the Password box and Confirm Password box, type the password for this account.

7. Click OK.

Figure 9-3

The Default Content Access Account dialog

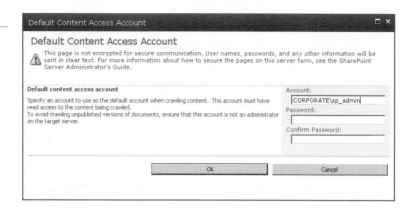

 SPECIFY THE CRAWL CONTACT E-MAIL ADDRESS

GET READY. To specify the contact e-mail address, perform the following steps:

1. Open Central Administration.
2. In the Application Management section, click Manage service applications. The Manage Service Application page displays.
3. Click the Search Service Application. The Search Administration page displays.
4. In the System Status section, click the link for the Contact *<e-mail address>*.
5. In the Search Email Setting dialog box, in the E-mail Address textbox, type the e-mail address that you want to appear in the logs of servers that are crawled by the search system.
6. Click OK.

The contact e-mail address is written to the logs of crawled servers. By default, the contact e-mail address is someone@example.com. It is recommended that you change this to an account that an external administrator can contact when a crawl might be contributing to a problem such as a decrease in performance on a server that the search system is crawling.

Creating Content Sources for Crawling Content

> After the Search Service Application is configured, you have to define at least one content source. A content source called Local SharePoint sites is created by default during installation and is automatically configured for crawling all of the sites in the server farm.

CERTIFICATION READY
What are the two types of crawls that you can schedule?
1.4.2

CERTIFICATION READY
How do you define how deep a crawl will dig into a directory?
1.4.5

CERTIFICATION READY
What are the different content types of data that you can crawl?
1.4.8

If you perform a stand-alone installation of SharePoint Server 2010, a full crawl of local SharePoint sites is automatically performed following installation and an incremental crawl is scheduled for every 20 minutes after that. A *full crawl* crawls all content that is specified by the content source, regardless of whether the content has changed. During an *incremental crawl*, only new or changed items are crawled and indexed. If you perform a Server Farm installation of SharePoint Server 2010, no crawls are automatically scheduled or performed.

A *content source* is a set of options that you can use to specify what type of content is crawled, what URLs to crawl, and how deep and when to crawl. You must create at least one content source before a crawl can occur. After you create a content source, you can edit or delete it at any time.

➔ CREATE A CONTENT SOURCE FOR CRAWLING

GET READY. To create a content source for crawling, perform the following steps:

1. Open Central Administration.
2. In the Application Management section, click Manage service applications. The Manage Service Application page displays.
3. Click the Search Service Application. The Search Administration page displays.
4. In the Crawling section, click Content Sources. The Manage Content Sources page displays (see Figure 9-4).

Figure 9-4

The Manage Content Sources page

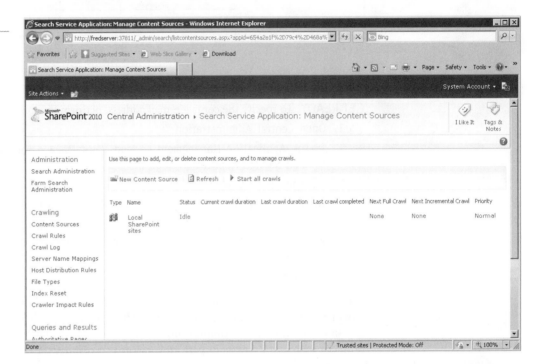

5. Click New Content Source. The Add Content Source page displays (see Figure 9-5).
6. In the Name section, in the Name box, type a name for the new content source.
7. In the Content Source Type section, select the content type that you want to crawl.
8. In the Start Addresses section, in the Type start addresses below (one per line) box, type the URLs from which the crawler should begin crawling.
9. In the Crawl Settings section, select the crawling behavior that you want (see Figure 9-6).
10. In the Crawl Settings section, specify a schedule for full crawls, select a defined schedule from the Full Crawl list (see Figure 9-7).
11. To define a full crawl schedule, click Create schedule to open the Manage Schedules page (see Figure 9-8). You can change a defined schedule by clicking Edit schedule. Click OK to accept your changes and return to the Add Content Source page.
12. To specify a schedule for incremental crawls, select a defined schedule from the Incremental Crawl list. To define a schedule, click Create schedule. You can change a defined schedule by clicking Edit schedule. Click OK to accept your changes and return to the Add Content Source page
13. To prioritize this content source, in the Content Source Priority section, on the Priority list, select Normal (the default) or High.
14. To immediately begin a full crawl, in the Start Full Crawl section, select the Start full crawl of this content source check box.
15. Click OK.

Figure 9-5

Add Content Source page

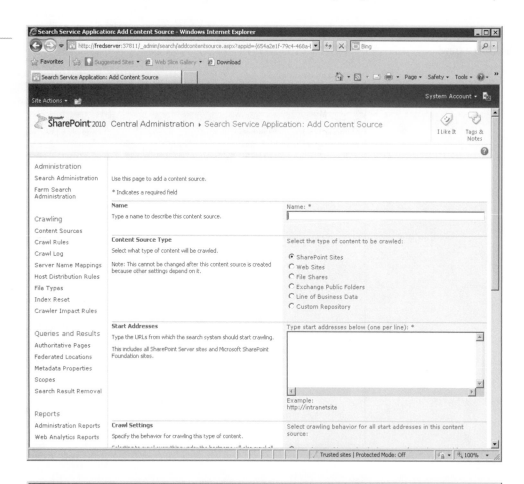

Figure 9-6

Configuring crawl settings

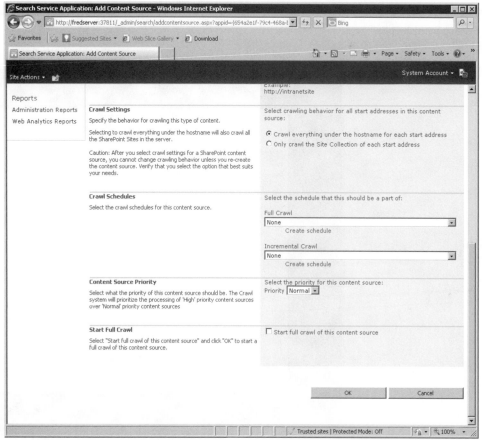

Figure 9-7

Scheduling a crawl

Figure 9-8

The Manage Schedules page

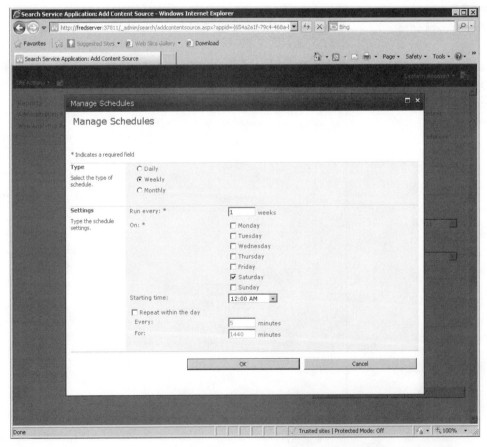

You can start a crawl at any time by opening the Manage Content Sources page, clicking the context menu of the content source, and then selecting either **Start Full Crawl** or **Start Incremental Crawl** (see Figure 9-9). You can also resume, pause, or stop crawls and delete content sources.

Figure 9-9

Starting a crawl

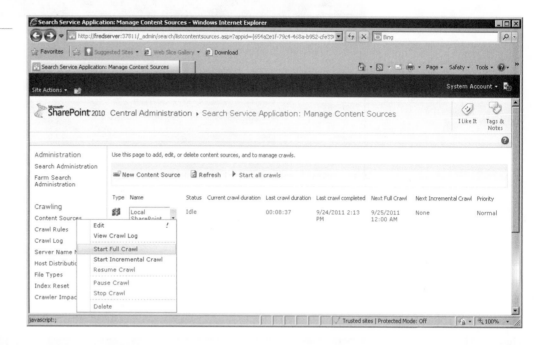

When you create a content source, you can only define one type of content. For example, you can add URLs for multiple SharePoint sites or add URLs for multiple file shares, but you cannot do both in a single content source.

Crawl rules allow you to include or exclude specific paths in a URL from being crawled and also allow you to specify different authentication accounts. Rules are applied in the order in which they are written during a content crawl, but you must perform a full crawl of the content source for the new rule to be implemented.

 CREATE A CRAWL RULE

GET READY. To create a crawl rule, perform the following steps:

1. Open Central Administration.

2. In the Application Management section, click Manage service applications. The Manage Service Application page displays.

3. Click the Search Service Application. The Search Administration page displays.

4. In the Crawling section, click Crawl Rules. The Manage Crawl Rules page displays (see Figure 9-10).

5. Click New Crawl Rule. The Add Crawl Rule page displays (see Figure 9-11).

6. In the Path section, in the Path box, type the hostname or hostnames of the sites on which you want the rule to apply, specifying the sites on the URLs to be affected by the rule. Use these formats: http://hostname/*; http://*.*; :// hostname/.

7. If desired, select the Use regular expression syntax for matching this rule check box or the Match case check box (or select both).

8. In the Crawl Configuration section, include or exclude all items in the path you used in the previous set.

CERTIFICATION READY
What is used to exclude certain paths when performing a crawl?
1.4.4

Figure 9-10

The Manage Crawl Rules page

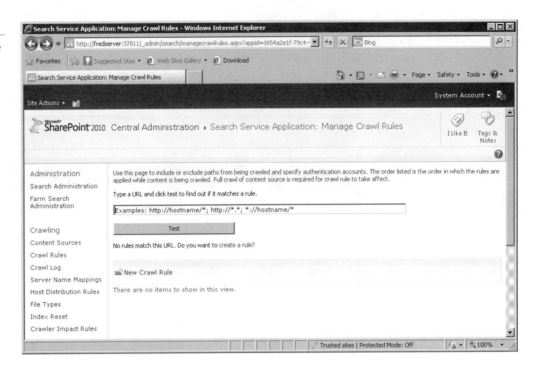

Figure 9-11

The Add Crawl Rule page

9. If you choose to exclude all items, you can choose to select Exclude complex URLs, such as those containing question marks.

10. If you choose to include all items, select the Follow Links on the URL without crawling the URL Itself option, the Crawl complex URLs (URLs that contain a question mark - ?) option, and the Crawl SharePoint content as http pages option.

11. Click OK.

12. When the rule is configured, you can type the URL in the test field on the Manage Crawl Rules page and then click the Test button to verify the rule matches the URL.

Content crawls can affect the performance of the SQL server as well as the Web sites and servers hosting the crawls. If necessary, you can define ***crawler impact rules*** to minimize the impact of the crawls. A crawler impact rule defines the rate at which the SharePoint Search service requests documents from a Web site during crawling. The rate can be defined as the number of simultaneous documents requested or as the delay between requests. In the absence of a crawler impact rule, the number of documents requested is 5 to 16 (depending on the hardware resources).

⊕ CREATE A CRAWLER IMPACT RULE

GET READY. To create a crawler impact rule, perform the following steps:

1. Open Central Administration.

2. In the Application Management section, click Manage service applications. The Manage Service Application page displays.

3. Click the Search Service Application. The Search Administration page displays.

4. On the Search Administration page, in the Crawling section, click Crawler Impact Rules. The Crawler Impact Rules page displays (see Figure 9-12).

Figure 9-12

The Crawler Impact Rules page

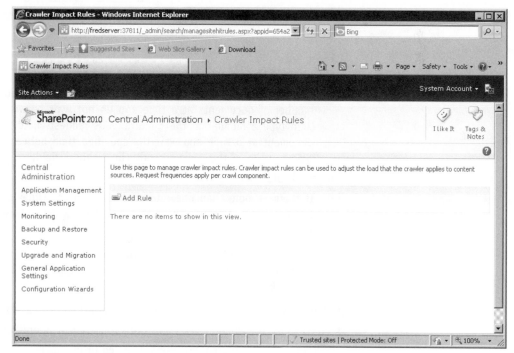

5. Click Add Rule. The Add Crawler Impact Rule page displays (see Figure 9-13).

Figure 9-13

The Add Crawler Impact Rule page

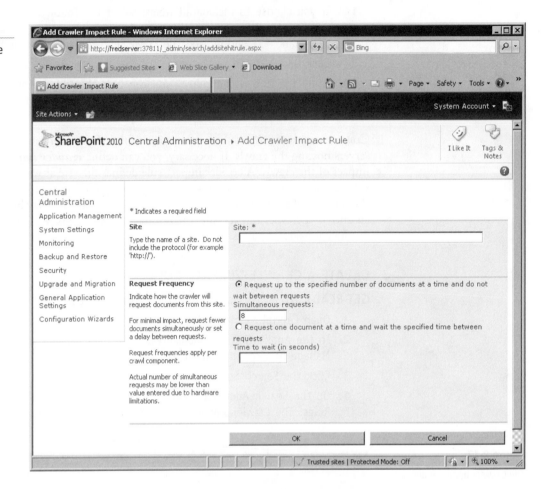

6. In the Site box, type the site's name without entering the protocol (such as http://).

7. In the Request Frequency section, either select the Request up to the specified number of documents at a time and do not wait between request radio button and then type a number in the Simultaneous requests field, or select the Request one document at a time and wait the specified time between requests option and then type a value in the Time to wait (in seconds) field.

8. Click OK.

9. If there is more than one rule configured in the Order column on the Crawler Impact Rules page, use the menus to select which rule will be evaluated first, second, and so on.

If there is a problem with crawling (including why content was not indexed and any errors that were encountered during the crawl), it can be found in the crawl logs. Some of the reasons include:

- A permission error whereby the crawl account does not have access to the SharePoint item
- An iFilter error whereby the file is not supported by SharePoint
- A protocol error, such as a possible blocked protocol

Creating a Search Center Site

At top of each page, there is already a search box available for you to perform searches within your SharePoint site. For more advanced searches, however, the Search Center (see Figure 9-14) provides an interface for users to submit search queries.

Figure 9-14

The Search Center

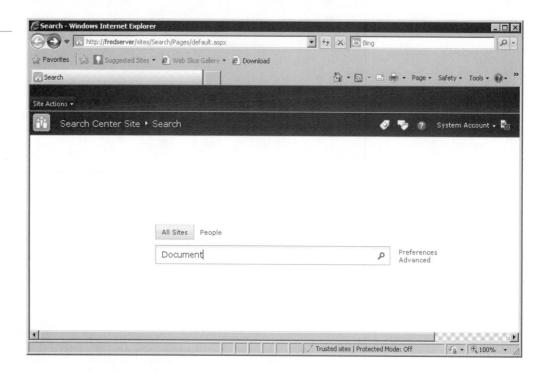

If you use the Enterprise Search center template for the Search Center Site, you can also perform people searches. To create the Search Center site, you must be a member of the Farm Administrators group.

 CREATE A SEARCH CENTER SITE

GET READY. To create a Search Center Site, perform the following steps:

1. Open Central Administration.
2. In the Application Management section, click Create site collections.
3. Type the name for this Search Center site and the description (optional).
4. In the Web Site Address section, type the last part of the URL for this site (such as Search).
5. In the Template Selection section, click the Enterprise tab and then select the Enterprise Search Center template or the Basic Search Center template. If you intend to use people search, you must select the Enterprise Search Center template (see Figure 9-15).

Figure 9-15

Selecting the Enterprise Search
Center template

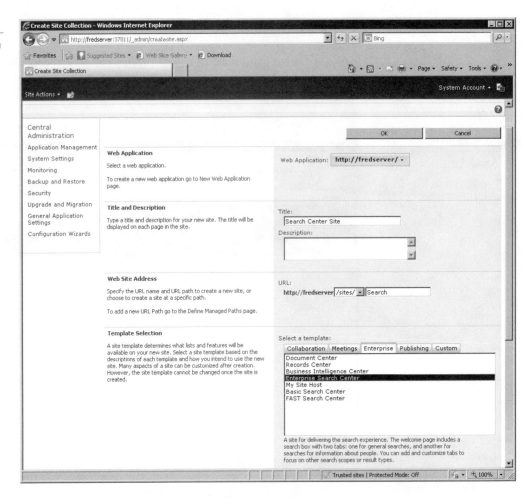

 TAKE NOTE*   The SharePoint Server Publishing Infrastructure feature must be active to create a Web
site using the Enterprise Search Center site definition. In addition, the SharePoint Server
Standard Site Collection Features feature must also be active before you can create a Web
site with either site definition.

6. In the Primary Site Collection Administrator section, in the User name box, type
   the user name of the primary site collection administrator for this site collection in
   the form of domain\user name.
7. In the Secondary Site Collection Administrator section, type the user name of a
   secondary site collection administrator.
8. In the Quota Template section, select a predefined quota template to limit
   resources that are used for this site collection.
9. Click OK.

GRANT ALL AUTHENTICATED USERS ACCESS TO THE SEARCH CENTER

GET READY. To grant all authenticated users access to the Search Center, perform the following
steps:

1. Open the Search Center Site.
2. Click the Site Actions menu and choose Site Settings.
3. In the Users and Permissions section, click People and groups.

4. Click either Enterprise Search Center Visitors or Basic Search Center Visitors.
5. Click the New menu and choose Add Users.
6. In the Users/Groups text box, type NT Authority\authenticated users.
7. Click OK.

Managing Enterprise Search Topology for Large Organizations

While SharePoint 2010 can scale up to 100 million index items, you must plan for a large-scale search architecture, including using multiple servers to host the different search components.

When looking at larger implementation of SharePoint 2010, you need to ensure that the search capability of your farm includes the following:

- Low crawl time
- Good index freshness
- Low query latency
- High crawl availability
- High query availability

By having a low crawl time and good index freshness, when a new item is added to the SharePoint farm, it will not be long before it is added to the index so that it can be searched for and found by SharePoint users. Of course, users always want to perform a search that quickly returns results. Lastly, high crawl and high query availability means that a server can fail yet the search capabilities will still be available to users.

Therefore, to ensure this, you may need to use multiple crawl servers so that multiple sources can simultaneously be crawled. To determine the number of crawl servers and how often crawls occur, you must look at how long a full crawl takes to complete and how fresh the indexes must be.

If you administer SharePoint for a large organization with offices throughout the world, links between countries or continents are slow or intermittent. Therefore, you should consider deploying separate Search service applications in different geographical areas such that crawls and queries do not cross a slow WAN link.

If you have a SharePoint environment that supports multiple tenants, you want it to appear that each client or tenant has its own farm. In addition, when a user from one organization searches for something, she should not see the results for another organization. While security trimming will help, you should also create separate Search Service applications for each tenant.

Lastly, if you are hosting Internet and intranet sites, you may not want confidential internal documents to be displayed to Internet users.

Using Index Partitions

CERTIFICATION READY
What can you use to divide a large crawl database and improve performance?
1.4.10

As your SharePoint environment grows, your search indexes will grow and the time to perform a search will increase. To scale the search components as your environment grows, SharePoint 2010 supports index partitions to divide the index into multiple partitions. To increase performance, each partition uses its own query server. Microsoft defines that the maximum number of items for an index partition is 10 million items.

If you performed a farm installation, you can modify the search topology. In Search Server 2010 Express, the topology components of each Search service application must be on one server.

In Search Server 2010, an ***index partition*** is a group of query components. Each query component holds a subset of the full text index and returns search results when a query is performed. Each index partition is associated with a specific property database that contains metadata associated with a specific set of crawled content. You can distribute the load of query servicing by adding index partitions to a Search service application and placing their query components on different farm servers.

 ADD AN INDEX PARTITION TO A SEARCH SERVICE APPLICATION

GET READY. To add an index partition to a Search Service Application, perform the following steps:

1. Open Central Administration.

2. In the Application Management section, click Manage service applications. The Manage Service Application page displays.

3. Click Search Service Application. The Search Administration page displays.

4. In the Search Application Topology section, click the Modify button. The Manage Search Topology page displays (see Figure 9-16).

Figure 9-16

The Manage Search Topology page

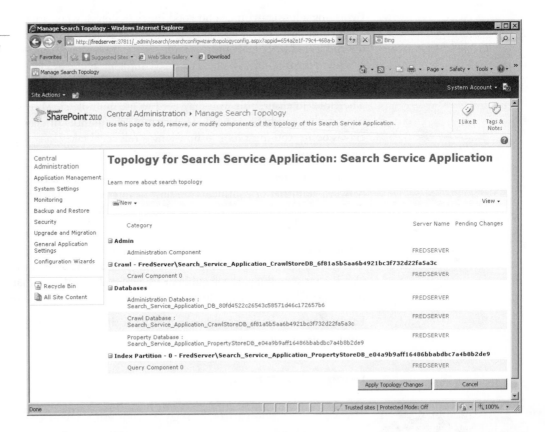

5. Click New and then click Index Partition and Query Component. The Add Query Component page displays (see Figure 9-17).

Figure 9-17

The Add Query Component page

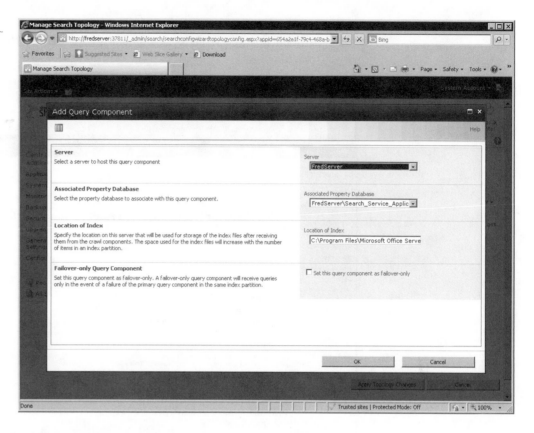

6. Click the farm server to which you want to add the first query component of the new index partition.

7. In the Associated Property Database list, click the property database that you want to associate with the new index partition.

8. In the Location of Index field, you can optionally type the location on the server that you want to use for storage of the index files after the index partition receives them from the crawl components.

9. If you want to provide a failover-query component, select the Set this query component as failover-only check box. If you are creating a new index partition, you should leave this box unchecked.

10. Click OK.

11. When you return to the Search Service Application page (refer to Figure 9-16), click the Apply Topology Changes button to start the SharePoint timer job that will add the new index partition and its first query component to the specified server.

If you want to balance the load of servicing queries across multiple farm servers, add query components to an index partition and then associate them with the servers that you want to service queries.

 ADD A QUERY COMPONENT TO AN INDEX PARTITION

GET READY. To add a query component to an index partition, perform the following steps:

1. Open Central Administration.

2. In the Application Management section, click Manage service applications. The Manage Service Application page displays.

3. Click the Search Service Application. The Search Administration page displays.

4. In the Search Application Topology section, click the Modify button. The Manage Search Topology page displays.

5. On the Manage Search Topology page, click a query component in the index partition that you want to modify, and then click Add Mirror (see Figure 9-18).

Figure 9-18

Adding a mirror query component

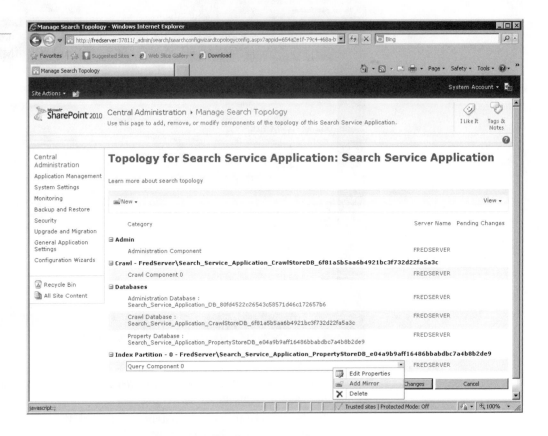

6. Click the farm server to which you want to add the first query component of the new index partition.

7. In the Associated Property Database list, click the property database that you want to associate with the new index partition.

8. In the Location of Index field, you can optionally type the location on the server that you want to use for storage of the index files after the index partition receives them from the crawl components.

9. If you want to provide a failover-query component, select the Set this query component as failover-only check box. If you are creating a new index partition, leave this box unchecked.

10. Click OK.

11. On the Manage Search Topology page, click the Apply Topology Changes button to start the SharePoint timer job that adds the new mirror query component to the selected index partition.

File Types and iFilters

By design, SharePoint only reads certain files during crawling, including commonly used Web pages and office documents. However, since SharePoint could not know about every possible data file that could be loaded in SharePoint, SharePoint has the ability to add iFilters to read those files.

CERTIFICATION READY
What is used to read a new type of document when performing a crawl?
1.4.3

An *iFilter* is a plugin that allows the Windows Indexing Service to read and index different file formats so that they become searchable. Without an appropriate iFilter, contents of a file cannot be parsed and indexed by the search engine.

By default, SharePoint only indexes certain files, including ASP documents, asp.net server pages (aspx), Microsoft Office Documents, HTML documents, JSP documents, OpenDocument documents, PHP documents, TIFF documents, URL documents, XML documents, and compressed zipped files/folders. If you need to add or remove file types, click the **File Types** option on the Search Administration page (see Figure 9-19).

Figure 9-19

The Manage File Types page

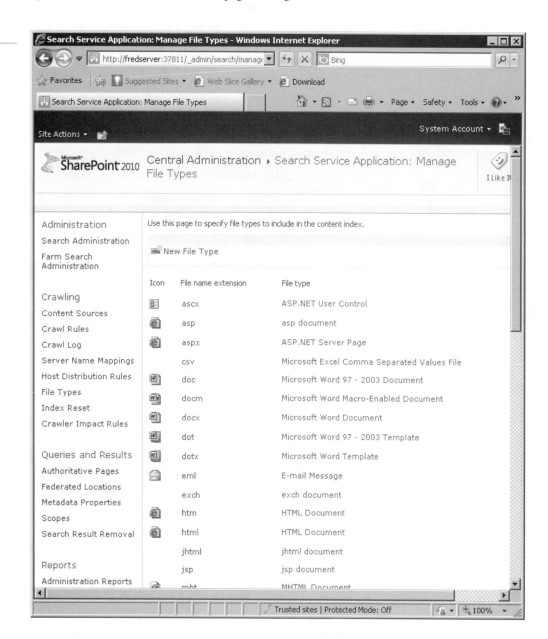

When it indexes the specified file types, each file must be stripped of formatting before its content can be added to the content index. SharePoint 2010 uses iFilters to remove embedded formatting from the content that is extracted from crawled items. Each iFilter must be associated with the kind of file that it can filter as identified by the three- or four-letter extension of the file name.

One popular file type that is not automatically included in SharePoint is Adobe's Portable File Format (PDF). Besides adding the PDF files using the the New File Type button, you must install the PDF iFilter to properly index PDF files.

 INSTALL ADOBE PDF iFILTER 9 FOR 64-BIT PLATFORMS

GET READY. To install the Adobe PDF iFilter, perform the following steps:

1. Install PDF iFilter 9.0 (64 bit) from http://www.adobe.com/support/downloads/detail.jsp?ftpID=4025

2. Download the PDF icon picture from http://www.adobe.com/misc/linking.html and copy it to C:\Program Files\Common Files\Microsoft Shared\Web Server Extensions\14\TEMPLATE\IMAGES\

3. Add the following entry in the C:\Program Files\Common Files\Microsoft Shared\Web Server Extensions\14\TEMPLATE\XML\docIcon.xml file

   <Mapping Key="pdf" Value="pdf16.gif" />

4. Open regedit.

5. Navigate to the following location:

   HKEY_LOCAL_MACHINE\SOFTWARE\Microsoft\Office Server\14.0\Search\Setup\ContentIndexCommon\Filters\Extension

6. Right-click Extension, click New, choose Key, and then create a key called .pdf (see Figure 9-20).

Figure 9-20

Creating a new key

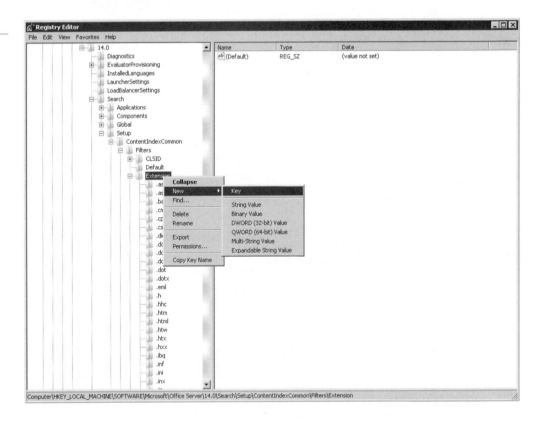

7. Add the following GUID in the default value:

   {E8978DA6-047F-4E3D-9C78-CDBE46041603}

8. Restart the SharePoint Server Search service or restart the SharePoint servers on the farm.

9. Perform a crawl.

> **TAKE NOTE***
>
> By default, SharePoint 2010 prevents you from opening PDF documents. If you wish to open PDF documents from within SharePoint, you must open the Central Administration, select Manage Web Applications, select the appropriate Web application, and then select General Settings. Then, for Browser File Handling, select Permissive (instead of Strict).

TIFF (Tagged Image File Format) is a graphics image format that is common within electronic faxes. By adding a TIFF iFilter to Windows, you can scan those images for text by using optical character recognition (OCR). Then use a group policy (or local policy) to force TIFF iFilter to OCR every page in a TIFF document.

⊙ INSTALL AND ENABLE A TIFF iFILTER

GET READY. To install a TIFF iFilter and configure Windows to automatically read TIFF documents with the OCR, perform the following steps:

1. Click Start > Administrative Tools > Server Manager.
2. Click Features.
3. Click Add Features.
4. Select Windows TIFF IFilter (see Figure 9-21) and click Next.

Figure 9-21

Selecting the TIFF IFilter

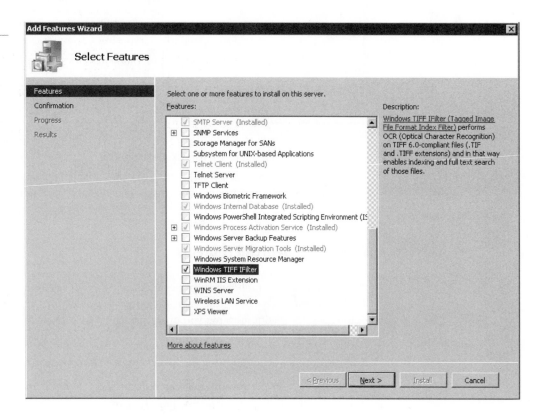

5. Click Install.
6. When the installation is complete, click Close.
7. Close Server Manager.
8. Open the Local Group Policy Editor by clicking the Start button and in the Start Search text box, typing gpedit.msc and then pressing Enter.
9. In the Computer Configuration section, expand Administrative Templates.
10. Expand Windows Components, expand Search, and then click OCR.

11. Double-click Force TIFF IFilter to OCR every page in a TIFF document (see Figure 9-22).

Figure 9-22

Forcing TIFF IFilter to perform OCR

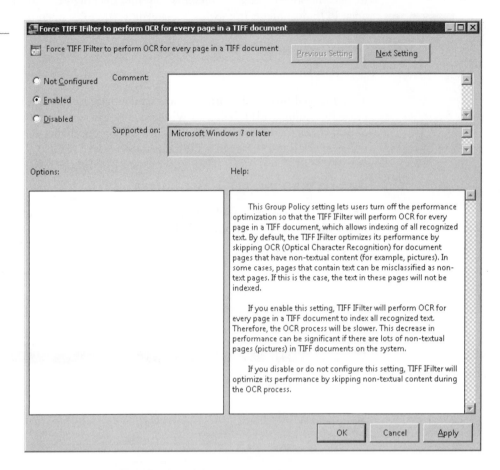

12. Select Enabled and then click Next Setting.

13. The default language for the server is the default language for OCR. Therefore, if you need to select additional languages, select Enable and select one or more languages.

14. Click OK.

Looking at Search Problems

It can become frustrating when you cannot find what you are looking for. Since a SharePoint environment can quickly grow, it is easy to misplace a document or other SharePoint item. As a SharePoint administrator, you must ensure that each SharePoint site is searchable.

If an item cannot be found using the SharePoint search items, you must first check the following:

- Does the user performing the search have access to the SharePoint item?
- Is the file or SharePoint item being crawled?
- Does the crawl account have access to the SharePoint item?
- Has a crawl occurred since the document or SharePoint was added or last modified?
- Is the file or SharePoint item a managed file type?
- Is the associated site, list, or library marked as searchable?
- Does the managed file need an iFilter loaded?
- Are the documents checked out?
- Is the file corrupted or otherwise unreadable?

By default, lists and items are configured as searchable. However, if you have a list or library, you can configure the list or items to not be visible in search results.

 CONFIGURE A LIST OR LIBRARY SEARCH OPTION

GET READY. To configure the search option for a list or library, perform the following steps:

1. In SharePoint, open the list or library.
2. On the Ribbon, click the List tab or Library tab and then select List Settings or Library Settings.
3. Click the Advanced Settings option.
4. In the Search section, select Yes (see Figure 9-23) if you want to allow the item from the document list or library to appear in search results. Select No if you do not.

If you still cannot find an item using a search, you should look at the crawl logs.

Figure 9-23

The Advanced Settings page

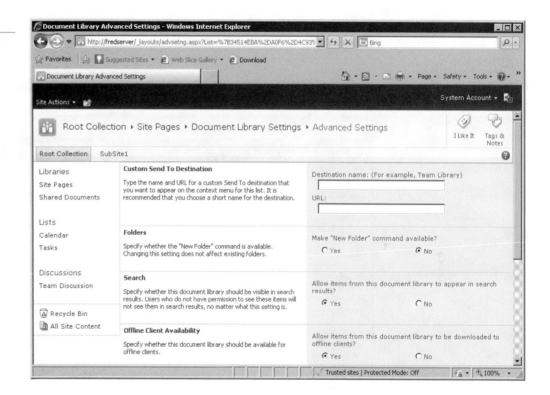

 VIEW THE CRAWL LOGS

GET READY. To view the crawl logs, perform the following steps:

1. Open Central Administration.
2. In the Application Management section, click Manage service applications. The Manage Service Application page displays.
3. Click the Search Service Application. The Search Administration page displays.
4. In the Crawling section, click Crawl Log. The Crawl Log—Content Source page displays (see Figure 9-24).

The first thing you should notice is the **Successes**, **Warnings**, and **Errors** columns. If you click on any of these numbers, you can review the individual successes, warnings, and errors (see Figure 9-25). You can also click **URL** or **Host Name** to drill down on a specific site, list, or library.

Figure 9-24

The Crawl Log—Content Source page

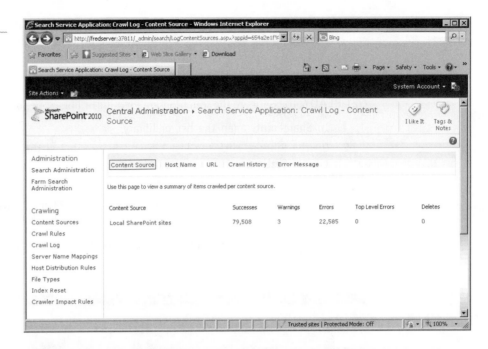

Figure 9-25

The Crawl Log—URL page

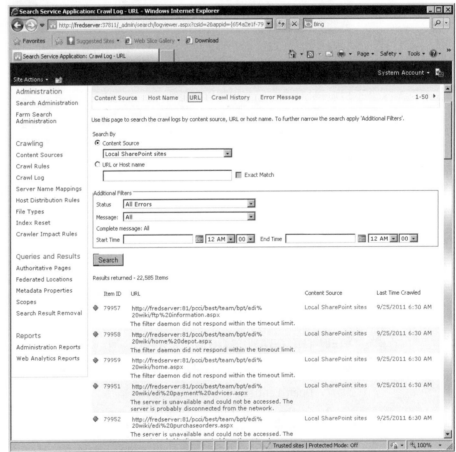

Queries and Results

When configuring searches, you want to make the search results as strong as possible so that users will find what they need so that they can do their jobs without losing valuable time to searches.

The Search Administration page for any search service contains a Queries and Results section with links to various features that can be configured to tweak Search results.

AUTHORITATIVE PAGES

Authoritative pages are the pages that you determine link to the most relevant information. Search uses these pages to determine the search rank of every page in the index. You use the Authoritative Pages utility to organize most authoritative to non-authoritative sites. Therefore, when performing searches, the most authoritative pages will rank higher than lower-level authoritative pages.

 ## MANAGE AUTHORITATIVE PAGES

GET READY. To manage authoritative pages, perform the following steps:

1. Open Central Administration.

2. In the Application Management section, click Manage service applications. The Manage Service Application page displays.

3. Click Search Service Application. The Search Administration page displays.

4. In the Queries and Results section, click Authoritative Pages. The Specify Authoritative Pages page displays (see Figure 9-26).

5. Type the appropriate URL in the appropriate box.

Figure 9-26

The Specify Authoritative Pages page

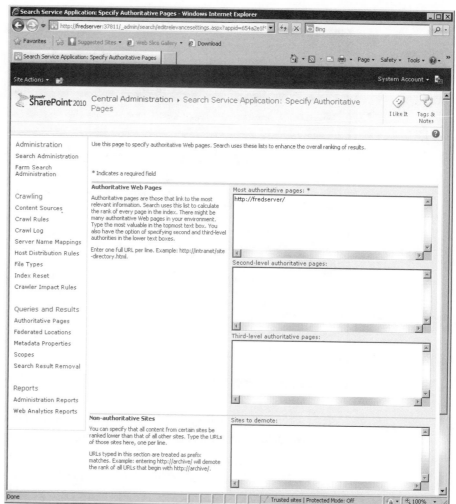

ADDING FEDERATED LOCATIONS

Federated search connectors enable the Microsoft enterprise search solution to pass a query to a target system (another SharePoint system or external Web site or service) and display results returned from that system. When you federate one search solution with another, user queries are sent to both indexes and results are displayed in the same page. Federated results are displayed in the federated results Web Parts, so users can clearly differentiate them from results from the local SharePoint index.

Federated search connectors work for all Microsoft enterprise search products and search connections are available for www.bing.com, YouTube, TechNet, and Wikipedia, to name a few. You might also want to create different Search service applications for servers in different geographical locations and have one geographical location federate the search center from another geographical location.

⊕ IMPORT A FEDERATED LOCATION SEARCH CONNECTOR

GET READY. To import a Federated Location Search Connector, perform the following steps:

1. Open Central Administration.
2. In the Application Management section, click Manage service applications. The Manage Service Application page displays.
3. Click the Search Service Application. The Search Administration page displays.
4. In the Queries and Results section, click Federated Locations. The Managed Federated Locations page displays (see Figure 9-27).

Figure 9-27

The Managed Federated Locations page

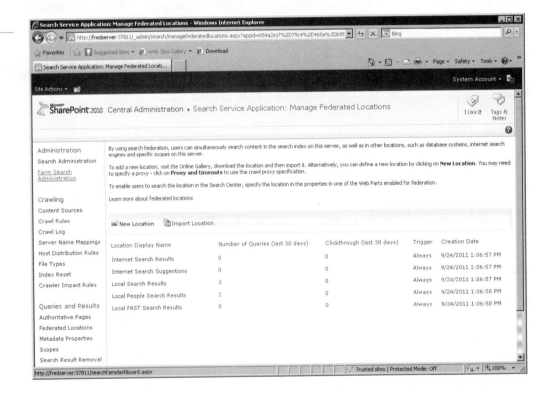

5. Click Online Gallery to find a new Federated Search Connector from Microsoft's Federated Search Connector Gallery for Enterprise Search Web site.

6. Download and save the Connector (FLD file) to your computer by clicking the desired connector.

7. Close the Web page.

8. Back on the Manage Federated Locations page, click Import Location. The Import Federated Location page displays (see Figure 9-28).

Figure 9-28

The Import Federated Location page

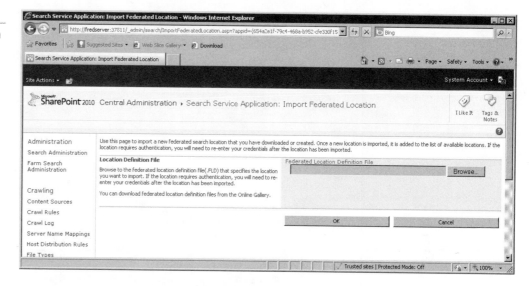

9. Click Browse and navigate to the location where you saved the FLD file. Select the FLD file and then click Open.

10. When the path to the FLD file populates the FLD file, click OK.

11. Click the Edit button to modify the settings for the Federated Location so that you can choose to modify items such as the display name, the description, the trigger that determines how the user's query matches the location, the location information, and so on. Click OK when you are done.

12. When you are back to the Edit Federated Location page, click Done.

13. Click OK to complete the import and return to the Manage Federated Locations page.

➔ CONFIGURE A FEDERATED LOCATION SEARCH CONNECTOR

GET READY. To configure a Federated Location Search Connector, perform the following steps:

1. Open Central Administration.

2. In the Application Management section, click Manage service applications. The Manage Service Application page displays.

3. Click the Search Service Application. The Search Administration page displays.

4. In the Queries and Results section, click Federated Locations. The Managed Federated Locations page displays.

5. On the Manage Federated Locations page, click New Location. The Add Federated Location page displays (see Figure 9-29).

6. In the General Information section, type the Location Name, Display Name, and Description in the available fields.

7. In the Author section, type an optional author (which can be a person or an organization) for the location.

Figure 9-29

The Add Federated Location page

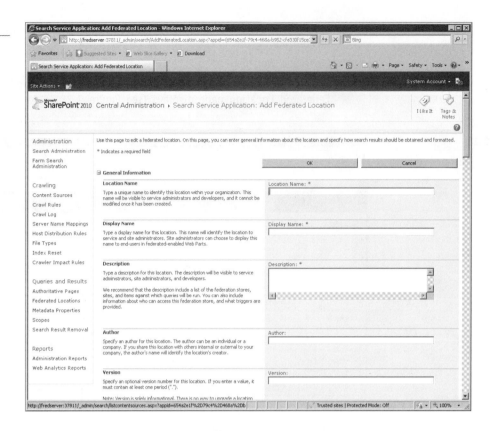

8. In the Version section, type a version number, which is typically 1.0.0.0 for the first version of a location connector.

9. In the Trigger section (see Figure 9-30), accept the default Always: Query should always match option or select Prefix: Query must begin with a specified prefix. Then type the prefix in the Add Prefix field or select Pattern: query must match a specified pattern. In the Add Pattern field, type the pattern, which can be a regular expression.

Figure 9-30

Defining triggers

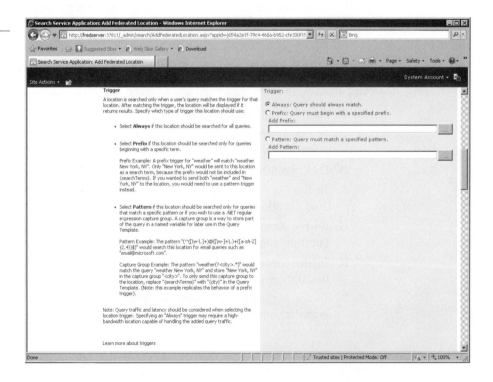

10. In the Location Information section (see Figure 9-31), select a Location Type, such as Search Index on this Server (the default), FAST Index, or OpenSearch 1.0/1.1.

Figure 9-31

Choosing a location type

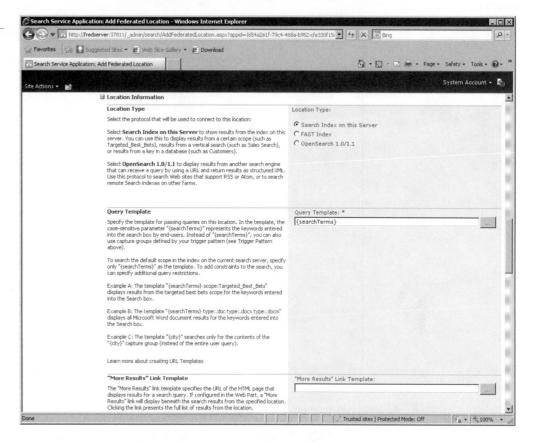

11. In the Query Template field, click the ellipsis button (...) to open the editor and then type a template name for passing queries to the location type's URL, which specifies not only the location but also the specific data to be queried. For example, type {searchTerms} scope:Targeted_Best_Bets.

12. In the "More Results" Link Template field, click the ellipsis button (...) to open the editor and type an optional URL for a Web page that offers additional search results for the query. For example, type http://server/SearchCenter/Pages/Results.aspx?k={searchTerms}.

13. In the Display Information section (see Figure 9-32), leave Use Default Formatting selected for Federated Search Results Display Metadata or clear the Use Default Formatting check box and manually configure the formatting in the XSL, Properties, and Sample Data editors.

14. In the Core Search Results Display Metadata section, leave Use Default Formatting selected or clear the Use Default Formatting check box and manually configure the formatting in the XSL, Properties, and Sample Data editors.

15. In the Top Federated Results Display Metadata section, leave Use Default Formatting selected or clear the Use Default Formatting check box and manually configure the formatting in the XSL, Properties, and Sample Data editors.

16. In the Restrictions and Credentials section, select No Restrictions if anyone can access and use the location, or select Use restriction if only site administrators access specific URLs.

17. In the Specify Credentials section, you might need to define credentials based on the type of authentication selected.

18. When done, click OK.

Figure 9-32

Setting display information
options

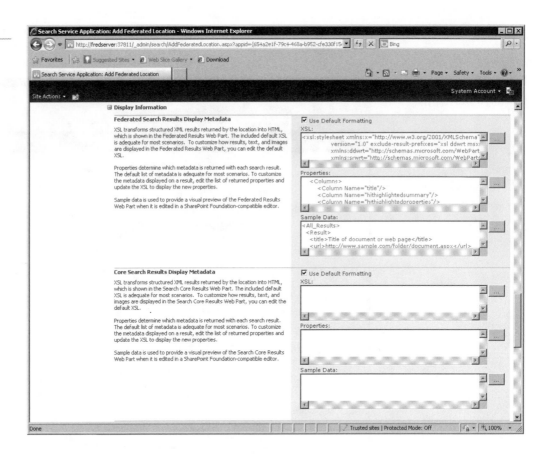

(→) **ADD FEDERATED RESULTS WEB PARTS**

GET READY. To add federated results Web parts, perform the following steps:

1. Open an Enterprise Search Center site.
2. To display a results page, type any search term and click the Search button.
3. Click Site Actions and then click Edit Page.
4. On the desired Web part, click Add a Web Part.
5. In the Web Part Categories list, click Search.
6. In the Web Parts list, click Federated Results, and then click Add.
7. Next to the new Federated Results Web Part, click the down arrow and then click Edit Web Part. The Properties sheet for the Federated Results Web Part displays.
8. In the Location drop-down list, select the federated location.
9. Click OK.
10. On the Ribbon, click Save and Close.

CERTIFICATION READY
What term best describes document properties that can be added or removed from a search?
1.4.7

USING METADATA PROPERTIES

Metadata property mappings are used to map properties used during the crawling of SharePoint sites and are used by users when performing search queries. For example, if you open one type of document, it might have a property or field that defines the author of a document. However, another document might use a different property or field to define the author. If you have a new property that you want to be searched, you must map the property as a crawled property.

➔ EDIT A METADATA PROPERTY MAPPING

GET READY. To edit a metadata property mapping, perform the following steps:

1. Open Central Administration.

2. In the Application Management section, click Manage service applications. The Manage Service Application page displays.

3. Click the Search Service Application. The Search Administration page displays.

4. In the Queries and Results section, click Metadata Properties. The Metadata Property Mappings page displays (see Figure 9-33).

Figure 9-33

The Metadata Property Mappings page

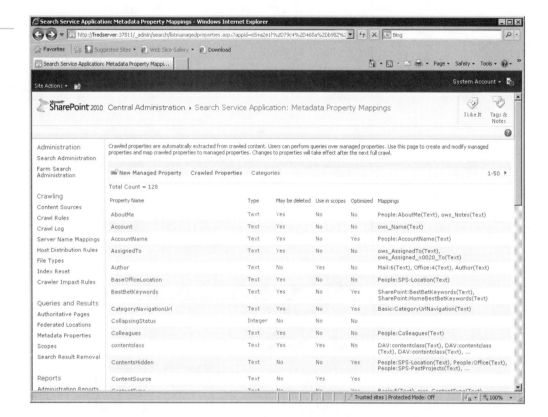

5. Click the desired Property Name to display the Edit Managed Property page (see Figure 9-34).

6. In the Name and type section, type or edit the Property Name and Description and then either select or deselect the Has Multiple Values check box.

7. In the Mappings to crawled properties section, leave Include values from all crawled properties mapped selected or select Include values from a single crawled property based on the order specified.

8. In the Crawled properties mapped to this managed property field, you can select any of the crawled properties present and then use the Move Up or Move Down buttons to change the list order. You can also use the Remove Mapping button to remove the crawled property from the list.

9. Click the Add Mappings button to open the Crawled Property Selection page (see Figure 9-35).

10. Select the desired Category and Crawled property name, and then click OK to add the new crawled property.

11. In the Use in scopes section, select or deselect the Allow this property to be used in scopes check box. Scopes are explained in the next section.

Figure 9-34

The Edit Managed Property
page

Figure 9-35

Crawled Property Selection
page

12. In the Optimize managed property storage section, you can select or deselect the
    Reduce storage requirements for text properties by using a hash for comparison
    check box if you only need this property to have equality/inequality comparisons.
    Leave the check box cleared if you need to enable other types of comparisons
    (such as less than, greater than, and order by).

13. Deselect the Add managed property to custom results set retrieved on each query
    check box to add this property to the restricted set of properties for optimized
    queries that use a custom results page to show special managed properties.

14. Click OK.

CONFIGURING SCOPES

To help users search only those sites or pages that are relative to them, you can define **search scopes**. If a user uses the Search Center site, she can select the scope. Common default scopes include the All Sites scope and the People scope. Once a scope has been created, you can add one or more rules to the scope to define its behavior.

ADD A SEARCH SCOPE

GET READY. To add a search scope, perform the following steps:

1. Open Central Administration.
2. In the Application Management section, click Manage service applications. The Manage Service Application page displays.
3. Click the Search Service Application. The Search Administration page displays.
4. In the Queries and Results section, click Scopes. The View Scopes page displays (see Figure 9-36).

Figure 9-36

The View Scopes page

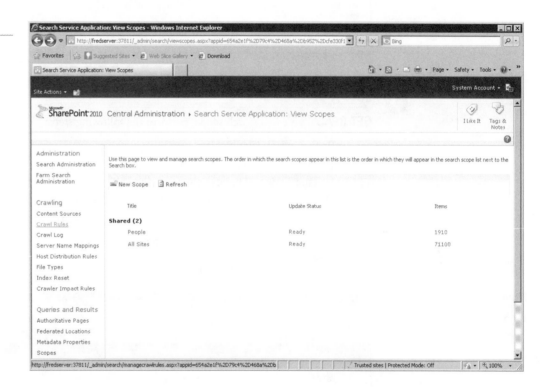

5. Click New Scope. The Create Scope page displays (see Figure 9-37).
6. In the Title and Description section, type a Title and Description.
7. In the Target Results Page section, leave Use the Default Search Results Page selected or choose Specify a different page for searching this scope.
8. In the Target results page box, type your desired URL (such as testing.aspx).
9. Click OK.

You can also edit an existing scope on the View Scopes page by clicking to the right of the scope name to open the menu, selecting **Edit Properties and Rules**, and then clicking **Change Scope Settings**. You can also copy a scope, assign a different name, and then edit the properties and rules as needed.

Figure 9-37

The Create Scope page

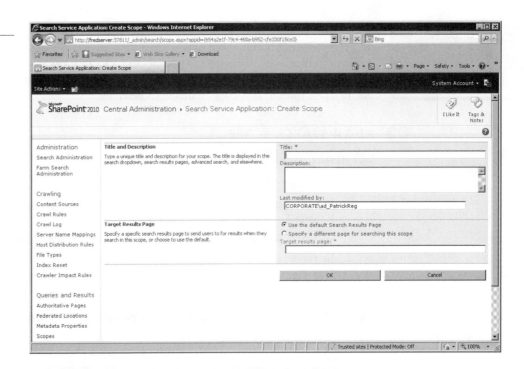

EDIT A SEARCH SCOPE

GET READY. To edit a search scope, perform the following steps:

1. Open Central Administration.
2. In the Application Management section, click Manage service applications. The Manage Service Application page displays.
3. Click the Search Service Application. The Search Administration page displays.
4. In the Queries and Results section, click Scopes. The View Scopes page displays.
5. Click a scope that you want to modify. The Scopes Properties and Rules page displays (see Figure 9-38).

Figure 9-38

The Scope Properties and Rules page

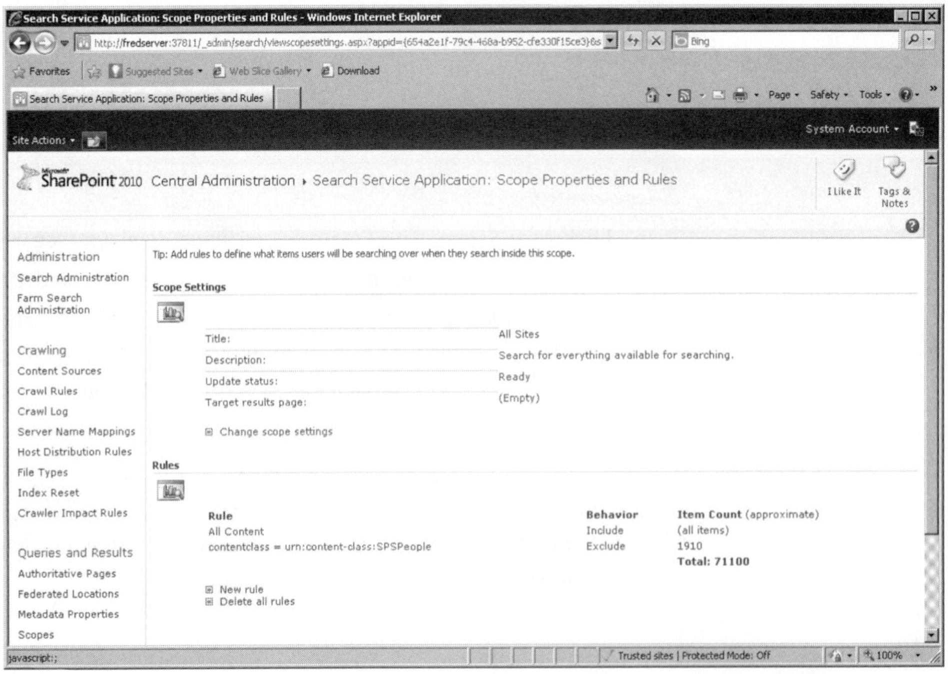

6. In the Rules section, click New rule. The Add Scope Rule page displays (see Figure 9-39).

Figure 9-39

The Add Scope Rule page

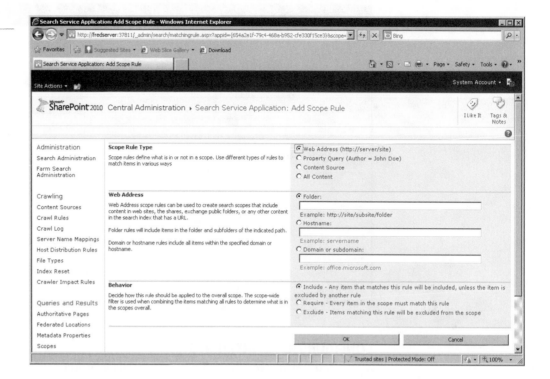

7. In the Scope Rule Type section, select the type of rule you want to define (such as Web Address, Property Query, Content Source, or All Content).

8. Depending on the option selected in Step 7, various options become available. For example, if you select Web Address, type the URL or the path to the resource. If you select Property Query, you will include or exclude content that has a managed property with a particular value. For example, you can select Author="John Doe".

9. In the Behavior section, select Include, Require, or Exclude to determine what action is applied to the Web address, property, or content source rule.

10. Click OK.

CONFIGURING SEARCH RESULT REMOVAL

Lastly, in the **Queries and Results** section, you can choose **Search Result Removal**. The Search Result Removal page allows you to specify the URLs for sites that you want removed from any search results returned in SharePoint. Specifying a URL in this field also automatically creates a crawl rule that excludes the specified URL from any future crawls (see Figure 9-40).

Figure 9-40

The Remove URLs From Search Results page

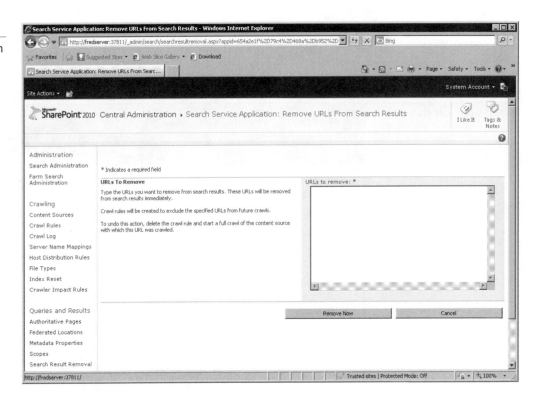

CONFIGURING REFINEMENTS

As an administrator, you can influence the results by working with keywords and Best Bets. Keywords and Best Bets are configured by site administrators at the site-collection level. Keywords with Best Bets allows users to search for terms (keywords) that are specific to your organization and find commonly used Web sites (Best Bets). You can use keywords with Best Bests to direct users to sites that you think might be most helpful to them depending on the keywords they have used in their queries.

To use keywords, you first add the keyword, and then add Best Bets, visual Best Bets, document promotions or demotions to it. When a user searches for the keyword, the search result will be displayed with these improvements.

 CONFIGURE KEYWORDS AND BEST BETS SETTINGS

GET READY. To configure keywords and Best Bets, perform the following steps:

1. Open a Search Center site.
2. Click the Site Actions menu and choose Site Settings.
3. In the Site Collection Administration section, click Search keywords.
4. To add a Keyword, click the Add Keyword option.
5. In the Keyword phrase text box, type a word or phrase.
6. In the Synonyms text box, type the appropriate synonyms.
7. In the Keyword Definition text box, type the keyword definition for the word.
8. To add a Best Bet for the keyword, click the Add Best Bet link.
9. In the URL text box, type a URL that represents a Best Bet Web site.
10. In the Title text box and Description text box, type a title and description.
11. Click OK to close the Add Best Bet page.
12. Click OK.

To add the Best Bets/Visual Best Bet and document promotions/demotions, click the keyword that you just entered. The Keyword Details page displays.

Removing the Search Service Applications

> While it does not happen often, you might want to remove the search service application. If the service application is not removed using the Central Administration Service Applications page, you must remove it using the **stsadm** or PowerShell.

The easiest way to remove any service application is to use the **stsadm** command at the command prompt. The syntax for removing the search application is as follows:

```
stsadm -o deleteconfigurationobject -id "<GUID>"
```

For example:

```
stsadm -o deleteconfigurationobject -id "005a02e9-aa38-4bc4-8973-a41cc08cc58d"
```

To determine the GUID, you can navigate to the service application page and mouse-over the search application link in the status bar. You can also use the following PowerShell command:

```
Get-SPServiceApplication |?{$_.name -eq "<name of Search Service Application>"}
```

For example:

```
Get-SPServiceApplication |?{$_.name -eq "Search Service Application"}
```

■ Configuring FAST Search Server

The Bottom Line

> FAST Search Server 2010 for SharePoint 2010 is an add-on product for Microsoft that upgrades the search capabilities of SharePoint to a whole new level, including richer query language, deep refiners, document thumbnails and previews, custom search experiences per user/profile, and metadata extraction. Different from the previous discussion on search technology, FAST Search requires a separate server license and a separate installation. It also requires that users have an Enterprise Client Access License to access the FAST features.

CERTIFICATION READY
What search technology allows for thumbnails for search results?
1.4.1

To install FAST Search Server 2010 for SharePoint, you must install SharePoint as a farm. The Complete (Advanced Installation) option must also be selected. In addition, if you want to preview Word and PowerPoint documents in the Search results, you need to install Microsoft Office Web Applications before running the SharePoint product configuration wizard.

Similar to installing SharePoint, you must be a member of the local administrators to perform the installation. The installation is similar to installing SharePoint. The full installation process for FAST Search Server involves three parts:

1. Running the Prerequisite Installer.
2. Installing FAST Search Server 2010 for SharePoint.
3. Running the post-installation configuration.

After you install FAST Search Server, you must perform the following steps before you can start using it:

1. Create and set up a Content Search Service Application.
2. Create and set up the Query Search Service Application.
3. Create a FAST Search Web site.

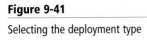

➕ MORE INFORMATION

For a detailed, step-by-step deployment of Fast Search Server 2010 for SharePoint, visit http://technet. microsoft.com/en-us/library/ff381267.aspx

⊙ INSTALL FAST SEARCH SERVER

GET READY. To install the FAST Search Server, perform the following steps:

1. Execute the splash.htm file.
2. Click Install Software Prerequisites.
3. When the Welcome screen displays, click Next.
4. When the license agreement displays, click I accept the terms of the License Agreement(s) and then click Next.
5. When the prerequisites are installed, click Finish.
6. Back on the splash screen, click Install FAST Search Server 2010 for SharePoint.
7. When the Welcome screen displays, click Next.
8. When the agreement displays, click I accept the terms of the License Agreement(s) and click Next.
9. When prompted for the Destination Folder, click Next.
10. When prompted to start the installation, click Next.
11. When the installation is complete, click Finish.
12. Click the Start button, select Programs, select Microsoft FAST Search Server 2010 for SharePoint, and then select Microsoft FAST Search Server 2010 for SharePoint Configuration Wizard.
13. When the Welcome screen displays, click Next.
14. When prompted for the deployment type (see Figure 9-41), select Single server (stand-alone) and then click Next.

Figure 9-41

Selecting the deployment type

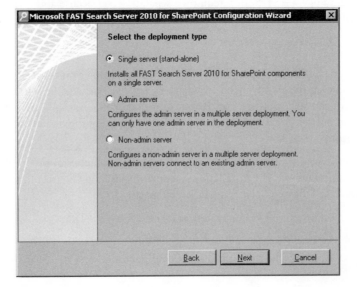

 **Configuring Indexes and Searches** | 373

15. Specify a Username and Password for the Fast Search Server 2010 to run on and then click Next.

16. A certificate is sometimes moved between servers. To allow the moving of certificates between servers, type a Password and then click Next.

17. When prompted for a Server name (see Figure 9-42), type the full name of the server you are currently on and then click Next.

Figure 9-42

The Server name and Base port number dialog

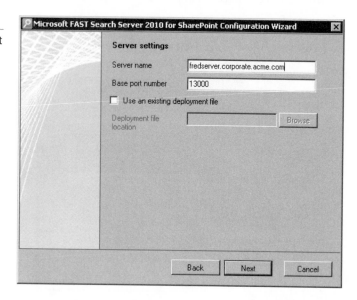

18. When prompted for the Database settings (see Figure 9-43), in the Database connection string box, type the name of the database server (if you're not using the default instance, be sure to include the instance) and then click Next.

Figure 9-43

Configuring database settings

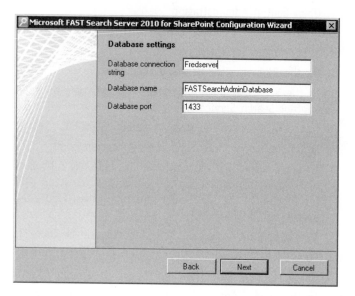

19. To transfer the click-through relevancy data from the SharePoint server or farm, select either Standalone or Server Farm (see Figure 9-44). If you select Standalone, type the Microsoft SharePoint Server name. If you select Server Farm, select the Microsoft SharePoint Server username. If you don't wish to transfer relevancy data, select Do not enable click-through relevancy. Click Next.

20. Review the summary and then click Configure.

21. When the Post-setup configuration is successful, click Finish.

Figure 9-44

Configuring click-through relevancy settings

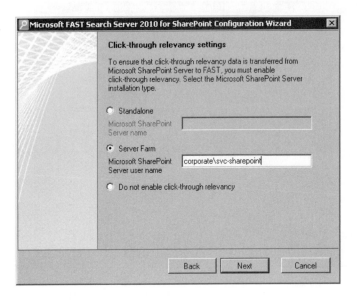

DEPLOY THE FAST SERVICE APPLICATION

GET READY. To deploy the FAST Service Application, perform the following steps:

1. Open Central Administration.

2. Click Application Management.

3. Click Manage Service Applications.

4. On the Ribbon, click New and then click Search Service Application.

5. In the Service Application Name text box, type an appropriate name for the FAST Content Search Service Application.

6. In the FAST Service Application section, select FAST Search Connector (see Figure 9-45).

7. Configure a service account and application pool.

8. In the Content Distributors text box, type the fully qualified domain name and port of the content distributors. If you do not know the values, open the install_info.txt file located in the FASTSearch program folder. Figure 9-46 shows a sample install_info.txt file.

9. Type a Content Collection Name. It can also be found in the install_info.txt file.

10. Click OK.

11. On the Ribbon, click New and then choose Search Service Application.

12. In the Service Application Name text box, type an appropriate name for the FAST Query Search Service Application.

Figure 9-45

Selecting the Fast Search Connector

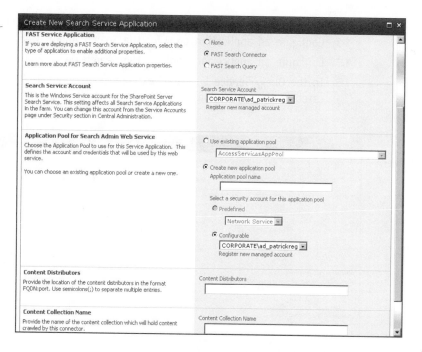

Figure 9-46

The install_info.txt file

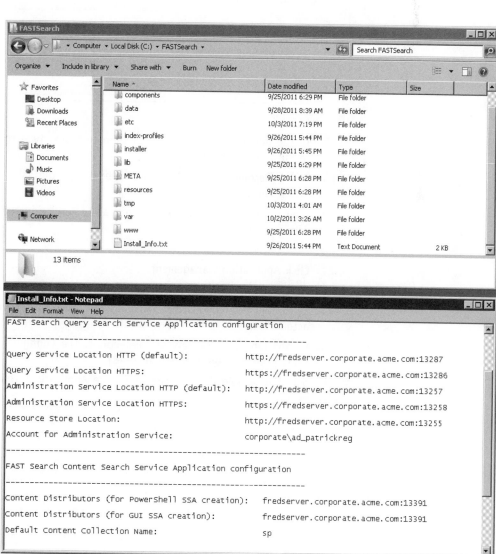

13. In the FAST Service Application section, select FAST Search Query.

14. Configure an application pool for the Search Admin Web Service.

15. Configure an application pool for the Search Query and Site Settings.

16. In the Query Service Location text box (see Figure 9-47), type the value (as indicated in the install_info.txt file).

Figure 9-47

Configuring FAST Search Query settings

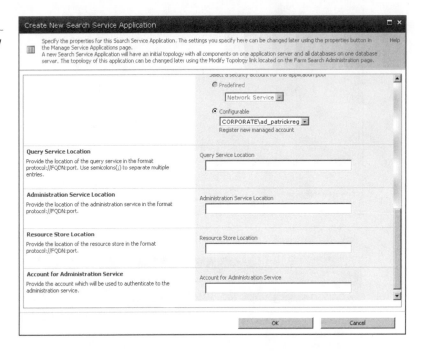

17. In the Administration Service Location text box, type the value (as indicated in the install_info.txt file).

18. In the Resource Store Location text box, type the value (as indicated in the install_info.txt file).

19. Type the user name for the administration service in the Account for Administration Service text box.

20. Click OK.

21. Click Application Management.

22. Click Manage Web applications.

23. Select the Web application that you want to enable search for without clicking the actual link.

24. On the Ribbon, click Service Connections. The Configure Service Application Associations page displays (see Figure 9-48).

25. Select to enable the two Search Service Applications that you just created.

26. Click OK.

Figure 9-48

Configuring service
connections

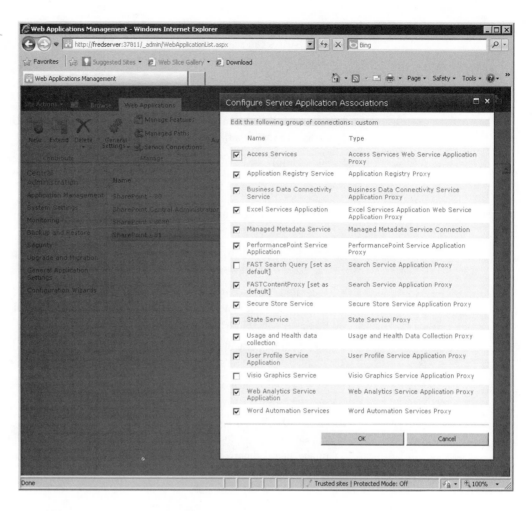

CREATE A FAST SEARCH CENTER SITE

GET READY. To create a FAST Search Center Site, perform the following steps:

1. Open the SharePoint Server 2010 site where you want to create a new site.
2. Click the Site Actions menu and then choose Site Settings.
3. Click Site collection features.
4. Make sure SharePoint Server Publishing Infrastructure and SharePoint Server Enterprise Site Collection features are enabled.
5. Click the Site Actions menu and then choose New Site.
6. Select the FAST Search Center template.
7. Click Create. A FAST Search Center is created.

SKILL SUMMARY

IN THIS LESSON, YOU LEARNED:

- SharePoint offers several enterprise search tools to quickly find items within SharePoint.

- To provide the search capability in SharePoint 2010, start with content sources found in the content databases.

- To add content to the search databases, each item must be crawled and indexed. Crawling is the process of traversing the URL namespace associated with content sources and looking for links to content that should be indexed.

- Before users can search for content by using Microsoft SharePoint Server 2010, you must create and configure the Search Service Application.

- After the Search Service Application is configured, you have to define at least one content source.

- Crawl rules allow you to include or exclude specific paths in a URL from being crawled as well as to specify different authentication accounts.

- At the top of each page, there is a search box available for you to perform searches within your SharePoint site. For more advanced searches, however, the Search Center provides an interface for users to submit search queries.

- To scale the search components as your environment, SharePoint 2010 supports index partitions to divide the index into multiple partitions.

- SharePoint 2010 uses iFilters to remove embedded formatting from the content that is extracted from crawled items.

- Federated search connectors enable the Microsoft enterprise search solution to pass a query to a target system (another SharePoint system or external Web site or service) and display results returned from that system.

- Metadata property mappings are used to map properties used during the crawling of SharePoint sites and are used by users when performing search queries.

- To help users search only those sites or pages that are relative to them, you can define search scopes.

- FAST Search Server for SharePoint 2010 is an add-on product for Microsoft that upgrades the search capabilities of SharePoint to a whole new level, including richer query language, deep refiners, document thumbnails and previews, custom search experiences per user/profile, and metadata extraction.

■ Knowledge Assessment

Fill in the Blank

Complete the following sentences by writing the correct word or words in the blanks provided.

1. To provide search capability in SharePoint, you must first add the _____.

2. _____ scales up to 500 million documents, provides advanced sorting, and offers scrolling preview and document thumbnails.

3. The _____ builds and stores the index file.

4. The _____ is used by users to submit queries to find content stored in the index.

5. The default content source created by default during installation is _____.

6. The _____ crawl is quicker than a full crawl.

7. To have SharePoint connect to another Internet search engine to retrieve results, you must load the appropriate _____.

8. To help users search only those sites or pages that are relative to them, you can define _____.

9. When you add a federated location search connector, you are downloading and installing a file with a _____ filename extension.

10. Review the _____ to determine if there is a problem with the logs.

Multiple Choice

Circle the letter that corresponds to the best answer.

1. Which of the following can SharePoint search? (Choose all that apply)
   a. Encrypted Oracle databases
   b. SharePoint sites
   c. file shares
   d. Exchange Public folders

2. How many documents does the Enterprise Search solution support in Microsoft SharePoint Server 2010?
   a. 1 million
   b. 10 million
   c. 100 million
   d. 500 million

3. What is the Web part that is created to display common search terms?
   a. Refinement panel
   b. Search Statistics
   c. Favorites
   d. Best Bets

4. What allows you to include or exclude specifics paths in a URL from being crawled?
   a. Crawl schedule
   b. Crawl rules
   c. Content direction
   d. Crawl directive

5. What would you use to divide a large index so that you can scale it to multiple servers?
   a. index partition
   b. split query
   c. query scope
   d. index scope

6. What type of pages are used to link to the most relevant information, which search users to determine the search rank of every page in the index.
   a. Federated location
   b. Best Bet page
   c. Authoritative page
   d. Metadata page

7. When you upload a new type of document to SharePoint, what can you add to SharePoint so that SharePoint knows how to read and crawl the documents?
   a. Index partition
   b. document reader
   c. crawl converter
   d. iFilters

8. What is used to map properties used during the crawling of SharePoint sites and are used by users when performing search queries?
   a. index partition
   b. metadata property mappings
   c. iFilter
   d. scope

9. When installing FAST service applications, what text file contains the necessary configuration information?
    a. install_info.txt
    b. config.txt
    c. web.config
    d. FAST.cfg

10. Which of the following are the default search scopes in SharePoint? (Choose all that apply)
    a. People
    b. All Local Sites
    c. All Sites
    d. Favorites

True / False

Circle T if the statement is true or F if the statement is false.

T | F **1.** You must perform a full crawl before performing an incremental crawl.

T | F **2.** To perform a search, you have to create a Search Center Site.

T | F **3.** To install FAST search, you only have to add the single FAST Search service application.

T | F **4.** A crawl has very little effect on the SQL server.

T | F **5.** Performing a query has little effect on the SQL server.

■ Case Scenario

Scenario 9-1: Increasing Crawl Performance

Over the past two years, the SharePoint farm has seen some significant growth where you have added multiple front-end servers and you have to upgrade the SQL server to handle the load. The number of documents has also grown significantly; you have about a million documents. Unfortunately, the searching of these documents has become slow and the crawling has affected the performance of other SharePoint components. What would you recommend?

By using enterprise search solutions that come with the SharePoint Server 2010, your SharePoint solution can handle up to 100 million documents. However, as your SharePoint environment grows, you will have to create multiple index partitions so that you can use multiple servers to divide the workload.

Scenario 9-2: Expanding SharePoint 2010

You have a company that has four large departments. Each department uses SharePoint heavily. Unfortunately, some users are complaining that it is becoming difficult to find what they are looking for because of the high volume of search results. What can you do?

There are several things you can do. First, you can create search scopes for each department. You can then tweak the search results by performing some result removal, adding key words, and adding Best Bets.

Monitoring and Analyzing the SharePoint Environment

OBJECTIVE DOMAIN MATRIX

TECHNOLOGY SKILL	OBJECTIVE DOMAIN DESCRIPTION	OBJECTIVE DOMAIN NUMBER
Monitoring and Analyzing a SharePoint Environment	Manage Operational Settings	2.1
	Configuring Logging	2.1.1
	Configuring Monitoring Levels	2.1.3
	Configuring Health Reports	2.1.4
	Configuring SQL Server Reporting Services (SSRS) Integration	2.1.6
	Monitoring and Analyzing a SharePoint Environment	4.2
	Generating Health, Administrative, and Web Analytics Reports	4.2.1
	Interpreting Usage and Trace Logs	4.2.2
	Identifying and Resolving Health and Performance Issues	4.2.3
Optimizing the Performance of a SharePoint Environment	Configuring Quotas	2.1.2
	Configuring Site Collection Quotas and Locks	3.2.7
	Optimizing the Performance of a SharePoint Environment	4.3
	Configuring Resource Throttling (Large List Management, Object Model Override)	4.3.1
	Configuring Remote Binary Large Objects (BLOB) Storage and BLOB and Object Caching	4.3.2
	Optimizing Services	4.3.3

KEY TERMS

binary large object (BLOB)

BLOB cache

boundaries

Event Viewer

Health Analyzer

locks

Object Cache

Output Cache

performance

Performance Monitor

quota

Remote BLOB
    Storage (RBS)

resource throttling

SQL Server Reporting
    Services (SSRS)

supported limits

threshold

timer job

trace logs

Unified Logging
    Service (ULS)

usage reports

Web Analytics

As SharePoint has become used more by the users of your organization, you have noticed certain performance problems, particularly during peak working hours. You need to make sure that SharePoint is always running well so that users can focus on doing their jobs.

■ Monitoring and Analyzing a SharePoint Environment

THE BOTTOM LINE

As you have learned so far, SharePoint can become a complex system with multiple servers, many roles and services, and complex configurations. When figuring out problems, you are not always provided with an obvious error message indicating the problem. Therefore, you must use your troubleshooting skills to gather the symptoms of the problem, determine the extent of the problem, and isolate the problem. While doing that, you sometimes need to go through the logs to gain insight into the problem.

CERTIFICATION READY
What SharePoint built-in tools allow you to monitor the health and performance of SharePoint?
2.1

There are many types of logs to view. To stick with basic troubleshooting of a Windows environment, the first logs to view are the logs displayed in the Event Viewer. Then for logs that are specific to SharePoint, you need to view the SharePoint logs. In addition, SharePoint includes several tools to help you troubleshoot SharePoint.

Using the Event Viewer

CERTIFICATION READY
What tools are available for troubleshooting SharePoint problems?
4.2

Every Windows system already has a logging system, which is viewed using the Event Viewer. The *Event Viewer* is a Microsoft Management Console (MMC) snap-in that enables you to browse and manage event logs. It is included in the Computer Management and Server Manager and is included in Administrative Tools as a standalone console. You can also execute the `eventvwr.msc` command.

The Event Viewer (see Figure 10-1) enables you to view events from multiple event logs. The Windows Logs directory includes the logs that were available on previous versions of Windows. They include:

- **Application**: Contains events logged by applications or programs.
- **Security**: Contains events such as valid and invalid logon attempts as well as access to designated objects (such as file and folders, printers, and Active Directory objects). By default, the Security log is empty until you enable auditing.
- **Setup**: Contains events related to application setup.

Figure 10-1

The Event Viewer

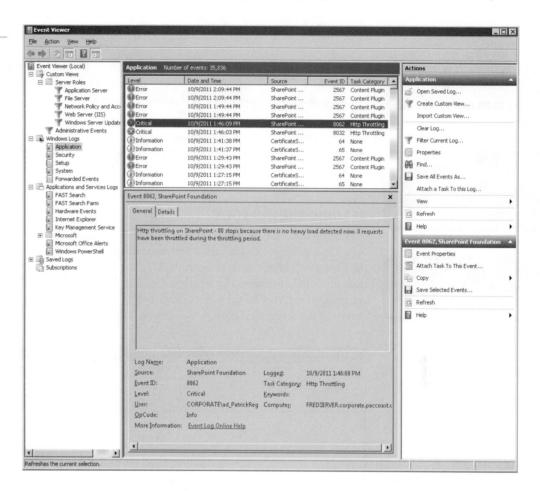

- **System**: Contains events logged by Windows system components, including errors displayed by Windows during boot and errors related to services.

- **Forwarded Events**: Stores events collected from remote computers. To collect events from remote computers, you must create an event subscription.

When looking at problems with SharePoint, you will usually focus on the application and system logs. If you have enabled security auditing in Windows (different from SharePoint audit logs), you will look in the security logs.

Application logs and System logs were first introduced with Windows Vista and are included with Windows Server 2008 servers. These logs store events from a single application or component rather than events that might have system-wide impact.

- **Admin**: These events are primarily targeted at end users, administrators, and support personnel. The events that are found in the Admin channels indicate a problem and a well-defined solution that an administrator can act on.

- **Operational**: Operational events are used for analyzing and diagnosing a problem or occurrence. They can be used to trigger tools or tasks based on the problem or occurrence.

- **Analytic**: Analytic events are published in high volume. They describe program operation and indicate problems that cannot be handled by user intervention.

- **Debug**: Debug events are used by developers to troubleshoot issues with their programs.

When you open any of these logs, particularly the Application, Security, and System logs, they will display thousands of entries. If you look entry by entry, you will need some time to find what you are looking. To reduce this time, you can use a filter to reduce the number of entries displayed. To filter a log, click the **Action** menu and choose **Filter Current Log**.

Managing the SharePoint ULS Logs

The primary logging mechanism for SharePoint is **_Unified Logging Service (ULS)_**, which writes SharePoint events to the SharePoint Trace Log and stores them in the file system. ULS logs are also sometimes referred to as **_Trace Logs_**.

Unified Logging Service (ULS) creates a detailed trace output of the events that occur in SharePoint in real time. It is dependent on SharePoint 2010 Tracing, which is a Windows service. By default, SharePoint logs are located at C:\Program Files\Common Files\Microsoft Shared\Web Server Extensions\14\LOGS.

READING THE ULS LOGS

When you open the ULS logs with Microsoft Notepad, you might find it difficult to read the logs. Often the error displayed on-screen (see Figure 10-2) includes the Correlation ID and the Date and Time. You must open the ULS log that covers the date and time of the error and then find the Correlation ID, which is a unique GUID string (see Figure 10-3). Related events are grouped together by the same Correlation ID. However, if you generate the same error by repeating the action that generated the error, a different non-sequential Correlation ID displays.

Figure 10-2

An error message with a Correlation ID

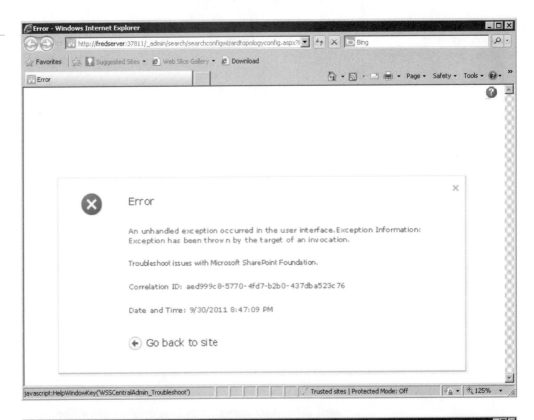

Figure 10-3

A log entry based on a Correlation ID

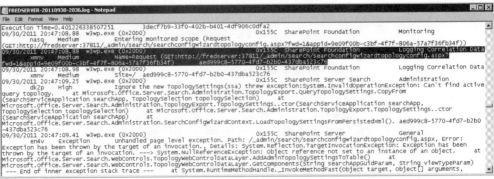

While you cannot view the logs with Central Administration, you can view and filter the logs with Windows PowerShell. The `Get-SPLogEvent` returns the results from a Unified Logging Service trace log.

 VIEW AND FILTER LOG EVENTS WITH WINDOWS POWERSHELL

GET READY. To view and filter log events with Windows PowerShell, perform the following steps:

1. Click Start > All Programs.
2. Click Microsoft SharePoint 2010 Products.
3. Click SharePoint 2010 Management Shell.
4. To view all trace events, execute the following command:

   `Get-SPLogEvent`

5. To display trace events by level (such as Error), execute the following command:

   `Get-SPLogEvent | Where-Object {$_.Level -eq "Error"}`

6. To display error entries that are between 5:00 and 6:00 p.m. on 12/04/2011, execute the following command:

   `Get-SPLogEvent -StartTime "12/04/2011 17:00" -EndTime "12/04/2011 18:00"`

To open the ULS logs and display its contents in a user-friendly format, you can use a ULS viewer, such as one located at http://archive.msdn.microsoft.com/ULSViewer. Similar to the Event Viewer, users can then perform advanced functions (such as filtering, sorting, and highlighting the logs) so that you can focus on what is important.

CONFIGURING THE ULS LOGS

When you configure diagnostic logging, you can specify where the location logs are stored as well as the logging level for events of different types. These logging levels apply to both diagnostic logs and the event logs. This is also where you enable event log flood protection, which configures the system to detect repeating events and suppresses the repeating event until the event stops. Flood protection prevents logs from growing too rapidly and makes it a little bit easier to search through logs.

 VIEW AND FILTER LOG EVENTS BY USING WINDOWS POWERSHELL

GET READY. To view and filter log events, perform the following steps:

1. Open Central Administration.
2. Click Monitoring. The Monitor page displays.
3. In the Reporting section, click Configure Diagnostic Logging. The Diagnostic Logging page displays (see Figure 10-4).
4. To view the Event and Diagnostic logging level for an event category, expand the appropriate category.
5. To alter the logging levels for a category, select the check box for a category, and then select the least critical event to report to the event logs and the diagnostic logs.

Figure 10-4

The Diagnostic Logging page

6. To disable event log flood protection, clear the Enable Event Log Flood Protection check box (see Figure 10-5).

Figure 10-5

Clearing the Enable Event Log Flood Production check box

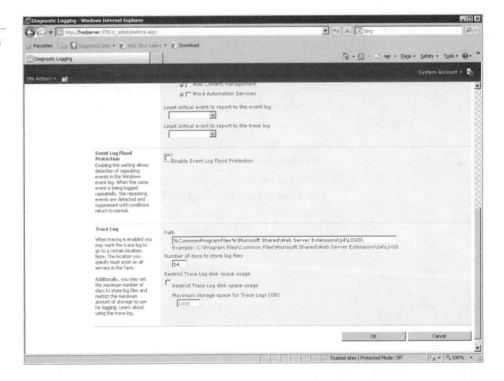

TAKE NOTE *

The path you use for diagnostic logs must exist on all SharePoint servers in the farm.

7. To configure the location of diagnostic logs, in the Trace Log section, type your preferred location in the Path text box.

8. To configure a maximum time to retain diagnostic logs and a maximum for the logs, specify the Number of days to store log files (between 1 and 366).

9. Click OK.

You can set the level of diagnostic logging for the event log and for the trace log. By specifying the level of diagnostic logging, you limit the types and amount of information that will be written to each log. The Event Log levels include the following levels:

- **None**: No logging occurs.
- **Critical**: A serious error has caused a major failure.
- **Error**: An urgent condition that should be investigated.
- **Warning**: A message that might indicate a potential problem or issue that might require attention. Warning messages should be reviewed and tracked for patterns over time.
- **Information**: Information messages do not require any action, but they can provide valuable data for monitoring the state of your solution.
- **Verbose**: The highest level of logging that corresponds to lengthy events or messages.

The trace log levels are as follows:

- **None**: No trace logs are written.
- **Unexpected**: Log messages about critical events that cause solutions to stop processing. When set to log at this level, the log only includes events at this level.
- **Monitorable**: This level is used to log warning messages about any unrecoverable events that limit the solution's functionality but do not stop the application. When set to log at this level, the log also includes critical errors (Unexpected level).
- **High**: This level is used to log any events that are unexpected but which do not stall the processing of a solution. When set to log at this level, the log includes unexpected and Monitorable messages.
- **Medium**: The trace log includes everything except Verbose messages. This level is used to log all high-level information about operations that were performed. At this level, there is enough detail logged to construct the data flow and sequence of operations. This level of logging could be used by administrators or support professionals to troubleshoot issues.
- **Verbose**: When set to log at this level, the log includes messages at all other levels. Almost all actions that are performed are logged when you use this level. Verbose tracing produces many log messages. This level is typically used only for debugging in a development environment.

Alternatively, you can use the `Set-SPLogLevel` PowerShell command to set the trace and event level for a set of categories.

When you plan and install SharePoint, you need to change the drive that logging writes to for production systems. By default, diagnostic logging is configured to write logs to the same drive and partition that SharePoint Server 2010 was installed on. Logs—particularly when problems are occurring—can use lots of disk space in a short amount of time and the writing of the logs can affect overall performance. To control how much disk space is used, you should restrict log disk space usage. However, plan for enough disk space to last a couple of weeks. You should also enable event log flooding protection.

Lastly, since Verbose mode records every action that SharePoint 2010 takes, you should use verbose settings sparingly. You should only use it to troubleshoot a particular problem or make a critical change to the system so that you have maximum logging to help you find and troubleshoot problems. You then re-configure logging back to the default values.

Using SharePoint Health Analyzer

The *Health Analyzer* runs automatic checks on the configuration of the SharePoint farm. It was created to identify common configuration mistakes and, in some situations, repair problems automatically.

The Health Analyzer enables you to diagnose and resolve configuration, performance, and usage problems as determined by predefined health rules. A health rule runs a test and returns an alert that tells you the outcome of the test. If the Health Analyzer detects critical issues, it displays a red banner at the top of the Central Administration (see Figure 10-6).

Figure 10-6

The Health Analyzer's red banner

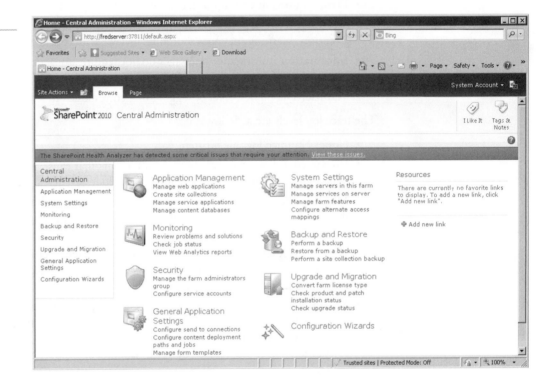

The Health Analyzer consists of the following components:

- Timer jobs
- SharePoint list
- Health rules

The timer jobs are jobs that are scheduled to run hourly, daily, weekly, or monthly, checking the status of the system and SharePoint components. The health rules are stored in a dedicated list called Health Analyzer Rule Definitions.

 VIEW THE SHAREPOINT HEALTH ANALYZER ALERTS

GET READY. To view the SharePoint Health Analyzer alerts, perform the following steps:

1. Open Central Administration.
2. Click Monitoring. The Monitoring page displays (see Figure 10-7).

Figure 10-7

The Monitoring page

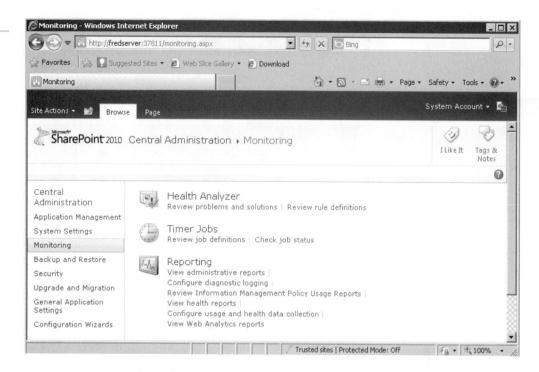

3. In the Health Analyzer section, click Review problems and solutions. The Review Problems and Solutions page displays (see Figure 10-8).

Figure 10-8

The Review Problems and Solutions page

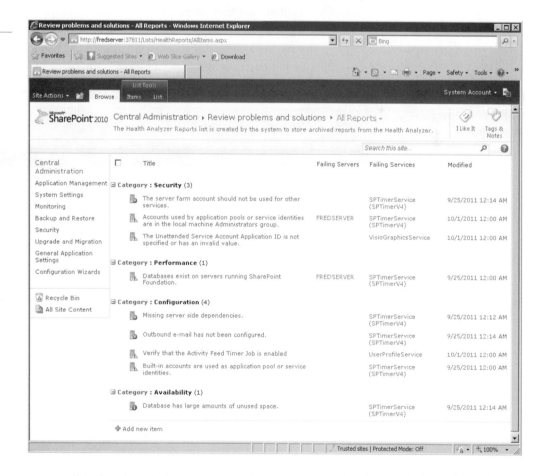

4. Click the alert that you want to view and resolve. The details of the problem display (see Figure 10-9).

Figure 10-9

Viewing and resolving
problems

This page reveals the error, provides an explanation, and offers a remedy. Health rules are categorized and presented on this page within their categories, which you can expand or collapse.

 CONFIGURE ALERT RULE DEFINITIONS

GET READY. To configure alert rule definitions, perform the following steps:

1. Open Central Administration.
2. Click Monitoring.
3. In the Health Analyzer section, click Review Rule Definitions. The Health Analyzer Rule Definitions page displays (see Figure 10-10).

Figure 10-10

The Health Analyzer Rule
Definitions page

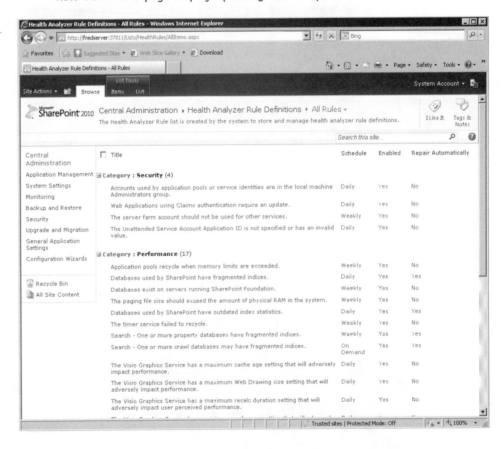

4. Click the rule you wish to configure and examine the details. The Rule Definitions page displays (see Figure 10-11).

Figure 10-11

The Rule Definitions page

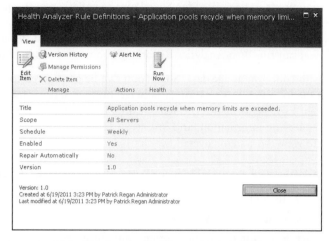

5. Click Edit Item to edit a rule definition (see Figure 10-12).

Figure 10-12

Editing a rule definition

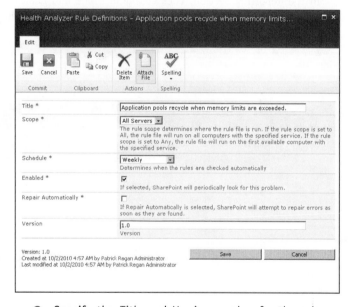

6. Specify the Title and Version number for the rule.

7. In the Scope field, specify whether the rule should run on All Servers that host the relevant service or on the first server that becomes available.

8. In the Schedule drop-down, select how often you want the rule to be executed.

9. Specify to enable or disable the rule by checking or unchecking the Enabled box.

10. If you want the rule to automatically repair the problem (if possible), select to check the Repair Automatically option.

11. Click Save.

Using Usage Reports and Web Analytics

If a component fails and you try to it use it, you will usually get an error message. Often, however, a problem might occur that affects performance. If SharePoint is slow, it might be obvious as you try to access a SharePoint site and you have to wait for the page to load. However, you can use *usage reports* and *Web Analytics* to give you a view in performance of how SharePoint is being used. In addition, SharePoint can gather data to create health reports.

CERTIFICATION READY
What type of report allows you to see what sites users are using the most and what sites are the slowest?
2.1.4

As detailed previously in this lesson, SharePoint can be configured to record error messages in a log, which can be expanded to record all events (Verbose mode). The Web Analytics service application needs to be created for SharePoint to collect, report, and analyze the usage and effectiveness of SharePoint 2010 sites. Usage data collection/Web Analytics tracking will log events whenever the selected events occur on your SharePoint system. After the data is collected, you can run Web Analytics Reports to show you how your system is being used.

Along with collecting usage data, SharePoint can be configured to collect health data. By default, the following information is gathered from all servers in the farm, including ULS logs, Event logs, performance counters, feature usage, timer job usage, search crawling information, querying information, and inventory. Once the information is compiled, run health reports to view the system's overall health.

CONFIGURE WEB ANALYTICS AND HEALTH DATA COLLECTION

CERTIFICATION READY
What service application is needed to run the Usage reports?
4.2.1

GET READY. To configure Web Analytics and health data collection, perform the following steps:

1. Open Central Administration.
2. Click Monitoring. The Monitoring page displays.
3. In the Reporting section, click Configure usage and health data collection. The Configure Web Analytics and health data collection page displays (see Figure 10-13).

Figure 10-13

The Configure Web Analytics and health data collection page

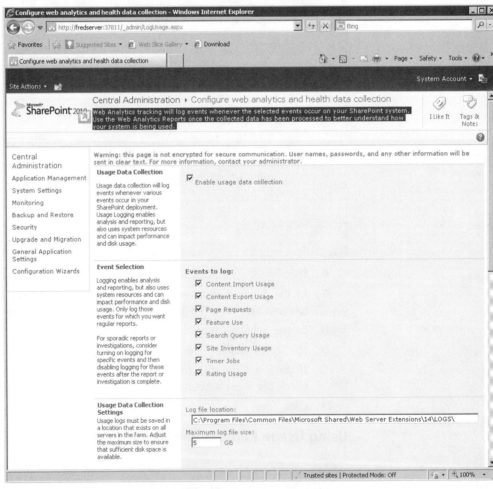

4. In the Usage data collection section, enable usage data collection by selecting the Enable usage data collection check box.
5. In the Event Selection section, select the events to log by selecting the check box next to the events in the Events to log list.

6. In the Usage Data Collection Settings section, in the Log file location box, type the path of the folder to which you want usage and health information to be written. The path must exist on all farm servers.

7. In the Maximum log file size box, type the maximum disk space for the logs in gigabytes (between 1 and 20 GB).

8. To take snapshots of various resources, data, and processes at a specific point in time so that it can be used in evaluating the overall health of the system, select the Enable health data collection check box (see Figure 10-14).

Figure 10-14

Selecting the Enable health data collection option

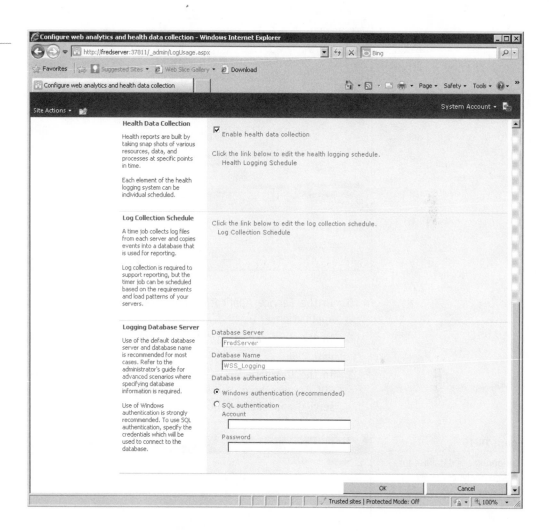

9. To change the collection schedules, click the Health Logging Schedule link. A list of timer jobs that collect health data is displayed. Click any timer job to change its schedule or disable that timer job.

10. In the Logging Database Server section, the Database Server and Database Name is displayed. To change the Database authentication used, select either Windows authentication or SQL authentication.

11. Click OK.

 CREATE A WEB ANALYTICS SERVICE APPLICATION

GET READY. To create a Web Analytics service application, perform the following steps:

1. Open Central Administration.

2. Click Application Management. The Application Management page displays.

3. In the Service Applications, click Manage Service Applications. The Manage Service Applications page displays.

4. Click New, and then click Web Analytics Service Application. The Create New Web Analytics Service Application page displays (see Figure 10-15).

Figure 10-15

The Create New Web Analytics Service Application page

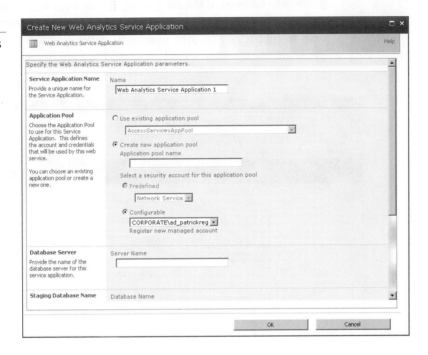

5. In the Service Application Name text box, type an appropriate name for the service application.

6. In the Application Pool section, select an existing application pool or create a new one.

7. In the Database Server section (see Figure 10-16), type the Server Name of the SQL Server where you want to create the two databases that the Web Analytics service application requires.

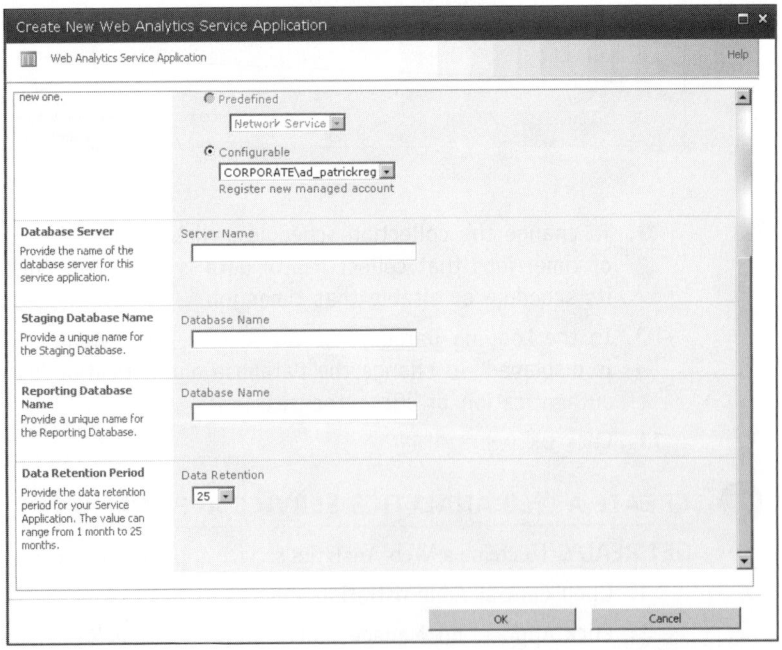

Figure 10-16

Configuring the database for the Web Analytics Service Application

8. In the Staging Database Name section, type a Database Name for the Web Analytics staging database.

9. In the Reporting Database Name section, type a Database Name for the Web Analytics reporting database.

10. In the Data Retention Period section, in the Data Retention drop-down, choose the number of months you want data to remain in the reporting database.

11. Click OK.

12. Click System Settings.

13. In the Servers section, click Manage Services on Server.

14. In the Server box, select the SharePoint server where you want the Web Analytics services to run.

15. To the right of the Web Analytics Web Service, click Start.

16. To the right of the Web Analytics Data Processing Service, click Start.

After enabling usage reporting and after the timer job has run to generate the logs, you can open the Monitoring page and click **View health reports** to view two reports: the Slowest Pages and the Top Active Users. You can select the type of report to display by clicking **Slowest Pages** or clicking **Top Active Users**, which are displayed at the upper-left of the page.

 VIEW WEB ANALYTICS REPORTS

GET READY. To view Web Analytics Reports, perform the following steps:

1. Open Central Administration.

2. Click Monitoring. The Monitoring page displays.

3. Click View Web Analytics reports. The Web Analytics Reports—Summary page displays (see Figure 10-17).

Figure 10-17

The Web Analytics Reports—Summary page

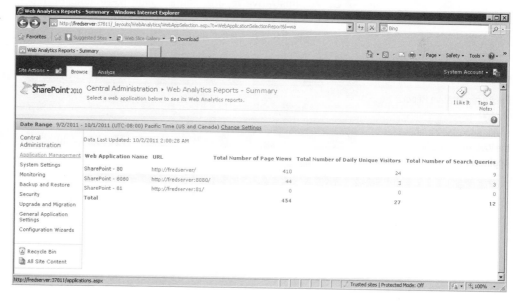

4. Click a Web Application Name to view additional metrics (see Figure 10-18).

Figure 10-18

Web Analytics Reports showing metrics

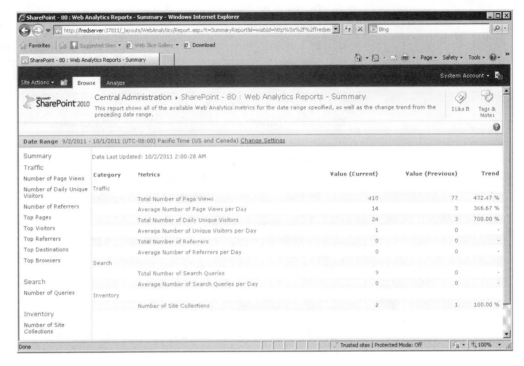

5. To see more detailed reports, select a Summary Traffic option on the left, such as Top Pages, Top Visitors, Top Browsers, Number of Queries, or Number of Site Collections.

6. Administrative reports contain multiple diagnostic reports. To view the Administrative Reports, click the Customized Reports link. The Administrative Report Library page displays (see Figure 10-19).

Figure 10-19

The Administrative Report Library

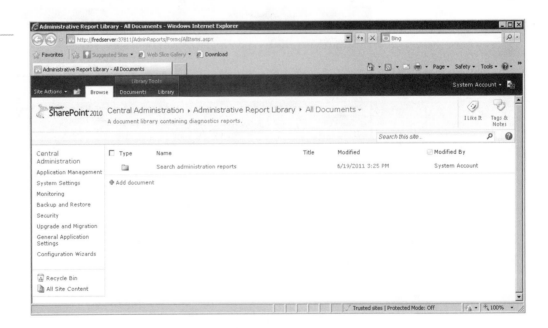

7. Click the Search Administration reports folder. The Search Administration Reports page displays (see Figure 10-20).

Figure 10-20

Search Administration Reports page

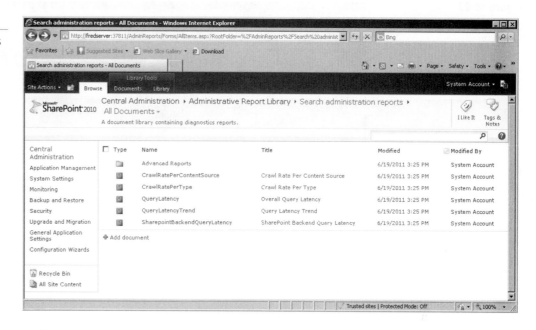

8. To run a report, click the report.

Web Analytics reports can also be accessed from the root collections site settings in the Site Actions.

 VIEW HEALTH REPORTS

GET READY. To view health reports, perform the following steps:

1. Open Central Administration.

2. Click Monitoring. The Monitoring page displays.

3. Click View health reports. The Slowest Pages page displays (see Figure 10-21).

Figure 10-21

The Slowest Pages page

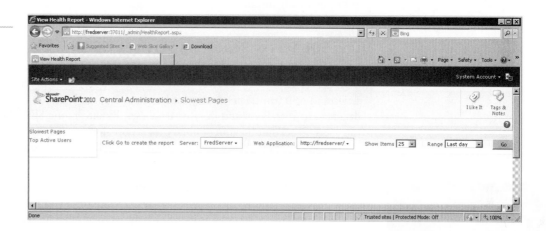

4. To run the report for slowest pages, click the Go button. See Figure 10-22.

Figure 10-22

The Slowest Pages report

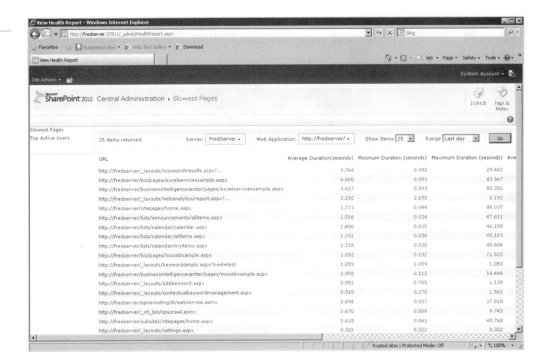

5. To show the top active users, click the Top Active Users link.
6. To run the report for the top active users, click the Go button.

Web Analytics analyzes usage data to provide insight into Web usage patterns. The Web Analytics Service Application requires the Usage and Health Data Collection Service and the State Service to be configured in the farm. You can also use the Web Analytics Web Part to view health reports from other SharePoint sites.

Before you can use Web Analytics reports and before you can use the Web Analytics Web Part, you must create and configure the Web Analytics services application. Of course, you can configure the Web Analytics services application using the Farm Configuration wizard or you can manually install it.

Using SQL Server Reporting Services (SSRS)

SQL Server Reporting Services (SSRS) provides a full range of ready-to-use tools and services to help you create, deploy, and manage reports. It can be used to analyze and visualize data held in SharePoint and in other databases. By integrating SharePoint with SSRS, you can use a SharePoint document library for report storage, making it easy to publish and execute reports. Reports can also be added to SharePoint dashboards and other pages.

CERTIFICATION READY
What tool allows you
to create and deploy
customized reports using
SharePoint?
2.1.6

To integrate SSRS and SharePoint 2010, you must install SQL Reporting Services. For smaller implementations, this is installed at the same time you install the SQL Server. If it is a larger installation, you can install SSRS on its own separate server. If it was not installed when you installed the SQL server and you wish to install it, you must rerun the SQL Server Installation wizard and add the Reporting Services feature to your existing instance.

Next, you must install the Reporting Services Add-In on SharePoint Web front-end servers and make several configuration changes. After the add-in is installed, the SharePoint front-end servers will consist of the following three components:

- **The SSRS Proxy**: The component that allows SharePoint to communicate with SSRS.
- **The Report Management User Interface**: The application pages that enable administrators to view, store, and manage report server content on the SharePoint farm.
- **The Report Viewer Web Part**: The Web part that can be used on a Web page to present reports.

For integrating with SharePoint 2010, you must use SSRS 2008 R2 or later.

To use the SQL Server Reporting Services with SharePoint, you must perform the following steps:

1. Make sure the SQL Server Reporting Services is installed.
2. Download and install the Reporting Services add-in.
3. Activate the report server integration feature.
4. Configure the report dataset in SharePoint Integrated Mode.
5. Configure the SSRS Proxy connection.

 INSTALL AND ACTIVATE THE REPORTING SERVICES ADD-IN

GET READY. To install and activate the Reporting Services add-in, perform the following steps:

1. Download the Reporting Services add-in on each SharePoint server in the farm from http://www.microsoft.com/download/en/details.aspx?id=622.
2. Double-click the rsSharePoint.msi file.
3. If a security warning box displays, click Run.
4. When the Welcome page displays, click Next.
5. Type your name and company and then click Next.
6. Click Install. The add-in is installed and configured.
7. Click Finish.
8. Open the top-level site in the site collection where you want to publish SSRS reports using your browser.
9. Open Site Actions and then click Site Settings.
10. In the Site Collection Administration, click Site Collection Features.
11. Scroll down to locate the Report Server Integration Feature. To the right of this feature, click Activate.

 CONFIGURE THE REPORT DATABASE IN SHAREPOINT INTEGRATED MODE

GET READY. To configure the Report Database in SharePoint Integrated Mode, perform the following steps:

1. Click Start > All Programs > SQL Server 2008 R2 > Configuration Tools > Reporting Services Configuration Manager.
2. Select the server name and report server instance and click the Connect button.

3. In the Connect pane, click Database (see Figure 10-23).

Figure 10-23

Selecting Database in
the Reporting Services
Configuration Manager

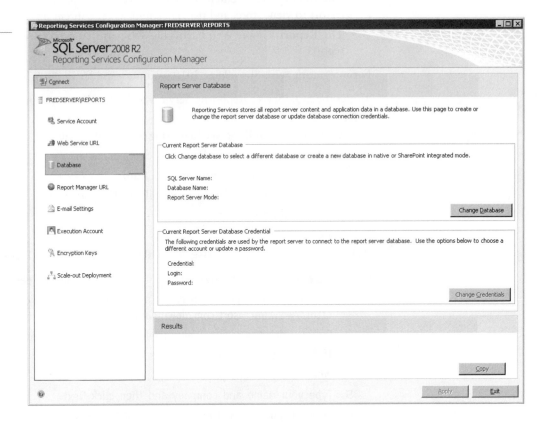

4. Click Change Database. The Change Database page displays.

5. Ensure that the Create a new report server database option is selected (see Figure 10-24), and then click Next.

Figure 10-24

Creating a new report server
database

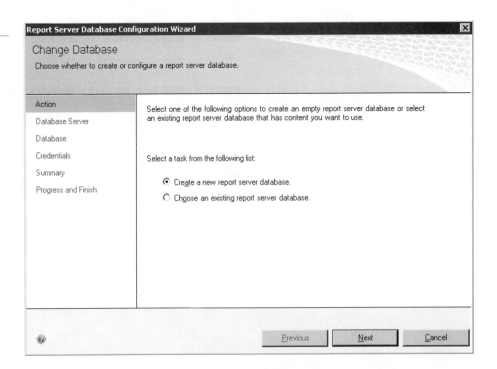

6. Specify the Server Name and authentication type. Click Next.

7. In the Database Name text box (see Figure 10-25), type a descriptive name for the reporting database.

Figure 10-25

Typing a Database Name

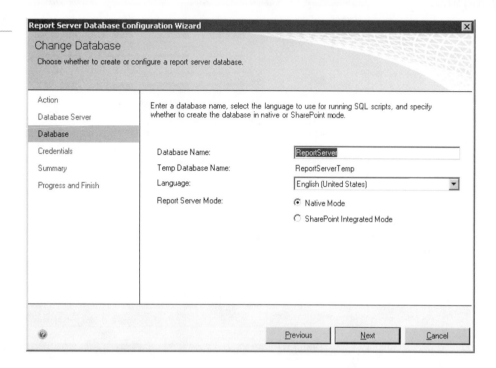

8. Select the SharePoint Integrated Mode option, and then click Next.

9. Click the Credentials section, and then specify the username and password of an existing user account that report services will use to connect to the reporting database. Click Next.

10. Review your specifications and then click Next.

11. Click Finish.

12. Click Exit to close the Reporting Services Configuration Manager.

 CONFIGURE THE SSRS PROXY COMPONENT

GET READY. To configure the SSRS proxy component, perform the following steps:

1. Open Central Administration.

2. Click General Application Settings. The General Application Settings page displays (see Figure 10-26).

3. In the Reporting Services section, click Reporting Services Integration. The Reporting Services Integration page displays (see Figure 10-27).

Figure 10-26

The General Application
Settings page

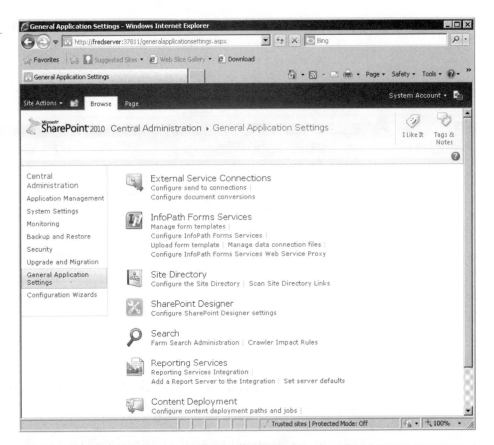

Figure 10-27

The Reporting Services
Integration page

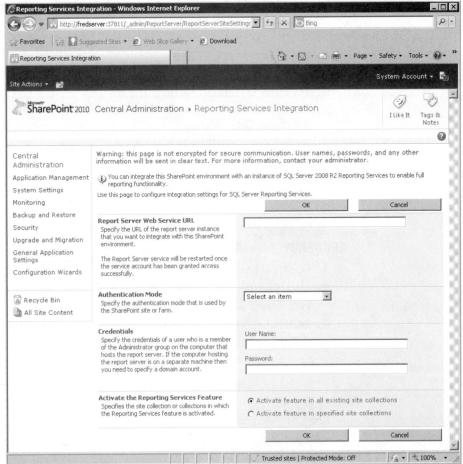

4. In the Report Server Web Service URL section, type the URL of the reporting server. It is usually http://<servername>/reports.

5. Use the Authentication Mode section and the Credentials section to configure the user account that SharePoint will use to connect to the reporting server. This account must be a member of the Administrators group on the reporting server.

6. If desired, leave Activate feature in all existing site collections default value or choose Activate feature in specified site collections.

7. Click OK.

8. When the feature activation is complete, click Close.

Managing Timer Jobs

Many of the automated tasks performed by SharePoint—such as sending e-mail alerts or trimming the audit database—are done by a timer job. A **timer job** contains a definition of the service to run and specifies how frequently the service is started. Many features in SharePoint rely on timer jobs to run services according to a schedule. Timer jobs are handled by the Windows SharePoint 2010 Timer service.

For the general administration of all jobs, the SharePoint Central Administration Web site has a Timer Job Status page and a Job Definitions page. From the View menu, you can filter the timer jobs at the following levels:

- **All**: Displays all timer jobs for the farm.
- **Service**: Displays all the timer jobs for a particular service. If you select this command, use the Service menu to select the service by which you want to filter the listed jobs.
- **Web Application**: Displays all the timer jobs for a Web application. If you elect this option, use the Web Application menu to select the Web application by which you want to filter the listed jobs.

+ MORE INFORMATION

For a list of default timer jobs, visit http://technet.microsoft.com/en-us/library/cc678870.aspx

 MANAGE TIMER JOBS

GET READY. To manage timer jobs, perform the following steps:

1. Open Central Administration.

2. Click Monitoring.

3. To see when a job is scheduled to run next, click Timer Job Status. The Timer Job Status page displays (see Figure 10-28).

4. To see jobs that are currently running, click Running Jobs. The Running Jobs page displays (see Figure 10-29).

5. To see history of jobs, click Job History. The Job History page displays.

6. To see the current timer jobs, click Review job definitions. The Job Definitions page displays (see Figure 10-30).

7. To modify a job, click on a job to open the Edit Timer Job page (see Figure 10-31).

Figure 10-28

The Timer Job Status page

Figure 10-29

The Running Jobs page

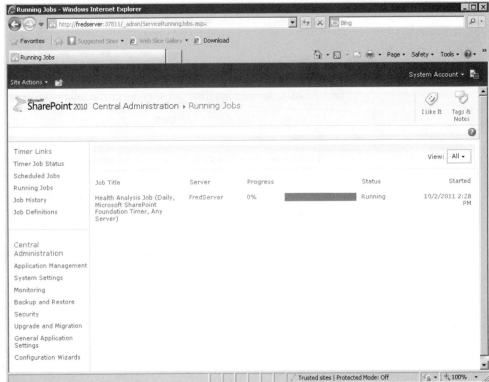

Figure 10-30

The Job Definitions page

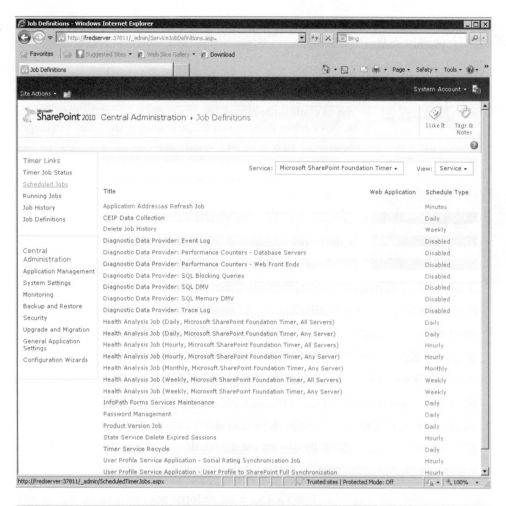

Figure 10-31

The Edit Timer Job page

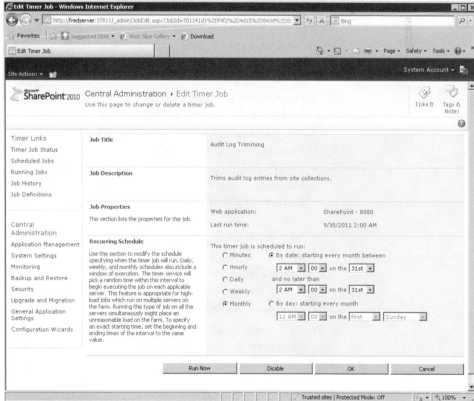

■ Optimizing the Performance of a SharePoint Environment

The Bottom Line

Since SharePoint is a complex environment, there are several areas that you can monitor, configure, and manage within SharePoint that directly affect performance. These allow you to control the SharePoint environment to make sure that a single user, or group of users, does not consume all of the resources, and that a manageable size is maintained for SharePoint collections or lists.

CERTIFICATION READY
What is the difference between boundaries, thresholds, and supported limits?
4.3

While capacity planning is beyond the scope of this course, as a SharePoint administrator, you need to be familiar with SharePoint boundaries, thresholds, and supported limits. This knowledge helps ensure that you have the proper hardware selected and you can better identify performance problems that are caused by exceeding the boundaries, threshold, and supported limits.

- *Boundaries* are concrete limits that are by design and cannot be exceeded. Examples of boundaries include:
  - The maximum file size of a document is 2 GB.
  - You can only have 5 zones per Web application.
  - Each list or library item can occupy only 8,000 bytes in the database.
- *Thresholds* are those limits that have a default value that cannot be exceeded unless the value is modified. Examples of thresholds include:
  - The List view threshold is 5,000, which specifies the maximum number of list or library document size limit.
  - By default, the default document size threshold is set to 50 MB, but can be changed to support the maximum boundary of 2 GB.
  - There are 2,000 subsites per site view. Similarly, the All Site Content page and the Tree View Control performance will decrease significantly as the number of subsites grows.
- *Supported limits* are limits that are not represented by a configurable value, such as the number of site collections per Web application. Examples include:
  - 20 managed paths per Web application are supported. Since managed paths are cached on the Web server and CPU resources are used to process incoming requests against the managed path list, exceeding 20 managed paths per Web application adds more load to the Web server for each request.
  - 10 application pools per Web server. The maximum number is determined by hardware capabilities, particularly the amount of RAM allocated to the Web servers.
  - 2,000 recommended (5,000 maximum) site collections per content database. Microsoft strongly recommends limiting the number of site collections in a content database to 2,000. However, as many as 5,000 site collections in a database are supported.
  - 30,000,000 documents per library.
  - Microsoft strongly recommends limiting the size of site collections to 100 GB. If multiple site collections larger than 100 GB are contained in a single content database, backup and restore operations can take a long time and are at risk of failure.
  - Microsoft strongly recommends limiting the size of content databases to 200 GB.
  - 300 content databases per Web application. Exceeding this supported limit might affect performance when users open a site or site collections.

➕ **MORE INFORMATION**

The SharePoint Server 2010 capacity management: Software boundaries and limits can be found at http://technet. microsoft.com/en-us/library/cc262787.aspx

Looking at Performance

Performance is the overall effectiveness of how data moves through the system. Of course, it is important to select the proper hardware (processor, memory, disk system, and network) to satisfy the expected performance goals. Without the proper hardware, hardware bottlenecks limit the effectiveness of software. While hardware is often to blame for performance, it can be caused by misconfiguration or heavy loads on the application. To help you diagnose performance problems, you can use the tools that were previously discussed in the lesson and you can use Performance Monitor.

When a component limits performance, that component is known as a bottleneck. What you do to relieve one bottleneck might cause other bottlenecks. For example, one of the most common bottlenecks is the amount of memory a system has. By increasing the memory, you can often increase the overall performance of a system (up to a point). However, when you add more RAM, the RAM needs to be fed more data from the disk, and now the disk becomes the bottleneck or the processor cannot keep up with the additional data. Overall, the system might become faster, but if your performance is still not where you want it to be, you need to then look for the possibility of another bottleneck.

You cannot identify performance problems by just taking a quick look at performance. Instead, you need a baseline, which can be created by analyzing the performance when the system is running normally and within design specifications. Then when a problem occurs, compare the current performance to your baseline to see what is different. Since performance can also change gradually over time, it is highly recommended that you baseline your server regularly so that you can chart your performance measures and identify trends. Then you will know when the server needs to be upgraded or replaced or the server workload reduced.

USING PERFORMANCE MONITOR

Performance Monitor is a Microsoft Management Console (MMC) snap-in that provides tools for analyzing system performance. It is included in the Computer Management and Server Manager consoles and it can be executed using the `perfmon` command. From a single console, you can monitor application and hardware performance in real time, specify which data you want to collect in logs, define thresholds for alerts and automatic actions, generate reports, and view past performance data in a variety of ways.

Performance Monitor (see Figure 10-32) provides a visual display of built-in Windows performance counters, either in real time or as a way to review historical data.

Figure 10-32

Performance Monitor

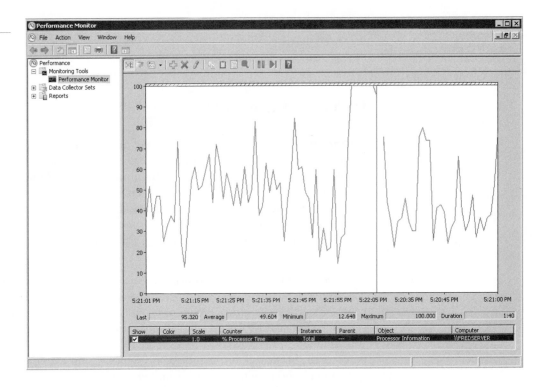

You can add performance counters to Performance Monitor by right-clicking the main pane and selecting **Add Counters** or by creating custom Data Collector Sets (see Figure 10-33). It features multiple graph views that enable you to visually review performance log data. You can create custom views in Performance Monitor that can be exported as Data Collector Sets for use with performance and logging features.

Figure 10-33

Performance Monitor counters

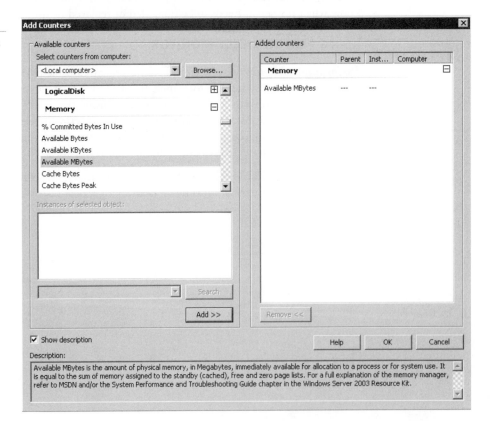

There are hundreds of counters that can be added. The most commonly used counters that show you the overall performance of a system are:

- **Processor: % Processor Time**: Measures how busy the processor is. Although the processor might jump to 100% processor usage, the processor should not be above 80% all of the time. If it is, you should upgrade the processor (using a faster processor or adding additional processors) or move some of the services to other systems.

- **System: Processor Queue Length**: Processor Queue Length is the number of threads in the processor queue. If the processor queue is 2x the number of processors/processor cores, you need to upgrade the processor.

- **Memory: Pages/sec**: A page fault occurs when a process attempts to access a virtual memory page that is not available in its working set in RAM. If the pages/sec is 20 or higher, you should increase the amount of memory.

- **Paging file: % Usage**: The paging file (Pagefile.sys) is a hidden file on your computer's hard disk that Windows uses as if it were RAM. The paging file and physical memory (RAM) make up virtual memory so that you can run more programs than if you were using just the physical memory. If the % Usage is more than 70%, you should increase the amount of RAM.

- **PhysicalDisk: Avg. Disk Queue Length**: The Disk queue length is the average number of read requests or write requests queued for the disk in question. A sustained average higher than 2 indicates that the disk is being over utilized.

＋ MORE INFORMATION

For more information about optimizing SharePoint performance, including Performance Monitor values, visit http://tk5bpsweb01.partners.extranet.microsoft.com/en/sdps/Documents/SharePoint%202010%20-%20Core%20Platform%20Guidance.docx

---

TAKE NOTE*

While the Windows Task Manager can show most of these performance counters live, the Performance Monitor allows you to look at hundreds of counters that are not available in the Task Manager. In addition, you can record the counter values over time and save them for later retrieval.

If you appear to have the necessary hardware (processor, memory, disk, and network) to run SharePoint, you might need to dig deeper into Performance Monitor. This would include looking at specific SharePoint counters, including applications, caches, and other components. In addition, you can also look at IIS, ASP.NET, and .NET CLR counters on front end-servers and SQL counters on the database servers.

Before you dig deep into Performance Monitor to diagnose performance problems, don't forget the other tools introduced earlier in this lesson (including running usage reports, health reports, and Web Analytic reports) as well as Developer Dashboard, which is covered in Lesson 6.

LOOKING AT SHAREPOINT PERFORMANCE

Since SharePoint is a complex environment with many components working together to provide a wide range of functionality for the users, one service or task can dramatically affect SharePoint performance.

Remember that SharePoint runs on IIS, .NET Framework, and SQL server, which runs on Windows servers. Therefore, any of these can cause problems—including performance problems—with SharePoint. Since multiple servers can be used in SharePoint, you must look at processor, memory disk, and network performance on all servers involved, particularly the front end-servers that are being accessed, and the SQL server. Next, you must check the performance of ASP.NET, .NET Framework, and IIS, including looking at the application pools on the front-end server.

You should work with your SQL administrator to make sure the SQL server is running at its best. Databases should be running on separate physical disks or logical unit number (LUN) for storage area networks (SANs). Separating the log files from the data files and having more spindles/disks will improve performance. You should also defragment the database indexes as part of a maintenance plan. Lastly, make sure that the SharePoint server and the SQL server have sufficient available bandwidth. If you do not, you must increase the bandwidth or isolate the communications between the SharePoint server and the SQL server to its own physical network or VLAN.

If SharePoint is only slow at certain times, you will likely need to look at the load and current tasks or jobs. You must look at how many users are accessing SharePoint, which pages are frequently accessed, and which pages take the longest to load. If you determine that some pages take too long to load, you need to examine the Web parts and workflows being used on the page. Lastly, since the bulk of the data is within content databases, you should distribute user data across multiple content databases.

When trying to figure out the SharePoint bottlenecks, you should always check if any of the following are occurring:

- Indexing/crawling
- Backups (SQL and/or SharePoint backups)
- Inefficient views/large list views
- Large list or library operations, such as delete and update
- Large databases
- Exceeding other thresholds and supported limits

To manage or at least influence performance, you can use the following:

- Quotas
- List view threshold
- Resource throttling
- Remote BLOBS
- BLOB caching
- Output and Object Caching

TAKE NOTE *

Backups are discussed in Lesson 12.

Using Quotas

A *quota* specifies the maximum amount of data that can be stored in a site collection. You can configure an e-mail that alerts the site collection administrator when the specified storage size is reached.

CERTIFICATION READY
What tool can be used to prevent a site from growing too big, which may affect overall performance and consume too much disk space on the SQL server?
2.1.2

CERTIFICATION READY
How do you notify the SharePoint administrator that a site is approaching its size limits?
3.2.7

To define a quota for a site collection, create a quota template that is then applied to any site collection in a SharePoint farm. The defined storage limit applies to the total size of the content for the top-level site and all subsites within the site collection, including versions of SharePoint items and the Recycle Bin. After you have created your quota templates, you can apply them to site collections.

CREATE OR EDIT A QUOTA TEMPLATE

GET READY. To create or edit a quota template, perform the following steps:

1. Open Central Administration.
2. Click Application Management.
3. In the Site Collections section, click Specify Quota template. The Quota Templates page displays (see Figure 10-34).

Figure 10-34

The Quota Templates page showing the Personal Site template

The Personal Site template is the only pre-defined template that is included with SharePoint 2010. If you create a new template, the values within the template begin with 0.

4. In the Template Name section, you can select Edit an existing template or Create a new quota template. If you select Create a new quota template, you can create the template from a blank template or you can start from an existing template. You can specify the name of the template in the New template name text box.

5. To limit the storage for the template, select the Limit site storage to a maximum of option and then specify the size in MB.

6. To specify when a warning email is sent to the site collection administrator, select the Send warning E-mail when Site Collection storage reaches option and then specify the threshold in MB.

7. In the Sandboxed Solutions With Code Limits section, specify the number of points to limit the maximum usage per day.

8. If you wish to send a warning e-mail, select the Send warning e-mail option and then select the number of points.

9. If you wish to delete an existing quota, click Delete.

10. Click OK.

 ASSIGN A QUOTA TO A SITE COLLECTION

GET READY. To assign a quota to a site collection, perform the following steps:

1. Open Central Administration.

2. Click Application Management.

3. Click Site Collection Quotas and Locks. The Site Collection Quotas and Locks page displays (see Figure 10-35).

Figure 10-35

The Site Collection Quotas and Locks page

4. To change the site collection, click the Site Collection box, click Change Site Collection, select the site collection that you want to configure (for example, http://fredserver), and then click OK.

5. To set a quota, you can select the quota template (such as the Personal Site template) from the Current quota template box or you can select Individual Quota to specify individual limit site storage and e-mail warning threshold in the Site Quota Information section.

6. Click OK.

When the site collection reaches the maximum storage level, an e-mail message that contains information about the issue is sent to the site collection administrator. You can then choose to delete unused content from the site collection or you can change the limits by doing one of the following:

- Change the storage limit on the quota template that the site collection is using. The modified quota template will not be automatically applied to any existing site collections that use the quota template.

- Designate a new quota template that has a higher storage limit to the site collection, which automatically increases the limits for the site collection to the limits in the newly designated quota template.

- Change the storage limit for the site collection manually, which overrides the limits set in the quota template that is currently applied to the site collection.

The preferred method is to designate a new quota template that has a higher storage limit to the site collection.

 **SharePoint Server** 2010 **Monitoring and Analyzing the SharePoint Environment | 413**

CERTIFICATION READY
How can you prevent a
site collection from being
changed?
3.2.7

Using Locks

You can apply *locks* to a site collection to prevent users from updating content or you can temporarily prevent users from accessing a site collection. While locks do not affect performance, they are usually discussed when your quotas are discussed because locks are established on the same page as quotas.

By opening the Site Collection Quotas and Locks page, you can put a lock on a site collection to prevent certain uses of the site. The locking options include:

- **Not locked**: Unlocks the site collection and makes it available to users.
- **Adding content prevented**: Prevents users from adding new content to the site collection. Updates and deletions are still allowed.
- **Read-only (prevents additions, updates, and deletions):** Prevents users from adding, updating, or deleting content.
- **No access:** Prevents users from accessing the site collection and its content. Users who attempt to access the site receive an error.

 LOCK OR UNLOCK A SITE

GET READY. To lock or unlock a site, perform the following steps:

1. Open Central Administration.
2. Click Application Management.
3. Click Site Collection Quotas and Locks. The Site Collection Quotas and Locks page displays (see Figure 10-36).

Figure 10-36

Selecting a lock status

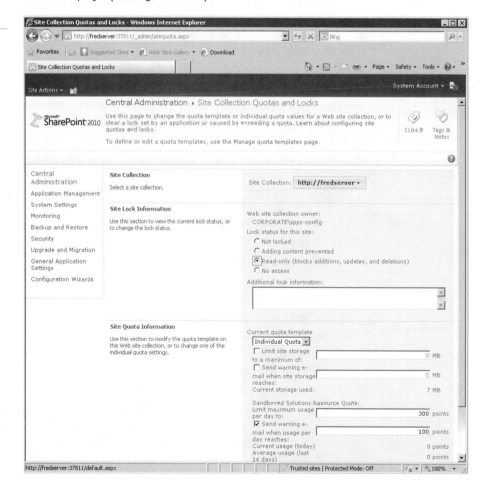

4. To change the site collection, click the Site Collection box, click Change Site Collection, select the site collection, and click the OK button.

5. Select the appropriate lock status. If you specify any option except the Not locked option, type a reason for the lock in the Additional lock information box.

6. Click OK.

Configuring and Managing Large Lists and Resource Throttling

Resource throttling provides options for monitoring and throttling server resources and large lists for Web applications. By performing resource throttling, you can control resource utilization so that user activities do not negatively affect server performance.

The biggest performance bottleneck in SharePoint Web applications is usually large lists. If you have a hundred users on a site and two users access large lists, *all* users can experience slow performance. Therefore, by default, SharePoint is configured to not display more than 5,000 items at one time for a list. A list can be larger than 5,000 items, but only 5,000 can be displayed on the screen at one time. Of course, you would use a view that users filters to show only some of the items within a list.

There might be some instances where you would like to override this limit, particularly when performing certain administrative tasks. To allow this, you would allow object model override. By default, auditors and administrators have a maximum limit of 20,000 list view items.

You also have the option of improving SharePoint performance by adjusting the resource-throttling settings that a Web application uses. At times, users might request pages from SharePoint at the same time that high-load, low-priority requests occur (such as when the search indexing service is indexing content). Under certain conditions, performance might suffer for users.

If HTTP request monitoring and throttling is enabled, the resource-throttling job monitors system resources such as CPU, memory, and wait time every five seconds. If the system is experiencing a high load after three unsuccessful checks, the low-priority HTTP requests will be suspended until the server load falls back to manageable levels.

CONFIGURE LIMITS FOR LARGE LISTS AND RESOURCE THROTTLING

GET READY. To configure limits for large lists and to enable/disable resource throttling, perform the following steps:

1. Open Central Administration.

2. In the Application Management section, click Manage Web applications.

3. Click to select the Web application that you want to configure.

4. Click the General Settings menu (see Figure 10-37) and choose Resource Throttling. The Resource Throttling page displays (see Figure 10-38).

5. In the List View Threshold text box, type the maximum number of items to view on a list.

6. If you wish to allow object model override, select Yes in the Allow object model override section.

7. In the List View Threshold for auditors and administrators text box, specify the maximum number of items to view on a list for administrators and auditors.

8. In the List View Lookup Threshold text box, specify the maximum number of lookup, person/group or workflow status fields that a database query can involve at one time.

Figure 10-37

The General Settings menu

Figure 10-38

The Resource Throttling page

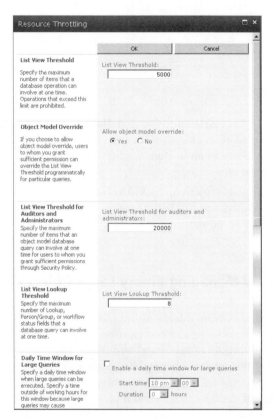

9. If desired, select the Enable a daily time window for large queries and then select the Start time and the Duration of the window for large queries for when you want large queries to be executed.

10. In the List Unique Permissions Threshold text box (see Figure 10-39), specify the number of unique permissions that a list can have at one time.

11. Backward-Compatible Event Handlers allows certain event handlers that were developed for SharePoint 2007 to work. Select On or Off.

Figure 10-39

The Resource Throttling page, showing the List Unique Permissions Threshold text box

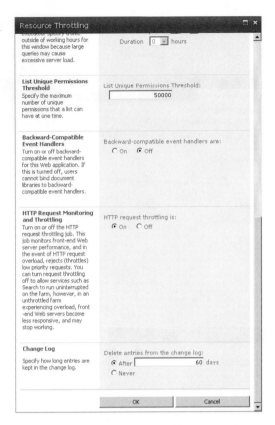

12. In the HTTP Request Monitoring and Throttling section, leave On (the default value) selected to enable this feature, which will then reject low-priority HTTP requests at times when a high number of such requests would otherwise affect Web server performance.

13. In the Change Log section, click After and specify the number of days after which entries in the change log will be deleted in order to preserve disk space. The default is set to 60 days.

14. Click OK.

Configuring and Managing Binary Large Object (BLOB) Storage

In SharePoint 2010, a ***binary large object (BLOB)*** is a large block of data stored in a database that is known by its size and location instead of by its structure. By default, BLOBs are stored directly in the SharePoint content database. BLOBs are very large and BLOB data can consume lots of space. Because server resources are often optimized for database access patterns and not large file patterns, it might be better to store BLOBs outside the content database to a shared folder. BLOBs that are stored outside of the content database are stored in a ***Remote BLOB Storage (RBS)***.

CERTIFICATION READY
How can you optimize performance when dealing with large files that need to be stored in SharePoint?
4.3.2

To use the RBS, perform the following steps:

1. Enable FILESTREAM on the database server. By default, FILESTREAM components are installed but are not enabled.

2. Provision a BLOB store for each content database.

3. Install the RBS client library on each Web server, which stores the BLOB data on the file system, enables fidelity checks, and performs other tasks.

4. Enable RBS for each content database.

5. Test the RBS installation.

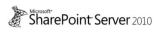

→ ENABLE FILESTREAM ON THE DATABASE SERVER

GET READY. To enable FILESTREAM on the database server, perform the following steps:

1. Click Start > All Programs > Microsoft SQL Server 2008 R2 > Configuration Tools > SQL Server Configuration Manager (see Figure 10-40).

Figure 10-40

The SQL Server Configuration Manager

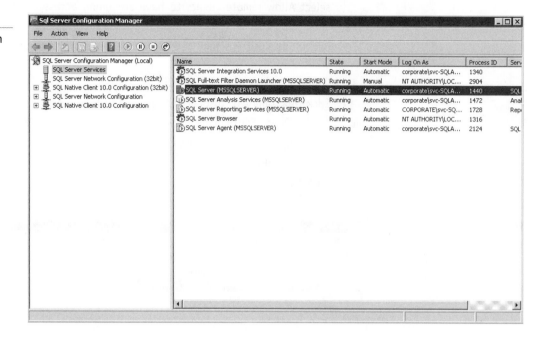

2. In the list of services, right-click SQL Server Services, and then click Open.

3. Right-click the instance of SQL Server on which you want to enable FILESTREAM and then click Properties. If it is the default instance, it will be MSSQLSERVER. The SQL Server Properties dialog box displays.

4. In the SQL Server Properties dialog box, click the FILESTREAM tab. The FILESTREAM tab displays (see Figure 10-41).

Figure 10-41

The FILESTREAM tab

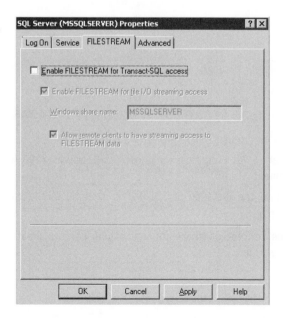

5. Select the Enable FILESTREAM for Transact-SQL access check box.

6. If you want to read and write FILESTREAM data from Windows, click Enable FILESTREAM for file I/O streaming access. In the Windows share name box, type the name of the Windows share.

7. If remote clients must access the FILESTREAM data that is stored on this share, select Allow remote clients to have streaming access to FILESTREAM data.

8. Click Apply.

9. Click Start > All Programs > Microsoft SQL Server 2008 R2 > SQL Server Management Studio.

10. Connect to the instance of SQL Server that hosts the SharePoint databases.

11. Click New Query to display the Query Editor.

12. In the Query Editor pane, type the following Transact-SQL code (see Figure 10-42):

```
EXEC sp_configure filestream_access_level, 2
RECONFIGURE
```

13. Click Execute.

Figure 10-42

Using the Query Editor

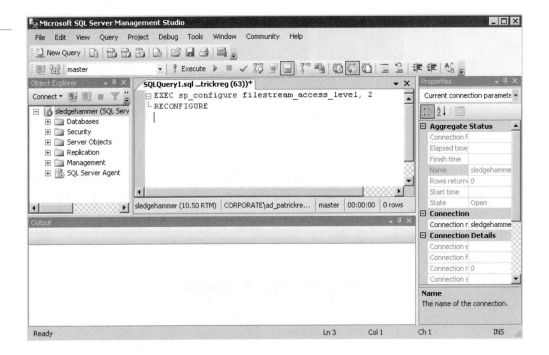

PROVISION A BLOB STORE FOR A CONTENT DATABASE

GET READY. To provision a BLOB store for a content database, perform the following steps:

1. Click Start > All Programs > Microsoft SQL Server 2008 R2 > SQL Server Management Studio.

2. Connect to the instance of SQL Server that hosts the content database.

3. Expand Databases.

4. Click the content database for which you want to create a BLOB store, and then click New Query.

5. Execute the following SQL query in the Query Editor pane (see Figure 10-43). (Replace [WSS_Content] with the content database name and replace c:\BlobStore with the volume\directory in which you want the BLOB store created.)

```
use [WSS_Content]

if not exists (select * from sys.symmetric_keys where name =
N'##MS_DatabaseMasterKey##')

create master key encryption by password = N'Admin
Key Password !2#4'
```

Figure 10-43

Provisioning a BLOB store for a content database

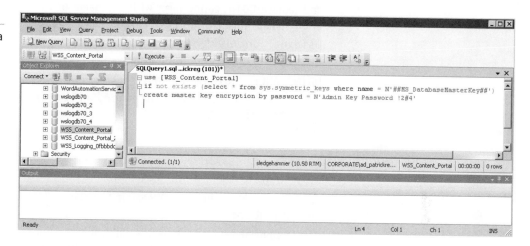

6. Execute the following SQL query in the Query Editor pane. Again, replace [WSS_Content] with the content database name and replace c:\BlobStore with the volume\directory in which you want the BLOB store created.

```
use [WSS_Content]

if not exists

(select groupname from sysfilegroups where groupname=N'RBSFilestre
amProvider')

alter database [WSS_Content]

add filegroup RBSFilestreamProvider contains filestream

use [WSS_Content]

alter database [WSS_Content]

add file (name = RBSFilestreamFile, filename = 'c:\Blobstore') to
filegroup RBSFilestreamProvider
```

⊙ INSTALL THE RBS CLIENT LIBRARY ON THE FIRST WEB SERVER

GET READY. To install the RBS Client Library on the first Web server, perform the following steps:

1. On any Web server, browse to http://go.microsoft.com/fwlink/?LinkID=165839&clcid =0x409 and then download the RBS_x64.msi file.

2. Click Start, click Run, type cmd into the Run/Search text box, and then click OK.

3. Execute the following command. (Replace WSS_Content with the database name, and replace DBInstanceName with the SQL Server instance name.)

```
msiexec /qn /lvx* rbs_install_log.txt /i

RBS-x64.msi TRUSTSERVERCERTIFICATE=true

FILEGROUP=PRIMARY DBNAME="WSS_Content"

DBINSTANCE="DBInstanceName"

FILESTREAMFILEGROUP=RBSFilestreamProvider
FILESTREAMSTORENAME=FilestreamProvider_1
```

INSTALL THE RBS CLIENT LIBRARY ON ALL ADDITIONAL WEB AND APPLICATION SERVERS

GET READY. To install the RBS client library on all additional Web and application servers, perform the following steps:

1. On a Web server, download the RBS_x64.msi at http://go.microsoft.com/fwlink/?LinkID=165839&clcid=0x409.

2. Click Start, click Run, type cmd into the Run/Search text box, and then click OK.

3. Execute the following command. (Replace WSS_Content with the database name, and replace DBInstanceName with the name of the SQL Server instance. The operation should finish within approximately one minute.)

   ```
   msiexec /qn /lvx* rbs_install_log.txt /i
   RBS_x64.msi DBNAME="WSS_Content"
   DBINSTANCE="DBInstanceName"
   ADDLOCAL=Client,Docs,Maintainer,ServerScript, FilestreamClient,
   FilestreamServer
   ```

 ENABLE RBS

GET READY. To enable RBS, perform the following steps:

1. Click Start > All Programs > Microsoft SharePoint 2010 Products > SharePoint 2010 Management Shell.

2. At the command prompt, type the following command (whereby <ContentDatabaseName> is the name of the content database).

   ```
   $cdb = Get-SPContentDatabase <ContentDatabaseName>
   $rbss = $cdb.RemoteBlobStorageSettings
   $rbss.Installed()
   $rbss.Enable()
   $rbss.SetActiveProviderName($rbss.GetProviderNames()[0])
   $rbss
   ```

Configuring BLOB, Output, and Object Caching

In Lesson 5, object cache settings, page output cache settings, and profile cache settings were discussed for a site collection. As you recall, when a resource is requested, a copy is placed in the cache. If the user requests the same resource that is in cache a second time, it will pull it from the cache instead of retrieving the resource from the SQL server or execute ASP.NET code to render a page. As a result, you see a faster response.

SharePoint uses the following three caches on Web front-end servers to temporarily store content as it is served to a user:

- BLOB cache
- Output cache
- Object cache

When configuring and using cache, you can increase the cache time, which means the resource will be in the cache longer. However, if the item changes in the content database, the resource remains in the cache until it expires. As a result, out-of-date items can be returned to users. Therefore, the cache settings must be balanced between performance and content freshness.

BLOB Cache

As introduced earlier in this lesson, the BLOB files store large documents, images, and videos. The **BLOB cache** reduces the load on SQL servers and accesses BLOBs faster if they have been used recently. To configure the BLOB cache, you must edit the web.config file for the Web application.

⊙ ENABLE THE BLOB CACHE

GET READY. To enable the BLOB cache, perform the following steps:

1. Click Start > Administrative Tools > Internet Information Services (IIS) Manager.
2. In the Connections pane, expand the server that hosts the Web application.
3. Expand the Site container.
4. Right-click the Web application you want to configure, and then click Explore.
5. Right-click the web.config file and then click Open.
6. Locate the line that begins with <BlobCache.
7. In the Location attribute, specify a folder on a disk that has enough space for the cache. This location should not be on the same disk as the operating system swap file or the SharePoint diagnostic logs.
8. For the maxSize attribute, type the maximum size of the BLOB Cache in GB.
9. Set the Enabled attribute to "true" (see Figure 10-44).
10. Save the web.config file and then close it.

Figure 10-44

Enabling the BLOB cache

Output Cache

The **Output cache** stores rendered versions of Web pages to accelerate their distribution to users and reduce load on content database servers. To maintain security, different versions of each page are stored depending on the permissions of the user who made the request. Different from the other caches, the output cache is available only if you have activated the Publishing feature in all the relevant sites. To enable the Output cache, edit web.config. The cache profile settings that you configure at the Web application level will be used for all cache profiles in the site collections for that Web application.

 ENABLE THE OUTPUT CACHE

GET READY. To enable the Output cache, perform the following steps:

1. Click Start > Administrative Tools > Internet Information Services (IIS) Manager.
2. In the Connections pane, expand the server that hosts the Web application.
3. Expand the Site container.
4. Right-click the Web application you want to configure, and then click Explore.
5. Right-click the web.config file and then click Open.
6. Locate the line that begins with <OutputCacheProfiles.
7. Set the useCacheProfileOverrides attribute to "true".
8. Save the web.config file and close it.

Object Cache

The **Object cache** reduces traffic between the SharePoint front-end servers and the SQL server by storing SharePoint objects such as lists, libraries, site settings collections, page layouts, content types, and so on. The object cache stores objects. Similar to the Output cache, the Object cache can only be figured if you enable the Publishing feature on all the relevant sites. Object cache settings can be configured at the Web application level and at the site collection level. To configure at the Web application level, edit web.config.

 ENABLE THE OUTPUT CACHE

GET READY. To enable the Output cache, perform the following steps:

1. Click Start > Administrative Tools > Internet Information Services (IIS) Manager.
2. In the Connections pane, expand the server that hosts the Web application.
3. Expand the Site container.
4. Right-click the Web application you want to configure, and then click Explore.
5. Right-click the web.config file and then click Open.
6. Locate the line that begins with "<ObjectCache".
7. In the maxSize attribute, set the memory size you want the Object Cache to be in MB.
8. Save the web.config file and close it.

Adjusting IIS Performance

Since SharePoint operates on top of IIS, it is important to configure IIS for the best performance possible.

When configuring the services and service applications, be sure to minimize the number of application pools. While application pools are used to isolate bad applications, more application pools consume more memory. If you find that you have a bad application, place the application in its own application pool, limit the amount of memory and CPU the application pool can use, and then configure the application pool to recycle. You should then work with the developer to get the application problems fixed.

➕ **MORE INFORMATION**

For more information about configuring application pool settings, visit http://technet.microsoft.com/en-us/library/cc745955.aspx

SharePoint content consists of two primary sources:

- Static files for the SharePoint root directories located in C:\Program Files\Common Files\Microsoft Shared\14 for 2010
- Dynamic data stored in content databases

Of course, users don't know the difference because SharePoint merges the page content and transmits the HTTP response to the user. You can enable and adjust IIS compression to optimize SharePoint Web page load times. When you enable static content compression, the default settings will only compress files larger than 2,700 bytes and will create a per-application pool disk space limit of 100 MB.

 ENABLE AND CONFIGURE IIS COMPRESSION

GET READY. To enable and configure IIS compression, perform the following steps:

1. Click Start > Administrative Tools > Internet Information Services (IIS) Manager.
2. In the Connections pane, select the desired server.
3. Make sure the Feature View is selected.
4. In the IIS section, double-click Compression (see Figure 10-45). The Compression page displays (see Figure 10-46).
5. Select the Enable dynamic content compression check box or select the Enable static content compression check box (or select both).
6. In the Static Compression section, if desired, select the Only compress files larger than (in bytes) check box and then type the desired value in bytes.
7. In the Cache directory field, accept the default path or type the path to the directory used for caching.
8. If desired, select the Per application pool disk space limit (in MB) check box and then type a value in megabytes.
9. In the Actions pane on the right, click Apply.

Figure 10-45

The IIS Server page

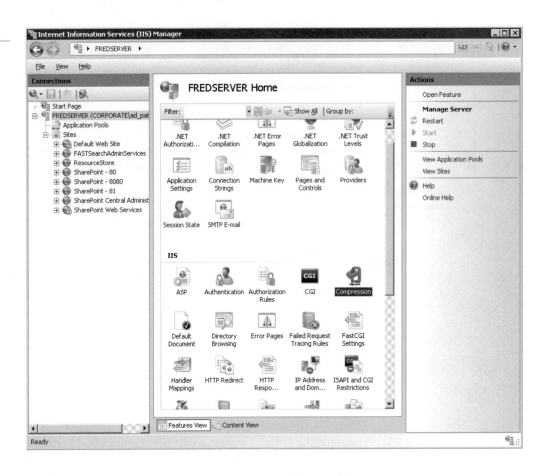

Figure 10-46

The Compression page

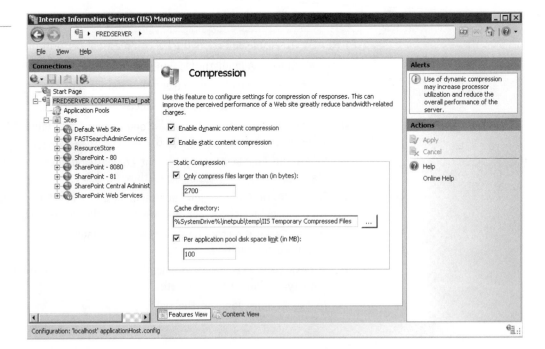

Optimizing Services

> Much of the functionality built into SharePoint is based on services, which are split into separate management units called Service Applications. Each Service Application can have its own database. Any of these services/Service Applications can cause performance problems.

CERTIFICATION READY
Which SharePoint
Service Applications are
processor and memory
intensive?
4.3.3

When configuring the SharePoint service, you should always use a different user account for each SharePoint service. While it does not necessarily improve performance, it might help you identify if a particular service is running slowly or is down.

For larger SharePoint implementations, you will have multiple front-end servers, a separate, hefty SQL server, and one or more multiple application servers to handle the different service applications. You should be aware that different application server roles place different demands on your server farm infrastructure. Therefore, you should take a closer look at the following service applications:

- The crawl server is highly processor intensive. In addition, the disk hardware should be optimized for writing. A RAID 10 disk configuration should be used for the optimal combination of fast write speed and disk redundancy.

- The query server role is memory intensive. Because the server loads as much of the index as possible into memory, the disk hardware should be optimized for fast input/output (I/O) times on disk read operations.

- Excel Calculation Services is processor-intensive and potentially memory-intensive depending upon your Excel Calculation Services caching configuration and usage.

- The word automation service is processor-intensive.

- Business Connectivity Services (BCS) can put a load on the processor, memory, and network when it accesses line-of-business systems.

SKILL SUMMARY

IN THIS LESSON, YOU LEARNED:

- Every Windows system already has a logging system, which is viewed using the Event Viewer. The Event Viewer is a Microsoft Management Console (MMC) snap-in that enables you to browse and manage event logs.

- The primary logging mechanism for SharePoint is Unified Logging Service (ULS), which writes SharePoint events to the SharePoint Trace Log and stores them in the file system. ULS logs are also sometimes referred to as Trace Logs.

- The Health Analyzer is a feature that is designed to run automatic checks on the configuration of the SharePoint farm. It was created to identify common configuration mistakes and, in some situations, repair problems automatically.

- You can use usage reports and Web Analytics to give you a view in performance of how SharePoint it is being used.

- After enabling usage reporting and after the timer job has run to generate the logs, you can open the Monitoring page and click View health reports to view two reports: the slowest pages and the top active users.

- Web Analytics analyzes usage data to provide insight into Web usage patterns.

- SQL Server Reporting Services (SSRS) provides a full range of ready-to-use tools and services to help you create, deploy, and manage reports.

- Many of the automated tasks that SharePoint performs (such as sending e-mail alerts or trimming the audit database) are performed by a timer job. Many features in SharePoint Server rely on timer jobs to run services according to a schedule.

- Since SharePoint is a complex environment, there are several areas that you can monitor, configure, and manage within SharePoint. These areas directly affect performance and allow you to control the SharePoint environment to make sure that a user or group of users does not consume all of the resources and that a SharePoint collection or list is a manageable size.

- A quota specifies the maximum amount of data that can be stored in a site collection.

- You can apply locks to a site collection to prevent users from updating content or you can temporarily prevent users from accessing a site collection.

- Resource throttling provides options for monitoring and throttling server resources and large lists for Web applications. By performing resource throttling, you can control resource utilization so that user activities do not negatively affect server performance.

- By default, SharePoint is configured to not display more than 5,000 items at one time for a list.

- A binary large object (BLOB) is a large block of data stored in a database that is known by its size and location instead of by its structure.

- BLOB data can consume lots of space while using server resources that are optimized for database access patterns (and not large file patterns). It might be better to store BLOBs outside the content database to a shared folder.

- BLOBs that are stored outside the content database are stored in Remote BLOB Storage (RBS).

- SharePoint uses three caches on Web front-end servers to temporarily store content as it is served to a user: BLOB cache, Output cache, and Object cache.

■ Knowledge Assessment

Fill in the Blank

Complete the following sentences by writing the correct word or words in the blanks provided.

1. The MMC that allows you to view Windows logs is _____.

2. The primary logging mechanism for SharePoint is _____.

3. The _____ logging mode shows all events that occur on the server.

4. The _____ enables you to diagnose and resolve configuration performance and usage problems.

5. _____ provides a full range of ready-to-use tools and services to create, deploy, and manage reports.

6. To integrate SSRS and SharePoint 2010, you must install SQL Reporting Services and the _____.

7. _____ are default values that cannot be exceeded unless the value is modified.

8. By default, you cannot display more than _____ list items at once in a view.

9. You can have only _____ zones per Web application.

10. _____ monitors and temporarily suspends low-priority HTTP requests.

Multiple Choice

Circle the letter that corresponds to the best answer.

1. ULS logs are also known as _____.
   a. system logs
   b. Web analytics logs
   c. trace logs
   d. performance logs

2. When looking up an error on the screen in the ULS logs, you must use the _____.
   a. correlation ID
   b. server name
   c. user name
   d. failed service

3. To configure the ULS logs, click Monitoring and then click _____.
   a. Configure Diagnostic Logging
   b. Web Analytics Logs
   c. Timer Jobs
   d. Health Logging

4. When you open Central Administration, what generates a red banner when a critical issue is detected?
   a. Timer detector
   b. Diagnostic Labs
   c. Web analytics service
   d. SharePoint Health Analyzer

5. What is used to collect, report, and analyze the usage and effectiveness of SharePoint 2010 sites?
   a. Health Logging service
   b. Performance Monitor
   c. Usage Logger
   d. Web Analytics service

6. What contains a definition of a service to run and specifies how frequently the service is started?
   a. Diagnostic Job
   b. Timer Job
   c. Start Job
   d. Service Job

7. What are concrete limits that cannot be exceeded in SharePoint?
   a. Boundaries
   b. Thresholds
   c. Supported limits
   d. Hard recommendations

8. Microsoft recommends limiting the size of content databases to _____.
   a. 50 GB
   b. 100 GB
   c. 200 GB
   d. 500 GB

9. What prevents a user from updating content in a site collection?
   a. A quota
   b. A lock
   c. A cache
   d. A throttle

10. What is a large block of data stored in a database that is known by its size and location instead of by its structure?
    a. descriptor
    b. binary large object
    c. construct
    d. binary log

True / False

Circle T if the statement is true or F if the statement is false.

T | F 1. Log files should be stored on the same drive and partition that SharePoint 2010 is installed on.

T | F 2. To enable BLOB caching, you should modify the web.config file.

T | F 3. The processor utilization should never be above 80%.

T | F 4. The Enable Event Log Flood Protection option detects repeating events and suppresses the repeating event until the repeating event stops.

T | F 5. When alerts are sent, the alerts are sent via a Timer Job.

■ Case Scenarios

Scenario 10-1: Looking at SharePoint Performance

You have been running SharePoint for several months with no problem. Then suddenly, when users try to access SharePoint, SharePoint appears to be very slow. What would you use to troubleshoot the problem?

The first thing you should do is to log in to the SharePoint servers and the SQL server to quickly look at processor and memory utilization using Task Manager. If it is high on either server, check to see which processes are utilizing the processor and memory the most. Then move over to the front-end SharePoint servers to look at the health reports and look at the Event Viewer. You should also look at what Timer Jobs are running and if a search crawl or backup is running. Then look at Web Analytic reports to see how SharePoint is being used and which pages are the slowest to respond. If you still cannot find the problem, you must use Performance Monitor to try to identify the bottleneck.

Scenario 10-2: Expanding SharePoint 2010

You get the following error when you try to access a SharePoint site:

An unhandled exception occurred in the user interface. Exception Information has been thrown by the target of an invocation.

Troubleshooting issues with Microsoft SharePoint Foundation

Correlation ID: bec923c-2-5710-2fd3-c2b0-237ab443d32

Date and Time: 12/23/2012 8:43:03 AM

How would you troubleshoot this error?

You will first need to determine what the real error message is. Therefore, you will have to go to your log folder where the ULS logs are kept. The first log that is the date after 12/23/2012 8:43:03 AM. Then search for the bec923c-2-5710-2fd3-c2b0-237ab443d32 string and read the associated error messages. Then you can research the error using your search engine if necessary. Then use Health Analyzer and Event Viewer to dig deeper, looking for any related events that might have caused this problem.

Managing Authentication Providers

OBJECTIVE DOMAIN MATRIX

TECHNOLOGY SKILL	OBJECTIVE DOMAIN DESCRIPTION	OBJECTIVE DOMAIN NUMBER
Manage Authentication Providers	Manage Authentication Providers	2.3
	Managing NTLM	2.3.1
	Managing Kerberos	2.3.2
	Managing Claims-Based Authentication	2.3.3
	Managing Forms-Based Authentication	2.3.4
	Configuring Secure Store Service (SSS)	2.3.5
	Configuring Active Directory Federation Services (AD FS)	2.3.6

KEY TERMS

Active Directory Federation Service (AD FS)

anonymous access

authentication

authentication provider

Basic Authentication

Claims-Based Authentication

Classic-Mode Authentication

Forms-Based Authentication (FBA)

Kerberos

NTLM

Secure Store Service (SSS)

service principal name (SPN)

You are attending a meeting with your manager. During the meeting, you are informed that senior management created a new policy that requires that the authentication used in Web sites sharing confidential information must use the most secure form of authentication. In addition, your manager would like to simplify logins for the users by using a single sign-on login for SharePoint and other Web services used within your company.

■ Manage Authentication Providers

THE BOTTOM LINE

As mentioned in Lesson 5, *authentication* is the act of confirming the identity of a user and is an essential part used in authorization. *Authentication providers* are software components that support specific authentication methods. You can configure a Web application to support many different types of authentication depending on the access method.

CERTIFICATION READY
What is the default authentication provider for SharePoint 2010?
2.3

The role of the authentication provider is to define which type of authentication is aligned to a specific zone in a Web application. By default, all zones are created with Windows NTLM (NT LAN Manager). Available authentication options include the following:

- Windows
- Negotiate (Kerberos or NTLM)
- Anonymous Access
- Forms
- Web Single Sign-On via federated authentication mechanisms such as ADFS (Active Directory Federation Services)

Classic-Mode Authentication is the same type of authentication used in SharePoint Server 2007. *Claims-based Authentication* is a new authentication mode that is built on the Windows Identity Foundation (WIF) and that uses an identity system that allows users to present claims that include information about who the user is and what system and content the user can access. The claim must be validated against a trusted source, such as Active Directory, LDAP, application specific databases, and user-centric identity models (such as LiveID and OpenID). In addition to supporting Windows authentication, it also supports Forms-Based Authentication (FBA) and Security Assertion Markup Language (SAML) token-based authentication.

Configuring Anonymous Access

In some instances, you might need to configure *anonymous access*, whereby users can access SharePoint content without validating user identities. This is similar to most Web sites that can be accessed on the Internet without logging in.

To help maintain security, anonymous access is disabled by default. Therefore, any user who tries to use anonymous access is automatically rejected without the actual request being processed. To enable anonymous access, you must configure the following settings:

- Anonymous authentication for the Web application
- Permissions assigned to anonymous users for sites, lists, and libraries
- Anonymous access restriction policies for the Web application's zones

You can enable anonymous authentication when you create a Web application or after creating a Web application. You just have to click **Yes** for the **Allow Anonymous** setting on the Create New Web Application page. When you enable anonymous authentication for a Web application, SharePoint automatically enables anonymous authentication for the Web site in IIS. As with other IIS Web site settings, you should not make the change directly in IIS Manager. Lastly, to grant access for anonymous, IIS uses the IUSR_*computername* account to provide users with access to resources under the IUSR account.

⊖ ENABLE ANONYMOUS AUTHENTICATION FOR A WEB APPLICATION

GET READY. To enable anonymous authentication for a Web application, perform the following steps:

1. Open Central Administration.
2. Click Application Management.
3. In the Web Applications section, click Manage Web Applications. The Web Applications Management page displays (see Figure 11-1).

Figure 11-1

The Web Applications Management page

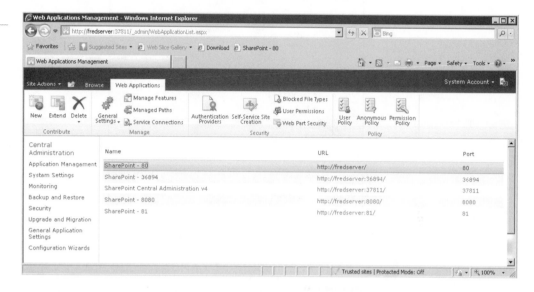

4. Click the Web application for which you want to enable or disable anonymous access.
5. On the Ribbon, click Authentication Providers. The Authentication Providers dialog displays (see Figure 11-2).

Figure 11-2

The Authentication Providers dialog

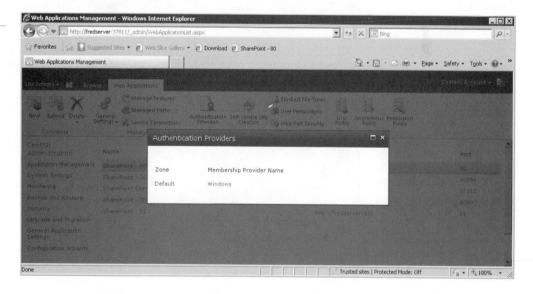

6. Click the name of the zone (such as Default) for which you want to enable or disable anonymous access. The Edit Authentication page displays (see Figure 11-3).
7. Select or clear the Enable anonymous access check box. (The enable anonymous access is deselected by default.) Click Save at the bottom of the page.

Now that the Web application is not ready to accept anonymous access, you need to grant permissions so that the IUSR account can access content. Of course, before you grant permissions to anonymous users to access content, you should consider the security implications to make sure that there is not sensitive data that will be opened up to everyone.

Figure 11-3

The Edit Authentication page

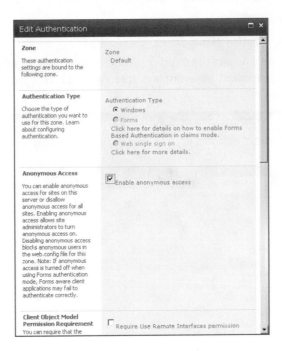

 GRANT PERMISSIONS TO ANONYMOUS USERS

GET READY. To grant permissions to anonymous users, perform the following steps:

1. Open the Site Actions menu and click Site Permissions. The Permissions page displays (see Figure 11-4).

Figure 11-4

The Permissions page

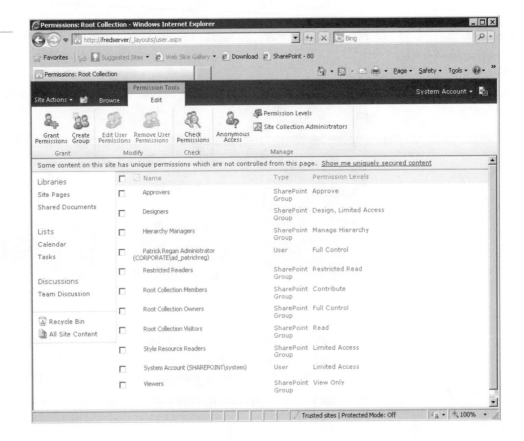

2. On the Ribbon, click Anonymous Access. The Anonymous Access page displays (see Figure 11-5).

Figure 11-5

The Anonymous Access page

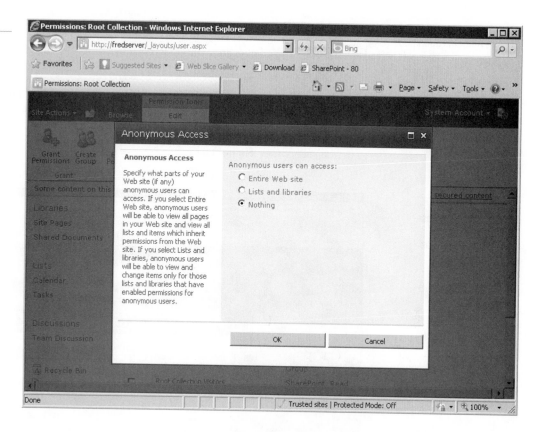

3. In the Anonymous users can access group, choose one of the following options:
- Entire Web Site: Anonymous users can view content on the entire Web site.
- Lists and libraries: Anonymous users can view content in certain lists or libraries.
- Nothing: Anonymous users have no access to the site. This is the default value.

4. Click OK.

You shouldn't configure anonymous access at the per-list and library level. Instead, you should design your site structure so that content that should be accessed by anonymous users is in separate sites.

 GRANT ANONYMOUS ACCESS TO A LIST OR LIBRARY

GET READY. To grant anonymous access to a list or library, perform the following steps:

1. Navigate to a list or library for which you want to configure anonymous access.

2. On the Ribbon, click the List tab or the Library tab.

3. Click the List Permissions button or Library Permissions button. The Permissions page displays.

4. Click Stop Inheriting Permissions.

5. Click Anonymous Access. The Anonymous Access page displays.

6. In the Anonymous Users Can list, select the check boxes for the permissions you want to assign to anonymous users. In a document library, anonymous users cannot be granted add, edit, or delete item permission; anonymous users can only view.

7. Click OK.

Farm administrators can enforce permissions related to anonymous access across all sites in a Web application by using anonymous access restrictions.

 CONFIGURE ANONYMOUS ACCESS RESTRICTIONS

GET READY. To configure anonymous access restrictions, perform the following steps:

1. Open Central Administration.
2. Click Web Applications. The Web Applications page displays.
3. Select the Web application that you want to configure.
4. On the Ribbon, click Anonymous Policy. The Anonymous Access Restrictions page displays (see Figure 11-6).

Figure 11-6

The Anonymous Access Restrictions page

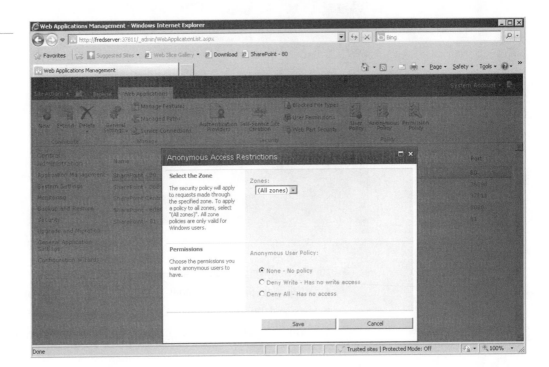

5. In the Zones list, select (All zones) or select the zone to which the policy will apply.
6. In the Permissions section, click one of the following options:
   • None—No Policy: No policy is defined. Instead, access will be determined by permissions granted to sites, lists, and libraries.
   • Deny Write—Has no write access: Anonymous users will be unable to modify content. This policy overrides access granted on content within the Web application.
   • Deny All—Has no access: This policy overrides all permissions granted on content within a Web application. As a result, anonymous users will not have access.
7. Click Save.

Configuring and Managing NTLM

As described in Lesson 5, *NTLM* (NT LAN Manager) is a suite of Microsoft security protocols that provides authentication, integrity, and confidentiality to users. NTLM is an integrated single sign-on mechanism. NTLM is the most established form of authentication found in Windows and is the easiest to implement.

Although Kerberos is the default authentication protocol for today's domain computers, NTLM is the default authentication protocol for Windows NT, stand-alone computers that are not part of a domain, and situations in which you are authenticating to a server using an IP address. NTLM also acts as a fallback authentication protocol if Kerberos authentication cannot be completed, such as when it is blocked by a firewall.

NTLM uses a challenge-response mechanism for authentication in which clients prove their identities without sending a password to the server. After a random, eight-byte challenge message is sent to the client from the server, the client uses the user's password as a key to generate a response back to the server using an MD4/MD5 hashing algorithm (one-way mathematical calculation) and DES encryption (a commonly used encryption algorithm that encrypted and decrypted data with the same key).

As covered in Lesson 5, NTLM is slightly less secure than Kerberos. However, it is the easiest to set up since it works out of the box.

Configuring and Managing Kerberos

Kerberos protocol is a secure protocol that supports ticketing authentication. While Kerberos is considered more secure than NTLM, it is more complicated than NTLM in that it requires additional configuration—such as requiring a service principal name (SPN) for the domain account that SharePoint is using.

When you create a Web application in SharePoint, you can choose between Negotiate or NTLM. The Negotiate authentication method will first attempt to use Kerberos authentication. If Kerberos authentication is not supported by the client, authentication falls back to NTLM.

When a user logs in to a network resource using Kerberos, the client transmits the username to the authentication server, along with the identity of the service the user wants to connect to (for example, a file server or a SharePoint server). The authentication server constructs a ticket, which contains a randomly generated session key, which is encrypted with the file server's secret key. The ticket is then sent to the client as part of its credentials, which includes the session key encrypted with the client's key/password. If the user types the right password, the client can decrypt the session key, present the ticket to the file or SharePoint server, and give the user the shared secret session key to communicate between them. Tickets are time-stamped and typically expire after only a few hours.

For all of this to work and to ensure security, the domain controllers and clients must have the same time. Windows operating systems include the Time Service tool (W32Time service). Kerberos authentication will work if the time interval between the relevant computers is within the maximum enabled time parameters. The default is five minutes. You can also turn off the Time Service tool and install a third-party time service. Of course, if you have problems authenticating, you should make sure that the time is correct for the domain controllers and the client that is experiencing the problem.

Kerberos offers several benefits. When the client connects to a server or service, Kerberos uses the current client ticket proving that the client is authenticated. As a result, the service does not have to perform authentication to a domain controller. In addition, Kerberos can perform a double-hop authentication, which forwards Kerberos tickets from one service to a supporting service. Both of these improved authentication performance.

To secure the double-hop authentication, you can configure Kerberos constrained delegation. Constrained delegation restricts which services are allowed to delegate user credentials by specifying, for each application pool or service, the services to which a Kerberos ticket can be forwarded.

When a client wants to connect to a Web application that uses Kerberos authentication, the client request connects by specifying the service's *service principal name (SPN)*. The SPN is made up of three components:

1. The service class, which is always HTTP. HTTP includes both the HTTP and HTTPS protocols.
2. The host name.
3. The port (if port 80 is not being used).

To establish an SPN for https://portal.contoso.com on port 443, you would use HTTP/portal.contoso.com:443.

When a domain controller's KDC receives the service ticket request from a client, it looks up the requested SPN. The KDC then creates a session key for the service and encrypts the session key with the password of the account with which the SPN is associated. The KDC issues a service ticket, containing the session key, to the client. The client presents the service ticket to the service. The service, which knows its own password, decrypts the session key and authentication is complete.

If a client submits a service ticket request for an SPN that does not exist in the identity store, no service ticket can be established and the client throws an access denied error. For this reason, each component of a SharePoint infrastructure that uses Kerberos authentication requires at least one SPN. For example, the intranet Web application app pool account must have an SPN of HTTP/intranet.contoso.com.

The SPN is associated with the application pool, not the server. In addition, for each Web application, you should assign two SPNs, one with the fully qualified domain name for the service, and one with the NetBIOS name of the service.

You can use ADSI Edit to add SPNs to an account. To configure an SPN for a service or application pool account, you must have domain administrative permissions or a delegation to modify the servicePrincipalName property. In addition, you must run ADSI Edit from a domain controller or load the Windows Server 2008 R2 Remote Server Administration Tools feature.

 ADD AN SPN TO AN ACCOUNT

GET READY. To add an SPN to an account, perform the following steps:

1. Click Start > Administrative Tools > ADSI Edit.
2. Right-click ADSI Edit in the console tree, and then click Connect To (see Figure 11-7).

Figure 11-7

Right-clicking ADSI Edit

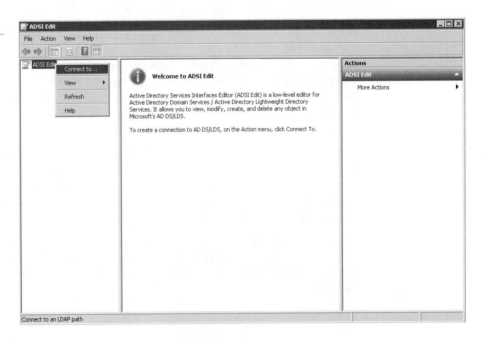

3. When the Connection Settings dialog displays, click OK (see Figure 11-8).

Figure 11-8

The Connections Settings dialog

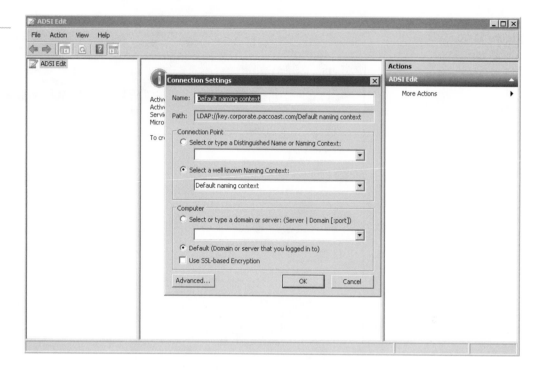

4. Expand Default Naming Context in the console tree, expand the domain, and then expand the nodes representing the OUs in which the account exists. Click the OU in which the account exists.

5. In the Details pane, right-click the service or application pool account and then click Properties (see Figure 11-9).

Figure 11-9

Selecting account properties

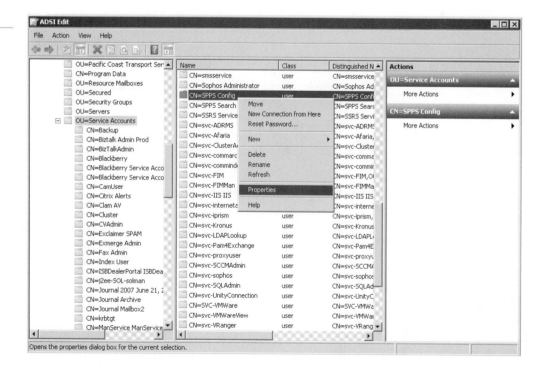

6. In the Attributes list, double-click servicePrincipalName to display the Multi-valued String Editor dialog (see Figure 11-10).

Figure 11-10

Adding SPN

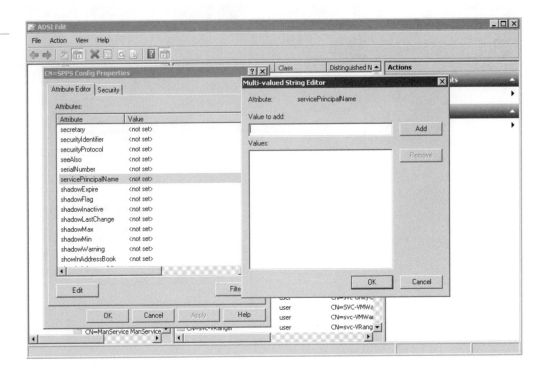

7. In the Value to add field, type the SPN and then click Add.
8. Click OK twice.

Alternatively, you can use the setspn.exe to add SPNs to an account. The syntax is as follows:

```
setspn <domain\user> -s <SPN>
```

Whereby:

- <domain\user> identifies the security principal to which you want to add an SPN.
- <SPN> is the service principal name that you want to add.

For example, to add SPNs for the intranet Web application to the app pool account, type the following commands:

```
setspn CONTOSO\SP_WebApps -s HTTP/portal.contoso.com
```

```
setspn CONTOSO\SP_WebApps -s HTTP/portal
```

Enabling Basic Authentication

Basic Authentication is a simple authentication protocol that sends a username and password over the network in clear text. Since clear text can be read by any protocol analyzer that sees the packets, it is considered unsecure. Therefore, to make it secure, Basic Authentication is often used with SSL certificates to provide encryption.

X REF

Installing a digital certificate and enabling SSL was discussed in Lesson 5.

Certain browsers and connection scenarios (such as users working behind certain proxy servers) will not support NTLM and Kerberos. In this situation, you have no choice but to use Basic Authentication. Of course, you should always enable Secure Sockets Layer (SSL) encryption.

You cannot select Basic Authentication when you create a SharePoint Web application. Instead, you must do so after creating the Web application.

 ENABLE BASIC AUTHENTICATION

GET READY. To enable Basic Authentication, perform the following steps:

1. Open Central Administration.
2. Click Application Management.
3. In the Web Applications section, click Manage Web Applications. The Web Applications Management page displays.
4. Click the name of the Web application for which you want to enable Basic Authentication.
5. On the Ribbon, click Authentication Providers. The Authentication Providers page displays.
6. Click the name of the zone for which you want to enable Basic Authentication. The Edit Authentication page displays.
7. In the IIS Authentication Settings section, select the Basic Authentication check box (see Figure 11-11).

Figure 11-11

Selecting the Basic Authentication option

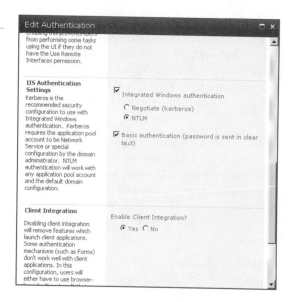

8. At the bottom of the page, click Save.

Configuring and Managing Claims-Based Authentication

Claims-Based Authentication, introduced with SharePoint 2010, is a flexible framework based on Security Assertion Markup Language (SAML) tokens and is built on the Windows Identity Foundation (WIF). Tokens are used to identify a user's identity and are generated by a trusted authentication provider such as Windows, Windows Live ID, or Active Directory Federated Services 2.0. By extending the reach of trusted authentication providers, you can provide authentication for Windows-based systems and systems that are not Windows based.

When a user needs to access a server (such as a file server or a SharePoint server), he will use a claim that asserts information about him, including his identity and group membership. The Web application accepts a claim and translates the claim into the SharePoint User object. While Classic Mode Authentication relies on IIS to pass the user's Windows security token to the Web application, in Claims-Based Authentication, the Web application relies on the farm's Security Token Service (STS) to deliver a token that contains claims, including claims about the user's identity.

Different than what you might think, STS does not actually perform authentication. Instead, it relies on a trusted authority, such as Active Directory or a number of other authentication providers.

- If the claims based application uses the Windows authentication provider, the STS performs essentially the same function as IIS does in Classic Mode Authentication.
- If Kerberos is available, the service ticket is processed and turned into a set of claims about the user's identity and group memberships.
- If NTLM, Basic, or Digest authentication are used, STS authenticates the credentials against Active Directory and then the NT token is translated into a set of claims about the user's identity and group memberships.

The resulting claims are provided to the Web application as a token that is translated into a SPUser object within the Web application.

One advantage of using claims: if you need to give access to a partner, you can use SAML to authenticate users against credentials stored in Active Directory Federated Services 2.0 (ADFS 2.0), by Windows Live ID, or by a custom trusted source. Claims-Based Authentication thus allows SharePoint Web applications to be extended to more diverse sets of users across domains, forests, and non-Windows environments. You can change the authentication provider or the methods of authentication without changing the Web application itself.

When you attempt to access a Web application that uses Claims-Based Authentication, you are transparently redirected to a sign-in page for the STS, at which you are authenticated. In some cases, such as Windows authentication, you might never even see this transaction when your browser's security settings are configured to authenticate silently to trusted sites or when the Web site is in a trusted zone. STS authenticates you and provides a token to your browser. Your browser then returns to the original Web site, submits the token, and the Web application then knows who you are.

In SharePoint, the Web application is configured to trust STS. In addition, in an AD DS domain, each component of Windows trusts the local security subsystem, which, in turn, trusts the domain—which, in turn, trusts other domains in the forest and means that the system trusts other domains in the forest.

While a claim can provide user and group information, it can also include other information. For example, it can include email addresses, department names, job titles, ages, genders, or telephone numbers. The Web application does not need to maintain local copies of the attributes, nor does it need to look up attributes in an external source. Instead, STS is configured to collect the attributes and to create claims. An advantage of Claims-Based Authentication is that it reduces the burden on applications by not having to maintain or look up information about users.

Lastly, you can assign permissions to content which are based on a claim and you can use claims to find users. Therefore, you can specify what users can make changes to other users or what users can view certain content.

⊕ **CREATE A WEB APPLICATION WITH WINDOWS-CLAIMS AUTHENTICATION**

GET READY. To create a Web application with Windows-Claims Authentication, perform the following steps:

1. Open Central Administration.

2. Click Application Management. The Application Management page displays.

3. In the Web Applications section, click Manage Web Applications.

4. On the Ribbon, click New to display the Create New Web Application page.

5. In the Authentication section, select Claims Based Authentication (see Figure 11-12).

Figure 11-12

Selecting the Claims Based Authentication option

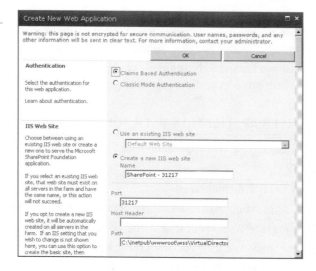

6. In the Claims Authentication Types section, select the Enable Windows Authentication check box.

7. If you want to use NTLM or Kerberos as the authentication method, select the Integrated Windows Authentication check box. Then, in the drop-down menu, select Negotiate (Kerberos) or NTLM.

8. If you want users' credentials to be sent over a network in a nonencrypted form, select the Basic Authentication (Password Is Sent In Clear Text) check box. If you use Basic Authentication, you should select Yes to Use Secure Sockets Layer (SSL) option.

9. Configure other settings for the new Web application.

10. Click the OK button at the bottom of the page.

Configuring and Managing Forms-Based Authentication

Forms-Based Authentication (FBA) is an identity management system that is based on ASP.NET membership and role provider authentication. When an unauthenticated user attempts to access a SharePoint Web application that is configured for FBA, that user doesn't see a popup login box; the user is redirected to a logon form/page to which the user submits credentials. The credentials are authenticated against an identity store, such as AD DS, an SQL Server database, or an LDAP data store, such as Active Directory Lightweight Directory Services (AD LDS), Novell eDirectory, Novell Directory Services (NDS), or Sun ONE.

CERTIFICATION READY
What type of
authentication has the
credentials entered on
a logon page and can
be authenticated with
AD DS or an SQL Server
database?
2.3.4

SharePoint Server 2010 uses the standard ASP.NET membership provider interface to authenticate the user and uses the standard ASP.NET role manager interface to gather group information about the user. Each ASP.NET role is treated as a domain group by the authorization process in SharePoint Server 2010. The resulting information about the user is converted into claims by the STS, thus FBA is also called Forms-Claims Authentication.

To configure FBA, perform the following steps:

1. The Web application's authentication mode must be configured as Claims-Based Authentication.
2. You must modify the web.config file of the Security Token Service (STS), the component that actually performs the authentication so that it knows which provider and data source to use.
3. You must modify the web.config file of the Web application's IIS site to register the membership provider and role manager.
4. You must modify the web.config file of the Central Administration IIS site to register the membership provider and the role manager.

CREATE A WEB APPLICATION WITH FORMS-CLAIMS AUTHENTICATION

GET READY. To create a Web application with Forms-Claims Authentication, perform the following steps:

1. Open Central Administration.
2. Click Application Management. The Application Management page displays.
3. Click Manage Web Applications. The Manage Web Applications page displays.
4. On the Ribbon, click New. The Create New Web Application page displays.
5. In the Authentication section, click Claims Based Authentication.
6. Specify if you want to allow anonymous or to use Secure Sockets Layer (SSL).
7. Select Create a new IIS site.
8. In the Port text box, type a port. In the Host Header text box, type a host header (if necessary).
9. Leave the Enable Windows Authentication option selected and the Integrated Windows authentication option selected. Select either NTLM or Negotiate (Kerberos).
10. If necessary, select Basic authentication.
11. In the Claims Authentication Types section, select the Enable Forms Based Authentication (FBA) check box (see Figure 11-13).

WARNING If you clear the Enable Windows Authentication check box, the "If Windows authentication is not selected on any Zone of this Web application" warning appears and the crawling for this Web application will be disabled. The crawler requires a zone that uses Windows authentication to index SharePoint content.

Figure 11-13

Selecting the Enable Forms Based Authentication (FBA) option

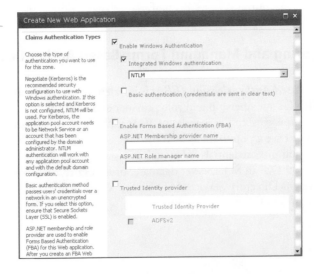

12. Type names for the ASP.NET membership provider and the role manager.

TAKE NOTE* Remember the names that you have typed because you will need to refer to them in the web.config file. Also, keep in mind that these names are case-sensitive.

13. Select the Default Sign In Page option or select the Custom Sign in Page option and then select the URL for the sign in page (see Figure 11-14).

Figure 11-14

Selecting the Sign In Page URL options

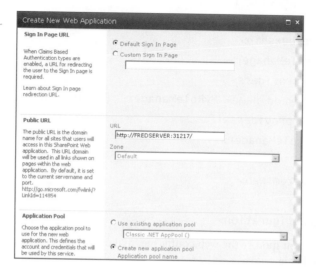

14. Specify the Public URL and Application Pool settings.

15. In the Database Name and Authentication section, specify the Database Server settings and the Database Name settings.

16. Select if you will be using Windows Authentication or SQL authentication. If you select SQL authentication, specify the SQL Account and Password.

17. If necessary, specify the name of the failover database server in the Failover Database Server text box.

18. Click OK.

After you have successfully created a Web application that uses Claims-Based Authentication, you must manually configure the specifics of the authentication provider by modifying the web.config file of the IIS site. Parts of the web.config file are:

```
<configuration>
. . .
  <SharePoint>
    <PeoplePickerWildcards>
      <clear />
      <add key="AspNetSqlMembershipProvider" value="%" />
      <add key="MyMembershipProvider" value="*"/>
      <add key="MyRoleManager" value="*"/>
    </PeoplePickerWildcards>
  </SharePoint>
```

```
<connectionStrings>
    <add name="MyConnectionString" [define the connection] />
</connectionStrings>
<system.web>

. . .

  <membership>
    <providers>
      <add name="MyMembershipProvider" [define the membership
      provider] />
    </providers>
  </membership>
    <roleManager>
      <providers>
        <add name="MyRoleManager" [define the role manager] />
      </providers>
    </roleManager>

. . .

  </system.web>

. . .

</configuration>
```

Any time you modify the web.config file, make only the changes specified by instructions
from a reliable source.

 CONFIGURE THE WEB.CONFIG FILE FOR THE CENTRAL ADMINISTRATION

GET READY. To configure the web.config file for the Central Administration, perform the following steps:

1. Start IIS Manager by typing INETMGR at a command prompt.
2. Go to the SharePoint Central Administration site in IIS.
3. Right-click SharePoint Central Administration and then click Explore.
4. Open the web.config file with Notepad.
5. Find the <Configuration> <system.Web> nodes and type the following entry:

```
<membership defaultProvider="AspNetSqlMembershipProvider ">
  <providers>
    <add name="membership"
    type="Microsoft.Office.Server.Security.LdapMembershipProvider,
    Microsoft.Office.Server, Version=14.0.0.0, Culture=neutral,
    PublicKeyToken=71e9bce111e9429c"
    server="yourserver.com"
    port="389"
    useSSL="false"
    userDNAttribute="distinguishedName"
    userNameAttribute="sAMAccountName"
    userContainer="OU=UserAccounts,DC=internal,DC=yourcompany,DC=
    distinguishedName (of your userContainer)"userObjectClass="person"
    userFilter="(ObjectClass=person)"
```

```
        scope="Subtree"
        otherRequiredUserAttributes="sn,givenname,cn" />
    </providers>
  </membership>
  <roleManager enabled="true"
  defaultProvider="AspNetWindowsTokenRoleProvider">
    <providers>
      <add name="LdapRole"
      type="Microsoft.Office.Server.Security.LdapRoleProvider,
      Microsoft.Office.Server, Version=14.0.0.0, Culture=neutral,
      PublicKeyToken=71e9bce111e9429c"
      server="yourserver.com"
      port="389"
      useSSL="false"
      groupContainer="DC=internal,DC=yourcompany,DC=distinguishedName
      (of your groupContainer)"
      groupNameAttribute="cn"
      groupNameAlternateSearchAttribute="samAccountName"
      groupMemberAttribute="member"
      userNameAttribute="sAMAccountName"
      dnAttribute="distinguishedName"
      groupFilter="((ObjectClass=group)"
      userFilter="((ObjectClass=person)"
      scope="Subtree" />
    </providers>
  </roleManager>
```

6. Save the changes.

⊙→ **CONFIGURE THE WEB.CONFIG FILE FOR THE SECURITY TOKEN SERVICE**

GET READY. To configure the web.config file for the Security Token Service Web application, perform the following steps:

1. Start IIS Manager by typing INETMGR at a command prompt.
2. Go to the SharePoint Web Services site in IIS.
3. Go to the Security TokenServiceApplication subsite.
4. Right-click SecurityTokenServiceAppliction and then click Explore.
5. Open the web.config file with Notepad.
6. Find the <Configuration> <system.Web> nodes and type the following entry:

```
<membership defaultProvider="AspNetSqlMembershipProvider">
  <providers>
    <add name="membership"
    type="Microsoft.Office.Server.Security.LdapMembershipProvider,
    Microsoft.Office.Server, Version=14.0.0.0, Culture=neutral,
    PublicKeyToken=71e9bce111e9429c"
    server="yourserver.com"
    port="389"
    useSSL="false"
```

```
                    userDNAttribute="distinguishedName"
                    userNameAttribute="sAMAccountName"
                    userContainer="OU=UserAccounts,DC=internal,DC=yourcompany,
                    DC=distinguishedName (of your
                    userContainer)"userObjectClass="person"
                    userFilter="(ObjectClass=person)"
                    scope="Subtree"
                    otherRequiredUserAttributes="sn,givenname,cn" />
            </providers>
        </membership>
        <roleManager enabled="true"
          <providers>
                    <add name="LdapRole"
                    type="Microsoft.Office.Server.Security.LdapRoleProvider,
                    Microsoft.Office.Server, Version=14.0.0.0, Culture=neutral,
                    PublicKeyToken=71e9bce111e9429c"
                    server="yourserver.com"
                    port="389"
                    useSSL="false"
                    groupContainer="DC=internal,DC=yourcompany,DC=
                    distinguishedName (of your groupContainer)"
                    groupNameAttribute="cn"
                    groupNameAlternateSearchAttribute="samAccountName"
                    groupMemberAttribute="member"
                    userNameAttribute="sAMAccountName"
                    dnAttribute="distinguishedName"
                    groupFilter="((ObjectClass=group)"
                    userFilter="((ObjectClass=person)"
                    scope="Subtree" />
            </providers>
        </roleManager>
```

7. Save the changes.

⊙➔ **CONFIGURE THE WEB.CONFIG FILE FOR THE SHAREPOINT WEB APPLICATION**

GET READY. To configure the web.config file for the SharePoint Web application, perform the following steps:

1. Start IIS Manager by typing INETMGR at a command prompt.
2. Go to the Claims Forms site.
3. Right-click SecurityTokenServiceAppliction and then click Explore.
4. Open the web.config file with Notepad.
5. Find the <Configuration> <system.web> section.
6. Find the <membership defaultProvider="i"> section and type the following entry:

```
    <add name="LdapMember"
        type="Microsoft.Office.Server.Security.LdapMembershipProvider,
        Microsoft.Office.Server, Version=14.0.0.0, Culture=neutral,
        PublicKeyToken=71e9bce111e9429c"
```

```
        server="yourserver.com"
        port="389"
        useSSL="false"
        userDNAttribute="distinguishedName"
        userNameAttribute="sAMAccountName"
        userContainer="OU=UserAccounts,DC=internal,
        DC=yourcompany,DC=com"
        userObjectClass="person"
        userFilter="(&amp;(ObjectClass=person))"
        scope="Subtree"
        otherRequiredUserAttributes="sn,givenname,cn"/>
```

7. Find the `<roleManager defaultProvider="c" enabled="ttrue" cacheRolesInCookie="false">` section and type the following entry:

```
    <add name="LdapRole"
        type="Microsoft.Office.Server.Security.LdapRoleProvider,
        Microsoft.Office.Server, Version=14.0.0.0, Culture=neutral,
        PublicKeyToken=71e9bce111e9429c"
        server="yourserver.com"
        port="389"
        useSSL="false"
        groupContainer="DC=internal,DC=yourcompany,DC=com"
        groupNameAttribute="cn"
        groupNameAlternateSearchAttribute="samAccountName"
        groupMemberAttribute="member"
        userNameAttribute="sAMAccountName"
        dnAttribute="distinguishedName"
        groupFilter="(&amp;(ObjectClass=group))"
        userFilter="(&amp;(ObjectClass=person))"
        scope="Subtree" />
```

Converting Web Applications to Claims-Based Authentication

If you create a Web application with Classic Mode Authentication, you can convert the Web application to Claims-Based Authentication. In addition, if you upgrade a SharePoint 2007 Web application that uses FBA, the upgraded Web application will be configured to use Classic-Mode Authentication and FBA will not function. Therefore, must convert the Web application to Claims-Based Authentication.

TAKE NOTE*

You cannot convert a Web application from Claims-Based Authentication to Classic-Mode Authentication.

To convert a Web application to Claims-Based Authentication, use PowerShell to first convert the authentication type and then to migrate the users and permissions. As with any Web application that you upgrade, it is highly recommended that you test the process in a lab environment.

To change the authentication type, execute the following commands in the SharePoint 2010 Management Shell, (whereby `<WebApplicationURL>` is the URL of the Web application that you want to convert to Claims-Based Authentication):

```
$w = Get-SPWebApplication "http://<WebApplicationURL>/"
$w.UseClaimsAuthentication = 1
$w.Update()
$w.ProvisionGlobally()
```

To migrate users and permissions, execute the following commands in the SharePoint 2010 Management Shell, (whereby `<WebApplicationURL>` is the URL of the Web application for which you want to migrate users and permissions):

```
$w = Get-SPWebApplication "http://<WebApplicationURL>/"
$w.MigrateUsers(True)
```

Configuring and Managing Secure Store Service (SSS)

The **Secure Store Service** (SSS) is a service application that acts as a credential manager. It is needed by various service applications, including PerformancePoint, to connect to external data sources on behalf of users or groups using the unattended service account.

CERTIFICATION READY
What Service Application acts as a credential manger that is needed for PerformancePoint and other Service Applications?
2.3.5

Much like you do with other service applications, you should configure the Secure Store Service as part of the initial farm configuration. Fortunately, when you configure SSS, you need only to open the Service Application and generate a new key. The key is used to encrypt and decrypt the credentials that are stored in the Secure Store database. When you generate the key, you must specify a passphrase for the hash. Be certain to record this passphrase in a safe place.

 CONFIGURE THE SECURE STORE SERVICE (SSS)

GET READY. To configure the Secure Store Service (SSS), perform the following steps:

1. Open Central Administration and, in the Application Management section, click Manage Service Applications.

2. From the list of service applications, select Secure Store Service Application. The Secure Store Service Application page displays (see Figure 11-15). If the Secure Store Service application doesn't display in the list of service applications, you'll have to create the service application and its associated proxy.

Figure 11-15

The Secure Store Service Application page

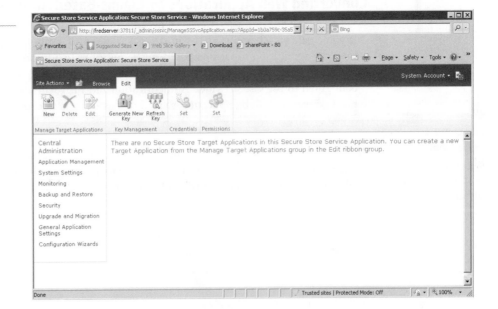

3. In the Key Management group, click Generate New Key. The Generate New Key page displays (see Figure 11-16), requesting a pass phrase from which a new key is generated.

Figure 11-16

The Generate New Key page

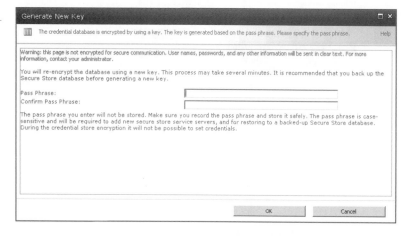

4. In the Pass Phrase text box and the Confirm Pass Phrase text box, type your pass phrase. The pass phrase must be a strong password consisting of at least three of the following: an uppercase character, a lowercase character, a number, and a special character. Examples include T1g3rRoar5! and TTm#AS53.

5. Click OK.

Configuring Active Directory Federation Services (AD FS)

Active Directory Federation Services (AD FS) provides secure sharing of digital identity and permissions across security and enterprise boundaries (such as outside forests, outside domains, and with remote networks. AD FS expands single sign-on (SSO) functionality within a single security or enterprise boundary or with Internet applications, customers, and partners.

CERTIFICATION READY
What form of authentication allows access to other Web sites and services from within SharePoint while providing single sign-on?
2.3.6

The AD FS service provides extensible, reliable, scalable, and secure identity federation and supports SAML token types as well as other client authentication methods (such as Kerberos, X.500) and username/password methods. AD FS can also use multiple identity store types, including Active Directory Domain Services (AD DS) and Active Directory Lightweight Directory Services (AD LDS). In other words, you can use AD FS to configure SharePoint to connect to a Web service that is internal or external and AD FS will authenticate using Windows authentication. Windows Live ID authentication is another example of federated identity. You can configure SharePoint's STS to trust tokens issued by Windows Live ID, just as some Microsoft sites do.

When a user attempts to access a Web site, he or she is redirected to the AD FS Web site, which issues a token. The AD FS token is then presented to SharePoint, which can augment the token with additional claims before giving the client the token. The token is is then submitted to the Web application.

AD FS 2.0 is included with Windows Server 2008 R2 as a role (see Figure 11-17). The AD FS administrator then runs a wizard to configure AF DS. The last task that the AD FS administrator must complete is to provide the digital certificate to the SharePoint administrator so that that SharePoint administrator can use the digital certificate when configuring SharePoint to use AD FS.

When configuring SharePoint to use AD FS, you must acquire the digital certificate, which you then place on the local drive. Second, you need a Web application that was created using Claims-Based Authentication. Then to configure AD FS, you will configure SharePoint using the SharePoint PowerShell.

Figure 11-17

Adding the AD FS role

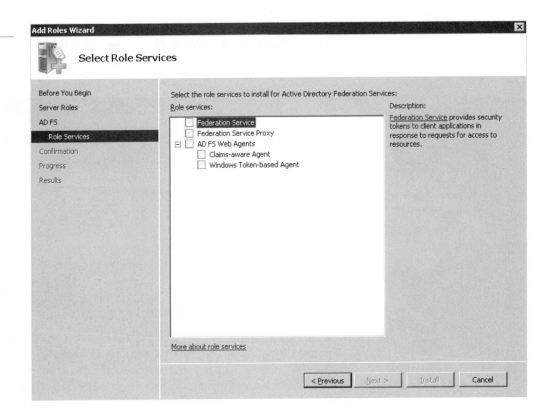

CONFIGURE SHAREPOINT TO USE AD FS

GET READY. To configure SharePoint to use AD FS, perform the following steps:

1. Click Start > Microsoft SharePoint 2010 Products > SharePoint 2010 Management Shell.

2. To add the Digital certificate, execute the following two commands at the shell:

   ```
   $certPath = "<path to cert>\<cert>.cer"
   $cert = New-Object System.Security.Cryptography.X509Certificates.
   X509Certificate2("$certPath")
   ```

3. To create a new trusted root authority provider within SharePoint, execute the following command:

   ```
   New-SPTrustedRootAuthority "ADFS Token Signing
   Trusted Root Authority" -Certificate $cert
   ```

4. A new claim-type mapping will uniquely identify the user (such as a user name or email address). To create a new claim-type mapping to an email address, execute the following command:

   ```
   $map1 = New-SPClaimTypeMapping -IncomingClaimType
   "http://schemas.xmlsoap.org/ws/2005/05/identity/claims/
   emailaddress" -
   IncomingClaimTypeDisplayName "EmailAddress" -SameAsIncoming
   ```

5. To specify the realm or unique URI for your site and the sign-in URL for your site, execute the following two commands:

   ```
   $realm = "https://www.fredserver.contoso.com"
   $signinurl = "https://fredserver.contoso.com/adfs/ls"
   ```

6. To create the actually trusted identity token issuer (provider), execute the following command:

```
$ap = New-SPTrustedIdentityTokenIssuer -Name
"ADFSv2" -Description "ADFSv2 Federated Identity" -
Realm $realm -ImportTrustCertificate $cert -
ClaimsMappings $map1 -SignInUrl $signinurl -
IdentifierClaim $map1.InputClaimType
```

After SharePoint has been configured for AD FS, you can open Central Administration and click **Manage Web Applications**. When you click on a Web application and click the **Authentication Providers** button in the Ribbon, you can choose the zone you want to configure, select **Trusted Identity Provider**, and then select the AD FS identity provider.

SKILL SUMMARY

IN THIS LESSON, YOU LEARNED:

- Authentication is the act of confirming identity of a user and is an essential part of authorization.

- Authentication providers are software components that support specific authentication methods. You can configure a Web application to support many different types of authentication depending on the access method.

- Classic-Mode Authentication is the same type of authentication used in SharePoint Server 2007.

- Claims-Based Authentication is a new authentication mode that is built on the Windows Identity Foundation (WIF) and that uses an identity system that allows users to present claims that include information about who the user is and what system and content the user can access.

- NTLM is slightly less secure than Kerberos. However, it is the easiest to set up since it works out of the box.

- The Kerberos protocol is a secure protocol that supports ticketing authentication. While Kerberos is considered more secure than NTLM, it is more complicated than NTLM in that requires additional configuration (such as requiring a service principal name (SPN) for the domain account that SharePoint is using).

- Basic Authentication is a simple authentication protocol that sends a username and password over the network in clear text.

- Forms-based Authentication (FBA) is an identity management system that is based on ASP.NET membership and role provider authentication. When an unauthenticated user attempts to access a SharePoint Web application that is configured for FBA, the user doesn't see a popup login box; the user is redirected to a logon form/page to which the user submits credentials.

- The Secure Store Service is a service application that acts as a credential manager. It is needed by various service applications, including PerformancePoint, to connect to external data sources on behalf of users or groups using the unattended service account.

- Active Directory Federation Service (AD FS) provides secure sharing of digital identity and permissions across security and enterprise boundaries. AD FS expands single sign-on (SSO) functionality within a single security or enterprise boundary or with Internet applications, customers, and partners.

Knowledge Assessment

Fill in the Blank

Complete the following sentences by writing the correct word or words in the blanks provided.

1. _____ Authentication was also available in SharePoint Server 2007.

2. The Claims-Based Authentication is built on the _____ and uses an identity system that allows users to present claims which include information about who the user is.

3. _____ is an authentication type that is the easiest to implement and is the default authentication for SharePoint 2010.

4. When you configure Kerberos, the user connects to the service via _____.

5. The _____ mode sends a username and password over the network in clear text.

6. _____ is an identity management system that is based on ASP.NET membership and role provider authentication, and it provides a Web form for users to supply usernames and passwords.

7. To enable Forms-based Authentication, you must configure the _____ file.

8. _____ provides secure sharing of digital identity and permissions across a security and enterprise boundary.

9. _____ are software components that support specific authentication methods.

10. To access a Web site or service through SharePoint using the same credentials but a different domain, you would use _____.

Multiple Choice

Circle the letter that corresponds to the best answer.

1. If you want a user to access SharePoint without logging in, you should use _____ authentication.
   a. anonymous
   b. digest
   c. NTLM
   d. Forms-Based

2. What account does the anonymous authentication use to access resources?
   a. domain\administrator
   b. computername\administrator
   c. IUSR_computername
   d. ASP_Net

3. What is used to enforce permissions across all sites in a Web application when using anonymous access?
   a. group policy
   b. anonymous access restrictions
   c. collection template
   d. access guideline

4. What command is used to add an SPN to an account?
   a. spn.exe
   b. setspnum.exe
   c. adsi.exe
   d. setspn.exe

5. To protect your Web site when using Basic Authentication, you should use _____.
   a. Basic encryption
   b. Kerberos
   c. Digest translation
   d. SSL

6. What type of tokens does WIF use when using Claims-Based Authentication?
   a. Game
   b. Security Assertion Markup Language (SAML)
   c. WIF
   d. Live ID

7. Which service application, including PerformancePoint, acts as a credential manager?
   a. NTLM
   b. AD FS
   c. SSL
   d. Secure Store Service (SSS)

8. When you configure the Secure Store Service, you must _____.
   a. assign the permissions to the Secure Store Service
   b. generate a seeding code
   c. generate a new key
   d. install a digital certificate

9. What is the act of confirming identity of a user and is an essential part used in authorization?
   a. negotiate
   b. auditing
   c. authentication
   d. accounting

10. When you configure the SPN for a SharePoint app pool account, you need to define the host name, port, and _____.
    a. encryption method
    b. authentication method
    c. token password
    d. service class

True / False

Circle T if the statement is true or F if the statement is false.

T | F 1. In a document library, you can only view a document when accessing the Web site using anonymous access.

T | F 2. Forms-based Authentication can only be used with Active Directory.

T | F 3. When granting anonymous access, you must check to see if any sensitive information will be accessible without authentication.

T | F 4. It is recommended that when you configure anonymous access, you should configure anonymous access at the per-list or per library level.

T | F 5. You can use ADSI Edit to add SPNs to an account.

■ Case Scenarios

Scenario 11-1: Switching to Kerberos

Your manager indicates a new directive came from the corporate office saying that whenever possible, you need to use Kerberos authentication. He would like to know which method is the default method, what advantage does Kerberos have, and what steps would you need to convert to Kerberos.

Scenario 11-2: Implementing SSL

Your manager tells you that he was at a customer site that uses SharePoint and they used a customized login page to access SharePoint. You tell your manager that they were most likely using Forms-Based Authentication. Your manager asks you to identify the basic steps in enabling Forms-Based Authentication (FBA). How do you respond?

Backing Up and Restoring a SharePoint 2010 Environment

OBJECTIVE DOMAIN MATRIX

TECHNOLOGY SKILL	OBJECTIVE DOMAIN DESCRIPTION	OBJECTIVE DOMAIN NUMBER
Backing Up and Restoring a SharePoint Environment	Backing Up and Restoring a SharePoint Environment	4.1
	Configuring Backup Settings	4.1.1
	Backing Up and Restoring Content, Search, and Service Application Databases	4.1.2
	Detaching and Attaching Databases	4.1.3
	Exporting Lists and Sites	4.1.4

KEY TERMS

backup

database snapshot

differential backup

full backup

Recycle Bin

restore

versioning

> Your manager wants to know what steps are needed to restore SharePoint if a disaster occurs. She also wants to know how long it takes to rebuild a system after a disaster occurs and how much data is lost in a disaster.

■ Backing Up and Restoring a SharePoint Environment

THE BOTTOM LINE

SharePoint is a powerful tool that can store and organize lots of information. As you have learned in the previous lessons, SharePoint can be a complex environment that takes time to install and configure and represents a huge investments of time and resources for users. SharePoint also can contain data that, if lost to disaster, might not be recoverable. As with any information system you administer within an organization, you must back up the data regularly and you must plan for data recovery in the event of disaster.

CERTIFICATION READY
What tools can you use
to back up SharePoint?
4.1

A disaster can occur at any time, often without warning. As an administrator, you must plan for these disasters and be ready to implement your plan to get the system back up and running as soon as possible without degradation.

In relatively minor data-loss incidents, you might have to restore only an individual item such as a list or document. A larger disaster, however, might require you to rebuild a server and restore the server data. A complete disaster is one in which you lose everything, including multiple servers, a server room, or an entire site. In any case, the cause of the disaster can be categorized as follows:

- **Component or system failure**: No matter what hardware you use, hardware failure can still occur at any time. You want to choose hardware that minimizes failures and minimizes the effects of the failure. Of course, you must weigh the levels of redundancy against the value of what is being protected.

- **Act of God**: This is a larger disaster (including fires, floods, earthquakes and storms) that causes power outages and/or physically damages one or more systems, the network that the systems connect to, the server room that holds the servers, or the entire site.

- **Incompetence**: Incompetence is caused by carelessness, such as situations in which an administrator or user mistakenly deletes an item (such as a site, list, or document) or an administrator misconfigures a system, unplugs the wrong cable, or creates a script that, when executed, results in loss of functionality or data.

- **Sabotage**: Sabotage is a malicious act that is usually done by a disgruntled administrator or user who has administrative permission or physical access to the system.

- **Malicious attack**: A malicious attack is an attack whereby a hacker tries to infiltrate a system so that he can retrieve confidential information or degrade (or even take down) a server.

Some disasters can be minimized by the following practices:

- Using redundant power supplies and uninterruptable power supplies (UPSs)
- Using RAID and/or spare disks
- Teaming of network adapters
- Clustering
- Database mirroring
- Creating back up sites

TAKE NOTE *

The best method for data recovery is backup, backup, backup!

And so on. When these are not enough, you might need to recreate a system and/or restore from backup.

A *backup* or the process of backing up refers to making copies of data so that these additional copies can be used to restore the original after a data-loss event. They can be used to restore entire systems following a disaster or to restore a small set of files or SharePoint items that were accidentally deleted or corrupted.

A *restore* is the process of retrieving the data from a backup and performing one of the following:

- Replacing lost or corrupted data
- Recreating a replacement system
- Creating a test or temporary system

Of course, you should be performing more backups than restores, but always plan for the worst.

In just about every situation, you must plan your backups, including where backup files will be stored, how they will be backed up, how often they will be backed up, and the type of backup performed. Of course, when you plan for backups, you must consider the following:

- The cost to perform and store the backups
- The importance of the data
- How often the data changes

- The time it takes to perform the backup
- The time it takes to perform a restore if a disaster occurs

Since data changes often, you will most likely need to figure out how to automate the backups so that they can occur automatically. In addition, you should plan for a method that allows you to perform impromptu backups that can be performed when you upgrade a system or make significant changes to the system.

While tapes are considered the traditional backup method, today's preferred methods include hard drives, optical drives, and Internet-based remote backup services. In most production environments, you should make sure that your backups are performed on a regular basis and that you verify that you have good backups. To verify that you have good backups, you should perform a test restore from time to time. In addition, by performing a test restore, you will verify the restore procedure. You also must select current server and backup hardware and software and schedule backups so that backups don't adversely impact system performance.

SharePoint backup tools include (but are not limited to) the following:

- SharePoint tools (Central Administration and SharePoint PowerShell)
- SQL Server tools
- Windows backup tools

In addition, you can purchase third-party backup utilities that allow you to back up file systems, SQL databases, and SharePoint. Many of these third-party backup utilities often have more bells and whistles to use when performing and scheduling backups. Many also provide you with more control over what you are backing up and restoring (data such as documents, lists, libraries, and sites).

When you create backups, they must be stored in a safe, secure place. You must protect access to backups because they contain confidential information. You also must ensure backups are available when you need them. You should consider storing some of the backups offsite, just in case your entire physical site is either destroyed severely damaged.

Before discussing the various SharePoint backup methods, you should also make sure that you document the SharePoint environment as well as the installation/configuration of the SharePoint environment in case you need to rebuild the system, troubleshoot problems, or train future administrators.

Backing Up and Restoring Using SharePoint Tools

The most popular tool for backing up and restoring SharePoint can be found in Central Administration. You can use Central Administration to perform a backup of the entire farm or to backup more granular objects, such as site collections, sites, shared services, lists, or libraries.

CERTIFICATION READY
What three things can Central Administration can back up?
4.1.1

Central Administration can back up the entire farm, any of its components, as well as lists and libraries. When you access the Farm Backup tool, you can select one of the following backup options:

- **Complete Farm**: Backs up the entire farm, including all content and configuration data.
- **Farm Configuration Only**: Backs up all configuration settings contained within SharePoint.
- **Farm Components**: Backs up individual SharePoint components that you select. The individual components include:
  - SharePoint_Config, which contains the configuration data for the entire farm
  - InfoPath Forms Services and all its subsettings

- SharePoint Server State Service
- Microsoft SharePoint Foundation Web application, which includes all Web applications containing site collections and the associated content databases
- WSS_Administration, which contains SharePoint Central Administration
- SharePoint Server State Service proxy
- SPUserCode, which contains the various groups of code collected for backup
- Global Search Settings
- Diagnostics Services
- Application Registry Service
- Shared Services, which includes Shared Services applications and Shared Services proxies

To perform a backup and restore using Central Administration, you must be a member of the Farm Administrators group.

Performing a backup does not affect the state of the farm. However, it might affect performance of SharePoint and/or the SQL server when the backups are running. To help avoid performance issues, you should perform backups during off hours, usually at night.

When you perform a backup using Central Administration, you choose between two types of backups:

- *Full backup*: A full backup copies all the content and configuration data. While it takes the longest to backup, it is also the quickest to restore (because it can restore all data in a single operation).
- *Differential backup*: A differential backup copies only the content that has changed since the last full backup. You can only perform a differential backup after you perform a full backup. Since it only backs up data since the last full backup, it is a quicker backup. However, to perform a restore, you must first restore the full backup and then restore the most up-to-date differential backup. That's why a restore takes longer.

➕ MORE INFORMATION

For more information on how to back up all or part of the farm and recover SharePoint, visit http://technet.microsoft.com/en-us/library/ee662536.aspx

---

BACKING UP AND RESTORING A FARM USING CENTRAL ADMINISTRATION

Backing up the farm backs up the configuration and content databases but does *not* back up any certificates used in trust relationships and does *not* back up any manual changes to the web.config files. After you complete the restore, you still must restore the digital certificates used in trust relationships and you still must restore any modified web.config files.

⊙→ BACK UP A SHAREPOINT FARM

GET READY. To back up a SharePoint farm, perform the following steps:

1. Open Central Administration.
2. Click Backup and Restore. The Backup and Restore page displays (see Figure 12-1).
3. To specify a backup location and the number of threads that are used to perform the backups, click Configure backup settings. Figure 12-2 shows the Default Backup and Restore Settings page. Click OK to return back to the Backup and Restore page.

Figure 12-1

Backup and Restore page

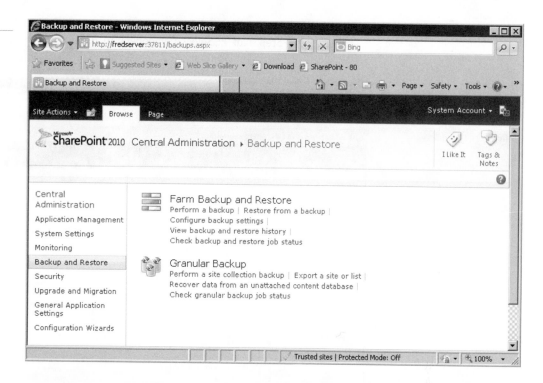

Figure 12-2

The Default Backup and
Restore Settings page

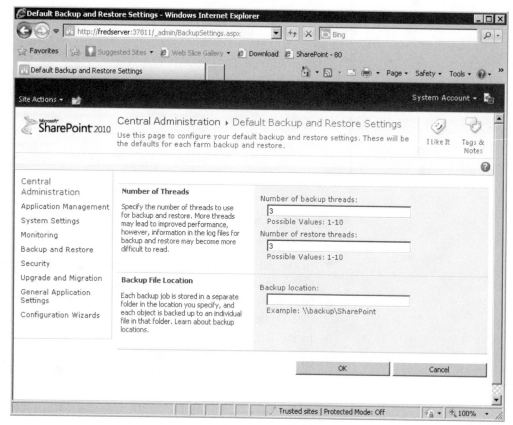

4. In the Backup File Location section, in the Backup location text box, type the
path to the folder where you want to save backups.

5. Click OK.